ADMINISTERING IIS 5.0

Administering
IIS 5.0

Patrick Santry

Mitch Tulloch

McGraw-Hill
New York   San Francisco   Washington, D.C.
Auckland   Bogotá   Caracas   Lisbon   London
Madrid   Mexico City   Milan   Montreal   New Delhi
San Juan   Singapore   Sydney   Tokyo   Toronto

McGraw-Hill

A Division of The McGraw·Hill Companies

4 5 6 7 8 9 0   QWF/QWF   0 7 6 5 4 3 2

ISBN 0-07-212328-1

The sponsoring editor for this book was Michael Sprague and the production supervisor was Clare Stanley. It was set in Century Schoolbook by D&G Limited, LLC.

Printed and bound by Quebecor/Martinsburg.

Throughout this book, trademarked names are used. Rather than put a trademark symbol after every occurrence of a trademarked name, we use names in an editorial fashion only, and to the benefit of the trademark owner, with no intention of infringement of the trademark. Where such designations appear in this book, they have been printed with initial caps.

 This book is printed on recycled, acid-free paper containing a minimum of 50 percent recycled de-inked fiber.

To my wife, Karyn; daughters, Katie and Karleigh; and my son, Patrick Jr. (a.k.a P.J.)

— Patrick

To my wife Ingrid

— Mitch

CONTENTS

Contents

Contents   **xi**

Chapter 8   Administering Indexing   243

Chapter 9   Administering the FTP Service   279

Contents

Contents

Contents

Contents

PREFACE

In February of 2000, Microsoft released the *Windows 2000 Operating System*. As part of the standard operating system, installation is version 5.0 of Microsoft's award-winning WWW server, *Internet Information Services 5.0 (IIS 5.0)*. IIS 5.0 is the platform of choice for system and network administrators planning on implementing corporate intranets and extranets, for Internet Service Providers hosting commercial Web services, and for programmers developing complex Web-based applications.

Who Should Read This Book?

IIS 5 is intended for network and system administrators who need to learn quickly how to install, configure, and administer IIS 5.0 in their networking environment. In today's fast-paced corporate world with consolidation and downsizing taking place everywhere, administrators are often expected to do more with less, work longer hours, and take on new responsibilities. They have less time to become familiar with the array of new products and upgrades flooding the market; yet learning is an essential part of their jobs as administrative duties expand to include developing and maintaining intranets, extranets, and various forms of Internet connectivity.

Although you try to keep abreast of Internet developments by learning HTML, PERL, and SSL, your job is made even harder by the fact that the Internet itself keeps evolving, making it necessary for you to acquire new skills, such as writing *Active Server Pages* (ASPs), VBScript and JavaScript, Dynamic HTML, ActiveX and Java, ODBC database connectivity, channels, streaming audio and video, and Internet telephony and fax gateways.

Who can keep up with such a rapid pace of development? Certainly not the overworked network administrator! Web servers, which started out as a welcome diversion from the mundane tasks of network tuning and maintenance, server upgrades and desktop support, have now turned into what some believe is the "next great thing," which others believe is a sinkhole of time, energy, money, and network bandwidth. A few years ago, setting up and maintaining a Web server was fun; now it's often overwhelming because of the high expectations of management.

This book is intended to bring some relief to your daily pressures. Rather than trying to cover everything for everyone, the focus is primarily on how to *quickly* get IIS 5.0 and related tools installed, configured, and running on your network—in other words, how to *manage* and *administer* IIS 5.0 servers within your organization. A *task-oriented* approach is used, with numerous *walkthroughs* emphasizing a *hands-on* approach for learning necessary skills. No previous familiarity with Web servers or earlier versions of IIS is assumed, although this is certainly helpful.

Administering IIS 5 also will be of use to anyone who needs or wants to learn how to configure and use IIS 5.0. MIS managers, Internet Service Providers, network consultants, and system integrators, hobbyists, and M.C.S.E.-track students will all benefit from this book's approach. Whether you have set up an IIS server before or not, this book will provide you with the skills and knowledge essential to set up an IIS-based intranet or extranet, administer clients and content-development tools, impart essential skills and knowledge to users, and generally get things up and running as quickly and as painlessly as possible.

An audience for which this book is *not* primarily intended is developers of advanced Web-based applications. Active Server Pages and COM+ demand a book all to themselves, because the field of Web-application development is rapidly becoming a separate discipline, requiring a knowledge of Windows architecture, ODBC, ActiveX, and high-level programming languages such as C++. Network and system administrators usually do not have the time for such things; their primary concern is supporting and maintaining the essential network infrastructure that supports all network applications (and putting out fires). Writing scripts to perform basic administrative tasks is one thing; high-level programming and distributed application development is another thing entirely.

Thus, information on advanced Web-based application development using tools like Active Server Pages and COM+ is discussed in Chapter 14 of this book but only briefly and at an introductory level. Knowledge of these tools is not required for performing most basic administrative tasks on IS 5.0, but the information is included to provide an introduction to these tools and what they can do. Serious Web-application developers will need to consult other sources for more information on using these advanced tools.

What Does This Book Cover?

This book covers three basic areas of system and network administration as it relates to implementing intranets, extranets, and Internet connectivity:

1. *Administering servers.* Covered in detail in this book are the core components relating to Internet Information Server 5.0 and related services included in Windows 2000:

   - Components of Internet Information Services 5.0: WWW service, FTP service, SMTP service, and NNTP service
   - Microsoft Indexing Services
   - Microsoft Certificate Services

   COM+ is covered but only briefly. Essential TCP/IP and DNS concepts are covered in the appendixes.

2. *Administering clients.* Administering Internet Explorer 5 using the *Internet Explorer Administration Kit* (IEAK) is covered. This tool is not included in the Windows 2000 but can be downloaded from the Microsoft Web site and is a valuable tool for network administrators planning on installing or upgrading client machines to Internet Explorer 5.0.

3. *Administering content developers.* Microsoft FrontPage 2000 is covered as a standard tool for introductory- and intermediate-level content developers to use for building Intranet and Web sites. Various methods for publishing Web content are explored, including Microsoft Office and WebDAV.

Simple Web-database connectivity is covered briefly using Access 2000 to create an Active Server Pages Web application for dynamically publishing a database to a Web site. Another method is provided for connecting to SQL Server databases using ASP. For many purposes these methods will be sufficient, but advanced Web-based application developers will want to consider such other tools as Microsoft Visual InterDev and Microsoft SQL Server, which are not covered in this book.

Developing Web applications with Active Server Pages is introduced briefly using examples. Developers who want to learn more about ASPs will need to consult other reference materials.

Features of This Book

Some of the features that make this book useful for administrators, both as a guide for setting up and configuring Internet Information Services 5.0 and as a reference guide for administering and troubleshooting purposes, are

■ *Walkthroughs*   Many of the book's chapters include step-by-step walkthroughs that readers can use as a starting point for gaining hands-on experience with the product. These walkthroughs can easily be customized for your particular network configuration.

■ *Task-based section titles*   Section titles usually indicate the administrative task that the section covers (e.g., configuring WWW logging, creating virtual servers, forcing a scan on a virtual directory, etc.).

■ *Screen shots*   Numerous screen shots complement the text, making the book useful for learning both at the console and away from it.

■ *For more info*   At the end of each chapter sources of additional information are suggested, including the Microsoft Web site, newsgroups, list servers, magazine articles, and TechNet.

Overview of Chapters

Chapter 1, "Installing IIS 5.0," looks at the various components included in Windows 2000, the system requirements for installation, and configuring. Also included is a checklist for administrators planning on implementing IIS 5.0 in a corporate environment.

Chapter 2, "Tools for Administration," provides an overview of the *Microsoft Management Console* (MMC), a Windows 2000 administrative tool that provides the core framework for managing Windows 2000 services. The MMC is an integral part of the Windows 2000 administrative management system. Also covered in this chapter are the HTML-based administration of IIS and the Windows Scripting Host.

Chapter 3, "Administering the WWW Service," examines the WWW service configuration options available to administrators; accessing these options through property sheets; and configuring settings at the Master, site, directory and file level. Also included is a basic introduction to the HyperText Transfer Protocol 1.1 supported by IIS 5.0.

Chapter 4, "Administering Security," looks at the various ways a Web site can be secured, including excluding IP addresses and domains, configuring authentication methods, setting IIS and NTFS permissions, disabling unnecessary services, auditing, security policies, and so on.

Chapter 5, "Administering Virtual Directories and Servers," covers creating, configuring, and deleting virtual servers; creating and configuring virtual directories for local and remote content; and understanding host headers.

Chapter 6, "Administering Content," examines establishing policies and procedures for developing Web site content, selecting tools for Web content development, administering and using FrontPage 2000 and Microsoft Office 2000 for Web content development, overviewing Web Distributed Authoring and Versioning (WebDAV), and publishing dynamic Web content from an Access database using Access 2000.

Chapter 7, "Administering Clients," looks at implementing Internet Explorer 5.0 as client software, configuring IE 5.0 security options, and using the Internet Explorer Administration Kit to create custom installation packages for administration-based installations of IE 5.0.

Chapter 8, "Administering Indexing," examines managing site indexing using Index Services, understanding how Index Services works, creating query pages, and a walkthrough of indexing a virtual server.

Chapter 9, "Administering the FTP Service," explains the FTP session, configuration of FTP settings using property sheets, and FTP security issues and gives a walkthrough of creating and connecting to an FTP site.

Chapter 10, "Administering Performance," looks at monitoring IIS performance using Windows 2000 Performance Monitor and other Windows 2000 administrative tools and techniques for tuning and optimizing performance of IIS servers.

Chapter 11, "Administering SSL with Certificate Services," looks at how the *Secure Sockets Layer* (SSL) protocol enables secure HTTP sessions, installing and configuring Certificate Services, generating and installing certificate requests, submitting a certificate request to a Certificate Authority, and a walkthrough of enabling SSL on a site.

Chapter 12, "Administering the SMTP Service," describes the mechanism of SMTP service installation of the SMTP service, configuration of the SMTP service settings using property sheets, and use of the SMTP service.

Chapter 13, "Administering the NNTP Service," covers installing and configuring the NNTP service using property sheets, understanding the NNTP service, creating newsgroups on IIS, setting newsgroup expiration policies, posting to newsgroups using Outlook Express, and a walkthrough of creating and posting to a newsgroup.

Chapter 14, "Administering Active Server Pages," covers the basic concepts of creating Web-based applications using Active Server Pages and understanding COM+. A number of examples of simple applications using Active Server Pages are demonstrated.

Chapter 15, "Troubleshooting," covers various tips and techniques for troubleshooting problems with Internet Information Services 5.0 and other

Windows 2000 components. Many of these tips are drawn from real-life situations experienced by administrators of IIS 5.0 servers.

Appendix A, "Essential TCP/IP," covers basic concepts of configuring TCP/IP for networks using Windows 2000, including subnetting concepts necessary for excluding IP addresses.

Appendix B, "Essential DNS," includes an explanation of the *Domain Name System* (DNS) and a walkthrough of setting up and configuring DNS on a network using Windows 2000 and its relation with Active Directory.

CHAPTER 1

Installing
IIS 5.0

Introduction

Microsoft Internet Information Services 5.0 are included as part of the Windows 2000 operating system, which is available from *Microsoft Value-Added Resellers* (VARs) everywhere. After completing this chapter, you will have a basic understanding of

- Internet components of Windows 2000
- System requirements for installing Windows 2000 Server with IIS 5.0
- Installation issues of IIS 5.0
- Installing IIS 5.0 on a fresh system
- Upgrading from previous versions of IIS on NT to Windows 2000 Server
- Adding and removing Internet components from Windows 2000
- Accessing release notes and online documentation

What Services Make Up IIS 5.0?

Microsoft has bundled IIS 5.0 as installation options of Windows 2000. We will be covering the following Internet components throughout this book:

- *Microsoft Internet Information Services 5.0 (IIS 5.0).* Includes a full-featured Internet server with WWW, FTP, SMTP, and NNTP services; support for Active Server Pages; support for *Web Distributed Authoring and Versioning* (WebDAV) and two administrative tools: an Internet Service Manager snap-in for *Microsoft Management Console* (MMC), and Internet Service Manager (HTML) for administration by Web browsers.
- *FrontPage 2000 Server Extensions,* which provides interfacing capability between clients running FrontPage 2000 and Web sites on IIS.

System Requirements for Installing IIS 5

Listed in this section are the *minimum* and *recommended* hardware and software requirements for systems to run IIS 5.0 or other Internet service components. Actual system requirements will depend upon factors such as

- The intended use for the server
- The server traffic load expected
- Other applications being run on the server
- Whether clustering is being used

To determine actual system requirements, administrators should perform a test installation using recommended hardware and software requirements, and then monitor server performance using Performance Monitor under real or simulated loads to determine what elements of hardware (processor, memory, disk, network) to upgrade. See Chapter 10 for information about load-testing IIS using the *Web Capacity Analysis Tool* (WCAT).

Hardware Requirements

Because IIS 5.0 is part of the Windows 2000 installation, the *minimum* hardware requirements for installing a Windows 2000 Server machine, as stated by Microsoft, are as follows:

Processor	Pentium/133
Memory	128MB
HD space available	2GB of hard disk space with 1.0GB of free space
Monitor	VGA

Here are some notes on these hardware requirements:

- Use the recommended requirements as your minimum or starting requirements. Performance with 128MB of RAM is unbearably slow, so start with 256MB of RAM and work upward.

- In addition, the stated hard disk space requirements should be at least doubled if a *custom* install is performed and most components are selected.

- The SVGA monitor is important for viewing Web content only.

- In general, production Web servers running IIS 5.0 probably want to have at least Pentium III 500 processors with 512 MB RAM and 100 MB Ethernet cards in most medium- and large-scale corporate intranet environments. Much of this depends on how much traffic you expect to receive to your Web site and the amount of processing overhead for your Web application if using Active Server Pages.

Software Requirements

Following are the software prerequisites for installing IIS 5.0.:

- Windows 2000 operating system or later
- TCP/IP protocol
- NTFS for all IIS drives (recommended for security reasons)

NOTE: *IIS 5.0 may also be installed on Windows 2000 Professional, but it installs as a scaled-down version and is missing some of the essential features it has when installed on Windows 2000 Server or Advanced Server, such as the ability to*

- *Host multiple Web sites on one machine*
- *Log to an ODBC-compliant database*
- *Restrict access by IP addresses*
- *Isolate processes*

Essentially, Windows 2000 Professional is not intended to be a production Web server, but may rather be used for

- *Publishing workgroup Web content within a LAN*
- *Performing remote administration of IIS on NT Server*
- *As a staging server for development of Web applications before going into actual production*

Software Recommendations

The following software is recommended if you plan to use IIS 5.0 in a medium- or large-scale corporate intranet production environment:

- *Name resolution services:* Either a WINS server or a DNS server (DNS recommended)
- *Client browser software:* Microsoft Internet Explorer 5 or higher
- *Content development tools:* Microsoft FrontPage 2000
- *Application development tools:* Microsoft Visual InterDev
- *Relational database management systems*: Microsoft SQL Server 7 or Access

Installation Issues for IIS 5.0

IIS 5.0 is installed by default as part of the Windows 2000 operating system installation. The following sections are items you should be aware of before doing your Windows 2000 installation with IIS 5.0.

Operating System Issues

IIS 5.0 can be installed on Windows 2000 Advanced Server, Server, or Professional. IIS 5.0 *cannot* be installed on any version of Windows NT 4.0 or Windows 95/98.

Compatibility Issues

If you are upgrading from Windows NT to Windows 2000, or wish to install Proxy Server 2.0 on a Windows 2000 installation, you will also need to upgrade your Proxy 2.0 installation. You can download the Proxy Server Setup Wizard to perform the upgrade from Microsoft's Web site. For more information, contact Microsoft or visit the TechNet article on the Web for performing the upgrade: `http://technet.microsoft.com/cdonline/Content/Complete/Internet/Server/Proxy/msp2wiz.htm`.

IIS 5.0 Windows 2000 Default Installation Configuration

After your machine has the operating system installed, there are certain configurations that pertain to the Internet services that you as an IIS administrator should be aware of.

Using Windows 2000 Explorer, you can examine some of the new directories installed on the machine, including the various subdirectories of the default content parent directory (Figure 1-1):

This assumes that the defaults were selected during setup. Content subdirectories under Inetpub include

AdminScripts	Contains VBScripts for managing IIS under Windows Scripting Host
ftproot	The default directory for the FTP publishing service
iissamples	Sample files to show off the capabilities of IIS

Figure 1-1
The default directory structure after installing Windows 2000.

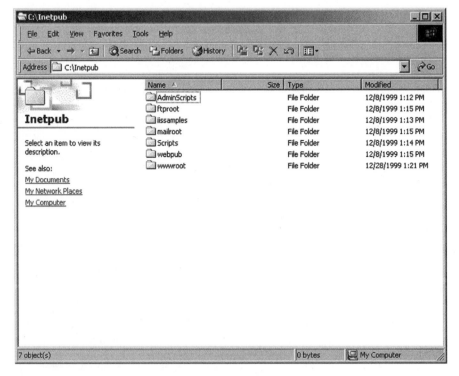

`Mailroot`	Contains directories for sending and receiving mail
`scripts`	Location for scripts belonging to the Default Web site
`wwwroot`	The default home directory for the WWW publishing service

New application files are located under

`C:\Program Files\`

Files for the Internet Service Manager (HTML) are located under

`C:\winnt\system32\inetsrv\`

Two accounts are created by the Windows 2000 installation. You should become familiar with them and how they affect the Internet services on the machine (Figure 1-2).

The new accounts are

■ IUSR_SERVERNAME (or IUSR_DOMAINNAME) where SERVERNAME is the name of the member server (or DOMAINNAME is the name of the domain). This account is called the *Internet Guest Account* and is used by IIS to enable users to connect to the WWW service using Anonymous Access as their authentication method. The account is a member of the *Guests* local group.

Figure 1-2
Accounts created by Windows 2000 to manage IIS.

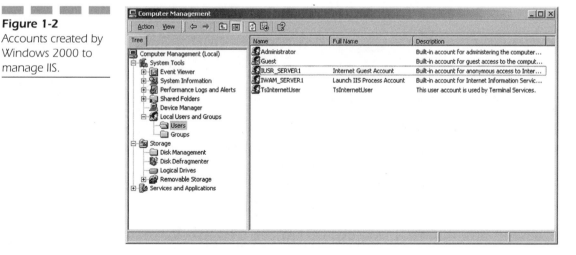

■ IWAM_SERVERNAME (or IWAM_DOMAINNAME) where
SERVERNAME is the name of the member server (or DOMAINNAME
is the name of the domain). This account is called the Web Application
Manager Account and is used by COM+ Services to run secure IIS
applications with process isolation. The account is a member of the
COM+ Trusted Process Identities local group, which is also created by
the Windows 2000 Setup.

Customizing Your IIS 5.0 Installation

After you install Windows 2000 Server on a new system, the Windows 2000
Configure Your Server application (see Figure 1-3) will start when you first
log onto your server. This allows you to customize the settings of various
services provided by the Windows 2000 operating system.

To customize your new installation of IIS 5.0, select Web/Media Server
from the left navigation options of the Configure Your Server application

Figure 1-3
The Configure Your
Web Server
application.

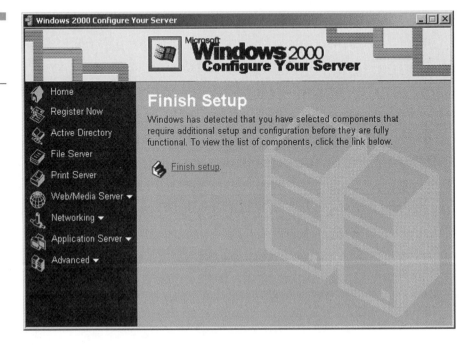

Figure 1-4
Step 2 of Configure
Your Web Server
application.

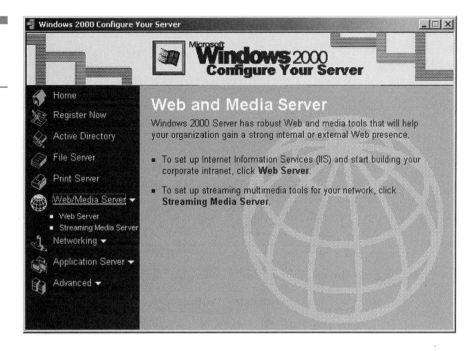

(see Figure 1-4). Select the Web Server option that has opened under the Web/Media Server menu option to view a list options for your IIS 5.0.

After you have selected the Web Server option, a screen will appear (see Figure 1-5) providing you with options for creating new virtual directories, starting your IIS Manager, and online help for IIS 5.0. These options will be discussed in detail in later chapters of this book.

Upgrading IIS 5.0

If you are currently running IIS 4 on Windows NT, when you perform your Windows 2000 upgrade, the installation will automatically detect your IIS 4 installation and upgrade your current Internet components with the configuration information intact.

Microsoft Transaction Server no longer exists under the Windows 2000 operating system. If you currently have Microsoft Transaction Server managing DCOM objects, your MTS packages will be upgraded to run under the new COM+ architecture.

Figure 1-5
Step 3 of Configure
Your Web Server
application.

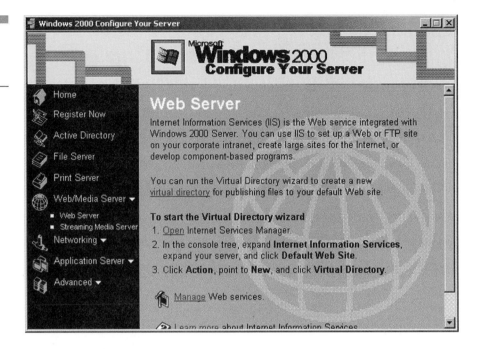

There are no other major issues relating to upgrading to IIS 5.0 from earlier versions of IIS. *Just make sure you do a full backup before performing the upgrade.*

NOTE: *When upgrading to Windows 2000 from an NT system, IIS 5.0 will only be installed by default if IIS was previously installed on the operating system. If you wish to add IIS 5.0 to the upgrade, you must select the custom installation option.*

Adding and Removing Components

You can add and remove components by using the Add/Remove program in the Control Panel of Windows 2000.

To add or remove components from Windows 2000, click Start, Settings, Control Panel, and then start the Add/Remove Programs application (Figure 1-6).

Select Configure Windows. Click the Components button, which will bring up online instructions to install, add, or remove Windows 2000 components. From here, select the services that you wish to change (see Figure

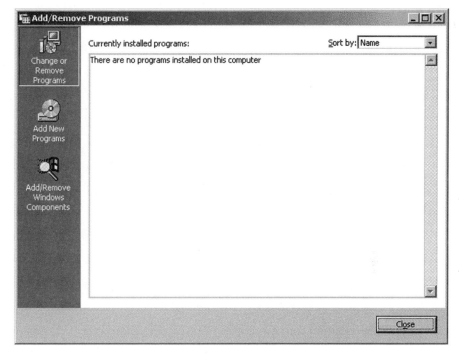

Figure 1-6
The Add/Remove
Programs application.

1-7). Table 1-1 shows the component name and short descriptions that are available with IIS 5.0.

NOTE: *Administrators removing Internet components from Windows 2000 should be aware that some services depend on others in order to run. For information on these dependencies, refer to the section of the Online Documentation entitled "Installing IIS."*

Uninstalling IIS 5.0

To remove IIS 5.0 from your Windows 2000 installation, use the procedure outlined in previous section "Adding and Removing Components." Select *Internet Information Services* (IIS) as your choice. This will then uninstall IIS as well as the underlying dependent components. By selecting the Details button, you can remove subcomponents of IIS 5.0 such as NNTP, SMTP, or FTP.

However, certain directories and files remain on the system after uninstalling IIS 5.0. They are listed below. These files may be safely removed

Figure 1-7
Removing
components of IIS.

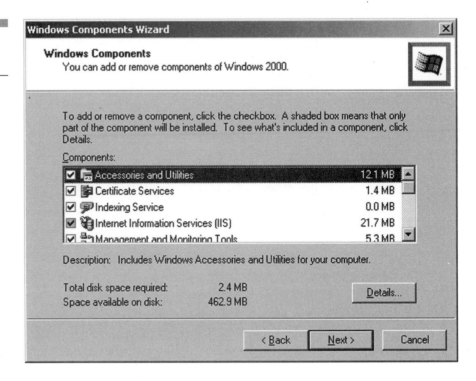

from the system (unless they contain Web content you have developed).
Note that some of these directories and files may not be present, depending
on the type of setup performed.

IIS content directories:

`\Inetpub\wwwroot\`

`\Inetpub\ftproot\`

`\Inetpub\Iissamples\`

`\Winnt\System32\inetsrv\iisfecnv.dll`

NNTP directories:

`\Inetpub\news\*.*`

`\Inetpub\nntpfile\*.*`

`\Winnt\Help\news\`

SMTP directories:

`\Inetpub\Mail\`

`\Inetpub\Mailroot\`

Table 1-1

Components and
subcomponents of
IIS 5.0

Component	Description
Common Files	Required files that are shared by several services
Documentation	Online help and documentation on IIS 5.0
File Transfer Protocol Services (FTP)	FTP service for transferring files
FrontPage 2000 Server Extensions	Used for remote content development and Web site management
Internet Information Services Snap-in	Microsoft Management Console snap-in for managing IIS 5.0
Internet Services Manager (HTML)	Web-based management utility for managing your Web server from a remote location
NNTP Service	Network News Transport Protocol, used for provided threaded newsgroup discussion services
SMTP Service	Simple Mail Transport Protocol, used for providing email services
Visual InterDev RAD Remote Deployment Support	For deployment of applications from a remote location—used for development servers, not recommended for production environments.
World Wide Web Server	Supports access to your Web sites.

Accessing Release Notes

If problems occur during the installation and use of IIS 5.0 or other Internet components of Windows 2000, you may want to view the *release notes* on these components. Release notes for IIS 5.0 can be obtained prior to installation at Microsoft's Web site at

`www.microsoft.com/windows2000/`

Accessing Online Documentation

Online documentation for IIS 5 is installed on the server as Web content to be read using Internet Explorer 5 (Figure 1-8). Thus, in order to read the documentation, IIS 5.0 must be successfully installed and the WWW service must start properly.

Figure 1-8
Accessing the IIS
online
documentation.

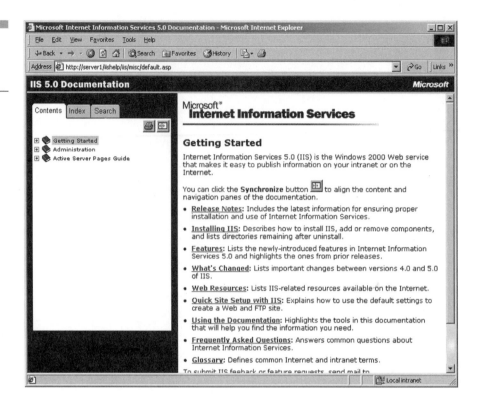

Online documentation may be accessed from remote browsers by using the URL

```
http://<server_name>/iisHelp/
```

where `<server_name>` is the NetBIOS name, fully-qualified domain name, or IP address of the IIS server.

Online documentation contains a facility for printing out entire sections of the documentation if desired.

Postscript: Checklist for Implementing IIS 5.0

Some final comments on implementing IIS 5.0 in your networking environment to help you keep your sanity. Implementing IIS 5.0 in a corporate environment as an intranet or Internet server is not a job that you as a network administrator should take lightly. Only a few years ago, the situation was much simpler and probably looked something like this:

- As network administrator, you installed and configured a basic Web server for Internet or intranet use, plus any associated tools needed such as a DNS server.
- As network administrator, you registered your company's domain name with Internic.
- As network administrator, you learned enough HTML to create the company Web site, which was probably 10-25 pages in size. You probably stole (borrowed) some graphics from other sites to make it look decent. You also had the responsibility of updating the site as needed.
- As network administrator, you learned enough Perl to write scripts for enabling forms on your site, and possibly created a simple discussion group as well. But when your boss asked if you could connect your Web site to the company database, you balked and said the tools were just not there yet for doing that.
- As network administrator, your email address was on your home page as Webmaster. You got all the accolades and all the flack from the people who visited your site.

Well, things are *much* different now. The Internet is big business, database connectivity is the norm, commerce systems are the future, Web servers have given way to Web farms, HTML has given way to RAD tools, legal issues abound, and expectations have gone through the roof. So before you implement your next web server, it's time to face facts: *You can't do it all anymore.* No single IT professional has the expertise or the time to become familiar with all the myriad aspects of Internet/intranet development these days. You would have to be manager, consultant, network administrator, database programmer, VB expert, graphic designer, trainer, and customer support all rolled up in one to be able to do it all. I don't know about you, but I'd rather not try.

So where do you begin? To help you implement IIS 5.0 in your network environment, here is a 12-step methodology that is useful for implementing any significant server upgrades or rollouts in a corporate environment:

1. Assess
2. Propose

3. Recruit

4. Train

5. Procure

6. Test

7. Deploy

8. Document

9. Monitor

10. Evaluate

11. Forecast

12. Maintain

This 12-step methodology is cast in the following section as a series of questions you should ask yourself and tasks you should perform as you progress through the stages of planning, designing, and implementing IIS 5.0 in your corporate network. As you read through it, ask yourself each question and visualize to yourself how each task will be performed. Check off each point as you consider it. Write down additional questions and tasks of your own in the space provided as they occur to you.

Step 1: Assess (Do You Need IIS 5.0?)

■ Are you familiar with aspects of your company's current network configuration as they relate to implementing IIS 5.0?

■ Do you have existing IIS 4.0 servers that will need to be upgraded?

■ Do you have existing Internet Explorer 4.0 browsers that will need to be upgraded to IE 5.0? Will end-user systems require additional memory to run IE 5.0?

■ Have you any concerns regarding the additional network traffic that will result from implementing IIS 5.0 for your intranet or the Internet?

■ Has your company any security policies in place regarding deploying Web servers?

■ Have you familiarized yourself with the features that are new in IIS 5.0? If necessary, visit Microsoft's Web site to review these new features:

`www.microsoft.com/windows2000/`

■ Have you reflected on why you want to upgrade your existing Web servers to IIS 5.0? Are the driving reasons valid concerns or pet cows?

Which of the following groups are pushing for the deployment? Are any of them resisting it? Why?

- Management
- IT department
- End users

- Have you the necessary resources at this time to consider implementing IIS 5.0?

  - Hardware (servers and peripherals)
  - Hardware (network infrastructure)
  - Software (rollout, site development, and maintenance)
  - Training (you and others)
  - Budget
  - Time
  - People (IT, programmers, Web developers)

- List any additional questions, concerns, or thoughts you may have regarding *assessing* your company's need for IIS 5.0 at this time.

  _____

  _____

  _____

Step 2: Propose (Why? What? How? When? Who? How Much?)

- List three reasons right now *why* your company needs to upgrade its existing intranet/Internet structure to IIS 5.0. If you can't do this, don't proceed any further.

  _____

  _____

  _____

- Describe briefly *what* will need to be purchased, upgraded, or reallocated to enable IIS 5.0 to be implemented on your network. Consider such things as

  - Servers
  - Peripherals

- Networking components
- Firewalls
- Software (administrative and end-user)
- Licenses (per-server and per-seat)
- Resource materials (administrative and end-user)
- Training courses (administrative and end-user)
- Other

■ Describe *how* and *when* you plan to implement IIS 5.0 on the network. Outline your plan as a series of steps with a target timeline, leaving yourself room for unforeseen circumstances.

■ Outline *who* has responsibility for what in your plan. Specifically, you should be able at this time to suggest names for each of the functions in Table 1-2, even though you may not plan immediately to use all the

Table 1-2

Implementation responsibilities

Function/Responsibility	Names(s)
Project leader (chief technical person, mastermind, and planner)	You—that's why you're reading this book!
Project leader's management counterpart (responsible for determining corporate needs, helping to procure funding, establishing policies regarding content and usage, etc.)	
Technical team (from your IT department; people you can delegate technical implementation tasks to)	
Database developer(s) (if you plan to implement database connectivity in your Web site)	
VBScript/Jscript developer(s) and programmer(s) (may be required for custom site development)	
Person(s) responsible for recruiting, training, and overseeing the Web site development team that will actually create the site content	
Graphic design company(s) for outsourcing of your Web site graphics needs (worth the money!)	
Training company(s) for outsourcing your technical and end-user training needs (also worth the money!)	
Person(s) responsible for ongoing technical support to Web site development team (from your IT department)	

features and functionality of IIS 5.0. Some names may appear in more than one place in the table—just make sure your name doesn't appear in every line!

- Estimate *how much* should be budgeted in order to implement your project. Provide a cost breakdown according to what you need and when you need it.

- List any additional questions, concerns, or thoughts you may have regarding *writing a proposal* and *preparing a presentation* on implementing IIS 5.0 in your corporate network at this time.

_____

_____

_____

Step 3: Recruit (Think Teamwork and Delegate!)

- Having had your proposal approved by management, begin by notifying both users and management of the following:
  - Purpose of deployment of IIS 5.0 in the company
  - Planned deployment date(s)
  - How deployment will affect users
  - Persons and groups responsible for specific functions or tasks
  - Whom to contact if problems are encountered

- Create a brief written description of goals and functions for each individual or group that will be involved in the project, including management contacts and end users.

- Meet with these individuals and groups to review their roles and responsibilities. Schedule regular meetings as appropriate and outline your expectations to them in advance of how they should document and report progress to you.

- List any additional questions, concerns, or thoughts you may have regarding *recruiting a team* for implementing IIS 5.0 in your corporate network at this time.

_____

_____

_____

Step 4: Train (Know Your Stuff!)

- Have you read through the online documentation of IIS 5.0?

- Do you feel a need to take any additional training before implementing IIS 5.0 in your corporate network? If so, you may want to check out the listing of *Microsoft Official Curriculum* (MOC) courses on Microsoft's Web site or contact your local *Microsoft Certified Technical Education Center* (CTEC) for a schedule of current courses. MOC courses are listed at

  `www.microsoft.com/train_cert`

- Will the people developing Web site content in your company require any training? You might want to sit down with management or department heads and assess training needs for end users and content developers at this time.

- Will end users migrating from IE 4.0 to IE 5.0 require training to enable them to make efficient use of the new browser's capabilities and potential?

- List any additional questions, concerns, or thoughts you may have regarding training individuals and groups for successful implementation and use of IIS 5.0 in your corporate network at this time.

  _____

  _____

  _____

Step 5: Procure (Buy It, Beg It, Borrow It, But Please Don't Pirate It!)

- Make your shopping wish list for implementing IIS 5.0 and try to get the invoice approved by management.

- List any additional questions, concerns, or thoughts you may have regarding *procuring* necessary hardware and software to allow a successful implementation of IIS 5.0 in your corporate network at this time.

  _____

  _____

  _____

Step 6: Test (Look Before You Leap!)

- Perform a testbed installation and fully familiarize yourself with the product. The test machine should be identical in hardware to your final production servers, and it should be either a fresh installation on a new or wiped machine or an upgrade onto a disk-image copy of an existing IIS 5.0 Web server complete with existing company intranet Web site content (if any).

- Perform a test installation of IE 5.0 on a machine similar to the average end-user machine. Apply any user restrictions you have decided to add by using Microsoft's Internet Explorer Administration Kit. Test these restrictions out.

- Try accessing all aspects of the migrated content to see if all the Web site functions still work (forms, Active Server Pages, database connectivity, and so on).

- Have you read the release notes on IIS 5.0? Check www.microsoft.com/windows2000 for the latest release notes regarding problems, patches, and workarounds to installation problems.

- Have you installed any patches and workarounds you found on Microsoft's Web site? Have you tested them out?

- Have you browsed the TechNet knowledge base concerning IIS 5.0 to see what other problems you might encounter?

- Have you posted to the Microsoft public newsgroups any problems you have encountered or any questions you might have? (It is cheaper than dialing Microsoft's support line!) You can find these newsgroups by pointing your news reader to the following NNTP server:

  msnews.microsoft.com

- List any additional questions, concerns, or thoughts you may have regarding *testing* your hardware and software to allow a successful implementation of IIS 5.0 in your corporate network at this time.

  _____

  _____

  _____

Step 7: Deploy (Roll It Out, But Don't Roll It Over Anybody!)

- Begin by notifying both users and management of the planned date for deployment of your new IIS 5.0 servers. Do this approximately one to two weeks in advance, and again two days before deployment. Ask them to notify you on or after that date if any network problems occur that might relate to the deployment.

- Back up your existing IIS servers before upgrading them to IIS 5.0 and Windows 2000. Back up your Web and FTP content directories, scripts, and applications as well.

- Having acquired the necessary hardware, software, and expertise, go ahead and install IIS 5.0 on your new production systems or upgrade your existing IIS 4.0 servers to IIS 5.0. Also apply any service packs, fixes, or patches that are available for this product at this time.

- Deploy or upgrade end-user systems to Internet Explorer 5.0, making sure you apply any service packs, fixes, or patches available for this product. Use the Internet Explorer Administration Kit to customize end-user browsers for your company's needs.

- Are you doing all the technical work yourself at this point? (Just checking.)

- After completing installation, check Windows 2000 Event Viewer to be sure there were no unforeseen problems with the installation.

- While your new servers are still off-line, perform a few basic standalone tests on them, including running each of the administrative tools and connecting to the WWW and FTP services using Internet Explorer 5.0.

- Configure the security settings on your new servers according to your company's network security policy. Consider all aspects of security, including

  - Administrative rights
  - Content-development rights
  - Browsing and access rights
  - IP address filtering
  - Firewall configuration
  - Remote-access methods

- Authentication methods
- Directory permissions

■ Install the IIS 5.0 administrative tools on your administrator consoles or install Internet Explorer 5.0 on them for remote administration capabilities.

■ Deploy the new server(s) on the network and monitor for any abrupt changes in network traffic patterns or user complaints.

■ Test remote administration of your new servers from your administrator consoles.

■ Test access from end-user stations that have browsing rights. Inform end users to contact you if they have problems accessing the new servers.

■ Test creation of content from end-user stations that have content-creation rights. Inform persons responsible for content creation to contact you if they have problems performing their duties.

■ Iron out any other bugs that appear during deployment.

■ List any additional questions, concerns, or thoughts you may have regarding *deployment* of IIS 5.0 in your corporate network at this time.

_____

_____

_____

Step 8: Document (Make Time for This!)

■ Document all problems and issues that appear during testing and deployment.

■ Document all security settings (users, groups, IP, authentication methods, directory permissions) implemented on your new servers. Indicate the order in which these settings were made.

■ Document responsibilities and functions of individuals and groups involved in both deployment and usage.

■ Document any user complaints that occur during the two weeks after deployment, even if they don't seem at the time to be directly related to the IIS 5.0 deployment.

■ List any additional questions, concerns, or thoughts you may have regarding *documentation* of your IIS 5.0 deployment at this time.

_____

_____

_____

Step 9: Monitor (How Does It Perform?)

■ Use Windows NT Performance Monitor to monitor selected objects and counters related to IIS 5.0 performance.

■ Run Performance Monitor and create log files for server analysis and optimization. Be sure you have sufficient disk space for logging.

■ Set alerts for objects and counters that critically affect performance and usability.

■ Use log files to create a baseline for both low- and high-usage periods of your IIS 5.0 servers. To allow for performance to settle as users become familiar with the new servers, wait one or two weeks after deployment before creating your baseline logs from an additional two weeks of logging server activity.

■ Continue logging to create a database of information for server analysis and optimization.

■ Identify any bottlenecks in server performance and try to correct them by implementing hardware upgrades, such as

- Adding additional memory
- Upgrading processors or adding additional processors
- Upgrading disk controllers and hard drives
- Upgrading network adapter cards

■ Tune server performance by changing configuration options on property sheets for WWW and FTP services. Monitor the effect of making these changes and try to optimize settings for best performance.

■ Tune performance of your proxy server, if you are using a proxy intermediary to run IIS 5.0 as an extranet server.

■ Develop a schedule and assign responsibility for long-term ongoing performance monitoring of your IIS 5.0 servers.

■ List any additional questions, concerns, or thoughts you may have regarding *monitoring and optimization* of your IIS 5.0 performance at this time.

_____

_____

_____

Step 10: Evaluate (Have We Met Our Goals?)

■ Approximately two to three months after deployment, meet with your implementation team and end-user contacts and evaluate the success of the project. Specifically address issues such as these:

- Are content developers comfortable working with the new platform?

- Are developers making use of the new features of IIS 5.0?

- Does any group feel that it needs more training to enable it to make full use of the potentialities of IIS 5.0?

- Are end users happy with the speed, accessibility, and functionality of the intranet/extranet?

- Are end users comfortable with any restrictions on IE 5.0 you have added using the Internet Explorer Administration Kit? Are they aware of the reasons for such customization?

- Are current security policies working? Any suggestions for modification?

- Has the time, energy, and money spent on the implementation been worthwhile?

- Have they any further thoughts, suggestions, or concerns they would like to express at this time?

■ Prepare a brief report for management summarizing developer and end-user satisfaction now that implementation is complete.

■ List any additional questions, concerns, or thoughts you may have regarding *evaluation* of your IIS 5.0 deployment at this time.

_____

_____

_____

Step 11: Forecast (Be Proactive!)

- Consider your evaluation meeting with content developers and end users and your ongoing performance monitoring, and discuss with your technical team how and when your current IIS 5.0 implementation might require further upgrading. Consider such issues as
  - Adding additional servers to accommodate user traffic
  - Repositioning servers to handle traffic more efficiently
  - Increasing network capacity (available bandwidth)
  - Adding new development platforms like Microsoft Visual InterDev
  - Adding new server functionality (for example, SQL Server, Site Server Commerce Edition, and so on)
  - Prepare a brief report for management outlining how and when such upgrades might need to be performed, depending on evolution of company and user needs.
  - List any additional questions, concerns, or thoughts you may have regarding *forecasting future growth* of your IIS 5.0 deployment at this time.

  _____

  _____

  _____

Step 12: Maintain (Keep on Top of Things!)

- Visit the Microsoft IIS Web site regularly for any news regarding
  - New or updated versions of IIS 5.0
  - Service packs, fixes, and patches for Windows 2000
  - New add-ons, controls, and tools to extend IIS 5.0 functionality
  - New or updated versions of IE 5.0
  - Service packs, fixes, and patches for IE 5.0
  - Conferences, events, newsletters, and newsgroups relating to IIS 5.0 and intranet development
- Train and establish a technical support group for IIS-5.0–related troubleshooting issues. Require monthly reports from this group

concerning the most frequently encountered problems and how they were resolved.

- Continue to monitor server performance and evaluate developer and end-user satisfaction on a regular basis. Make reports to management on a regular basis forecasting future requirements and assessing future needs.

- List any additional questions, concerns, or thoughts you may have regarding *maintaining* your IIS 5.0 deployment at this time.

_____

_____

_____

- Collect your paycheck—you deserve it!

SUMMARY

IIS 5.0 and other Internet components of Windows 2000 are installed by default with Windows 2000. Administrators should be aware of all issues that need to be addressed before installing IIS 5.0 in a production environment. This chapter has dealt with some of these issues; refer to the current release notes on the Microsoft Web site for further issues regarding each Internet component of Windows 2000.

For More Information

The following are a few suggested sources for getting additional information on installing and maintaining IIS 5.0.

Microsoft Web Site

For general information regarding IIS 5.0, visit the IIS section of the Microsoft Web site, located at

`www.microsoft.com/windows2000`

To download Internet Explorer 5, visit the site

```
www.microsoft.com/windows/ie/default.htm
```

Microsoft Public Newsgroups

For general newsgroups relating to IIS 5.0 issues, connect to the news server msnews.microsoft.com and subscribe to the following groups:

```
microsoft.public.inetserver.iis
microsoft.public.inetserver.misc
```

Microsoft TechNet

Consult the latest edition of Microsoft TechNet CD for information under the following category:

```
windowsproductfamily/mswindows2000/mswindows2000server/resourcekit/
windows2000internetinformationservices
```

Microsoft Certified Professional Magazine January 2000 has a feature article entitled "Web Wizardry! IIS 5.0 Lends Security and Speed to Your Online Efforts," which provides a useful overview of IIS 5.0. You can also visit the MCP Magazine Web site at:

```
www.mcpmag.com
```

Tools for Administration

Introduction

A core component of any Web server is the administrative tool used to manage its services, resources, and performance. Internet Information Services 5.0 comes with a complete set of administrative tools for both local and remote administration. After completing this chapter, you will have a basic understanding of the functionality and capabilities of the following administrative tools:

- The *Microsoft Management Console* (MMC), which allows administrators to manage IIS 5.0 servers from any computer on which the MMC and its snap-ins are installed.
- The HTML version of the Internet Service Manager, which allows administrators to remotely administer IIS 5.0 servers from any computer with a browser that supports frames and JScript.
- The *Windows Scripting Host* (WSH), which enables administrative scripts written in VBScript or JScript to run directly on any desktop or from a command line.

Understanding the Microsoft Management Console

The *Microsoft Management Console* (MMC) is a common management environment that provides a framework for specially designed network and server administration tools to run on. These specially designed tools are called *snap-ins,* and they provide the administrator the capability for managing a wide variety of network and server resources and services.

A snap-in is the smallest element of network management capability. Unless snap-ins are added to the MMC environment, the MMC is useless because it has no inherent management functionality. A collection of snap-ins saved as an .msc file is known as a *tool*.

All the standard Windows 2000 administrative tools (for example, User Manager, Server Manager, Event Viewer) run as snap-ins within the Management Console. The MMC will also run on Windows NT 4.0 and higher, and on Windows 95/98, allowing administrators to remotely manage network resources and servers even from a Windows 95/98 workstation.

The advantages of MMC-based administration include

- The capability to create custom management consoles that are *task-based*. Instead of being confronted with a bewildering array of separate tools, an administrator can create one management console specifically for Web server administration that has just those tools needed for administering Web servers, another console for remote access administration, and so on. Administration is simplified by reducing the clutter of unnecessary tools and providing only what is needed for the task at hand.

- The capability to *delegate* limited management tasks to others. A senior administrator can create a console for a junior administrator that allows limited functionality like backup and performance monitoring. The management console is saved as a simple .msc file that can be delivered by email or read from a network share.

- The existence of a *standardized framework* providing a single integrated interface for snap-ins to run on. All snap-ins must conform to the look and feel of the MMC, easing administration and shortening the amount of time required to learn new administrative tools.

Microsoft Management Console version 1.2 is part of the Windows 2000 operating system. This version of the MMC includes snap-ins to manage the various ISS 5.0 components that are part of the Windows 2000 operating system.

- Internet Information Server 5.0
- *Simple Mail Transfer Protocol* (SNMP) service
- *Network News Transfer Protocol* (NNTP) service
- *File Transfer Protocol* (FTP) service

Using the Microsoft Management Console

Starting the MMC

When IIS 5.0 is installed on a system, the appropriate snap-in for MMC is installed to provide tools for administering IIS. This Microsoft Management Console on an IIS server can be started in two ways:

Method 1   To start the Microsoft Management Console from the Internet Service Manager shortcut on the Start menu, choose Start, Programs, Administrative Tools, Internet Services Manager. This opens an MMC console window with the IIS 5.0 snap-in loaded. The Start Menu shortcut is mapped to a Microsoft Management Console configuration file, or *tool* (saved as an .msc file) that contains the saved MMC window configuration and layout settings. This configuration file is located by following this path on a Windows NT server:

```
C:\winnt\system32\inetsrv\iis.msc
```

Tools (.msc files) are small files that can be copied or emailed to workstations of administrators or server operators who have specific management tasks delegated to them, such as administering the SNMP service on an IIS server. As long as a senior administrator has the MMC installed on his or her machine, along with the snap-in files being present, the senior administrator can create a tailor-made tool and send it to junior administrator or operator, who will be able to start the console simply by clicking on the tool (.msc file).

Method 2   To start the MMC with no snap-ins installed (functionality to the empty console can be added by loading snap-ins), click Start, Run and enter the following path:

```
C:\winnt\system32\mmc.exe
```

Snap-ins will need to be loaded into the console to enable it to perform administrative tasks. See the section "Adding a Snap-in to the MMC" for more information on how to do this.

If method 1 is chosen, a console window opens showing the your IIS server name under the Internet Information Services node (see Figure 2-1).

The MMC Layout

The layout of the console window is similar to the familiar Windows Explorer format and consists of two panes: the *scope pane* and the *results pane*.

The scope pane (left pane) provides a hierarchical view of all the network elements that can be managed using the MMC. These network elements are called *nodes* and include servers, network services, directories, files, ActiveX controls, and so on. This collection of all manageable nodes is called the *namespace*.

Figure 2-1
The Internet Services
Manager.

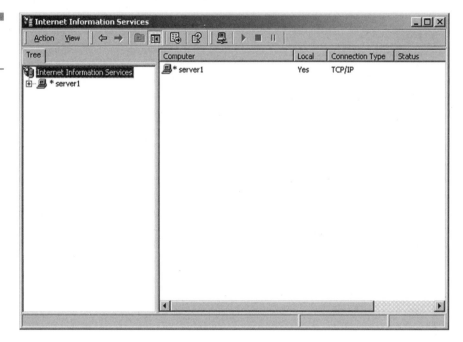

The results pane (right pane) shows the manageable properties of what-ever node is selected in the scope pane. In Figure 2-2, the Default Web Site node under the IIS server called server1 is selected in the scope pane (namespace), whereas the results pane shows all the manageable nodes that exist in the namespace hierarchy under the server1 node, including virtual directories and even files.

The MMC is a *Multiple Document Interface (MDI)* application. That is, you can create multiple child windows within the same console parent win-dow. Figure 2-2 shows the console with only one child window open; other windows can be added showing different views of the same namespace. These windows can then be tiled, cascaded, maximized, or minimized as in any MDI application.

The MMC console opened for managing IIS contains the rebar at the top of the window, which is context-sensitive based upon what node is currently selected in the MMC console.

Other elements of the console window that are not viewable in the IIS console, but will be covered later in this chapter, include the Menu bar, and the Main *toolbar* (see section *Creating a New MMC Console*).

The rebar (see Figure 2-3) is a customizable toolbar whose context-sensitive appearance depends on the currently selected node in the scope

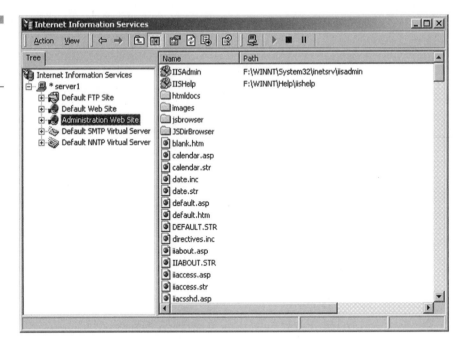

Figure 2-2
The Default Web Site node in the Internet Services Manager.

Figure 2-3
The rebar is a customizable, context-sensitive toolbar.

pane. A comparison between Figures 2-1 and 2-2 shows the varying appearance of the rebar.

For example, when the Default Web Site (or any other node in the IIS section of the MMC namespace) is selected, the rebar shows the following buttons:

- *Action* button   Clicking this button generates a drop-down menu that has essentially the same functionality as the shortcut menu that is accessed by right-clicking on a node in the namespace.

- *View* button   Clicking this button generates a drop-down menu that allows you to change the view of icons in the results pane (just as in Windows Explorer).

- *Delete* a node button.

- *Show properties* of a node button.

- *Up one level* button.
- *Show / Hide* the scope pane button.
- *Add a computer* to the list button.
- *Start* node button to start a Web site.
- *Stop* node button to stop a Web site.
- *Pause* node button to pause a Web site.

NOTE: *In previous versions of IIS, in order to stop all your Inet Services, you had to either go to Services and stop and start them from there, or use a net stop from the command line. You can now stop and restart all IIS processes from the IIS Manager.*

1. *Select the server name for the IIS services you wish to terminate. Right-click and select Restart Internet Services. This will bring up a dialog box (see Figure 2-4) for starting, stopping, and rebooting the selected server.*

2. *You can also use the net stop command to restart IIS processes:*

    1. *Open a command prompt.*

    2. *Type*

        ```
        net stop iisadmin
        ```

    3. *Type*

        ```
        net start w3svc
        ```

Figure 2-4
The
Stop/Start/Reboot
dialog box.

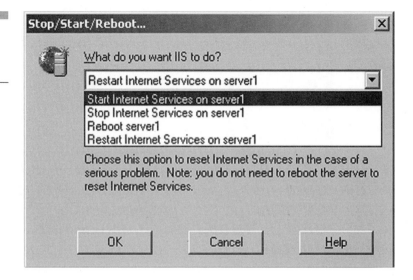

In most instances, you only need to stop an individual Web site. Selecting a Web site (virtual server) node in the MMC and clicking the Stop button only stops that site, not the WWW service itself.

The status bar (bottom of console) shows details concerning the currently selected node.

Creating a New MMC Console

To create a new (empty) console window, select Run from the Start menu and type in MMC. This will start a new occurrence of the MMC. An empty console window will appear (Figure 2-5). Notice the single child window within the parent console window. The only node in the console is the top-level node called Console Root.

The console window will have no management capability until we add snap-ins to it.

In this mode, you'll notice the addition of two new bars that weren't there when we were in the IIS Manager MMC console—the Menu bar and Main toolbar. The menu bar consists of the following options:

Figure 2-5
An empty console window appears.

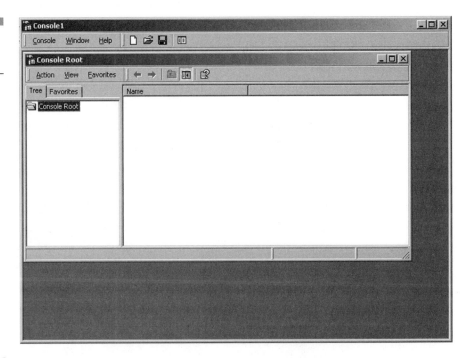

- Create a *new* tool (.msc file).
- *Open* an existing tool.
- *Save* a tool configuration.
- *Add* (or *remove*) a snap-in to the console.
- *Customize* the appearance of the MMC.
- *Access* the MMC help files.

The Main toolbar (below the Menu bar) serves essentially the same function as the menu bar. Contained on it are the following five buttons:

- *Create* a new console button.
- *Open* an existing console button.
- *Save* the current console button.
- *New* window button.
- *About* button.

Adding a Snap-in to the MMC

Next, we will add a standalone snap-in for Internet Services Manager to the console window. There are two basic types of snap-ins for the MMC:

- *Standalone snap-ins* (or just *snap-ins*) supply management capability for selected BackOffice products. An example would be the Internet Information Server snap-in, which provides the functionality of the Internet Service Manager.

- *Snap-in extensions* (or just *extensions*) supply additional functionality by extending the management capabilities of existing snap-ins. An example would be the Mail-SMTP extension for the Internet Information Server snap-in.

To add a new snap-in to the MMC, select Console, Add/Remove Snap-in from the menu bar. The Add/Remove Snap-in dialog box appears (Figure 2-6). To add a standalone snap-in, select the Standalone tab and click Add. The Add Standalone Snap-in box appears (Figure 2-7). Select Internet Information Services (for example) and click Add. Internet Information Services is now listed as a console snap-in in the Add/Remove Snap-in dialog box. The Internet Information Services snap-in provides the full functionality of the Internet Service Manager for configuring your IIS 5.0 server.

Figure 2-6
The Add/Remove
Snap-in dialog box.

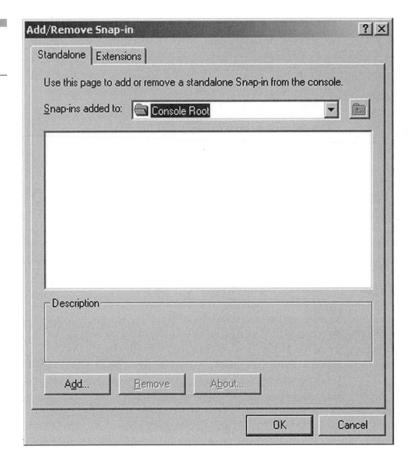

In addition to adding standalone snap-ins to your console namespace, the Add Standalone Snap-in dialog box also allows you to add

- *Folders,* which are virtual folders that can be used to organize your MMC namespace. Note that the Root Console and Internet Information Services nodes also appear as folder icons in the MMC namespace.
- *Links to Web addresses,* which are hyperlink URL nodes that will appear in the results pane when they are selected. An example appears below in the section *Adding a Node to the MMC.*
- *General controls* and *monitoring controls,* which are ActiveX controls that may be embedded in the namespace as the results node for the node you are currently installing (this functionality is provided as a

Figure 2-7
The Add Standalone
Snap-in dialog box.

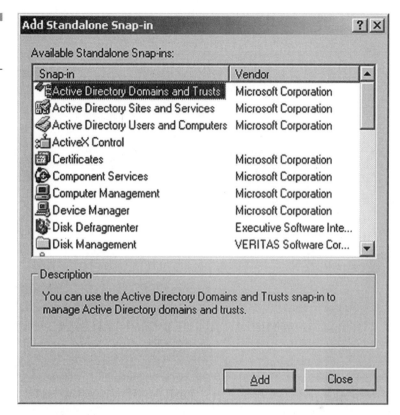

framework for developers, and will be further extended in later releases of the MMC).

To add a snap-in extension, select the Extensions tab on the Add/Remove Snap-in box (Figure 2-8). Select the snap-in you wish to extend from the drop-down list to get a series of checkboxes showing the extensions you can add. Select the desired extensions (for example, the Mail-SMTP extension) and click OK to return to the MMC console window. The Internet Information Server snap-in with the Mail-SMTP extension has now been added to the console window (Figure 2-9).

Customizing an MMC Console

Shown in Figure 2-9 is the new console created in the previous section. Notice that this console has one child window, titled *Console1—Console Root*.

Figure 2-8
The Add/Remove
Snap-in dialog box.

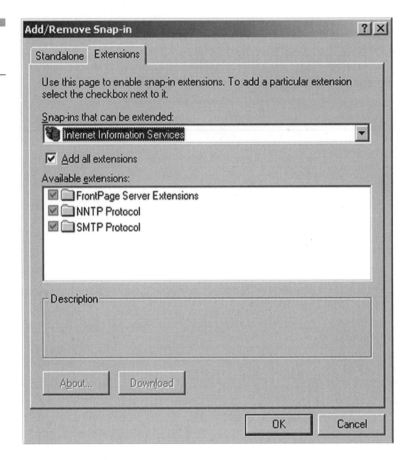

Our newly created console can be customized in a variety of ways. For example, you may want to create a new child window whose function is to allow administration of a single IIS 5.0 server. To do this, select the Internet Information Server node in the scope pane to show the IIS 5.0 servers that can currently be managed in the results pane. If the server you wish to administer doesn't appear in the results pane, you will need to connect to it first by right-clicking on the Internet Information Services node in the scope pane, selecting Connect from the shortcut menu, and entering in the name of the IIS 5.0 server you wish to connect to.

In the results pane, select the IIS 5.0 server you wish to create a MMC child window for and right-click on the server node. Select New Window from Here from the shortcut menu or click the Action button on the rebar and select New Window from Here from the drop-down menu.

Figure 2-9
The IIS snap-in with
the Mail-SMTP
extension has been
added to the console
window.

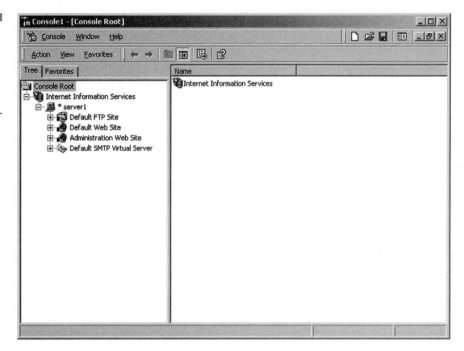

Figure 2-9
The IIS snap-in with
the Mail-SMTP
extension has been
added to the console
window.

Either of these actions retitles the original child window as 1:CONSOLE ROOT and creates a second child window titled 2:* <server name>. In this example, it's 2:*SERVER1 (see Figure 2-10). The second child window has the IIS 5.0 server you selected in the above steps as the top of its namespace.

Note that although the two windows have different root nodes, they both give views of the same namespace. An MMC console can show only one namespace at a time.

These two child windows can be resized, tiled, or cascaded as in any MDI application. For example, select the new 2:* SERVER1 window, maximize it, and then change the view in the results pane by clicking the View button on the rebar and selecting Large from the drop-down list as the icon size in the results pane. The result is shown in Figure 2-11.

After creating the second child window, you could close the original child window, which contains the Console Root node. If you do this, the top of your MMC namespace for your currently open console becomes a single IIS 5.0 server (server1 in Figures 2-10 and 2-11). The console settings can then be saved as an .msc configuration file, set to read-only mode, and delivered to a designated administrator or operator whose task is only to administer the single server called server1.

Figure 2-10
A second child
window is created.

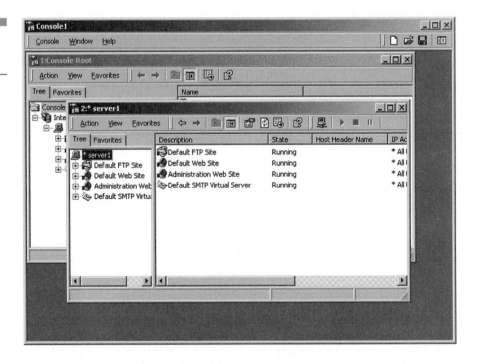

Figure 2-11
The child window
can be resized.

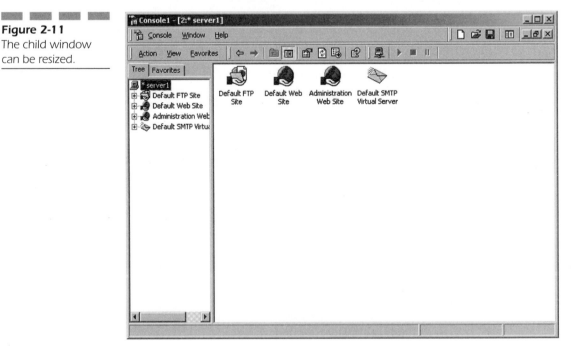

Adding a Node to the MMC

As mentioned earlier, several types of nodes may be added to the console, including virtual folders, links to Web addresses, and ActiveX controls. Here we give an example of adding a node to the console that functions as a link to the IIS server's home page on its default Web site. This node will be placed immediately beneath the Internet Information Services node in the namespace.

To add a new node to the MMC:

Select the Internet Information Services node in the scope pane and choose Console, Add-Remove Snap-in from the menu to open the Add/Remove Snap-in box. Click the Add button to open the Add Standalone Snap-in box, select Link to Web Address (for example), and click Add.

This method will open the Link to Web Address Wizard. Type in the URL

```
http://<server_name>
```

where <server_name> is the name (NetBIOS or fully-qualified domain name) of the IIS 5.0 server for which you wish to create a link to its home page on its default Web site (Figure 2-12).

Figure 2-12
The Link to Web Address Wizard.

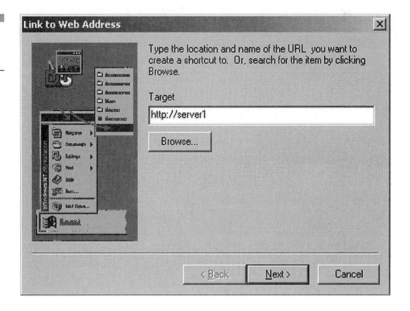

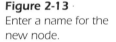

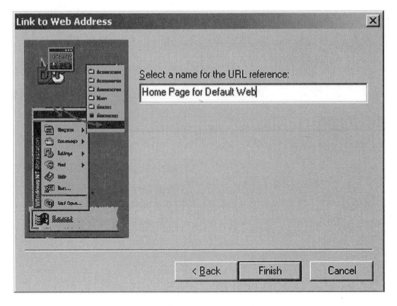

Click Next and enter a friendly name (description) for this new node (we have chosen the name *Home Page for Default Web* in this example). Then click Finish to create the new node (see Figure 2-13). Notice that a Web page icon appears in the results pane when the Internet Information Services node is selected in the scope pane.

Your console window can be further customized because nodes that have folder icons (for example, virtual folders and snap-ins), links to Web addresses, and ActiveX controls can be cut, copied, and pasted into different arrangements using the Action button on the rebar or using the shortcut menus that appear when you right-click these nodes.

Finally, click on the new Home Page for Default Web icon in the scope pane (or double-click on its node in the results pane), and the Web page will open up in the results pane, as shown in Figure 2-14.

Note that when a Web page is open in the results pane, additional Web navigation buttons are available on the rebar (refer to Figure 2-14). Remember that the appearance of the rebar changes in a context-sensitive manner depending on which node is currently selected.

Saving an MMC Console

To save your newly configured console:

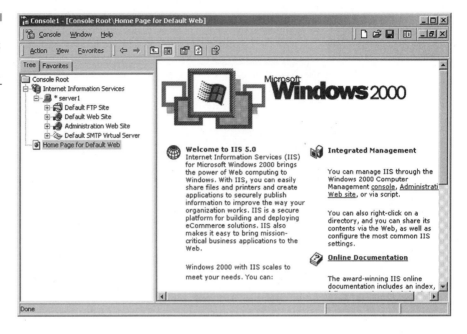

Figure 2-14
The Web page opens up in the results pane.

Choose Console, Save or Save As from the menu.

or

Click the Save button on the main toolbar.

The Save As dialog box appears. Type a filename for your new console and save it with the default extension of .msc in the location you specify. The .msc file you create is called a *tool*.
Possible locations for saving a tool include the following:

■ The folder Administrative Tools (the default location for saving .msc files), which appears in the Programs folder on the Start menu (see Figure 2-15). This will place your newly created tool in the Administrative Tools located in the following folder:

```
C:\Documents and Settings\Administrator\Start
Menu\Programs\Administrative Tools\
```

■ A network share on an NTFS volume accessible to other administrators and server operators. For example, if you create a custom console with only certain nodes added, you may want to set the

Figure 2-15
The newly created
tool can be saved to
the Administrative
Tools folder.

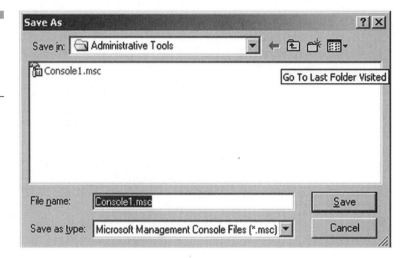

.msc file to read-only mode so the administrator or operator you
delegate the console to cannot permanently modify the file.

■ Attached to an email message mailed to a designated administrator
operator.

NOTE: *The designated administrator or operator who uses the .msc file
you created must have the MMC locally installed on her machine with the
necessary snap-ins added in order to be able to use the .msc file. The .msc
file contains configuration information only and has no intrinsic management capability.*

Further Examples of Using the MMC

Look back for a moment to Figure 2-2, which shows the default Web site
selected in the scope pane on the IIS 5.0 server called server1. The results
pane shows the contents (Web pages and files) that make up this Web site.
But where are the contents actually located? In other words, what is the
location (local or network) of the home directory for the default Web site?

To answer this question, in the screen of Figure 2-2, simply right-click on
the Default Web Site node in the MMC and select Explore to open Windows
Explorer (Figure 2-16). This action will open up Windows Explorer at the
home directory for the default Web site, in this case

        C:\winnt\inetpub\wwwroot\

Figure 2-16
Open Windows
Explorer at the home
directory for the
default Web site.

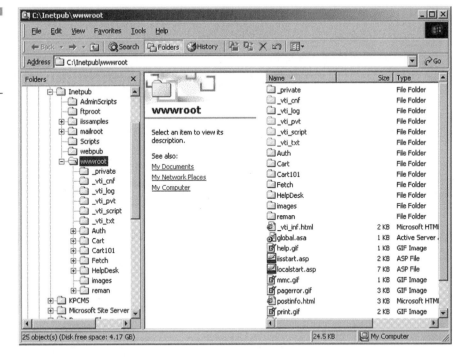

Configuring settings for a Web site is easy using the MMC. In the screen of Figure 2-2, simply right-click the Administration Web Site node and select Properties to access the Administration Web Site Properties box (see Figure 2-17).

In Chapter 3, *Administering the WWW Service*, we will see how to use these property sheets to configure a wide variety of settings for servers, Web and FTP sites, and even individual directories and files.

Settings that are made on these property sheets are stored in the *Metabase*. This is a hierarchical memory-resident database where IIS 5.0 settings and properties are stored. Many of these settings were stored in the Registry in previous versions of IIS, but these settings have now been migrated to the Metabase because it is more flexible and faster to access than the Registry. However, some IIS registry keys remain to provide backward compatibility with earlier versions of IIS.

In the Windows 2000 Server Resource Kit, you will find a tool called the Metabase Editor. This tool allows you to modify the IIS metabase in the same way you would modify the Windows 2000 system registry. The setup file for installing metaedit is locate at `<cdroot>\apps\metadit` of the Windows 2000 Server Resource Kit.

Figure 2-17

Access the
Administration Web
Site Properties dialog
box.

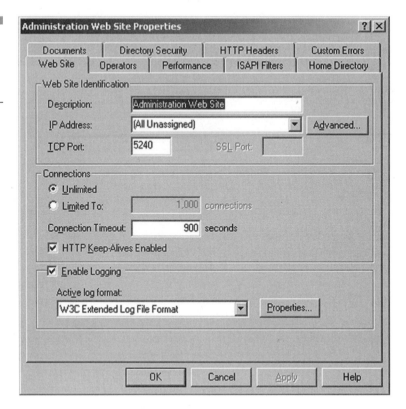

Just as with the Registry, configuring settings in the Metabase incorrectly may render your IIS 5.0 server inoperable, and should only be done with utmost care. For information on VBScript APIs for editing the Metabase, refer to the IIS online documentation.

Using MMC for Remote Administration

We went through customizing an MMC console by adding nodes for our local machine, but you can also easily use these same methods for administering other servers located on your *Local Area Network* (LAN). From any Windows 2000 machine, you can start MMC and create a console that contains the Internet Services Manager. You can connect to a remote server from MMC in one of two possible ways:

Select Internet Services Manager, right-click to bring up the
    menu options, select Connect, and type in the server you wish
    to connect to.

or

> Select Internet Services Manager, select Action, Connect from the
> menu options and type in the server you wish to connect to.

You must have the appropriate snap-in installed on the client machine
that you are locally logged on to in order to manage the remote machine.
You can see the results of having more than one machine in MMC in Figure
2-18.

Walkthrough: Using the MMC to Enable Internet Service Manager (HTML) for Remote Administration

You can use the MMC to configure Web and FTP sites you have created on
your IIS server. For example, in Figure 2-2, simply right-click on the Administration Web Site node and select Open or Browse from the shortcut menu.
This opens the home page of the administration Web site, used to remotely

Figure 2-18
The results of having
more than one
machine in MMC.

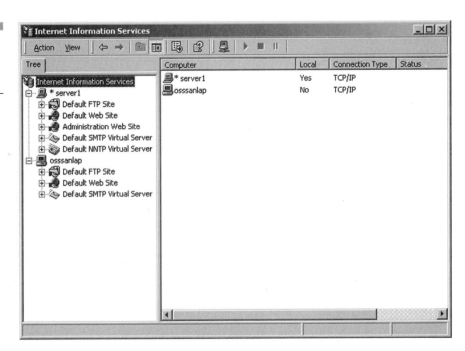

50

Chapter 2

administer IIS 5.0 servers using only a browser. The administration Web site is also known as the *Internet Service Manager HTML* and is a tool for remotely administering IIS servers using a standard Web browser. The Internet Service Manager (HTML) is covered in the next section of this chapter.

Notice in Figure 2-19 that what actually opens up if we try the above procedure is an *HTTP Error 403* page. This is because after a default installation of IIS 5.0, the security settings will need to be modified to enable remote administration of IIS 5.0 servers by accessing the administration Web site from a browser. The default settings for the administration Web site when IIS 5.0 is installed include an IP address restriction that allows the site only to be accessed by the following URLs:

```
http://localhost:<tcp_port_number>
```

or

```
http://127.0.0.1:<tcp_port_number>
```

Figure 2-19
The HTTP Error 403 page.

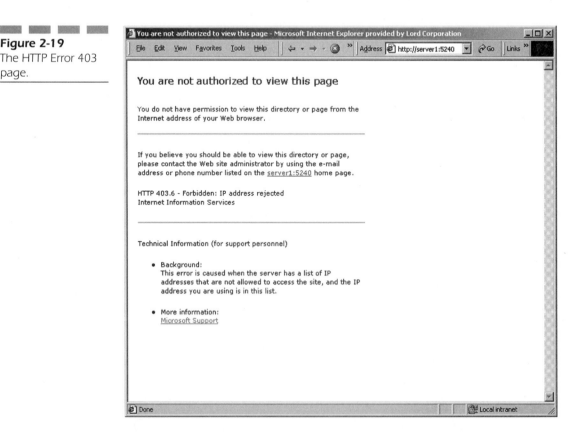

where `<tcp_port_number>` is the port number for the administration Web site. This can be found from the Web site tab of the Administration Web Site Properties sheet. In Figure 2-17, this port number is 5240, so the administration Web site can be accessed from the URL

```
http://localhost:5240
```

or

```
http://127.0.0.1:5240
```

However, the two URLs above work only if the browser is installed on the server itself. Furthermore, if you right-click on the administration Web site node in the MMC and select Browse, the browser tries to open up the site

```
http://<server_name>:<tcp_port_number>
```

or in this case

```
http://server1:5240
```

which fails to work locally and remotely because of the IP address restriction in place.

This default IP address restriction essentially means that when you install IIS 5.0, you can only use the Internet Service Manager (HTML) to manage the server from a browser that is installed locally on the IIS server. You must access it through localhost or the loopback address, not the server's NetBIOS name or fully qualified domain name. So if we want to enable administrators to use browsers on remote computers to administer their IIS servers, we need to reconfigure the default security settings.

To remove this IP address restriction, access the Administration Web Site Properties sheet (Figure 2-17), select the Directory Security tab, and click the Edit button for IP Address and Domain Name Restrictions. This brings up the IP Address and Domain Name Restrictions dialog box as shown in Figure 2-20.

Note the default setting for this Web site; namely, that all IP addresses are to be denied access except the *loopback* address 127.0.0.1. It is granted access to the site.

Select the radio button Granted Access to grant all computers access to this Web site. This way, an administrator will be able to administer the IIS server using the administration Web site from any computer regardless of its IP address, as long as that computer has a suitable browser installed on it.

Figure 2-20
The IP Address and
Domain Name
Restrictions dialog
box.

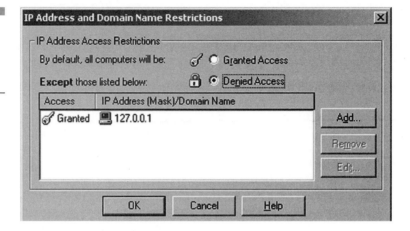

Of course, granting all computers access to the administration Web site creates a security hole; anyone who knows which port the administration Web site is running on can connect to the site and perform administrative tasks.

We need to close this hole. On the Administration Web Site Properties sheet, select the Directory Security tab again and click the Edit button for the Anonymous access and authentication control. This brings up the Authentication Methods dialog box as shown in Figure 2-21. Deselect Anonymous Access (if it is selected), making sure that only Integrated Windows authentication is enabled. By doing this, you add the further security restriction that in order to administer the site you will need to have a valid Windows user account. Then click on the OK button to commit your changes and close the dialog box.

Next, select the Operators tab and make sure that the only group that has been granted operator privileges on the administration Web site is the Administrators local group. This renders the site secure because only members of the Administrators local group have permission to access it.

Finally, to safeguard security, make sure that the Everyone group is removed from all files and subdirectories in the directory containing the Internet Service Manager (HTML) files, namely

```
C:\winnt\system32\inetsrv\
```

You should now be able to securely connect to the administration Web site locally or remotely by using the following URL from a suitable browser on any computer in the domain where you are logged on as administrator:

Figure 2-21
The Authentication
Methods dialog box.

```
http://<server_name>:<tcp_port_number>
```

or in this case

```
http://server1:7935
```

When you use this URL in Internet Explorer 5.0, the result is as shown in Figure 2-22.

Using the MMC to configure IIS 5.0 server property sheets for Web and FTP sites will be covered in more detail in Chapters 3 and 10.

Understanding the Internet Service Manager (HTML)

As mentioned above, included with IIS 5.0 is a browser-based version of the Internet Service Manager called *Internet Service Manager (HTML)*. The ISM (HTML) allows administrators to remotely administer IIS 5.0 servers

Figure 2-22
You can now
securely connect to
the administration
Web site locally or
remotely.

from browsers over an intranet or the Internet. The previous section dealt with using the MMC to modify IIS security settings in order to enable remote administration with the ISM (HTML).

In order to use the ISM (HTML), the administrator needs to know what TCP port the administration Web site is configured to use. This is because when IIS 5.0 is installed on a machine, it randomly assigns a port number between 2000 and 9999 to the administration Web site. However, the administration Web site will respond to all of the domain names configured on the IIS server, as long as the port number is appended to the request.

The ISM (HTML) will run from any browser that supports JScript and frames. Internet Explorer 3.02 or higher is supported.

The ISM (HTML) allows administrators to perform most of the management functions that the MMC provides. However, certain functions that can be performed on the MMC cannot be performed from the ISM (HTML), such as configuring the administration Web site itself.

Using the Internet Service Manager (HTML)

In the following sections, we will learn how to start the Internet Service Manager and how to use it to configure site properties.

Starting the Internet Service Manager (HTML)

To start the ISM (HTML) from the IIS server itself, access the URL:

```
http://<host>:<admin_port_number>
```

where <host> is either the IP address, NetBIOS name, or fully qualified domain name of the server, and <admin_port_number> is the TCP port number assigned to the administration Web site. The result is shown in the screenshot of Figure 2-22.

To access the ISM (HTML) from a remote machine, access the URL

```
http://<hostname>:<admin_port_number>
```

or

```
http://<hostname>/iisadmin:<admin_port_number>
```

Members of the Administrators group may use either method above; other Web site operators must use the second method only.

Configuring Site Properties with the Internet Service Manager (HTML)

Chapter 3 fully discusses the various options for configuring IIS 5.0. Chapter 3 deals only with using the MMC to administer IIS, but using the ISM (HTML) is essentially the same, except that instead of using tabbed property sheets, the ISM (HTML) uses hyperlinks to access different configuration pages. After learning how to administer IIS with the MMC, it is only a small step further to administering it with the ISM (HTML).

Nevertheless, here is one small example of using the ISM (HTML) to configure IIS. To configure the SERVER1\IIS Operators local group as Web

Figure 2-23
Configure the
SERVER1\IIS
Operators local
group as Web site
operators for the
default Web site.

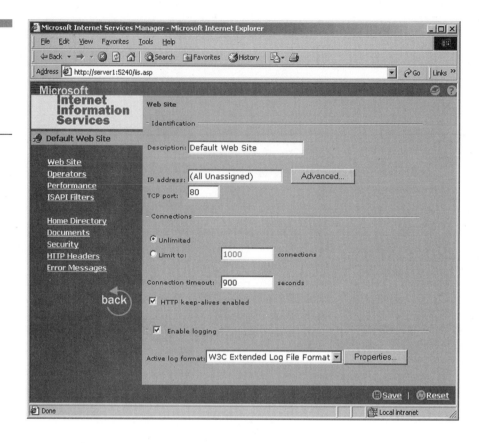

site operators for the default Web site, perform the following steps using the
ISM (HTML):

Select the Default Web Site icon in the right frame in Figure 2-23
and click the Properties hyperlink in the left frame.

or

Double-click on the Default Web Site hyperlink in the right frame in
Figure 2-23.

Either method causes a new page to load in the browser, which looks like
Figure 2-24.

To grant operator privileges for the default Web site to a local group
called IIS Operators on the SERVER1 server, click the Operators link on
the right frame in Figure 2-23. This will then display a new view in Internet Explorer that lists all the current operators for the default Web site as
in Figure 2-24.

Figure 2-24
A new page is
loaded in the
browser.

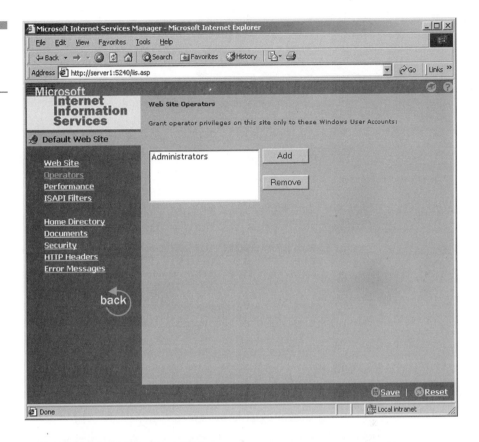

Figure 2-24
A new page is
loaded in the
browser.

Figure 2-25
The Explorer Use
prompt.

Then click on the Add button shown in Figure 2-23. The Explorer User Prompt dialog box appears, prompting you to enter in the name of the user or group to whom you want to grant operator privileges (see Figure 2-25). If you were granting permissions to a global group from a domain, you would enter the domain name followed by the global group name. In this example, we are using local groups, so you would enter in the local machine name and the corresponding local group in the following form:

```
<domain_name or machine_name>\<group>
```

For our example, you would enter

```
SERVER1\IIS Operators
```

Click OK to close the dialog box. To apply the settings, click the Save icon at the bottom of the ISM (HTML) page.

To check your work, open the MMC on the server and access the Property sheet for the default Web site. Select the Operators tab and verify that SERVER1\IIS Operators has been added to the list of operators.

Understanding the Windows Scripting Host

The third and last management tool included with Windows 2000 is the *Windows Scripting Host (WSH)*. This tool functions as a controller of ActiveX scripting engines, allowing administrative scripts to be run either from the command line or directly from shortcuts on the desktop.

Microsoft now has three products that run scripting languages:

- Internet Information Services runs Active Server Pages, which are server-side scripts that run on Web servers.
- Internet Explorer can run client-side scripts on the browser.
- The Windows Scripting Host can run scripts directly on administrator consoles.

The usual scripting languages for the Windows Scripting Host are *Visual Basic Scripting language* (VBScript) and *JavaScript* (JScript), but other scripting engines like Perl can be registered on the system and mapped to the WSH. Refer to the section of the online documentation entitled "Windows Scripting Host Programmer's Reference" for more information on how to register a new scripting engine for WSH.

The main advantage of using the WSH is that scripts written in VBScript and JScript are far more powerful than those written with the standard scripting language of MS-DOS command batch files. Using VBScript or JScript, the administrator can write either interactive or batch (that is, noninteractive) scripts that perform administrative tasks such as

- Creating users and groups
- Configuring environment variables

- Configuring Registry and Metabase keys
- Mapping network drives
- Performing additional user authentication

The WSH will run on Windows 2000 Server, Professional, Advanced Server, and Windows 98.

You can download the WSH separately and install it on your machine by visiting the following URL at the Microsoft Web site:

```
msdn.microsoft.com/scripting
```

Sample scripts are included with the installation of the WSH. These sample scripts are located in

```
C:\winnt\samples\WSH\ and C:\inetpub\AdminScripts\
```

Included are the samples listed in Table 2-1.

The scripts of Table 2-1 and other sample scripts are also available from the Microsoft Web site as a self-extracting file. To download these samples, open the URL

```
msdn.microsoft.com/scripting
```

Using the Windows Scripting Host

This section deals with configuring and running scripts using the WSH. Developing and testing scripts in VBScripts and JScript requires knowledge of these scripting languages and is beyond the scope of this book.

Running Scripts from the Command Line Using the WSH

Scripts written in either VBScript or JScript can be run from the command line using the command-line-only version of the WSH. This *command-line version of WSH* is called cscript.exe and is located in the path

```
C:\winnt\system32\cscript.exe
```

although it can be installed anywhere in the main system path.

Table 2-1

Scripts and functions

Script	What It Does
C:\winnt\samples\WSH\Chart.vbs C:\winnt\samples\WSH\Chart.js	Demonstrates how to access Microsoft Excel using the WSH
C:\winnt\samples\WSH\Excel.vbs C:\winnt\samples\WSH\Excel.js	Demonstrates the properties of WSH in Microsoft Excel
C:\winnt\samples\WSH\Network.vbs C:\winnt\samples\WSH\Network.js	Displays user and computer names, lists network drives, and maps new ones.
C:\winnt\samples\WSH\Registry.vbs C:\winnt\samples\WSH\Registry.js	Writes keys to the registry and then deletes them.
C:\winnt\samples\WSH\Shortcut.vbs C:\winnt\samples\WSH\Shortcut.js	Creates a shortcut to Notepad on the desktop.
C:\winnt\samples\WSH\Showvar.vbs	Lists server environment variables.
C:\InetPub\AdminScripts\adsutil.vbs	IIS administration utility that manipulates IIS through the use of ADSI.
C:\InetPub\AdminScripts\chaccess.vbs	Change access permissions on your Web sites.
C:\InetPub\AdminScripts\contftp.vbs	Unpauses an FTP server.
C:\InetPub\AdminScripts\contsrv.vbs	Unpauses an individual Web site.
C:\InetPub\AdminScripts\contweb.vbs	Unpauses the Web server.
C:\InetPub\AdminScripts\dispnode.vbs	Displays the properties of a specified node.
C:\InetPub\AdminScripts\disptree.vbs	Print a tree of administration objects from the root node of the local machine.
C:\InetPub\AdminScripts\findweb.vbs	Searches a computer for a Web you specify and displays its properties.
C:\InetPub\AdminScripts\mkw3site.vbs	Create a new Virtual Web site.
C:\InetPub\AdminScripts\mkwebdir.vbs	Creates a virtual Web directory off of a specified Web site.
C:\InetPub\AdminScripts\pauseftp.vbs	Pauses an FTP site.
C:\InetPub\AdminScripts\pausesrv.vbs	Pauses an individual Web site.
C:\InetPub\AdminScripts\pauseweb.vbs	Pause the Web services.
C:\InetPub\AdminScripts\startftp.vbs	Starts an FTP site.

Script	What It Does
`C:\InetPub\AdminScript\startsrv.vbs`	Starts an individual Web site.
`C:\InetPub\AdminScripts\startweb.vbs`	Start the Web services.
`C:\InetPub\AdminScripts\stopftp.vbs`	Stops an FTP site.
`C:\InetPub\AdminScripts\stopsrv.vbs`	Stops an individual Web site.
`C:\InetPub\AdminScripts\stopweb.vbs`	Stops the Web services.
`C:\InetPub\AdminScripts\synciwam.vbs`	Synchronizes the IWAM accounts. Used for object identities running under COM+.

To run the showvar.vbs sample script from the command line, open a Command Prompt window and type

```
cscript showvar.vbs
```

The result will be a series of dialog boxes displaying the currently defined environment variables on the IIS server.

Command-Line Options for the WSH

The full syntax for running scripts with the command-line version of WSH is as follows:

```
cscript <script_filename> <host_options> <script_options>
```

where

- `<script_filename>` is the path to the script (unless it is located in the current directory).
- `<host_options>` are options preceded by two forward slashes (//) that enable or disable certain aspects of WSH.
- `<script_options>` are parameters preceded by one forward slash (/) that are passed to the script for it to execute properly (depending on the script).

Table 2-1 explains the host options available with the command-line version of WSH.

Running Scripts from the Desktop Using the WSH

Scripts written in VBScript or JScript can be run from the desktop using the *Windows version of the WSH*. This version of WSH is called wscript.exe and is located in the path

```
C:\winnt\system32\wscript.exe
```

although it can be installed anywhere in the main system path.

To run the showvar.vbs sample script from the desktop, do one of the following:

- Double-click on the icon for showvar.vbs in Windows Explorer, My Computer, the Find box, or on the desktop. The WSH makes use of the file extensions .vbs and .js for executing scripts.

- Click Start, Run, type the path to the script, and click OK.

- Go to the command line and type

```
wscript showvar.vbs
```

Again, the result will be a series of dialog boxes displaying the currently defined environment variables on the IIS server.

Configuring .wsh Files for Windows-Based WSH Scripts

Just as DOS programs running on the old Windows 3.1 platform needed a PIF file to configure the environment in which they ran, scripts that are run with the Windows-based version of the WSH can make use of a configuration file called a .wsh file.

Settings can be configured at the per-script level by creating a .wsh file for each script. Scripts may have multiple .wsh files, allowing an administrator to create multiple configurations for running scripts and then assign different configurations to different people on the system.

To create a .wsh file for a script (for example, showvar.vbs), locate the script in Windows Explorer or My Computer, right-click on the script, and select Properties. Select the Scripts tab of the property sheet and select the runtime configuration options as desired for this particular script.

When you close the Properties box, a file called showvar.wsh is created in the same directory as the script. This file can be opened in any text editor and looks something like this, depending on what options were selected:

```
[ScriptFile]
Path5C:\winnt\Samples\wsh\showvar.vbs
[Options]
Timeout=10
DisplayLogo=1
BatchMode=0
```

While .wsh files set options for specific scripts, it is also possible to set global options for all scripts being executed by the WSH. To set global options for all scripts executed by the WSH, locate the file wscript.exe in the System32 directory and double-click on it to open the Windows Scripting Host box. Under the General tab, select the runtime options you desire as defaults for all scripts run on your machine. The options currently available with version 2.0 of the WSH are

■ Stop scripts after specified number of seconds.

■ Display logo when scripts are executed in command mode.

Because the available options are more limited, the Windows-based version of WSH is more suited to interactive scripts than batch scripts.

To run a script while making use of its .wsh file, double-click on the .wsh file to execute the script. If you double-click the script itself, it will ignore the .wsh file.

NOTE: *Be sure to keep the .wsh file in the same directory as the script. If you move the .wsh file to a different directory, you should edit the file and modify the Path statement inside it.*

SUMMARY

There are three primary tools to administer an IIS server, the HTML version of Internet Service Manager for remote administration using a browser, the Windows Scripting Host for batch and interactive scripting of administrative commands, which is run either from the desktop or from the command line, and the Microsoft Management Console. You can select the tool most suited to the administrative tasks that need to be performed. Administrators should also regularly visit Microsoft's Web site for updates to these management tools.

For More Information

For more information, try the following Internet and print resources.

Microsoft Web Site

For general information regarding Microsoft Management tools, visit the Microsoft Web site at

```
www.microsoft.com/management
```

Microsoft also provides Microsoft Terminal Services for a method of remotely administering a Windows 2000 Server. For information, refer to the Windows 2000 documentation.

The latest information on the *Microsoft Management Console* (MMC) can be found at

```
http://www.microsoft.com/management/mmc/helpmenu_productnews.htm
```

Microsoft Public Newsgroups

For newsgroups relating to the MMC, connect to the news server `msnews.microsoft.com` and subscribe to the following:

```
microsoft.public.management.mmc
```

Windows NT Magazine

The December, 1999 issue has a feature article titled "Windows Scripting Host 2.0—The Scoop on the Windows Script File Format" that provides a useful overview of the Windows Scripting Host.

The December, 1999 issue also has a feature article titled "A Tour Through Beta 3," that provides an overview of managing Windows 2000 using MMC.

The October, 1999 issue has an article available exclusively on the Web entitled "Getting the Most Out of MMC," that provides tips on MMC and its use with Windows 2000.

`www.winntmag.com/Articles/Content/7415_01.html`

You can also visit the Windows NT Magazine Web site at `www.winntmag.com`.

Administering the WWW Service

Introduction

The *World Wide Web* (WWW) Publishing Service is the core component of Internet Information Services 5.0, enabling the publishing of both static and dynamic Web content and enabling remote administration of IIS 5.0 through the Internet Explorer 5.0 Web browser. After completing this chapter, you will be able to

- Understand the *Hypertext Transfer Protocol* (HTTP), which underlies the WWW service and how HTTP 1.1 protocol is implemented in IIS 5.0.
- Configure the WWW service on IIS 5.0.
- Configure the Master, Site, Directory, and File properties for WWW sites.
- Back up IIS 5.0 configuration settings.

Understanding the Hypertext Transfer Protocol

The WWW Publishing Service is the server portion of the HTTP client/server protocol. HTTP is the application-layer protocol that underlies communication between WWW clients (called browsers) and WWW servers (or Web servers). Browsers make HTTP requests to Web servers, and the server responds with HTTP responses.

Most WWW servers support version 1.1 of HTTP. HTTP 1.1 is currently a Draft Standard proposed by the World Wide Web Consortium (W3C) and the *Internet Engineering Task Force* (IETF). A Draft Standard specification is considered to be one final step from being an Internet Standard. HTTP 1.1 has been implemented in latest generation Web servers (including IIS 4.0 and higher) and browser clients (including Internet Explorer 4.0 and higher).

Understanding HTTP

HTTP is a *stateless* protocol. In other words, a WWW client forms a connection with a WWW server, the server transfers the requested file to the client, and the connection is then terminated, with the server retaining no

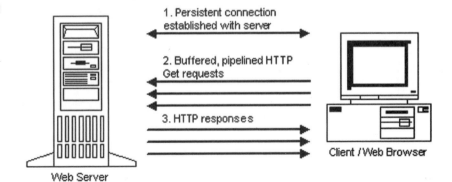

Figure 3-1
Details of an HTTP
1.1.

memory of the transaction. Here is the HTTP transaction process in more detail (see Figure 3-1):

1. A WWW client (such as Internet Explorer) uses a transport-level protocol (usually TCP) to establish a connection, usually on port 80, with the WWW service running on the WWW server (such as Internet Information Server).

2. After the connection is established, the client sends a request to the server, usually an HTTP Get request message, requesting a file from the server (the first file requested is the text of the Web page itself). The HTTP Get request includes a number of request headers that contain information about the type of transaction method requested, the capabilities of the WWW client (browser) that is making the request, and other data. The client can also send multiple requests to the server without waiting for a response—this is known as *pipelining*. Pipelining a recent implementation in the HTTP 1.1 draft results in fewer delays and faster file transfers. These requests can also be *buffered*, meaning several GET requests are collected together and then sent to the server.

3. The WWW service on the server responds to the request by transferring the requested file (an error code is returned if the requested file is unavailable).

4. The server has the ability to establish a *persistent connection* to the client, thus keeping the TCP connection open after they are established. This speeds the transfer of the files that make up Web pages by reducing the need to establish repeated or multiple connections. This is an improvement over the previous implementation of HTTP.

A Sample HTTP Session

Using a tool such as Microsoft's Network Monitor allows you to view the contents of HTTP packets directly and gain an understanding of what happens when a browser makes an HTTP request to a WWW server. Let's consider an example where Internet Explorer 5.0 is the client and Internet Information Server 5.0 is the server.

1. The user viewing a Web page in the browser clicks on a hyperlink that points to the URL

    ```
    Server1.anycorp.com/resumes/janet.htm
    ```

2. Clicking on this link causes the browser to send the following HTTP Get request message to the server:

    ```
    GET /resumes/janet.htm HTTP/1.1
    Accept: image/gif, image/x-xbitmap, image/jpeg, image/pjpeg,
      application/msword, application/vnd.ms-powerpoint, */*
    Accept-Language: en-us
    Accept-Encoding: gzip, deflate
    User-Agent: Mozilla/5.0 (compatible; MSIE 5.0; Windows NT)
    Host: server1
    Connection: Keep-Alive
    ```

    From the client's request headers, we can observe that

    - The name of the WWW server computer is server1.

    - The client (IE5.0) is an HTTP 1.1-compliant browser.

    - The client requests the file /resumes/janet.htm starting from the server's root.

3. The server receives the request and replies with a series of HTTP packets, the first of which contains response headers and the beginning portion of the requested file:

    ```
    HTTP/1.1 200 OK
    Server: Microsoft-IIS/5.0
    Connection: Keep-Alive
    Date: Thu, 06 Jan 2000 19:00:36 GMT
    Content-Type: text/html
    Accept-Ranges: bytes
    Last-Modified: Wed, 05 Jan 2000 17:45:28 GM
    ETtag: "d0293c63743cbc1:df3"
    Content-Length: 3097
    <HTML><HEAD><TITLE>Resume of Janet
    Smith</TITLE<</HEAD><BODY><H1>Janet Smith,
    M.C.S.E.</H1><P><HR><P>My name is Janet Smith, and I am
    currently a consultant with...
    ```

From the server's response headers, we can observe that

- The server (IIS 5.0) is an HTTP 1.1-compliant WWW server.
- The content-type being returned to the client is text/html.
- The length of the file being returned is 3097 bytes.

Understanding the WWW Service

IIS 5.0 has an HTTP 1.1-compliant WWW service with a wide range of settings that can be configured for optimal use as an intranet, extranet, or Internet server. The main tool for administering and configuring the WWW service on IIS 5.0 is the *Internet Service Manager* (ISM) snap-in for the *Microsoft Management Console* (MMC). Using the ISM snap-in for the MMC, an administrator can manage any number of IIS 5.0 servers on a local network.

For remote management of IIS 5.0 using a Web browser, the Internet Service Manager (HTML) provides most of the same functionality as the MMC. Because of the similarity in function of the two tools, only the ISM snap-in for the MMC will be covered in this chapter because it is the primary tool for server administration.

To start Internet Service Manager, choose Start, Programs, Administrative Tools, Internet Service Manager. This will open the Microsoft Management Console, from which you can expand the Internet Information Services node in the scope pane (left side) and select the locally installed IIS server—in this case, server1. The results pane (right side) shows the configurable nodes of IIS running on server1 (see Figure 3-2).

The WWW service running on the selected server (server1 in our example) is primarily managed by using *property sheets*. Each node in the server's namespace (which includes the IIS server itself, the default Web site, other virtual servers and virtual directories, and even individual Web pages and files) is a node in the MMC that has its own set of *properties*. These properties are accessed by

- Selecting the node and clicking the Properties button on the rebar
- Selecting the node, clicking the Action button on the rebar, and choosing Properties from the drop-down menu
- Right-clicking on the node and choosing Properties from the shortcut menu

Figure 3-2
The configurable
nodes of IIS

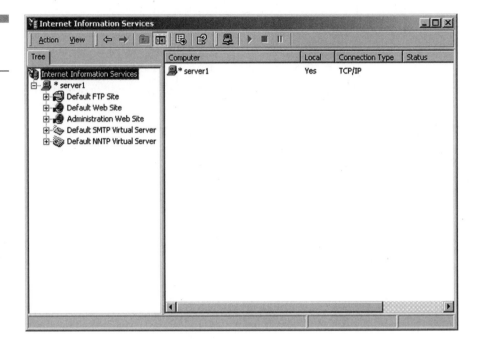

IIS 5.0 can be configured to have an unlimited number of Web sites running on it simultaneously, each responding to its own unique IP address and *fully qualified domain name* (FQDN). Each of these *virtual servers* (or Web sites) acts and behaves as if it were an entirely distinct machine, as if you had multiple IIS 5.0 machines on your network. Each can be configured separately and can be stopped, started, and paused independently. The creation of virtual servers (Web sites) will be covered in more detail in Chapter 5 *Administering Virtual Directories and Servers*.

Understanding Types of WWW Property Sheets

The property sheets for the WWW service on IIS 5.0 can be configured at four different levels:

Master property sheets

Site property sheets

Directory property sheets

File property sheets

Following is an explanation of the four levels of IIS property sheets for the WWW service, along with instructions on how you can access and configure property settings for each level.

1. *Master properties*   Master properties can be configured for all Web sites running on the IIS server. To access Master properties, right-click the IIS server node in the Microsoft Management Console and select Properties from the shortcut menu.

2. *Site properties*   Site properties (or virtual server properties) can be configured individually for each Web site running on the IIS server, including the default Web site that is created when IIS is installed. To access Site properties, right-click the Web site node in the MMC and select Properties from the shortcut menu.

3. *Directory properties*   Directory properties (or virtual directory properties) can be configured individually for each virtual directory defined within a Web site on the server. All files will inherit the property settings of the virtual directory that contains them. To access Directory properties, right-click the virtual directory within the Web site and select Properties from the shortcut menu.

4. *File properties*   File properties can be configured individually for each Web page within a virtual directory or Web site. To access File properties, right-click the selected Web page and choose Properties from the shortcut menu.

Settings for all of the WWW property sheets are stored in the *Metabase,* a database structure that replaces some of the functions of the Windows 2000 Registry for IIS 5.0.

The following sections describe how to access and configure the four types of property sheets using, as an example, the default Web site created when IIS 5.0 is installed.

Accessing the WWW Service Master Properties Sheet

Right-click the server node (server1 in Figure 3-2) and select Properties from the shortcut menu to bring up the Server Properties sheet (see Figure 3-3). From this sheet, select WWW Service and click Edit to bring up the WWW Service Master Properties sheet.

Any settings made to the Master Properties sheet are automatically inherited by the default (root) Web site and by all *new* virtual Web sites that

Figure 3-3
The Server Properties
sheet in Internet
Services Manager

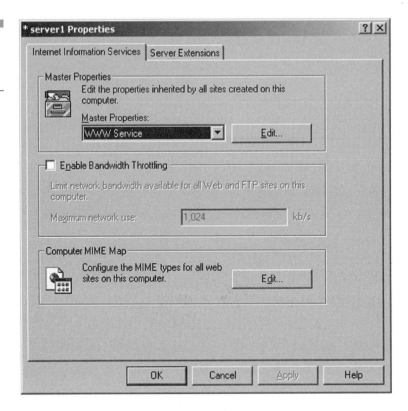

are created afterward. However, if the Master Properties are later changed, existing virtual Web sites do *not* inherit these changes unless they are specified to do so; only new virtual Web sites will automatically inherit them.

Accessing the WWW Site Properties Sheet

Right-click the Default Web Site node (see Figure 3-2) and select Properties from the shortcut menu to bring up the WWW Site Properties sheet (in this case, the Default WWW Site Properties sheet). Any settings made to this property sheet affect only the selected Web site and override any settings made in the WWW Master Properties sheet.

The Default Web site in Figure 3-2 can be accessed by a browser through the URL

```
http://server1/
```

Note that the WWW Site Properties sheet has the same tabs as the WWW Master Properties sheet, except for the absence of the Service tab for backward compatibility for IIS 3.0 Web applications.

Accessing the WWW Directory Properties Sheet

Right-click any virtual directory (such as the IISSAMPLES node under the default Web site) and select Properties from the shortcut menu to bring up the Virtual Directory Properties sheet (in this case, the IISSAMPLES Properties sheet). Any settings made to this property sheet affect only the selected virtual directory and override any previously made settings in the WWW Master Properties and WWW Site Properties sheets.

The IISSAMPLES virtual directory under the Default Web site in Figure 3-2 can be accessed by a browser through the URL

```
http://server1/IISSAMPLES/
```

Accessing the WWW File Properties sheet

Right-click any file node (Web page, image file, script file, and so on) and select Properties from the context menu to bring up the File Properties sheet. Any settings made to this property sheet affect the selected file only.

For the rest of this chapter, the figures will be taken from the WWW Master Properties and Default WWW Site Properties sheets because these two property sheets have the most options to configure. Most of what is said, however, applies to the WWW Directory Properties and WWW File Properties sheets as well.

Understanding Inheritance Overrides

To see how setting the properties of a node on the server namespace can affect the properties of child nodes beneath it, try the following exercise:

Access the WWW Service Master Properties sheet for your installed IIS 5.0 server. Change the Connection Timeout from the default value of 900 seconds to a new value of 450 seconds and click OK twice.

Next access the Default WWW Site Properties sheet and note that the Connection Timeout is now 450 seconds. Change this value to 1800 seconds and click OK.

Again, access the WWW Service Master Properties sheet. Change the Connection Timeout from 450 seconds back to 900 seconds and click OK. A dialog box called Inheritance Overrides will appear, indicating that the Default WWW Site Properties child node has overridden the Connection Timeout value you have just set, and asking you whether you want to select this child node to have its Connection Timeout value revert to the new default value. Select Default WWW Service and click OK twice.

Check that *both* the WWW Service Master Properties and the Default WWW Site Properties sheets now have a timeout of 900 seconds.

It works like this:

- When a *new* Web site is created, it automatically inherits the Master property settings of the IIS server on which it is created.
- When a *new* Web virtual directory is created, it automatically inherits the Site property settings of the Web site on which it is created.
- When a *new* Web page or subdirectory is created in a virtual directory or Web site, it automatically inherits the properties of the virtual directory or Web site that contains it.

However,

- When a Master property setting is changed, you are given the option of passing this change along to all *existing* Web sites on the IIS server.
- When a Site property setting is changed, you are given the option of passing this change along to all *existing* virtual directories on the Web site.
- *But* when a property on a virtual directory is changed, the changes are *automatically* passed along to all Web pages and subdirectories in the virtual directory.

Configuring WWW Property Sheets

The four different types of WWW property sheets have different options (tabs) available depending on whether they configure options at the Master, Site, Directory, or File level. Here are the property sheet tabs available for each level:

- *Web Site* tab (Master, Site, and Directory levels). Configures site identification, IP address, TCP port, limit connections, enables and configures logging.

- *Operators* tab (Master and Site levels). Grants operator privileges.

- *Performance* tab (Master and Site levels). Tune server-caching performance, throttles bandwidth for site, enables HTTP Keep-Alives.

- *ISAPI Filters* tab (Master and Site levels). Sets options for ISAPI filters.

- *Home Directory* tab (Master, Site, Directory, and File levels). Configures content location and access permissions, enables indexing, creates FrontPage Web, allows directory browsing, enables logging, configures application settings, sets execution permissions (at the Directory properties level, this is called the *Virtual Directory* tab; at the File properties level, it is called the *File* tab).

- *Documents* tab (Master, Site, and Directory levels). Specifies default documents, enables footers.

- *Directory Security* tab (Master, Site, Directory, and File levels). Configures authentication methods, configures SSL, grants or denies access to IP addresses and domain names.

- *HTTP Headers* tab (Master, Site, Directory, and File levels). Configures content expiration, specifies custom HTTP headers, configures content ratings, modifies MIME mappings.

- *Custom Errors* tab (Master, Site, Directory, and File levels). Configures custom HTTP error messages.

- *Service* tab (Master level only). Sets a default Web site for applications that still use IIS 3.0 settings and settings for HTTP compression of documents.

In addition to these, the IIS Server Properties sheet can be used to globally throttle WWW bandwidth and configure the global MIME mappings.

Configuring Default Properties for IIS

To configure the default properties for an IIS server, select a server node (for example, server1) under the Internet Information Services hierarchy in the scope pane of the MMC and click the Properties button on the rebar to access the Server Properties sheet (where "Server" is replaced by the actual name of the server, in this case server1—see Figure 3-3). From this property sheet, you can set default or global properties for all Web and FTP sites on the selected server. These properties include the maximum bandwidth used by the WWW and FTP services and the default MIME types recognized.

Configuring Default Bandwidth Throttling for IIS

To limit the amount of network bandwidth that the WWW and FTP services use, check Enable Bandwidth Throttling on this property sheet and enter a value for maximum network use in kilobytes per second (KB/s). The default value is 1024 MB/s or 1 megabyte per second (MB/s). Bandwidth throttling is useful if your IIS server fulfills multiple roles on your network, such as functioning as a domain controller or mail server.

A rule of thumb suggested by Microsoft is that you initially throttle the bandwidth at 50 percent and then adjust it upward or downward as necessary and monitor server performance. For a standard 100-Mbps backbone PCI Ethernet card, a good starting value for maximum network use would thus be 50 Mbps (6100 KB/s).

NOTE: *Bandwidth throttling of the WWW service applies only to the delivery of static Web pages (HTML) and not to dynamic pages such as Active Server Pages (ASPs).*

Configuring Default MIME Types for IIS

Another option you can configure from this property sheet is the MIME types that the WWW service sends to browsers in the HTTP response header. MIME stands for *Multipurpose Internet Mail Extensions* and was originally developed as an extension to the original Internet mail protocol defined by RFC 822 to allow the transmission of nontext content to be packaged and encoded within text-only email messages.

MIME is used in HTTP sessions as follows:

1. A browser client contacts a WWW server requesting a document, which could be text, HTML, images, audio, or some other format. For

example, say the client requests a sound file from the server given by the URL

`server1.anycorp.com/sounds/bullfrog.au`

2. The server looks up the file extension .au in its table of MIME mappings (a table that matches file extensions with MIME types) and then determines that the MIME type for the requested file is

`audio/basic`

3. The server returns the requested file, preceded by a series of response headers. One of the response headers indicates the MIME type of the document being returned, in the form of a content-type header:

`Content-type: audio/basic`

4. The client looks up this content type in its own table of MIME mappings to determine what to do with the file; that is, whether to

- Display the document in the browser window

- Invoke a helper application to render the document

- Ask for user intervention (that is, a dialog box appears requesting whether the user wants to save or open the file; if Open is selected, the user must then specify which application to use to open the file, as the client is unfamiliar with the MIME type returned)

To view a list of MIME mappings for the WWW service, click the Edit button on the Server Property sheet to get the File Types property sheet (Figure 3-4).

To configure a new MIME mapping, click New Type and enter the MIME content type and the file association to be mapped to this type. To edit an existing type, select the type and click Edit.

Why might you want to create your own MIME mapping? Say that you have a collection of Perl scripts that you want to make available as plain text files for browsing to users in your Developer global group. Perl scripts usually have the extension .pl, yet are saved in plain text format. What you can do is register a new MIME type for your WWW service by clicking New Type and entering the file extension and MIME type, as shown in Figure 3-5.

Now when a browser tries to access a URL such as

`server1.anycorp.com/scripts/sample.pl`

the server will return the file with a header indicating that the file is of type text/plain, and the browser will display the file as unformatted text within the browser window. Of course, you should make sure that the Perl scripts

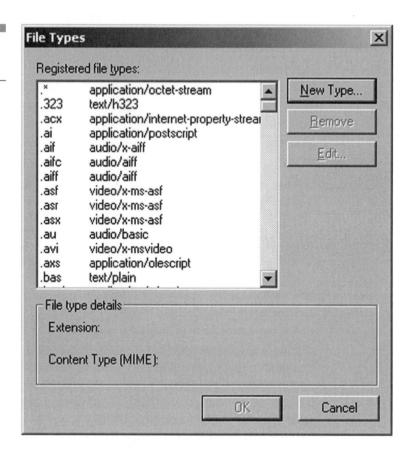

reside on an NTFS volume so only the Developer global group can be
assigned permission to read the directory containing the scripts.

Configuring WWW Server Master Properties

In addition to configuring default bandwidth throttling and default MIME types, the Server Properties sheet allows you to access and edit the server's Master properties. These Master properties settings will be inherited as defaults by all Web sites created afterward on the server (though these settings can be overridden by setting properties for the Web sites themselves).

To configure the WWW Master properties, select WWW Service in the Master Properties drop-down box on the Server Properties sheet and click the Edit button. The WWW Service Master Properties sheet will appear (see Figure 3-6). The ten tabs on this property sheet allow full customization of the default properties for all Web sites created afterward on the selected IIS server. The following sections give details on many of the settings that can be configured using this property sheet, although the settings operate in essentially the same way whether they are configured at the Master, Site, Directory, or File level.

Figure 3-6

The WWW Service Master properties sheet.

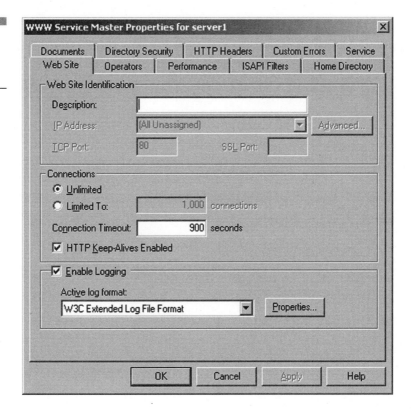

Configuring WWW Site Identification

Enter a friendly description in the Description textbox for the Web site selected. This description will appear attached to the Web site node in the MMC.

Certain settings on this WWW Service Master Properties sheet are grayed out in Figure 3-6 because a server has been selected to be configured rather than a specific Web site. The IP Address, TCP Port, and Advanced properties can be configured only from the WWW Site Properties sheet, not from the WWW Service Master Properties sheet. SSL Port can be configured only if the Web site is set up to use SSL.

On the WWW Site Properties sheet, use the IP Address drop-down box to assign a particular IP address to the selected Web site. If you leave the setting here at All Unassigned, the Web site will respond to all IP addresses that are not specifically assigned to other Web sites, in effect making this the default Web site. Only IP addresses that have been previously configured in the Network application of Control Panel will appear in the drop-down box here.

The default TCP port for HTTP is port 80. To change this value, enter a new number into the TCP Port box. Notify users of the change in port numbers because when they try to access this FTP site, they will have to include the port number.

For example, if the port is changed to 6800 and users are trying to access the site with Internet Explorer, they must browse with an URL such as

    http://139.53.5.118:6800

or

    http://super.santry.com:6800

(using DNS name resolution) or

    http://super:6800

(using NetBIOS name resolution).

NOTE: *Do not use any of the Well-Known Port Numbers other than port 80 for the HTTP port number. If you do, conflicts may occur with other TCP services. Well-Known Port Numbers are discussed in Chapter 9,* Administering the FTP Service.

The SSL Port box will be covered in Chapter 11.

The Advanced button is used to configure additional identities for the Web site. It allows you to configure Host Header Names, a feature of IIS 5.0 that allows multiple Web sites to each have their own fully qualified domain name but be mapped to the same IP address and TCP port number. This is covered in Chapter 5, *Administering Virtual Directories and Servers*.

Configuring WWW Connection Limits and Timeouts

Select either

- Unlimited, to allow an unlimited number of simultaneous connections to the server.

- Limited to, to specify the maximum number of simultaneous connections allowed to the server. The default value is 1000 connections.

NOTE: *To temporarily deny access to your Web server, you might set the Limited to field to zero. Then when a client tries to access a page on the server, the server will return a status code 403 message that will produce the following display in the browser window:*

```
HTTP Error 403
403.9 Access Forbidden: Too many users are connected
```

This error can be caused if the Web server is busy and cannot process your request due to heavy traffic. Please try to connect again later.
Please contact the Web server's administrator if the problem persists.
HTTP status codes will be dealt with later in this chapter.

Set the Connection Timeout Interval to the length of time, in seconds, until the server disconnects from an inactive user. The default value is 900 seconds (15 minutes). If HTTP Keep-Alive is enabled on the Performance tab, a client will request a page from the server, a connection is formed, the server delivers the page to the client, and the connection remains open in case the client requests another page (speeding up the process by eliminating the need for the client to establish a fresh connection). But if the client does not require an additional page, this timeout feature causes the connection to eventually be closed by the server, freeing up TCP ports for other uses.

Configuring WWW Logging Select Enable Logging to turn on the WWW Service logging features. Logging is enabled by default so administrators can keep track of which sites are being accessed by which users, how often these sites are being accessed, whether the server's responses have been successful, and so on.

Select an Active log format from the drop-down list. Microsoft IIS 5.0 offers logging in four possible formats:

- Microsoft IIS Log File Format
- NCSA Common Log File Format
- W3C Extended Log File Format (the default format)
- ODBC Logging

The first three formats produce simple ASCII text logs. These can be viewed in a simple text editor such as Notepad, imported into a database, or imported into and analyzed with various log analysis programs.

In addition, the W3C Extended Log File Format is customizable, allowing administrators to select which parameters to include in the log. The default format for IIS logging is the W3C Extended Log File Format.

To set the logging options for these three formats, select the desired format and click the Properties button to access the Microsoft Logging Properties sheet. Then use this sheet to select

- The logging time period, for example:
  - Create new logs on a daily, weekly, or monthly basis.
  - Allow the log file to grow to an unlimited size.
  - Create a new log file when the old one reaches a specified fixed limit.
- The location of the log files, which by default are in the directory

  `C:\winnt\system32\logfile\`

- Which parameters to include in the log (for W3C Extended Log File Format only)

Understanding the Microsoft IIS Log File Format This format is a comma-delimited fixed-field ASCII text file. A typical name for such a log file might be

In000109.log   Created on January 9, 2000

inetsv23.log   The twenty-third limited-size log file created

Typical output from such a log might be as follows:

```
10.107.3.201, -, 01/9/00, 11:02:22, W3SVC1, SERVER1, 10.107.3.200,
53998, 275, 5585, 200, 0, GET, /Default.asp, -,

10.107.3.201, -, 01/9/00, 11:02:28, W3SVC1, SERVER1, 10.107.3.200,
2354, 395, 2167, 200, 0, GET, /iissamples/default/nav2.gif, -,

10.107.3.201, -, 01/9/00, 11:02:28, W3SVC1, SERVER1, 10.107.3.200,
2634, 395, 644, 200, 0, GET,/iissamples/default/MSFT.GIF, -,
```

To help in interpreting the Microsoft IIS Log File Format, Table 3-1 lists the fields contained in the last entry of the preceding log and their meaning.

Understanding the NCSA Common Log File Format   The NCSA Common Log File Format is a space-delimited fixed-field ASCII text file. A typical name for such a log file might be

nc000109.log	Created on January 9, 2000
ncsa23.log	The twenty-third limited-size log file created

Table 3-1

Sample fields in Microsoft IIS Log File Format.

Data Element	Typical Value
Client's IP address	10.107.3.201
Client's username (- if anonymous)	-
Date of request	1/9/00
Time of request	01:02:56
Service requested (W3SVC1 is the WWW service)	W3SVC1
Server's name	SERVER1
Server's IP address	10.107.3.200
Server's elapsed processor time (ms)	1282
Bytes sent by client's request	395
Bytes returned by server's response	2167
HTTP status code returned	200
Win32 status code returned	0
Request method	GET
Document requested	/iissamples/default/nav2.gif

Typical output from such a log might be as follows:

```
10.107.3.201 - - [09/Jan/2000:11:06:39 -0600] "GET
/iissamples/default/iis3.GIF HTTP/1.0" 200 3558

10.107.3.201 - - [09/Jan/2000:11:06:42 -0600] "GET /default.asp
HTTP/1.0" 200 5518

10.107.3.201 - - [09/Jan/2000:11:06:46 -0600] "GET
/iissamples/default/IE.GIF HTTP/1.0" 200 8866
```

To help in interpreting the NCSA Common Log File Format, Table 3-2 lists the fields contained in the last entry of the preceding log and their meaning.

Understanding the W3C Extended Log File Format The W3C Extended Log File Format is a space-delimited variable-field ASCII text file with headers. A typical name for such a log file might be

Ex000109.log   Created on January 9, 2000

extend23.log   The twenty-third limited-size log file created

Typical output from such a log might be as follows when all extended logging options are selected:

```
#Software: Microsoft Internet Information Services 5.0

#Version: 1.0

#Date: 2000-01-10 01:02:54

#Fields: date time c-ip cs-username s-sitename s-computername s-
ip cs-method cs-uri-stem cs-uri-query sc-status sc-win32-status sc-
bytes cs-bytes time-taken s-port cs(User-Agent) cs(Cookie)
```

Table 3-2

Sample Fields in
NCSA Common
Log File Format

Data Element	Typical Value
Client's IP address	10.107.3.201
Client's domain\username	[blank]
Date and time of request	09/Jan/2000:01:02:56
GMT offset	-0600
HTTP request	"GET /iissamples/default/nav2.gif HTTP/1.0"
HTTP status code returned	200
Bytes returned by server's response	2167

```
cs(Referer)

2000-01-10 01:02:54 10.107.3.201 - W3SVC1 SERVER1 10.107.3.200
GET /Default.asp - 200 0 5585 275 4697 80
Mozilla/2.0+(compatible;+MSIE13.0;+Windows195) - -2000-01-10
01:02:56 10.107.3.201 - W3SVC1 SERVER1 10.107.3.200
GET /iissamples/default/IISTitle.gif - 200 0 21576 399 761 80
Mozilla/2.0+(compatible;+MSIE13.0;+Windows195)
ASPSESSIONIDGQGGGGYP5HILJEGPCGGLNFFKEKHEBCGHM http://server1/

2000-01-10 01:02:56 10.107.3.201 - W3SVC1 SERVER1 10.107.3.200
GET /iissamples/default/nav2.gif - 200 0 2167 395 1282 80
Mozilla/2.0+(compatible;+MSIE13.0;+Windows195)
ASPSESSIONIDGQGGGGYP5HILJEGPCGGLNFFKEKHEBCGHM http://server1/
```

To help in interpreting the W3C Extended Log File Format, Table 3-3 lists the fields contained in the last entry of the preceding log and their meaning.

Understanding ODBC Logging   The fourth log format is ODBC Logging, which is specific to IIS and allows administrators to log WWW transactions directly to an ODBC-compliant database such as Microsoft SQL Server or Microsoft Access. The steps involved in logging to a database are as follows:

1. Create a database and define a table within it. Give the table a name (the default suggested name is InternetLog).
2. Create the following fields within the table to hold the logged data:

Field	Data Type
ClientHost	varchar(255)
Username	varchar(255)
LogTime	datetime
Service	varchar(255)
Machine	varchar(255)
ServerIP	varchar(50)
ProcessingTime	int
BytesRecvd	int
BytesSent	int
ServiceStatus	int
Win32Status	int
Operation	varchar(255)
Target	varchar(255)
Parameters	varchar(255)

Table 3-3

Sample fields in W3C Extended Log File Format

Data Element	Typical Value
Date of request	2000-01-10
Time of request	01:02:56
Client's IP address	10.107.3.201
Client's username (- if anonymous)	-
Service requested (W3SVC1 is the WWW service)	W3SVC1
Server's name	SERVER1
Server's IP address	10.107.3.200
Request method	GET
Document requested	/iissamples/default/nav2.gif
Search query (if any)	-
HTTP status code returned	200
Win32 status code returned	0
Bytes returned by server's response	2167
Bytes sent by client's request	395
Server's elapsed processor time (ms)	1282
Server's TCP port	80
Type of client (a.k.a. user agent)	Mozilla/4.0+(compatible; +MSIE+4.0;+Windows+98
Cookie (if any)	ASPSESSIONIDGQGGGGYP= HILJEGPCGGLNFFKEKHEBCGHM
Referrer (the site containing the link that the user clicked to get this page)	http://server1

3. Use the System DSN property sheet of the ODBC option in Control Panel and give the database a system *data source name* (DSN). This is necessary so ODBC can reference the table. The default suggested DSN is HTTPLOG.

4. Select ODBC Logging as the Active log format on the Web Site tab of the WWW Service Master Properties sheet. Click the Properties button to access the ODBC Logging Properties sheet (Figure 3-7).

Figure 3-7
The ODBC logging sheet.

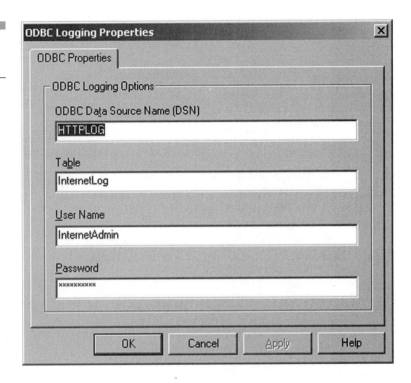

5. Enter the system DSN, table name, and the username and password, if these are necessary to connect with the database, and click OK to begin logging.

Configuring WWW Site Operators The Operators tab on the WWW Service Master Properties sheet is used to specify which Windows 2000 user accounts will have operator privileges for all Web sites on the IIS server (Figure 3-8). The Operators tab on a WWW Site Properties sheet can be used to specify which Windows user accounts will have operator privileges for a particular Web site selected. By default, the Administrators local group is assigned operator privileges on all Web sites on the IIS server. But Web site operators do *not* have to be members of the Administrators local group.

To add a user or group to the operators list, click Add and select the user or group from the Add Users and Groups property sheet.

Web site operators have the right to perform simple administrative tasks on the Web sites to which they are assigned. These tasks include

- Setting access permissions
- Enabling and configuring logging
- Enabling and configuring content expiration

Figure 3-8
Adding new WWW
Service Operators

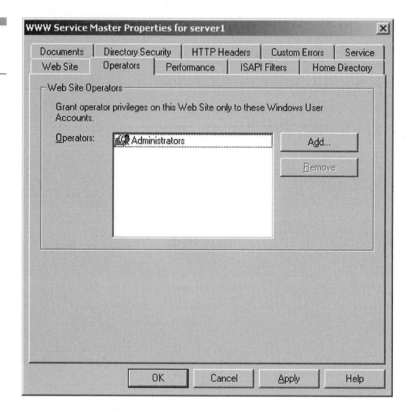

- Enabling and configuring content ratings
- Defining fault documents
- Adding footers to Web pages

Operators *cannot* perform the following tasks unless they are also members of the Administrators local group:

- Configuring IP address and port number
- Throttling bandwidth
- Changing the anonymous user account
- Creating and mapping virtual directories
- Configuring application settings

Typically, Web site operators include the Administrators local group and the company or departmental person responsible for managing the particular Web site. An administrator generally creates a *read-only mode* .msc file representing an MMC window with only one node in the scope pane; namely, the Web site to be administered. The Web site operator is then allowed to use this .msc file to open an MMC window to administer the Web site.

Configuring WWW Performance Tuning   The sliding control featured in the Performance tab (Figure 3-9) allows you to tune the performance of your server based on the expected number of hits per day. If the number selected is slightly greater than the actual number of hits, the server will perform well. But if the number selected is much greater than the actual number of hits, too much server memory will be used for caching server hits, and the result will be a decrease in overall performance of the server. Use the IIS logging capabilities to determine the number of hits per day on your server and adjust the setting here accordingly.

Configuring WWW Bandwidth Throttling   As Figure 3-9 illustrates, this option is grayed out for the WWW Service Master Properties sheet because it is configured globally on the Server Properties sheet (see Figure 3-3). On the WWW Site Properties sheet, the value selected here will always

Figure 3-9
Configuring performance tuning, bandwidth throttling, and HTTP Keep-Alives.

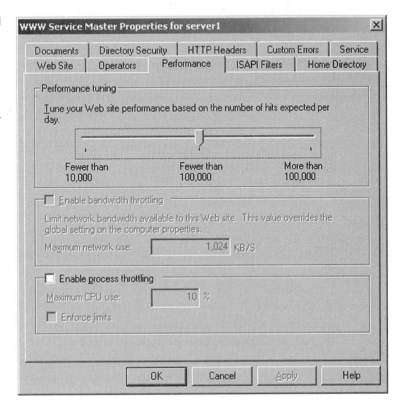

override the default value set on the Server Properties sheet, even if the value selected is greater than the value on the Server Properties sheet.

Configuring HTTP Keep-Alive   Check the checkbox shown in Figure 3-9 to enable or disable HTTP Keep-Alives on the server. When the box is checked, the server will keep a connection open with a client instead of opening and closing a new connection every time an HTTP Get request is made by the client. HTTP Keep-Alive is an enhanced form of HTTP 1.1 Persistent Connections and is enabled by default.

Configuring ISAPI Filters   IIS 5.0 supports a variety of ways of extending the functionality of the WWW service, including

- *Active Server Pages* (ASPs)
- *Internet Server Application Programming Interface* (ISAPI)
- *Common Gateway Interface* (CGI)
- *Internet Database Connector* (IDC)

Prior to the introduction of IIS, most WWW servers supported only *Common Gateway Interface* (CGI) applications. CGI is an early standard allowing WWW servers to communicate with server-side gateway applications. Typically, a Webmaster would write a CGI script in a scripting language such as Perl, and then save the script in the cgi-bin/ subdirectory of the Web site being developed. This CGI program might be a simple script to process the results of a submission from an HTML form. The basic problem is that each time a CGI program is called, a new process is started on the server. Thus, when CGI programs are called frequently, the added overhead due to multiple instances of the same CGI program running simultaneously on the server can easily cause the server's performance to decline noticeably.

Microsoft developed ISAPI as an alternative to CGI. Like CGI, ISAPI applications provide a way to extend the capabilities of a WWW server. Calling an ISAPI application does not create a new instance of the application, whereas invoking a CGI script always generates a new process, even if a similar process is already running on the server. ISAPI applications are multithreaded and can run within the same process space as IIS, thus making more efficient use of system resources and improving server performance considerably. ISAPI applications are usually written and compiled in C++ and provide much better performance than interpreted scripting engines such as Perl. Writing and developing ISAPI applications requires knowledge of a high-level programming language such as C++ and is beyond the scope of this book.

ISAPI applications fall into two categories:

■ *ISAPI extensions* are loaded on demand to provide additional functionality for specific Web sites running on the server. An example is a DLL that handles a form submission on a Web page. In general, ISAPI extensions are DLLs that process data received from an HTTP request, for example:

```
http://scripts/extension.dll?var1+var2+var...
```

■ *ISAPI filters* are loaded when the WWW service initializes and remain in memory until the IIS server is shut down. They are triggered when some system event occurs on the IIS server and provide additional functionality to all Web sites running on the server. Examples include DLLs that provide a custom authentication method, perform data encryption, generate custom logs, and perform traffic analysis.

Use the ISAPI Filters tab on the WWW Service Master Properties sheet (Figure 3-10) or WWW Site Properties sheet to add, remove, edit, or change

Figure 3-10
Configuring ISAPI filters.

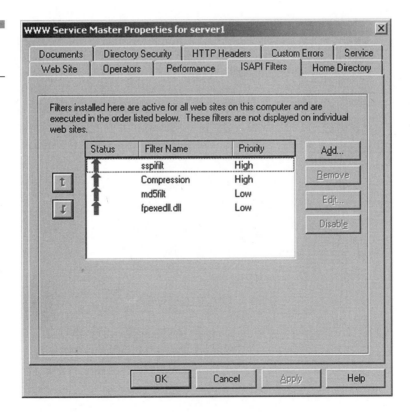

the order of ISAPI filters on the server or site. Click Add to add a new ISAPI filter by mapping a friendly name for the filter to the local or network path of the filter's executable file. Filters can be added, removed, or deleted, and assigned a priority rating and an order of execution.

The Details box shows the current status (loaded into memory, unloaded from memory, or disabled) of each ISAPI filter, its friendly name and executable file, and its priority.

Creating ISAPI filters involves high-level programming and is beyond the scope of this book. Refer to the Online Documentation for more information about creating ISAPI applications. IIS 5.0 comes with some sample ISAPI applications that can be compiled with a C++ compiler and tested on IIS 5.0. You'll find more information on these samples in the online documentation, if you're interested.

Configuring WWW Content Location   The Home Directory of a Web site is the location where its home page and other related content is stored. This setting is grayed out on the WWW Service Master Properties sheet (see Figure 3-11), but is available on the WWW Site Properties sheet.

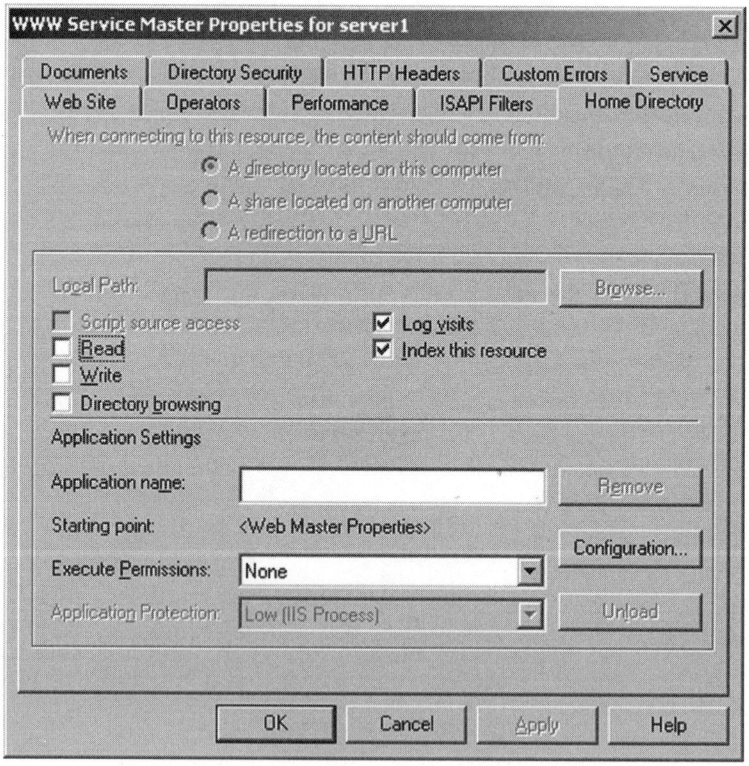

Figure 3-11
Setting the Home
Directory options.

When you install IIS, it creates a default Web site with a home directory located at

`C:\inetpub\wwwroot`

If you create a new Web site on the server, you have the option of specifying the location of the new site's home directory. Using the radio buttons on this property sheet, you can choose one of three possible settings:

- A *local directory* on this computer

  Enter the path or browse to the new home directory located on this server, for example:

  `C:\webstuff\newhome`

- A *network share* located on another computer

  Enter the UNC path to the share on the selected server, for example:

  `\\webcontent\newhome`

  Click Connect As and enter the username and password of the security credentials that will allow users to access the contents of the network share. Do not use an Administrator account here—it could pose a security risk.

- A *redirection* to a URL

  Redirection tells the client to look elsewhere for the document it seeks. You can redirect client requests for the home directory by entering a fully qualified URL in the textbox, such as

  `http://webserver2/newhome`

Creating new Web sites and configuring their home directories is covered in more detail in Chapter 5.

Configuring WWW Access Permissions If the home directory of a Web site is mapped to a local directory or a share on the network (options 1 and 2 in the preceding list), the following IIS access permissions can be enabled for that directory (refer to Figure 3-11):

- Enable Read access if you want users to be able to browse the contents of the home or a selected directory. Normally directories containing HTML files (Web pages) should be assigned Read access so users can view them; directories containing files you don't want users to be able to read (for example, CGI scripts and ISAPI applications) should have Read access disabled.

■ Enable Write access if you want clients to be able to upload content or edit files in the directory.

Note that the Web access permissions assigned to directories in this way must be combined with the NTFS permissions if the directory is on an NTFS volume. This is covered in more detail in Chapter 4, *Administering Security*.

NOTE: *To temporarily deny access to a Web site so you can make changes to it, select the WWW Site Properties sheet, select the Home Directory tab, and clear the Read checkbox.*

Configuring WWW Content Control   As illustrated in Figure 3-11, select Log Access if you want to have client visits to the home or selected directory logged. Note that logging must *first* be enabled on the Web Site tab of the properties sheet. This setting allows logging to be selectively enabled on different Web sites on the server and on different virtual directories within a site.

Select Directory Browsing Allowed if you want to allow users to browse your Web site's directory structure. Normally, directory browsing is disabled by leaving this option cleared. This is because allowing a user access to information about your Web site's directory structure could help them gain unauthorized access to content on your site.

If your home or selected directory lacks a default document (default.htm or default.asp or index.htm) and directory browsing is disabled, a browser trying to access your directory will receive an HTTP status code 403 message:

```
HTTP/1.1 403 Access Forbidden
```

If your home or selected directory lacks a default document but directory browsing is enabled, a browser accessing your directory will display a UNIX-style directory structure. Figure 3-12 illustrates a browser trying to access the /images directory on server1:

NOTE: *Virtual directories do not appear in directory listings. In order to browse the directory of a virtual directory, you must enter the full URL for the virtual directory in the browser.*

Figure 3-12
View of a directory
when directory
browsing is enabled
on the server.

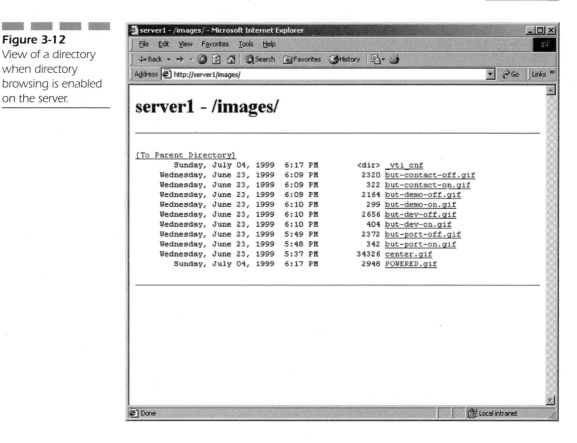

Select Index This Directory to have Microsoft Index Server include the home or selected directory for full-text indexing of your Web site. This will be covered in more detail in Chapter 8.

Select FrontPage Web to create a FrontPage Web for the home or selected directory. This will be covered in more detail in Chapter 6.

Configuring WWW Application Settings   Applications include all the directories and files in a directory that are specified as an application starting point, until another starting point is encountered. Configuring the home directory of a Web site ensures that all directories under the home directory, and all virtual directories within the site, are part of the same application. Application settings are particularly relevant for sites containing *Active Server Pages* (ASP) scripts.

Click the Remove button in the WWW Service Master Properties sheet (refer to Figure 3-11) to remove an existing application from the site. The Remove button now becomes a Create button. To create a new application for your site, click the Create button and enter a friendly name for your application in the Name textbox. Click the Configuration button to configure your application using the Application Configuration property sheet (see Figure 3-13).

The App Mappings tab on the Application Configuration property sheet can be used to map interpreters and script engines to certain filename extensions. For example, if a browser tries to access the URL

```
http://server1/default.asp
```

the application mappings settings determine that if a user tries to access the site's home directory, the server notices the file mapping *.asp and looks up which application deals with this type; namely

```
C:\inetpub\wwwroot\system32\inetsrv\asp.dll
```

Figure 3-13
Configuring a WWW application.

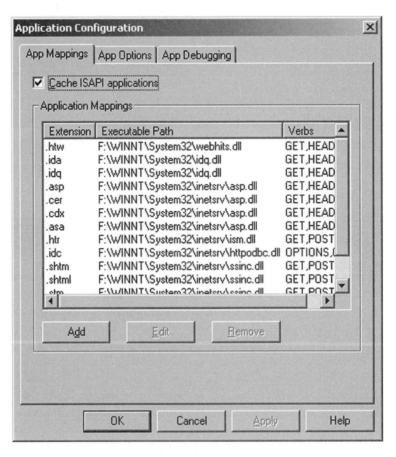

Selecting Cache ISAPI Applications allows ISAPI DLLs to be loaded and then cached, which speeds up operation of the server.

The App Options tab on the Application Configuration property sheet provides the following options:

- *Enable Session State*   Selecting this checkbox will enable ASP applications to create a new session for each user and allow the user to be tracked across multiple ASP pages.
- *Enable Buffering*   Selecting this checkbox will cause the server to collect ASP output and buffer it before sending it to the client.
- *Enable Parent Paths*   Selecting this checkbox allows ASPs to use relative paths to parent directories by using ../ to go one level up. If this is enabled, do not give the home directory execute permission; a security breach might occur if the user can browse up to the home directory and execute a binary within this directory.
- *Default ASP Language*   The default ASP language is VBScript. This may be changed here (for example, to JScript).
- *ASP Script Timeout*   This setting determines how long asp.dll will allow an ASP script to run.

The App Debugging tab on the Application Configuration property sheet can be used to

- Enable ASP server-side script debugging.
- Enable ASP client-side script debugging.
- Cause detailed ASP error messages to be sent to the client when an error occurs. Included with the error message is the file and the line number in the script that caused the error.
- Cause a text message to be sent to the client when an error occurs.

You can then set Application Protection, which allocates how the Web application will be processed. The default setting is medium (pooled), meaning it will run in the process or memory space of other applications. You can also select low (IIS process), meaning it will run in the same process as the IIS server, or high (isolated), meaning the application will run in its own space without affecting any of the applications running on the server.

Finally, permissions must be assigned for the application to run.

- Script permission allows the execution of scripts mapped to a script engine.
- Execute permission allows any binary executable to run in the directory.

NOTE: *Script permission is generally safer than execute permission and should always be used when a site contains scripts mapped to a script engine running on IIS 5.0.*

Configuring WWW Default Documents Under the Documents tab, select Enable Default Document (see Figure 3-14) to define that file is returned when a request from a browser contains a directory (for example, asdf) but not a specific file. If this setting is enabled, the requested URL.

```
http://server1/asdf/
```

will return one of the following files:

```
http://server1/asdf/default.htm
```

Figure 3-14
Configuring default documents and footers.

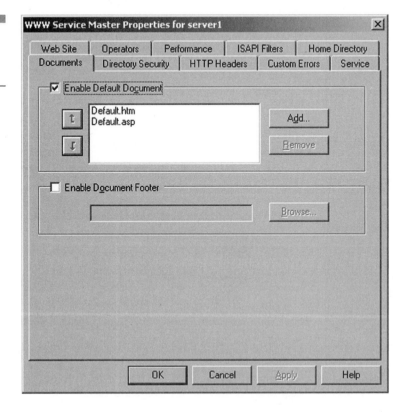

or

```
http://server1/asdf/default.asp
```

If both types of files exist in the home directory, the first one in the listbox (default.htm) will be returned to the browser. The order in the listbox can be modified by using the up and down arrow buttons.

Other default file types can be defined. A common one to define is *index.htm,* which can be either an index page or a home page. If no default document is found, the server will either return a status code 403 (Access Forbidden) message or provide a listing of files and subdirectories in the directory, depending on whether the server is configured to allow directory browsing.

Configuring WWW Document Footers   Select Enable Document Footer (see Figure 3-14) to have an HTML segment automatically appended to every document retrieved from the server. Specify the full local path to the footer segment.

Configuring WWW Anonymous Access and Authentication Control   Use the Directory Security tab in the property sheet (see Figure 3-15) to configure the kind of logon authentication to be used by browsers trying to access your Web site. These settings will be considered in detail in Chapter 4.

Configuring WWW IP Address and Domain Name Restrictions   The Directory Security tab of the property sheet can also be used to set your server's security properties (see Figure 3-15). These settings will be considered in detail in Chapter 4.

Configuring WWW Secure Communications   The Directory Security tab in the property sheet can also be used to help configure SSL settings for your Web site (see Figure 3-15). These settings will be considered in detail in Chapter 12.

Configuring WWW Content Expiration   In the HTTP Headers tab, select Enable Content Expiration (see Figure 3-16) to allow your server to return content expiration information in the response headers to an HTTP request. Use these settings for Web pages that regularly or frequently change their content (for example, announcement pages) and to speed up the browsing process.

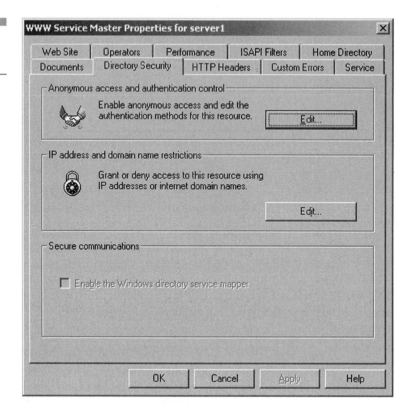

If content expiration is enabled, the next time a browser accesses a page
it will use the response header information to determine if the content on
the page is considered to have expired or not. If the content has expired, the
browser will request a new copy of the page with the expectation that the
page has been updated since the original was received. If the content has
not expired, the browser assumes that the current content is still valid and
will try to retrieve the page from its client-side cache, which speeds up the
browsing process.

The content expiration settings include

- *Expire Immediately*   A new copy of the page will be downloaded the
  next time the page is requested; the page will never load from the
  client-side cache.

- *Expire After* <minutes/hours/days>   The content will expire after
  the specified time interval. Until this interval passes, the client will try
  to retrieve the page from cache, which will speed up the browsing
  process.

Figure 3-16
Configuring content
expiration, custom
HTTP headers,
content ratings, and
MIME Map.

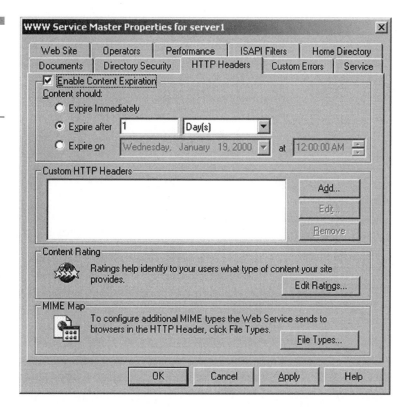

■ *Expire On* <date/time>   The content will expire on the specified date
and time. Until that time has passed, the client will try to retrieve the
page from cache, speeding up the browsing process.

Configuring WWW Custom HTTP Headers   As shown in Figure 3-16,
click Add to create custom HTTP response headers (name/value pairs) to
be returned to clients making HTTP requests to the home or selected directory. These headers can contain control information that invokes specialized responses from suitably configured browser clients, firewalls, and
proxy servers.

Configuring WWW Content Rating   As shown in Figure 3-16, select
Edit Ratings to establish content ratings for the home or selected directory.
These content ratings have been developed by the *Recreational Software
Advisory Council* (RSAC) and can be used by browsers such as Internet
Explorer 3.0 and higher versions to determine whether the client has the

privileges to view the site. For more information on RSAC, visit their Web site at

`www.rsac.org.`

Content ratings can be established in four areas (see Figure 3-17):

- Violence
- Sex
- Nudity
- Language

To test the Content Ratings system, try the following exercise:
Check the Enable Ratings for This Resource box, select the Language category, and move the slider to level 2 (moderate expletives). Enter your

Figure 3-17
The Content Rating property sheet with content ratings enabled.

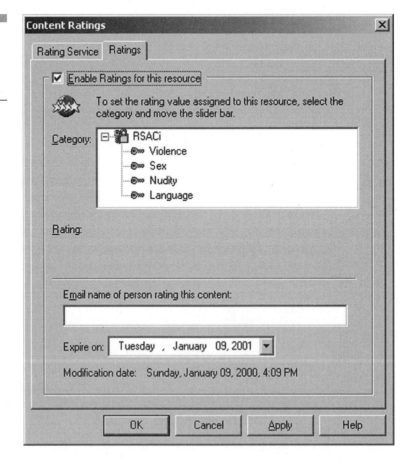

email address as the person rating the content of your server and set the expiration date for a week from today. Click Apply to configure the ratings for your server. This indicates that your site contains moderate expletives and should be viewed only by those with the corresponding privileges.

Now start a content ratings-enabled browser such as Internet Explorer 5.0 and choose Internet Options from the Tools menu on the browser. Select the Content tab on the Internet Options property sheet. Note that Content Advisor has a button labeled Enable; this indicates that Content Advisor has not yet been enabled on your browser. Try to access your server's default Web site using the browser; you should have no difficulty doing so.

Enable Content Advisor on your browser by clicking the Enable button on the Content tab of the Internet Options property sheet. You are requested to enter a supervisor password, which is used to prevent unauthorized personnel (such as your children) from altering the ratings you are about to set. Type `password` as your supervisor password, and retype it for confirmation.

The Content Advisor property sheet now appears, which is similar in appearance to the Content Ratings property sheet of IIS 5.0 shown in Figure 3-17. Select the Language category and verify that the slider is set at level zero (inoffensive slang). This indicates that sites specified as having a level 0 language rating are acceptable to the browser and will be displayed, but any sites with a higher-level language rating will be inaccessible. Click OK twice, and then close your browser; the Content Advisor will not take effect until the browser restarts.

Now test your site's rating by restarting your browser and trying to access your server's default Web site again. This time you should receive a message box like the one in Figure 3-18.

Notice that your browser will not allow you to access the site unless you enter the supervisor password. Enter password and view the site. Now configure your browser's Content Advisor to allow you to view sites with level 2 language ratings. Shut down and restart your browser, and try to access the site; this time you should succeed.

Finally, disable the Content Advisor feature on Internet Explorer 5.0 and disable content ratings on your server to return everything to the state you began with.

The Content Advisor property sheet for Internet Explorer 5.0 has a General tab with two important configuration options:

■ Select Users Can See Sites That Have No Rating if you are using your browser to view sites on the Internet. The vast majority of sites on the Internet are not rated under this system, so leaving this option

unchecked will mean that you will be able to access practically nothing at all on the Internet. Content Advisor is effective only if it is widely implemented on browsers such as Internet Explorer and on servers such as Internet Information Server.

■ Select Supervisor Can Type a Password to Allow Users to View Restricted Content if you want the option of viewing restricted content when you browse a site.

Configuring WWW Additional MIME Types You can configure other MIME types in addition to the ones already defined in the section "Configuring Default MIME Types for IIS." If MIME types are configured here for the home or selected directory and then the Master MIME types are changed, the Master MIME types overwrite the changes made to the home or selected directory; the changes are not merged.

Configuring HTTP Error Messages When a client (browser) makes an HTTP request to a server, the server responds by sending a series of response headers followed by the requested file or files. If the transaction is successful, the first request header sent by the server typically looks like this:

```
HTTP/1.1 200 OK
```

(Refer back to the section *A Sample HTTP Session* in this chapter if you need more information on HTTP request/response headers.) The number 200 in the response header is an HTTP status code signifying that the transaction was successful. HTTP status codes generally fall into one of three categories:

- 200 through 299 signify the transaction was *successful*.

- 300 through 399 signify that *redirection* has occurred.

- 400 through 599 signify that some sort of *error* has occurred.

IIS 5.0 allows the administrator to customize HTTP status code messages from the third category. To customize an HTTP status code, first select it on the property sheet (see Figure 3-19) and do one of the following:

Figure 3-19
Configuring custom
HTTP error codes.

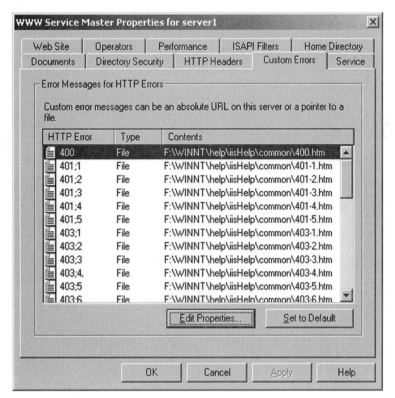

- Click Set to Default if you want the server to return the default (standard) status message.
- Click Edit Properties to access the Error Mapping Properties box.

Accessing the Error Mapping Properties box allows you to customize an HTTP status code in three possible ways, by selecting the message type as either:

- Default, to have the server display the default (standard) status message. These messages are defined by the HTTP specifications and are quite brief and sometimes uninformative (for example, "400 Bad Request").
- File, to have the server display a custom error page stored locally on the server or on a network drive. Microsoft supplies a set of customized error pages that are more informative than the default error messages (see Table 3-4). As an administrator, you may want to further customize these pages by adding the company logo, a mailto link to the site

Table 3-4

HTTP status codes and their meaning

Field	Data Type
ClientHost	Varchar(255)
Username	Varchar(255)
LogTime	Datetime
Service	Varchar(255)
Machine	Varchar(255)
ServerIP	Varchar(50)
ProcessingTime	Int
BytesRecvd	Int
BytesSent	Int
ServiceStatus	Int
Win32Status	Int
Operation	Varchar(255)
Target	Varchar(255)
Parameters	Varchar(255)

administrator, a feedback form, advertising, and so on. These custom error pages are located on your server in the directory

```
c:\winnt\help\iisHelp\common
```

■ URL, to have the server redirect the client to a URL, which must be an URL on a local server. This URL could point to a custom page or to a script or executable program that handles the error condition. The only requirement is that the URL must exist; otherwise, the server will return a "200 Request Successful" message to the client.

Configuring the Default IIS 3.0 Web Site   For each IIS 5.0 installation, one (and only one) Web site on the server can be selected for administration by a previous version of Internet Service Manager (version 3.0 or earlier). Choose which site (if any) you want to administer this way from the drop-down box in the Service tab (see Figure 3-20). This tab appears *only* on the WWW Service Master Properties sheet.

Figure 3-20

Configuring the IIS 3.0 Default Web site and HTTP compression.

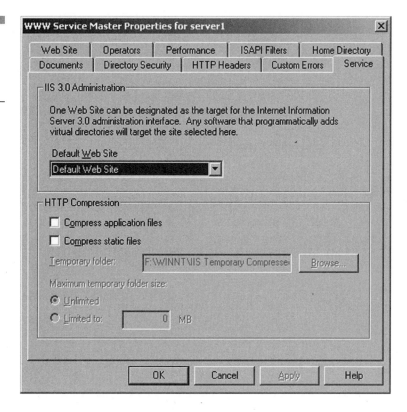

HTTP Compression   A new feature of IIS 5.0 is the ability to compress both static (HTML) and dynamic documents (ASP). HTTP compression works only if the client browser supports it, as does IE 5.0. Compression does increase the amount of processing that needs to be done on the server, but can reduce the size of the transmission by 80%. It would be best to monitor the performance of your Web server after implementing compression to see the impact of compression on your server's processor usage.

To enable compression, select Compress Static Files or Compress Application Files in the Service tab (see Figure 3-20). Then type in a directory where the compressed files should be kept. Note that the place where the documents are stored must be an NTFS partition and a local drive that is not compressed using NTFS file compression.

For More Information

For more information on *Hypertext Transfer Protocol* (HTTP), check out some of the following resources.

The World Wide Web Consortium (W3C)

The *World Wide Web Consortium* (W3C) is a group of international, vendor-neutral organizations whose goal is to promote the development of protocol standards for the World Wide Web. For information about the current status of HTTP, visit the W3C Web site at

```
www.w3.org
```

The W3C also publishes a magazine called the *World Wide Web Journal*. There is an online version of this magazine at

```
www.w3j.com
```

To participate in technical discussions regarding the development of HTTP and related software, you can subscribe to the mailing list at

```
www-talk@w3.org
```

Send an email message to `www-talk-request@w3.org` with the subject of SUBSCRIBE and nothing in the body of the message. There are literally dozens of mailing lists available from the W3C, but this one is probably the one of most general interest.

To post more general and less technical questions regarding HTTP, try posting to the newsgroup

```
comp.infosystems.www
```

or one of the other relevant `comp.infosystems` newsgroups.

The Internet Engineering Task Force (IETF)   The IETF is another organization concerned with developing the underlying architecture of the Internet protocols to increase the overall performance of the Internet. The IETF consists of individuals organized into working groups devoted to specific tasks, communicating mainly through mailing lists. The HTTP Working Group is one example. For more information about the IETF, visit their Web site at

```
www.ietf.org
```

Administering Security

Introduction

Security is a prime concern for network administrators, and Internet Information Services 5.0 running on Windows 2000 forms a reliable, scaleable environment for securely hosting Internet, intranet, and extranet Web sites. After completing this chapter, you will be able to

- Describe the various security methods available for Web sites hosted by IIS 5.0 running on Windows 2000.
- Configure IIS to grant and deny access to users based on their client IP addresses or Internet domain names.
- Understand and configure IIS authentication security, including anonymous access, basic authentication, and Integrated Windows Authentication.
- Understand and configure IIS permissions for Web sites and individual pages.
- Understand and configure NTFS permissions for Web sites and individual pages.
- Understand how to combine IIS and NTFS permissions.
- Understand other methods of increasing security of IIS servers, including disabling unnecessary protocols and services, and by monitoring effectiveness of security settings by implementing NTFS auditing and IIS logging.

Additional security for IIS can be realized by implementing *Secure Sockets Layer* (SSL) in combination with X.509 client certificates. This is covered in Chapter 11.

Understanding IIS Security

Administrators can control access to Web content hosted on IIS 5.0 running on Windows 2000 servers in four main ways:

- *IP address and domain name security* IIS allows administrators to control access by clients to Web sites, virtual directories, and individual files based upon the IP address or domain name of the client or group attempting to access the resource. IP address and domain name security applies to all users who try to access the resource, regardless of which groups they belong to.

- *IIS authentication security* IIS allows administrators to control access by clients to Web sites, virtual directories, and individual files based on the kind of user authentication methods configured for the resource. IIS authentication security applies to all users who try to access the resource, regardless of which groups they belong to.

- *IIS permissions* IIS allows administrators to control access by clients to Web sites, virtual directories, and individual files based on Web access permissions for the resource. IIS permissions apply to all users who try to access the resource, regardless of which groups they belong to.

- *NTFS permissions* Windows 2000 allows administrators to control access by clients to physical directories and files based on NTFS access permissions for the resource. Unlike the other three methods, NTFS permissions provide granularity by allowing different permissions to be assigned to different users and groups.

Of these four alternatives, the most fundamental method of securing access to Web sites is the *Windows NT File System* (NTFS). Prior to configuring any other form of security, make sure that the NTFS permissions for the content being published are set correctly. IIS is only as secure as the file system on which it runs.

NOTE: *The File Allocation Table (FAT) file system is not recommended for hosting Web content because it does not provide any directory- or file-level security. If you have Web content stored on a FAT partition, use the Windows 2000 utility convert.exe to change the file system to NTFS. The syntax for using this command is*

```
Convert C:/fs:ntfs
```

Figure 4-1 shows the process by which the four security methods are applied when IIS receives a request to access a resource. Based on this figure, each of the security schemes will be examined in detail in the order in which they are applied.

Figure 4-1
Applying the four
security methods
when a user tries
to access IIS.

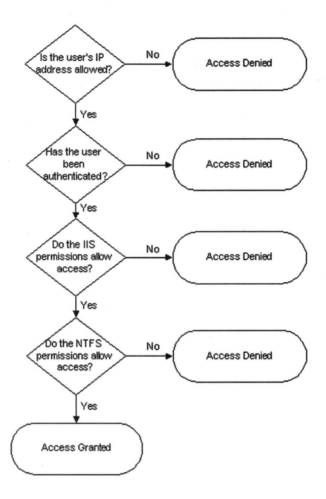

Understanding IP Address and Domain Name Security

IIS can be configured to grant or deny access to Web sites, virtual directories, or individual files depending upon the IP address or Internet domain name of the client. This is done by configuring IP address and domain name restrictions for the resource. The clients may be either individual hosts or all computers in a particular subnet. This is a global security setting for each resource, and is independent of the particular group that the user accessing the resource belongs to.

Configuring IP Address and Domain Name Restrictions

The method for configuring IP addresses and domain name restrictions varies depending on what you are configuring them for.

- To configure IP address and domain name restrictions for virtual servers (Web sites), virtual directories, and any physical subdirectories of a virtual server, right-click on the resource's node in the *Microsoft Management Console* (MMC), select Properties from the Context menu, choose the Directory Security tab on the property sheet, and click Edit under IP Address and Domain Name Restrictions.

- To configure IP address and domain name restrictions for any file in a virtual directory or server, right-click on the file's node in the MMC, select Properties from the Context menu, choose the File Security tab on the property sheet, and click Edit under IP Address and Domain Name Restrictions.

The IP Address and Domain Name Restrictions box allows administrators to grant or deny access to servers, sites, and pages based on IP addresses and Internet domain names (see Figure 4-2). Before configuring IP address and domain name security you must decide whether to *grant* access to all hosts *except* for those specified, or *deny* access to all hosts *except* for those specified.

To grant or deny access to hosts, click Add to bring up the Grant (or Deny) Access On dialog box, and then choose one of the following options:

Figure 4-2
Setting IP and domain name restrictions.

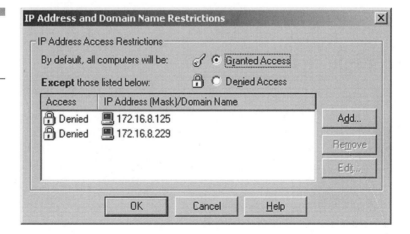

■ *Single computer* Enter the IP address of the individual host to which you want to grant or deny access. If your network supports DNS, you can also click DNS Lookup, enter the *fully qualified domain name* (FQDN) of the host to which you want to grant or deny access, and have your DNS server resolve the FQDN into an IP address.

■ *Group of computers* Enter the IP network address and subnet mask of the network to which you want to grant or deny access (see Figure 4-3).

■ *Domain name* Enter the domain name of the Internet domain to which you want to grant or deny access. A dialog box may appear warning you that this option requires DNS Reverse Lookup and may impact the performance of your server.

Strategies for Using IP Address and Domain Name Security

Try the following strategies for using IP address and domain name security.

■ If your Web server provides an extranet connection to another company, you might want to deny access to all computers except for the IP network addresses of the other company.

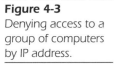

Figure 4-3
Denying access to a group of computers by IP address.

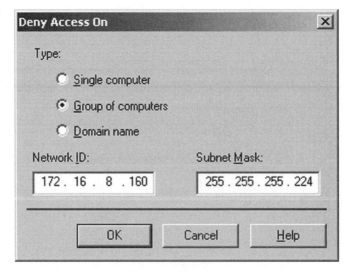

- If an attempt to hack into your network has come from 207.166.52.4, you might want to deny access to that IP address or to the entire 207.166.52.0 network.

- If your IIS server provides intranet services to your LAN and your LAN is also connected to the Internet outside, you might want to grant access to your own network numbers while denying access to everyone else.

Understanding IIS Authentication Security

IIS can be configured to control access to Web sites, virtual directories, or individual files, depending on the logon authentication method used by the client. This is done by configuring IIS authentication security for the resource. This is a global security setting for each resource, and is independent of the particular group to which the user accessing the resource belongs.

The four IIS authentication schemes available are

- *Anonymous access*   Everyone can access the Web site, virtual directory, or individual file configured with this setting.

- *Basic authentication*   Users must enter a valid Windows 2000 user account and password in response to a logon dialog box in order to access the Web site, virtual directory, or individual file configured with this setting.

- *Digest authentication*   This method sends the password over the network as hash value. This option can only be used for a Windows 2000 domain. This method can be used for passing logins over a network firewall or proxy. Currently this method can only be used if the browser is Internet Explorer 5 or higher.

- *Integrated Windows Authentication*   Users already logged on to their machines with a valid Windows user account are automatically authenticated and allowed to access the Web site, virtual directory, or individual file configured with this setting.

These four authentication schemes may be configured to control access to

- All Web content hosted on your IIS server
- Individual Web sites hosted on your IIS server

- Individual virtual directories in a Web site
- Individual physical subdirectories in a Web site
- Individual Web pages or other files in a Web site

To configure IIS authentication security as the default setting for *all Web sites* hosted on your IIS server, start the *Microsoft Management Console* (MMC), open the WWW Service Master Properties sheet for your IIS server, and select the Directory Security tab (Figure 4-4). Next click Edit to open the Authentication Methods dialog box (Figure 4-5). Select any combination of the four authentication methods available, and click OK to close the Authentication Methods property sheet.

Now click Apply on the WWW Service Master Properties sheet. If the default settings you have chosen differ from the settings of any child nodes on the server, *and* these child node settings have changed since the default settings were previously set, the Inheritance Overrides box will open, allowing you to select which child nodes should inherit the default settings you

Figure 4-4

The Directory Security tab of the WWW Service Master Properties sheet.

Figure 4-5
Selecting the
authentication
methods.

have selected for the parent node (see Figure 4-6). By default, *all* child nodes automatically inherit any settings made using the WWW Service Master Properties sheet.

To configure IIS authentication security for a *specific* Web site, virtual directory, or physical directory hosted on your IIS server, use the MMC and right-click on the node representing the resource to which you want to restrict access and select Properties to open the <resource_name> Properties sheet for your resource.

Next choose the Directory Security tab and click Edit to open the Authentication Methods property sheet. Select any combination of the four authentication methods available and click OK to close the Authentication Methods property sheet.

Now click Apply on the <resource_name> Properties sheet. If the settings you have chosen for this Web site differ from the settings of any child nodes under this site, *and* these child node settings have changed since the default settings were previously set, the Inheritance Overrides box will open, allowing you to specify which child nodes should inherit the settings you have selected.

Figure 4-6
The Inheritance
Overrides box.

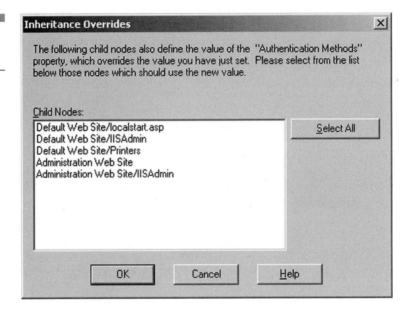

Finally, to configure IIS authentication security for a specific *file* within a virtual server or directory, use the MMC, right-click on the node representing the file you want to restrict access to, and select Properties to open the <resource_name> Properties sheet for this page. Choose the File Security tab and click Edit to open the Authentication Methods property sheet. Select any combination of the three authentication methods available and click OK.

Configuring Anonymous Access

The first IIS authentication scheme we examine is called *anonymous access*. When IIS is installed, the setup program creates a special user account called the *Internet Guest Account*. Using User Manager (if IIS is installed on a member server, or User Manager for Domains if IIS is installed on a domain controller), we can see that this account has the following properties:

■ The username is IUSR_SERVERNAME, where SERVERNAME is the name of the server on which IIS is installed.

■ The user cannot change the password.

■ The password never expires.

■ The user is a member of the Guests local group.

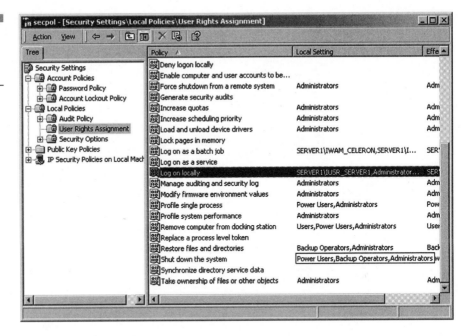

Figure 4-7
IUSR_SERVER1 must
have the right to log
on locally.

In addition, by using Local Security Policy MMC console and selecting User Rights Assignment node from the Local Policies node, in the right pane you can see the Log on Locally policy (see Figure 4-7). If we select the properties of the Log on Locally policy, we can see that the Internet Guest Account has this right (see Figure 4-7). If you were to check other policies, you would see that the Internet Guest Account is only part of the Log on Locally policy.

By default, Allow Anonymous Access is enabled on the Authentication Methods property sheet for your IIS server (see Figure 4-5). This means that all users, whether they have valid Windows user accounts or not, are allowed access to Web content on your IIS server. In other words, the IUSR_SERVERNAME account allows guest access to all users who access your server, without requiring a specific user account and password.

If necessary, the account used to allow anonymous access can be changed by selecting Edit on the Authentication Methods property sheet. This opens the Anonymous User Account box (see Figure 4-8). You might use this option in one of the following situations:

■ You accidentally deleted the existing IUSR_SERVERNAME account and you need to create a new account for anonymous access.

■ You wish to rename the IUSR_SERVERNAME account to prevent any security breach that might occur if someone changes the rights and

Figure 4-8
Configuring the
Anonymous User
Account.

permissions of the Guests group. Someone might try to hack the IUSR_SERVERNAME account on the chance that the settings for the Guests group are incorrect.

- If your IIS server is installed on a Windows 2000 *member server,* and IIS needs to provide anonymous access to Web content stored on other servers in your domain, you may need to replace the default IUSR_SERVERNAME, which is a local account on the member server, with a domain-wide account that can be assigned permissions on other servers in the domain. If IIS is installed on a *domain controller,* this is not an issue.

- If you have several IIS servers installed on Windows 2000 member servers, and you want to harmonize their various IUSR_SERVERNAME accounts so you have only one Internet Guest Account, you can create a new IUSR account on a domain controller and replace the existing local IUSR accounts with the new global IUSR account. This will simplify setting up ACLs for resources containing Web content on NTFS volumes.

Before you use this option, you need to create a new account for anonymous access using the Active Directory Users and Computers snap-in. Be sure to assign it the same right as IUSR_SERVERNAME has; namely, the right to log on locally to the IIS server(s) it applies to. Then use the Anonymous User Account box to assign a new user account for anonymous access to your IIS server. Leave the Enable Automatic Password Synchronization checkbox selected so Windows 2000 will automatically synchronize the IIS settings with the password defined in Active Directory Users and Computers snap-in.

Strategies for Using Anonymous Access

When should anonymous access be used? Some possible situations are as follows:

- Where security needs are low and the site is intended to be generally available to the public through the Internet
- On a corporate intranet with no connection to the Internet
- Where security needs are high and users must not be allowed to accidentally pass their credentials over WAN links to access the corporate Web site

NOTE: *If you have modified the rights and permissions of the Guests local group, the Internet Guest Account will inherit these new rights and permissions as well because it is a member of the Guests group. Always check what rights and permissions the Guests group has on your system before allowing anonymous access to your IIS Web server.*

Configuring Basic Authentication

The second IIS authentication scheme we cover is called *basic authentication*. Basic authentication is the standard HTTP method of user authentication and is supported by most Web browsers.

If Basic Authentication is selected on the Authentication Methods property sheet for a resource (see Figure 4-5), a client trying to access a virtual server, virtual directory, or individual file will be presented with an Enter Network Password dialog box (Figure 4-9). The user must then enter a valid Windows user account and password to be allowed to access the page they are trying to view. If an invalid account is successively entered three times into this box, the server will return the following message to the client browser:

```
HTTP Error 401.1 Unauthorized Logon Failed
```

Basic authentication is not a secure authentication scheme and should be used only in low-security environments. In basic authentication, the username and password are encoded into a string of ASCII characters using a process known as *uuencoding*. (The Authentication Methods dialog

box says that basic authentication sends the username and password as *clear text,* but this is not actually the case.) This uuencoded string, which is easily decipherable using a simple mathematical algorithm, is then included in the HTTP Get Request packet as an HTTP Request Header, such as

```
Authentication: Basic ZG9uYWxkOnBhc3N3b3Jk
```

Figure 4-10 shows a Network Monitor capture of a basic authentication request. Anyone with sufficient access to your network to capture such packets can easily decode the authentication string and then use the username and password to hack into your Windows network. So don't use basic authentication unless it is necessary on one of the following grounds:

- To provide a basic level of authentication in a low-security environment
- To provide authentication for non-Microsoft clients in a *heterogeneous network* (that is, a network that also includes UNIX workstations, Macintosh clients, and so on)

Basic authentication can be combined with *Secure Sockets Layer* (SSL) encryption to provide a secure authentication scheme in heterogeneous environments. This ensures that not just user authentication but *all* client/server traffic, including data transfer, is strongly encrypted. SSL encryption provides a greater degree of security but negatively impacts server performance. SSL is covered in Chapter 11.

Figure 4-10
Network Monitor
capture of a basic
authentication
session.

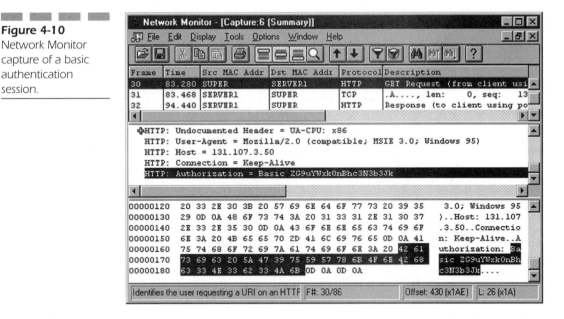

Figure 4-11
Configuring Basic
Authentication
Domain.

You can configure IIS to forward a request for basic authentication to a
domain other than the server's domain. To do this, select Basic Authentication on the Authentication Methods property sheet and click Edit to bring
up the Basic Authentication Domain dialog box. Browse to or enter the
name of the domain to be used for authentication and click OK (see Figure
4-11).

Strategies for Using Basic Authentication

When should basic authentication be used? Some possible situations are as follows:

- In a heterogeneous networking environment where security is low and authentication by non-Windows 2000 systems is required.

- In a low-security environment where some users use browsers such as Netscape Navigator that cannot use Windows Integrated Authentication.

- In a medium-security environment where companies need to provide extranet access to content that is not sensitive (for example, providing distributors with access to online catalogs). A single account is created by the supplier and is used by distributors to log on to the supplier's Web server. This account is changed on a regular basis.

- In a high-security environment combined with SSL to allow sensitive information to be securely transmitted via extranet connections between companies.

Configuring Digested Authentication

Digest Authentication is a step up from Basic Clear text in that it sends passwords over the Internet in a hashed format. Digest Authentication is not yet an Internet standard and is only supported by Internet Explorer 5 accessing a domain that is controlled by a Windows 2000 domain controller.

In order to use Digested Authentication, the following must be configured for your Windows 2000 domain:

- Your IIS 5.0 must be in a Windows 2000 domain.

- User accounts must have the Save Password as Encrypted Clear Text enabled in the User account properties dialog box in the Active Directory Users and Computers MMC snap-in.

NOTE: *Digest Authentication stores the passwords as plain text files on the domain controller. This file is used to compare the hashing sent by IIS. It is important to secure this file from access. Refer to the Windows 2000 documentation on securing your server.*

Strategies for Using Digested Authentication

When should Digested Authentication be used? The following are some suggestions:

- When you want more security than Basic Clear text can provide
- When you want to access a resource that is behind a firewall or proxy

Configuring Windows Integrated Authentication

The forth and last IIS authentication method is called *Windows Integrated Authentication*. In integrated authentication, the server authenticates the client through an interchange of encrypted packets, none of which contain the password in any form. This is the most secure of the four IIS authentication schemes from a network perspective, and it takes place in different ways, depending on the network configuration.

- If the user is logged on to a Windows 2000 system using a valid domain user account, the integrated security process is transparent to the user. The user simply tries to access the desired resource, a series of HTTP packets automatically authenticate the user based on his or her current logon credentials, and the user accesses the page. No logon box appears for the user to deal with. However, a domain controller must be accessible for integrated authentication to succeed.

- If the user is logged on to a Windows 95 system participating in a workgroup, he is confronted with an Enter Network Logon dialog box and must enter a valid Windows 2000 username and password to access the resource. Again, a domain controller must be accessible for the authentication method to succeed.

Windows Integrated authentication is supported by the client software Microsoft Explorer 2.0 and higher. It is not currently supported by any version of Netscape Navigator.

As in any password authentication scheme, simple guidelines must be followed to ensure that security is not breached. Administrators need to plan and enforce the proper account policy to ensure that passwords are not stolen or guessed. From the start menu select Administrative Tools, Domain Security Policy, to start the Domain Security Policy MMC snap-in. Expand

Figure 4-12
Setting policies in the
Domain Security
Policy MMC snap-in.

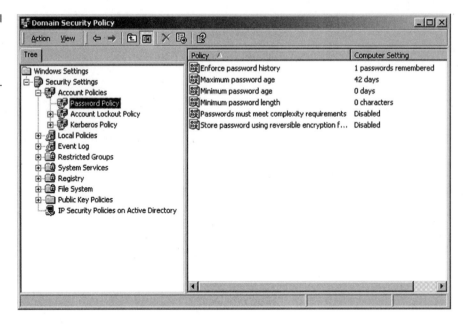

the Account Policies node and underneath you will see the Password Policy
node (Figure 4-12). From here you can set the policies on your accounts:

- Setting a minimum password length
- Establishing a maximum password age before expiration
- Ensuring password uniqueness by keeping password history
- Enabling account lockout after a few bad logon attempts
- Forcing users to log on before they can change a password

In addition to the preceding measures, make sure that you have a written network security policy in place, with clear guidelines for users on how
to choose a secure password, how to protect a password, and the consequences of violating the company security policy.

Strategies for Using Integrated Authentication

When should integrated authentication be used? Some possible situations
are as follows:

■ Where the security needs are high and only domain users are to be allowed access to the site

■ In a corporate intranet composed of Windows 2000 and Windows 98 workstations, to provide security and eliminate the need for users to enter logon information each time they access the intranet

Combining IIS Authentication Methods

Any two or all four of the authentication methods may be enabled on the same resource. The general rules for combining these methods are as follows:

■ If anonymous access and another authentication method (basic authentication or integrated authentication) are both enabled on the same resource, anonymous access is attempted first. If this fails (for example, if the NTFS permission on the resource has access explicitly denied to IUSR_SERVERNAME), the other method is attempted.

■ If basic authentication, digest authentication, and integrated authentication are all enabled on the same resource, integrated authentication has precedence and will be attempted first by the client browser.

Understanding IIS Permissions

IIS can be configured to control access to Web sites, virtual or physical directories, or individual files based on Web access permissions assigned to the resource. This is done by configuring IIS permissions for the resource. This is a global security setting for each resource, and is independent of the particular group that the user accessing the resource belongs to.

Configuring IIS Permissions

■ To configure IIS permissions for a virtual server, right-click on its node in the MMC, select Properties from the Context menu, and choose the Home Directory tab on the property sheet for the node.

- To configure IIS permissions for a virtual directory, right-click on its node in the MMC, select Properties from the Context menu, and choose the Virtual Directory tab on the property sheet for the node.

- To configure IIS permissions for a physical directory, right-click on its node in the MMC, select Properties from the Context menu, and choose the Directory tab on the property sheet for the node.

- To configure IIS permissions for an individual file, right-click on its node in the MMC, select Properties from the Context menu, and choose the File tab on the property sheet for the node.

Figure 4-13 shows the Virtual Directory tab for the IISSAMPLES property sheet as an example. Note that the *read* and *script* permissions are enabled on the virtual directory and its contents.

IIS offers two kinds of *access permissions* to restrict access to virtual directories, folders, and files (see Figure 4-13). Either or both of these may be selected for any resource.

Figure 4-13
Configuring IIS permissions for a virtual directory

IISSamples Properties

Virtual Directory | Documents | Directory Security | HTTP Headers | Custom Errors

When connecting to this resource, the content should come from:

- ⦿ A directory located on this computer
- ○ A share located on another computer
- ○ A redirection to a URL

Local Path: `c:\inetpub\iissamples`   [Browse...]

☐ Script source access   ☑ Log visits
☑ Read   ☑ Index this resource
☐ Write
☑ Directory browsing

Application Settings

Application name: [   ]   [Remove]

Starting point: <Default We...\IISSamples>

Execute Permissions: [Scripts only ▼]   [Configuration...]

Application Protection: [Medium (Pooled) ▼]   [Unload]

[OK]   [Cancel]   [Apply]   [Help]

■ *Read* Select this checkbox to allow clients to display the contents of your virtual directory or folder, or to allow them to display your file.

■ *Write* Select this checkbox to allow clients to write to the contents of your virtual directory or folder, or to allow them to overwrite an existing file.

In addition to access permissions, if your directory contains executable files or scripts, you can configure *Execute Permissions* for these files by choosing one of the following:

■ *None* No executables are allowed to run in this directory.

■ *Scripts* Scripts that are mapped to a script engine are allowed to run in this directory. This includes Active Server Pages, IDC scripts, CGI scripts, and so on.

■ *Scripts and Executables* Both scripts and executable binaries are allowed to run in this directory.

Strategies for Securing Your Site with IIS Permissions

IIS permissions are assigned depending on the kind of resource being accessed. Typical IIS permissions for various resources are listed in Table 4-1.

NOTE: *Be careful about assigning both write and execute permission to a folder. This may allow users to upload and run binary executables on your server. This level of permission should be assigned only to trusted developers. Wherever possible, use script instead of execute permission.*

Table 4-1

Suggested IIS Permissions.

Type of Web Content	Suggested IIS Permissions
Static Web Content	Read and none
Active Server Pages	Read and script
Other scripts	Read and script
Executable programs	Read and execute
Database content	Read, write, and none

Understanding NTFS Permissions

Windows 2000 can be configured to control access to physical directories and files based on NTFS permissions assigned to the resource. Unlike the other three methods described, NTFS permissions provide granularity by allowing different permissions to be assigned to different users and groups. For NTFS permissions to be used, volumes hosting Web content must be formatted with the *Windows NT File System* (NTFS).

There are six basic NTFS permissions:

- Read (R)
- Write (W)
- Execute (X)
- Delete (D)
- Change permissions (P)
- Take ownership (O)

These six permissions are rarely used individually, but are grouped to form what are called *NTFS standard permissions*. There are two different sets of NTFS standard permissions: those applying to folders (directories) and those applying to individual files. Tables 4-2 and 4-3 summarize these two types. In addition to these standard permissions, administrators can create *special access* permissions consisting of any grouping of the NTFS basic permissions RWXDP and O.

Table 4-2

NTFS Standard Permissions for folders.

	NTFS Standard Permissions	
Type of Access	**Folders**	**Files in the Folders**
No access	None	None
Read	RX	RX
Change	RWXD	RWXD
Add	WX	Unspecified
Add and read	RWX	RX
List	RX	Unspecified
Full control	RWXDPO	RWXDPO

	Type of Access	NTFS Standard Permissions
Table 4-3	No access	None
NTFS Standard Permissions for files.	Read	RX
	Change	RWXD
	Full control	RWXDPO

When a volume is formatted with NTFS, all resources (files and folders) on the volume have *access control lists (ACLs)* created for them. The ACL for a resource specifies which users and groups have what kind of access to the resource. Figure 4-14 shows the ACL for the folder C:\intepub\www-root on a typical IIS server.

Configuring NTFS Permissions

A user's access to a resource on an NTFS volume is determined by the ACL of the resource and the user's membership in Windows 2000 groups. For example, if the user has *full control* permission and a group the user belongs to has only *read* permission on the resource, the user has *full control* permission on the resource. In other words, when NTFS permissions are combined, the effective permission is the *least restrictive* permission:

```
Full control+Read=Full control
```

The exception to this rule is that when *no access* permission combines with any other NTFS standard permission, the result is always *no access:*

```
No access+Any NTFS permission=No access
```

When the ACL of a folder is modified, all files within that folder normally inherit the new settings. This can be toggled off by deselecting the Replace Permissions on Existing Files checkbox in the Directory Permissions dialog box (see Figure 4-14). This feature can also be applied recursively by checking the Replace Permissions on Subdirectories checkbox.

Figure 4-14

Permissions on the
root of the IIS Default
Directory.

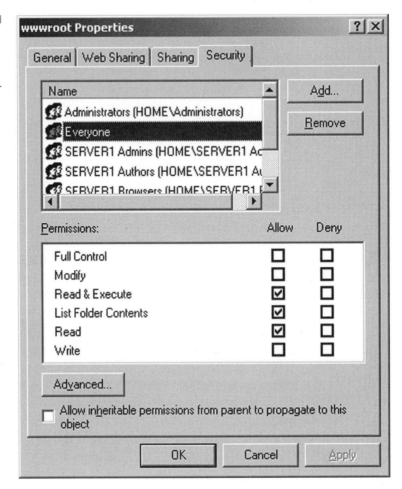

Strategies for Securing Your Site with NTFS Permissions

Configuring NTFS permissions should be your primary concern in securing access to a Web site. The first step in configuring NTFS security on an IIS server should be the removal of the Everyone group from the ACL for the virtual directory or Web page. The Everyone group means for exactly what it says—*everyone!* This includes the Internet Guest Account, the built-in Windows 2000 Guest Account, the Guests group, and so on. Removing the Everyone group eliminates the possibility of a security breach based on forms of guest account access.

If basic or integrated authentication is used, the simplest strategy is to assign the built-in Users group *read (RX)* permission to allow all valid Windows 2000 domain users read access to your Web sites. This might be the best strategy if your IIS server hosts Web content for employee access on the company intranet. Access could then be restricted for individuals or departments by individually assigning them *no access* permission on the resource, which overrides the previously assigned *read* permission. Access could be broadened for content developers, for example, by assigning them *modify (RWXD)* permission.

Another issue to consider is that the NTFS permissions assigned to a resource depend on the kind of resource being accessed. Similar to IIS permissions discussed earlier, typical NTFS permissions for various resources are listed in Table 4-4.

Combining NTFS and IIS Permissions

The most secure scheme is to employ both IIS and NTFS permissions. The simple rule for such a combination is that permissions that explicitly deny access take precedence over permissions that explicitly grant access. For intranets, a general strategy for planning combinations of IIS and NTFS permissions might include the following guidelines:

- Assign IIS read permission to the directory to allow browsing.
- Assign IIS script permission for directories containing Active Server Pages or other scripts.
- Assign NTFS read permission to the Users local group.
- Assign NTFS change permission to the group responsible for creating content in the directory.

Table 4-4

Suggested NTFS permissions.

Type of Web Content	Suggested NTFS Permissions
Static Web content	Read(RX)
Active Server Pages	Read (RX)
Other scripts	Read (RX) or special access (X)
Executable programs	Read (RX) or special access (X)
Database content	Change (RWXD)

- Assign NTFS full control permission to the Administrators local group and to any other group responsible for administering the server on which the directory resides.

- Assign NTFS no access permission to any group or user who should not be allowed to browse the contents of the directory.

- Remove the Everyone group from the ACL.

Walkthrough: Securing Your Web Using the IIS Permissions Wizard

You can use the IIS Permissions Wizard to secure your Web site. This wizard allows you to configure security settings for sites that are either targeted for external or internal use by going through a series of dialog boxes.

In this walkthrough, we will use the IIS Permissions Wizard to secure a Web site for an intranet use.

First, open the Internet Services Manager MMC snap-in and expand the Default Web Site node to display the IISSamples Virtual Directory (see Figure 4-15).

Figure 4-15
Securing the
IISSamples Virtual
Directory.

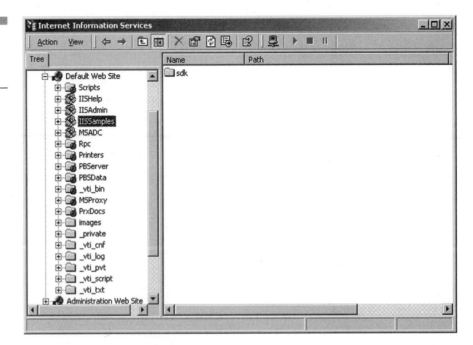

Figure 4-16
The IIS 5.0
Permissions Wizard.

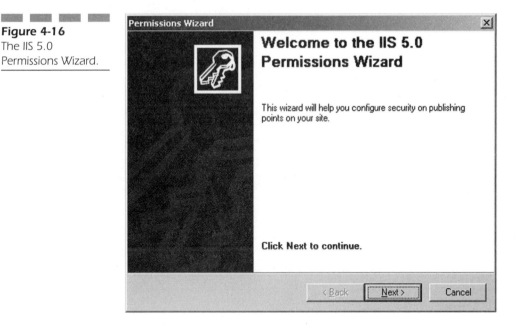

Right-click the IISSamples virtual directory and select All Tasks, Permissions Wizard to start the Permissions Wizard (see Figure 4-16). Click the Next button to begin the wizard.

From the screen shown in Figure 4-17, choose Select New Security Settings from a Template. This setting will allow you to customize the security settings of this virtual directory. Selecting the Inherit All Security Settings option will apply the parent directory's permissions to this virtual directory. Click the Next button to continue configuring the virtual directory.

The dialog box shown in Figure 4-18 is where you select what template type best fits the Web you want to secure. You have two possible options:

- *Public Web Site* Select this to allow anonymous access to your site from the outside world. This allows ASP pages to execute and for Internet users to access your pages via the IUSR_MACHINENAME account.

- *Secure Web Site* Select this option for a secure site such as an intranet or extranet site where all users accessing the site will have a valid Windows domain account.

For this walkthrough, select *Secure Web Site* and then click the Next button to continue.

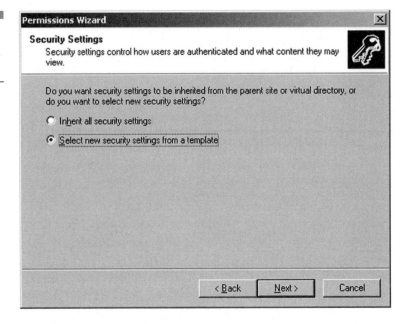

Figure 4-18
Select the template type to match your Web's function.

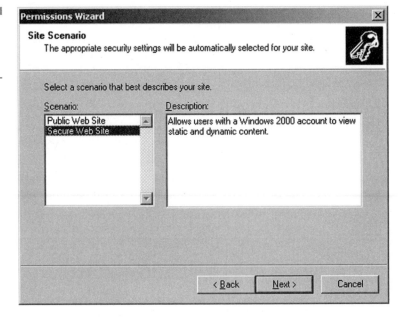

In this next screen (see Figure 4-19), select Replace All Directory and File Access Permissions. This option will apply the Wizard security settings to all folders and files branched off of the IISSamples virtual directory.

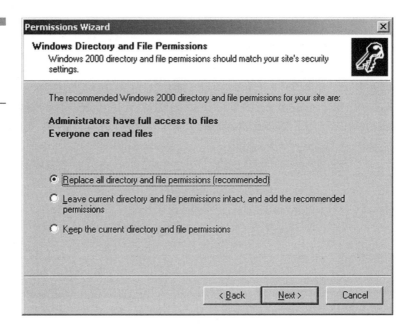

Figure 4-19
Replacing the
permissions on
all subdirectories
and files.

Other available options are to leave the permissions intact and allow it to apply the recommended permissions to the current virtual directory and not to the child directories, or to keep the current permissions without any modifications. Click the Next button to see an overview of the changes that will applied to the virtual directory after the wizard is complete (see Figure 4-20). Click the Finish button to close the wizard.

NOTE: *You should always go back and physically check the permissions that were applied using the Permissions Wizard to ensure that they comply with your security policies.*

Other Methods of Securing IIS Servers

This section discusses some additional actions that administrators can perform to enhance the security of IIS servers.

Figure 4-20
Summary of changes
that will be applied
by the Permissions
Wizard.

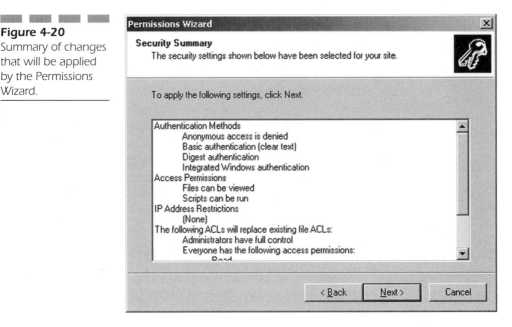

Securing IIS by Disabling Unnecessary Services, Protocols, and Bindings

Disabling unnecessary services on your IIS server has several advantages:

- Performance will improve due to the decreased demand on system resources.

- Fewer administrative errors will occur because there are fewer options to configure.

- Fewer system weaknesses exist to be exploited by malicious hackers.

Services can be disabled by right-clicking on the My Computer icon on the desktop and selecting Manage from the context menu. This will open the Computer Management snap-in (Figure 4-21). Expand the Services and Applications node to display the Services node. Click on the Services node to display the services available in the right pane of the MMC. Select the service you want to disable, right-click to bring up the context menu, select properties from the context menu to bring up the Service dialog box (Figure 4-22). Choose Disabled and click OK.

Figure 4-21
Listing of services
in the Computer
Management
snap-in.

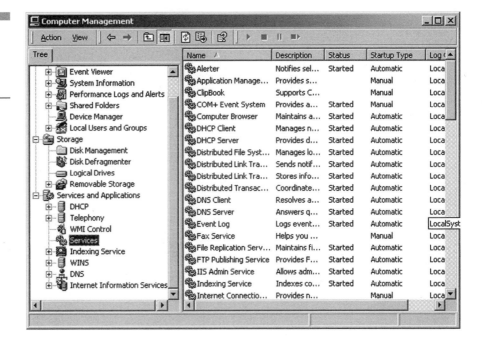

One service you may want to disable on your IIS server is that of the Server. The reason for doing so is that when this service is running, any shares that are created on the server will appear when users browse the network. These shares could form a potential point of entry to your server. For example, on an NTFS volume, Windows 2000 automatically shares the root as a hidden share for administrative purposes (for example, as \\SERVERNAME\C$). With the Server service disabled, hackers are prevented from attempting to connect to such shares.

An alternative is to install a second network card onto your IIS server, connecting one card to the LAN and the other to the Internet. The network card bindings can then be configured using Network in Control Panel so the Server service is bound only to the LAN-side network card.

Be aware that if the Server service is allowed to function over the Internet, not only may it serve as a possible security leak, but you also may no longer be fulfilling Microsoft licensing requirements. This is because IIS uses HTTP, whereas the Server service uses the *Server Message Block* (SMB) protocol. Microsoft's licensing requirements apply to SMB, but not to HTTP. Therefore, any SMB connections to your Server service from over the

Figure 4-22
Disabling
unnecessary
services.

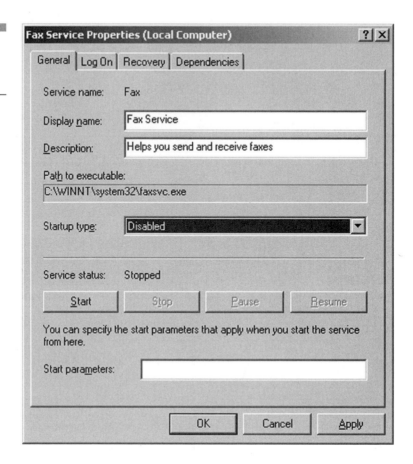

Internet will require a client license to comply with Microsoft's licensing requirements for Windows 2000 Server.

In addition, it is a good idea to remove or unbind unnecessary protocols for the obvious reason that the simpler your system is, the easier it is to configure and the less likely it is that something important will be overlooked or misconfigured.

NOTE: *Stopping the Server service also stops the Computer Browser service and Microsoft Message Queue service. Be sure you understand the consequences of stopping services on your system; otherwise, you may experience unexpected results.*

Securing IIS by Disabling Directory Browsing

In the previous chapter, I mentioned that directory browsing should normally be disabled so users cannot see and navigate around your server's directory structure, looking for weak points to probe. To disable directory browsing on a virtual server, virtual directory, or folder, access the node's Property sheet and select the Home Directory, Virtual Directory, or Directory tab, respectively. Make sure that Directory Browsing Allowed is deselected.

Securing IIS by Logging

Logging the HTTP activity on your server is another way of securing your site. Logging allows you to look for unusual patterns of server access that could indicate hacking attempts. For example, a log might indicate that a single client IP address attempted to log on to a particular site 600 times in a single day, which could indicate an attempt to break into the system.

Logging can also reveal other unusual client behavior patterns. For example, you may discover that clients are frequently visiting a relatively unimportant part of your Web site. You should probably check that section yourself in case the activity is associated with a security leak in that section of the site.

The important thing is to review your logs on a regular basis to detect possible security breaches. A good way to do this is to import your IIS log files into a log analysis application and use this to generate usage reports for your site.

Securing IIS by NTFS Auditing

NTFS volumes provide another form of logging called auditing. Together, IIS logging and NTFS auditing provide important information concerning the security performance of your IIS server.

To enable auditing on a file, folder, or drive, start the Local Security Policies snap-in and expand the Local Policies node. Select the Audit Policy node. In the right pane of the MMC, you'll see a listing of events that you can audit (see Figure 4-23). Select which kind of activity you want to track on your server from the right pane and double-click. This will bring up the

Figure 4-23
Local Security Policies
MMC snap-in.

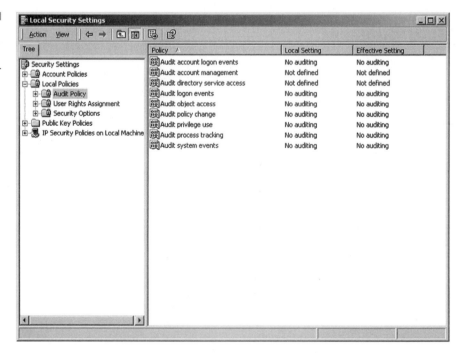

Local Security Policy Setting dialog box (see Figure 4-24). Select the options you want to log in this dialog and click OK. Events will be written to your Security log and can be viewed using Event Viewer.

Strategies for Auditing Web Content   Here are a few strategies for effective auditing:

- Check Success for Logon and Logoff to get statistics on the number of users connecting successfully to your IIS server.
- Check Failure for Logon and Logoff to detect possible attempts to hack your server.
- Check Failure for File and Object Access to track attempts to connect to content that is not intended to be generally available to everyone.

After auditing has been enabled, you can access the property of any auditing event by right-clicking on the resource (folders, files, and so on) and selecting Properties from the context menu (refer to Figure 4-14). This will bring up the Resource Properties dialog box. Click the Advanced button to bring up the Access Control Settings dialog box and click the Auditing

Figure 4-24
Establishing an
audit policy.

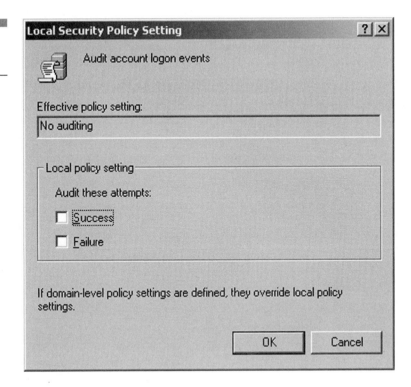

tab. Here you will see a listing of events that are being audited for that particular resource (see Figure 4-25). You can also add events to be audited by clicking on the Add button, which will bring up a listing of users and groups to select from to be audited. Select a group—another dialog box will appear listing those events that can be audited (see Figure 4-26).

Securing IIS by Applying Service Packs and Hotfixes

You should always apply the latest service packs, hotfixes, and upgrades for Windows 2000 to close any security holes that have been discovered in these products. No product is completely secure, and your continued vigilance as an administrator is critical to maintaining a secure, functioning Web server (and possibly to keeping your job as well). Be sure to check your system against the Windows Update periodically to keep your system up to date.

Figure 4-25
Viewing the audit
properties of the
resource.

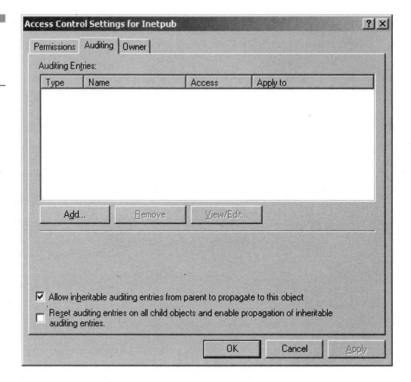

Securing IIS by Writing and Publishing a Corporate Security Policy

In corporate networks, it is critical that you not only configure security settings, but also establish a written company security policy. A good portion of network security breaches come not from outside hackers but from disgruntled employees, and a clearly communicated security policy outlining unacceptable conduct and its possible consequences can serve as an effective deterrent to employee sabotage of your servers.

SUMMARY

IIS 5.0 provides a number of mechanisms for securing access to your server, whether it is employed as an Internet, intranet, or extranet server. These include IIS authentication, IIS permissions, NTFS permissions, IP address and domain name restrictions, disabling and unbinding unnecessary ser-

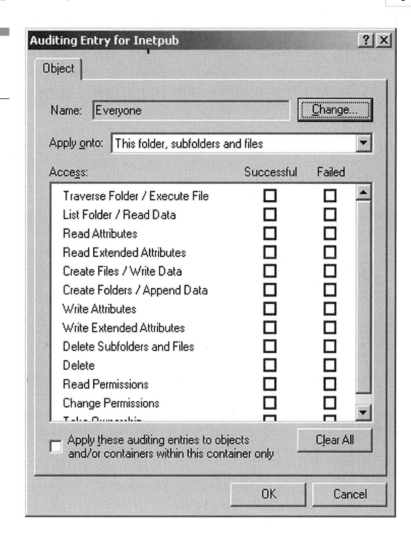

Figure 4-26
Configuring NTFS auditing for a directory.

vices and protocols, logging and auditing access to your site, applying updates, and establishing and communicating a company security policy. This chapter has outlined strategies for using these approaches in securing your server against unauthorized access.

For More Information

Try the resources on the following page for more information on administering security.

Microsoft Web Site

For an excellent source of information on security issues regarding IIS and Windows 2000, visit the Microsoft Security Advisor Web site at

```
www.microsoft.com/security
```

The site has white papers, case studies, information on security standards and technologies, and separate sections dealing with security issues for various Microsoft products.

Microsoft Public Newsgroups

General IIS issues including security are discussed in the newsgroups

```
microsoft.public.inetserver.iis
microsoft.public.inetserver.misc
```

Microsoft Windows 2000 Resource Kit

The *Internet Guide* component of the Windows 2000 Resource Kit has useful information on IIS security issues in the security section of the Internet Information Services 5.0 Resource Kit.

Microsoft TechNet

TechNet has some useful papers on Internet security located in

```
Technologies | Internet.
```

IETF draft specification for digest security can be found at

```
http://www.ietf.org/rfc/rfc2069.txt
```

Administering Virtual Directories and Servers

Introduction

Organizing your Web content is an important issue for corporate intranets spanning multiple departments and for Internet servers hosting content for more than one company. Internet Information Services 5.0 allows administrators to organize Web content in two ways: by using virtual directories and using virtual servers. After completing this chapter, you will be able to

- Understand what virtual directories are and what they are used for
- Create, configure, and delete virtual directories for content stored both locally and on remote servers
- Understand what virtual servers are and what they are used for
- Create, configure, and delete virtual servers for content stored both locally and on remote servers
- Understand host headers and how they are used to configure virtual servers

Understanding Virtual Directories

Virtual directories are a mechanism that allows Web content to be stored in locations other than the default directory

```
C:\inetpub\wwwroot
```

which is the home directory for the default Web site that is created on the local machine on which IIS is installed. This is accomplished by defining an *alias* for the virtual directory and mapping this alias to the physical location of the Web content. The actual Web content may be located in

- A directory on the local machine (hence a *local virtual directory*)
- A share on a remote server (hence a *remote virtual directory*)

Local Virtual Directories

For an example of a local virtual directory, consider the mapping

```
marketing ↔ D:\MarketingDept\Webstuff
```

which assigns the alias marketing to the Web content stored in the directory

```
D:\MarketingDept\Webstuff
```

which is on the local machine (that is, the machine on which IIS is installed). If the local machine is an intranet server called server1, the Marketing Department Web site would be accessed by the following URL:

```
http://server1/marketing
```

The previous example illustrates why the term virtual directory is used: the user attempts to access the subdirectory marketing, which appears to be a subdirectory of the home directory of the default Web site on the IIS server. In other words, the path for the Marketing directory appears to be

```
C:\inetpub\wwwroot\marketing
```

But this subdirectory doesn't actually exist. Instead, it is an alias representing the real directory:

```
D:\MarketingDept\Webstuff
```

So we could say that virtual directories are *mappings of URL space onto directory space.*

Remote Virtual Directories

For an example of a *remote virtual directory,* consider the mapping

```
sales ↔ \\Fileserv4\SalesWeb
```

which assigns the alias sales to the Web content stored in the share Sales-Web, which is on the remote machine Fileserv4.

Note that remote virtual directories are mapped to UNC network shares. Again, if IIS is installed on a machine called server1, the Sales Department Web site would be accessed by the following URL:

```
http://server1/sales
```

Why Use Virtual Directories?

Virtual directories, especially remote ones, are useful for several reasons:

- It's *easier* to allow existing content to be left on existing file servers instead of being moved to a new IIS server. Moving content from one server to another involves several administrative tasks: capacity planning and upgrading for the new server, establishing new drive mappings for non-Web access to the content, educating users concerning the change in location of content, and so on. A key rule of thumb for administrators is if it works OK, don't change it!

- Performing *backups* of content is simpler if the content is left on existing file servers. Your network has a backup scheme in place for its existing file servers; using remote virtual directories means you don't have to modify your existing backup scheme.

- *Upgrading* the capacity of servers storing the content for your intranet can be performed without shutting down the Web servers themselves, minimizing Web server downtime.

- *Security* is enhanced by allowing those who create content access only to servers hosting content, not the Web servers themselves. No shares need to be created on the Web servers, making the Web servers more impervious to attack from hackers.

- Content can be *segregated* between departments by using virtual directories. Each department can access its own Web content through a unique URL (http://<server>/<dept_alias>) that maps to a unique directory on a server. Departments can work independently on their sites and only need to have their home pages linked to the default home page of the company Web site (http://<server>/default.htm) in order for them to be located and viewed on the intranet.

- *Load balancing* can take place by storing content for different departments on different file servers.

- Content can be stored on the network in locations where it is *easily accessed and updated*. Web servers can be installed in locations where they are easily accessed by administrators (although the HTML version of Internet Service Manager allows most IIS management functions to be performed remotely from anywhere in the network).

Disadvantages of Virtual Directories

The main disadvantage of using virtual directories is the slight drop in performance that occurs when content stored on remote servers is accessed over the network. This can be minimized by

- Upgrading network cards in servers
- Locating Web servers physically close to stored content

Walkthrough: Creating a Virtual Directory

Virtual directories can be created and managed using any of the following tools:

- The *Internet Services Manager* (ISM)
- The HTML version of the Internet Service Manager
- The Windows Scripting Host

In this walkthrough, we will use the MMC with ISM snap-in to create and configure a virtual directory on the default Web site.

First create and store the Web content that needs to be published in either a local directory on your IIS server or on a remote network share. Assign appropriate NTFS permissions for controlling access to the folder containing your content.

From the Microsoft Management Console, right-click the Web site (here the Default Web Site) to which you wish to add a virtual directory. From the shortcut menu that appears, select New, Virtual Directory, and the New Virtual Directory Wizard will appear (Figure 5-1). Click Next to start the wizard. Enter the alias to be used to access the virtual directory and click Next (Figure 5-2).

Next, you will need to specify either the path to the content directory on the *local* machine if you are creating a *local* virtual directory (Figure 5-3) or the UNC path to the network share containing the Web content if you are creating a *remote* virtual directory (Figure 5-4). In either case, you can either type in the path or select Browse to locate it.

If you specify content stored on a remote server, the next step will be to enter credentials sufficient to allow access to the remote folder (Figure 5-5).

Figure 5-1
The New Virtual
Directory Wizard.

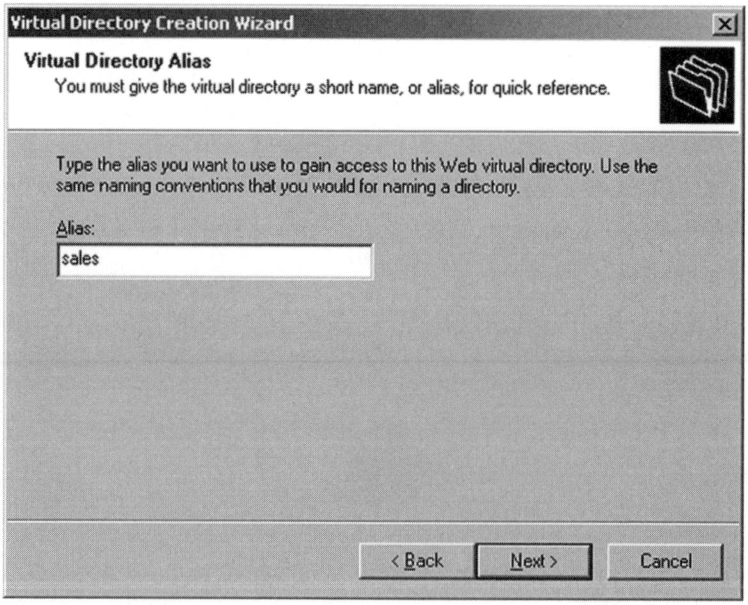

Figure 5-2
Specifying the
alias to use.

This can be a guest account, a specially defined domain user account, or an account belonging to the group that will have sole access to the virtual directory. Be careful to use an account with the minimum permissions nec-

Figure 5-3
Specifying the
path to use.

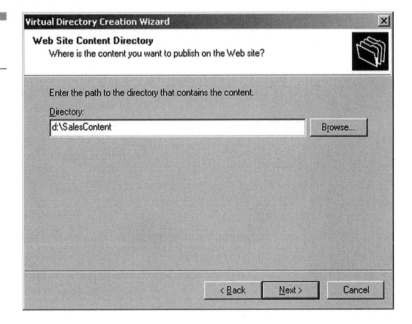

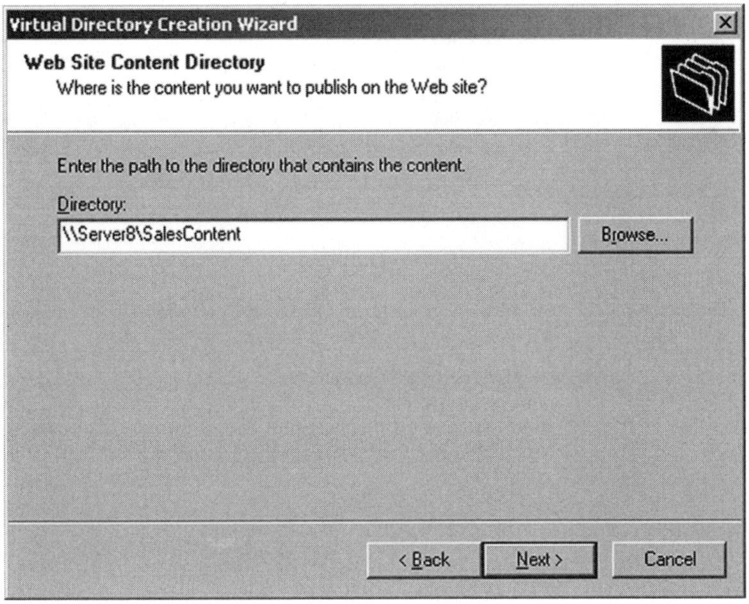

Figure 5-4
Specifying the UNC
path to remotely
stored content.

essary to provide access to the content. *Never use an administrator account to provide access to a virtual directory.*

Figure 5-5
Specifying the
credentials to access
remote content.

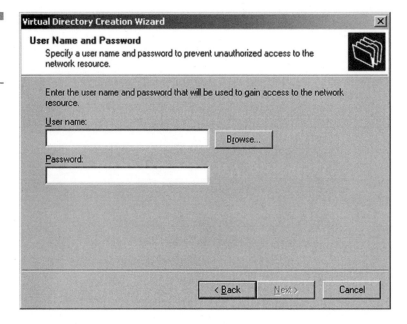

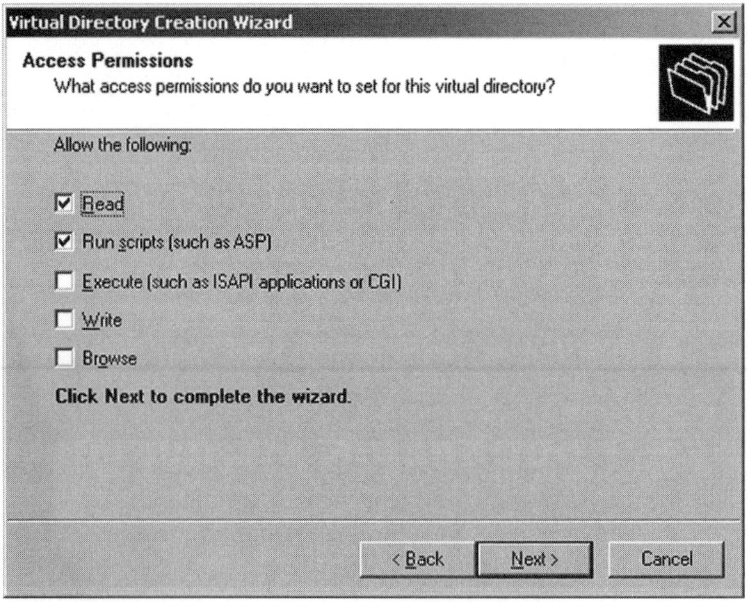

Figure 5-6
Specifying access
permissions for the
virtual directory.

Finally, specify the IIS access permissions you want for the virtual directory (Figure 5-6). These include whether or not to allow

- Read access
- Write access
- Script access
- Execute access
- Directory browsing access

By default, read and script access permissions are enabled.

Configuring Virtual Directories

When a virtual directory is created, it inherits the settings established in the Web Site Property sheet for the Web site to which the virtual directory belongs, which itself inherits the settings established in the Master Property sheet for the IIS server. To modify these settings for the virtual directory, right-click the virtual directory in the MMC and select Properties from the shortcut menu. This will open the Virtual Directory Property sheet (Figure 5-7), which has five tabs that allow you to configure settings as follows:

- *Virtual Directory* tab: location of mapped folder, access permissions, application settings
- *Documents* tab: default documents, footers
- *Directory Security* tab: authentication types, IP restrictions, SSL
- *HTTP Headers* tab: content expiration, custom headers, content ratings, MIME mappings
- *Custom Errors* tab: map to HTTP status code pages

For more information on configuring any of these settings, refer to Chapter 3, *Administering the WWW Service*.

Deleting Virtual Directories

To delete a virtual directory, right-click the virtual directory node in the Internet Services Manager Console and select Delete from the shortcut menu and confirm the deletion. You can also delete the virtual directory by selecting the node and pressing the Delete key on the keyboard, or choosing

Figure 5-7
Virtual Directory
Property sheet.

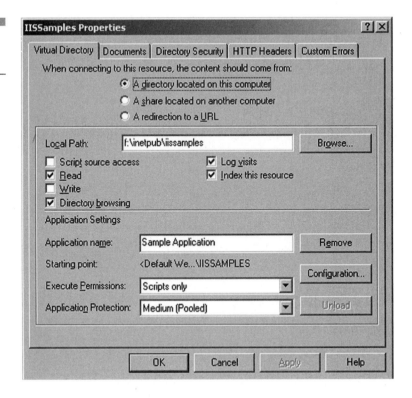

the Delete icon from the rebar, or selecting Delete from the Action drop-down menu on the rebar.

NOTE: *Deleting a virtual directory does not delete the Web content stored in the folder or share to which the home directory alias is mapped. It only deletes the mapping between the alias and the content folder.*

Using Virtual Directories

The following scenario illustrates the usefulness of using virtual directories in your intranet deployment.

Scenario

The management of MTIT LTD. assigns the company's network administrator the task of developing a corporate intranet. This intranet will contain content created by the following divisions: Planning, Records, and Design. Each division will be responsible for developing its own content. These divisions also have extensive legacy content (Word, Excel, and PowerPoint documents) stored on a file server called file2.mtit.com, which is working at near capacity. The network administrator is asked to employ minimal resources for building the intranet. Users currently have Office 95 and Netscape Navigator 3 on their desktops. The problem is how to proceed.

Possible Solution

Instruct content developers to store their Web content in their division's folder on `file2.mtit.com`. Provide them with HTML creation tools and enough training to get them going. This might be a good time to upgrade to Office 2000, which provides users with HTML creation capability. Or, you can download the Internet Assistants for Word 95, Excel 95, and PowerPoint 95 from Microsoft's Web site, which add HTML functionality to Office 95.

Install Internet Information Server on an existing server that is not being utilized near full capacity. As an example, choose `backup3.mtit.com`.

Create three virtual directories called *planning, records,* and *design* within the default Web site on the IIS server. Map these aliases to the appropriate shared folders on the remote file server to allow access through URLs such as

```
http://backup3.mtit.com /planning
http://backup3.mtit.com /records
http://backup3.mtit.com /design
```

Leave the NTFS permissions as currently set on `file2.mtit.com` and modify IIS security settings as seems appropriate, given the security needs of the company and the nature of the content being published.

Create a home page for the default Web site that identifies this as the company intranet, establishes policies and rules of use, and provides links to each division's home page in its own virtual directory.

Standardize on Internet Explorer 5.0 as the browser client to be used throughout the company. Save Office 2000 documents as HTML and view with Internet Explorer 5. Either way will provide the capability of viewing legacy documents from within Internet Explorer without necessitating the conversion of large quantities of legacy documents into HTML format first.

Understanding Virtual Servers

Virtual servers are different from virtual directories. On IIS, virtual servers are a mechanism by which several Web sites can be hosted on a single IIS 5.0 server. In effect, the IIS server behaves as if it were actually multiple IIS servers, each with its own properties, content, and assigned Web site operators. IIS 5.0 allows an unlimited number of virtual servers to be created. Virtual servers, in turn, may have one or more virtual directories contained in them. A virtual directory is always created within a virtual server or on the default Web site.

Virtual servers are created by defining a new Web site and mapping this site to the home directory of the Web content for the site. The home directory for the virtual server may be mapped to

- A directory on the local machine
- A share on a remote server

Virtual servers make it possible for multiple host or domain names to refer to the same physical IIS server. For example, the URLs

```
http://mis
http://marketing
http://sales
```

could all refer to the same physical intranet server. As another example, the URLs

```
http://www.mtit.com
http://www.santry.com
```

could likewise refer to the same physical Internet server. In this case, each Web site or virtual server belongs to a separate company.

NOTE: *Another name for a virtual server is a Web site. These two terms will be used interchangeably in this book.*

What Characterizes a Virtual Server?

Virtual servers (that is, Web sites) are uniquely identified by the following three parameters:

■ IP address
■ TCP port number
■ Host header name

As long as two virtual servers differ in one of these parameters, they can both exist and run on the same IIS server. For example, on an IIS server with only one IP address assigned and only one hostname defined on the DNS server, you can still host multiple Web sites by assigning them each a unique port number. These would be individually identified by URLs, such as

```
http://server6
http://server6:7200
http://server6:25803
```

In the first URL above, the port number is not specified, causing the server to respond to the default HTTP port, which is port 80. In the other two URLs, a port number has been randomly chosen from the numbers 1023 to 65535, excluding the well-known port numbers defined in the text file

```
C:\winnt\system32\drivers\etc\services
```

Similarly, multiple Web sites could be created on IIS 5—each with a different IP address, but the same (default) TCP port number (port 80).

The feature of Windows 2000 that makes virtual servers possible is the assignment of multiple IP addresses to a single server, a process known as *multihoming.* In order to host multiple domain names on a single IIS server, you can assign as many IP addresses to your server as you have Web sites to host. When you create each Web site, you assign it one of the IP addresses bound to your IIS server. To see how to add additional IP addresses to your Windows 2000 server, see Appendix A.

Multiple Web sites can also have the same IP address and TCP port number by using a feature called *host header names,* which is explained later in this chapter.

NOTE: *When you have multiple IP addresses assigned to an IIS server, each time you create a new virtual server, you must assign it an IP address. If you do not assign the virtual server an IP address but instead leave the IP address as "all unassigned" on the virtual server's property sheet, the virtual server responds to any IP addresses that are bound to the server but are not assigned to any other virtual server, making this virtual server the default Web site.*

Why Use Virtual Servers?

- Virtual servers are useful for many of the same reasons as virtual directories: security, easy backups and upgrades, content segregation and administration, and so on. However, virtual servers offer even more features than virtual directories do.

- Virtual servers are *completely configurable.* Each virtual server behaves as if it is a separate IIS server, and all the configuration options for the default Web site are available for any other Web site.

- Virtual servers may be *stopped, started,* and *paused* just like a real IIS server. For example, you may want to stop a virtual server while updating it with new content or changing its access permissions.

- Virtual servers may be assigned separate *Web site operators.* Each department could have its own virtual server and assign users who can fully administer its site. *Note:* From an administrator's point of view, this is probably the main benefit of using virtual servers—you can *delegate* administration of virtual servers to their Web site operators!

- *Bandwidth-throttling* and *performance-tuning* settings may be established for each virtual server.
- Virtual servers may contain any number of virtual directories. For example, the Marketing Web site could contain a home directory and several subdirectories whose content can be located in noncontiguous locations on various servers in the network, such as

    ```
    http://marketing.mtit.com/
    http://marketing.mtit.com/proposals/
    http://marketing.mtit.com/contacts/
    ```

Walkthrough: Creating a Virtual Server

Virtual servers can be created and managed using the same tools used for creating and managing virtual directories, namely

- The *Internet Service Manager* (ISM) snap-in of the *Microsoft Management Console* (MMC)
- The HTML version of the Internet Service Manager
- The Windows Scripting Host

In this walkthrough, we will use the MMC to create and configure a virtual server (Web site) on an IIS 5 machine.

First, create and store your primary Web content (the home page and pages of similar importance) that needs to be published in either a local directory on your IIS server or on a remote network share. Assign appropriate NTFS permissions for controlling access to the folder containing your content.

To create a virtual server using the Microsoft Management Console, right-click on the physical IIS server (the icon looks like a small computer) to which you would like to add a virtual server. From the shortcut menu that appears, select New, Web Site. The New Web Site Wizard will appear (see Figure 5-8). Click Next to begin the wizard. Enter a friendly name to describe the Web site (this name will appear beside the virtual server's node in the MMC) and click Next (Figure 5-9).

Figure 5-8
The New Web
Site Wizard.

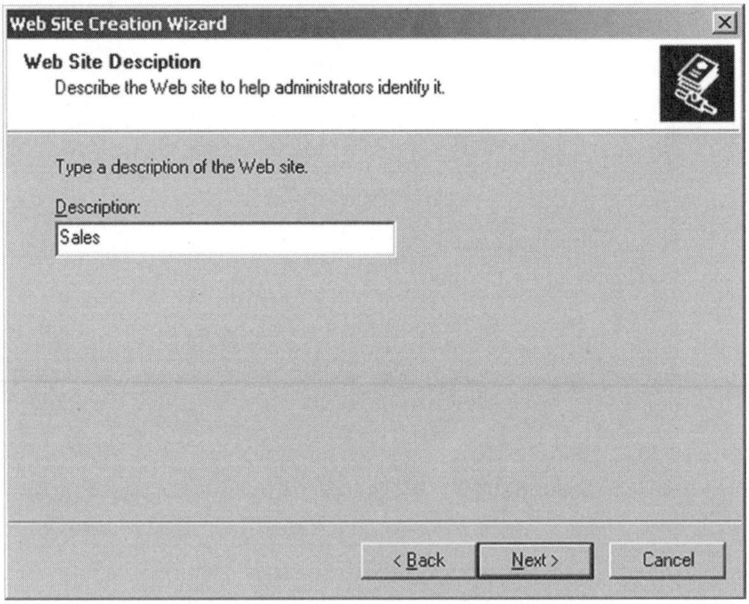

Figure 5-9
Entering a friendly
name for the site.

Use the drop-down box to select an available IP address from the IP addresses bound to your server or select All Unassigned if you wish this virtual server to be your new default Web site (Figure 5-10).

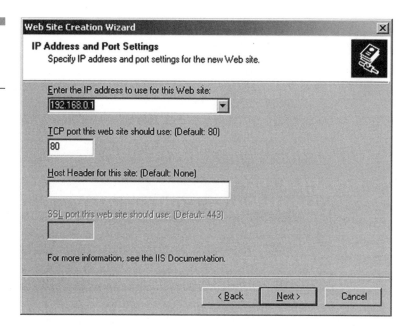

Figure 5-10
Assigning IP address and port number to the virtual server.

NOTE: *Be sure to select an IP address not already used by another virtual server or by your default Web site. If you select an IP address that is already in use, the New Web Site Wizard will not indicate any error at this point, but when you try to start the virtual server afterward, a dialog box will appear with the message, "A duplicate name exists on the network," and you will be unable to start the virtual server.*

Similarly, if the existing default Web site has "All Unassigned" as its IP address (see the Web Site tab on the Default Web Site Properties sheet), and you try to assign the same value "All Unassigned" as the IP address for your new virtual server, you will receive an error message when you try to start your virtual server: "The service could not be started because it is not correctly configured. Make sure that its server bindings do not conflict with other sites running on the same machine."

You can also configure which TCP *port* your virtual server is to be accessed from (the default port is 80).

If SSL is enabled, you can also configure which SSL port the virtual server should use (the default is 443).

Next, specify the location of the *home directory,* which is your virtual server's main content directory and contains your Web site's home page.

Figure 5-11
Mapping a virtual
server's home
directory to a
local folder.

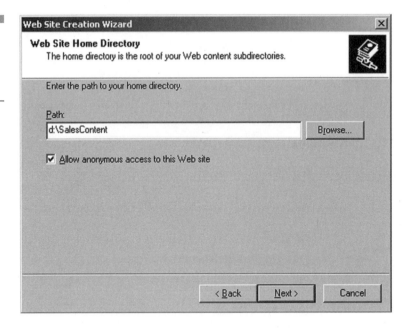

Figure 5-12
Mapping a virtual
server's home
directory to a
network share.

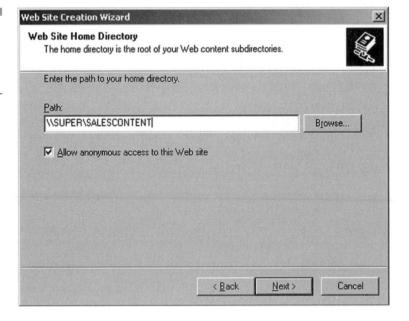

This can be either a folder on the local server (Figure 5-11) or a UNC path
to a share on a remote server (Figure 5-12). In either case, you can also

choose at this point to allow anonymous access to your Web site by check-ing the checkbox.

If you choose to map the virtual server's home directory to a network share, you will need to specify credentials that allow the proper level of access to the remote folder (Figure 5-13). Do not assign an administrator account to a virtual server.

Finally, specify the IIS access permissions you want for the virtual server (Figure 5-14). These include whether to allow

- Read access
- Write access
- Script access
- Execute access
- Directory browsing access

By default, read and script access permissions are enabled.

Your virtual server (Web site) is now created, but it is in a *stopped* con-dition. To start your virtual server, right-click on its node in the MMC and select Start from the shortcut menu.

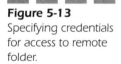

Figure 5-13
Specifying credentials for access to remote folder.

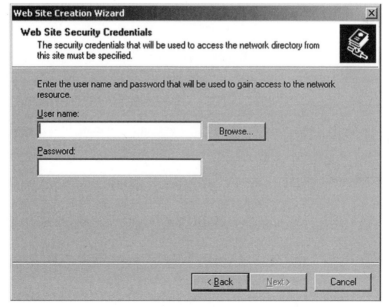

Figure 5-14
Assigning access
permissions to the
virtual server.

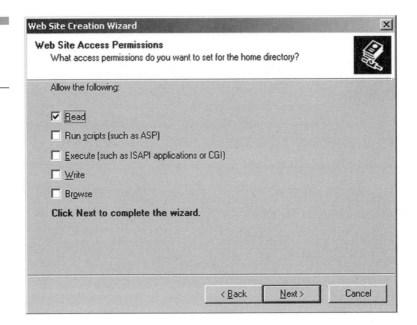

Configuring Virtual Servers

When a virtual server is created, it inherits the settings established in the
Master Property sheet for the IIS server on which it is created. To modify
these settings for the virtual directory, right-click the virtual server in the
MMC and select Properties from the shortcut menu. This will open the Web
Site Property sheet (Figure 5-15), which has the same nine tabs that the
Default Web Site Property sheet has, allowing you to fully configure the set-
tings for your Web site. For more information on any of these settings, refer
to Chapter 3.

Deleting Virtual Servers

To delete a virtual server, right-click its node in the Microsoft Management Console and select Delete from the shortcut menu to confirm the
deletion.

Figure 5-15
Web site properties
for a virtual server in
a stopped condition.

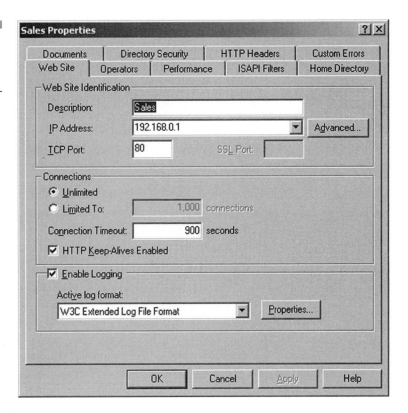

NOTE: *Deleting a virtual server does not delete the Web content in its home directory; it only deletes the mapping from the virtual server to the home directory.*

Using Virtual Servers

Below, we revisit the scenario given earlier in this chapter to illustrate the usefulness of using virtual servers in your intranet deployment.

Scenario

Management assigns the network administrator for MTIT Ltd. the task of developing a corporate intranet. This intranet will contain content created and managed by the following divisions: Planning, Records, and Design. Each division will be responsible for developing its own content and managing access to it. These divisions also have extensive legacy content (Word, Excel, and PowerPoint documents) stored in various folders on several file servers. Minimal resources are to be employed for building the intranet. What is the best way to proceed?

Possible Solution

Create a home directory for each division on a file server that has available space to house the home directories. Instruct content developers to store their home pages and other relevant pages in their home directories. Provide them with HTML creation tools and enough training to get them going.

Install Internet Information Server on an existing server that has sufficient free resources. Say, for sake of argument, that this server is called `www.mtit.com`. Create three virtual servers on the IIS server. Call these servers

```
planning.mtit.com

records.mtit.com

design.mtit.com
```

Map these virtual servers to their respective home directories.

Assign Web site operators for each virtual server. Give these individuals training on how to modify their Web site settings, how to create virtual directories, how to manage access to their sites, and so on. The operators will need to create virtual directories to allow access to legacy content without necessitating conversion of the content to HTML. For example, the Planning division might create a virtual directory accessed by the URL

```
http://planning.mtit.com/ppt
```

that maps to a folder containing PowerPoint files of planning session presentations.

Create a home page for the default Web site www.mtit.com that identifies this as the company intranet, establishes policies and rules of use, and provides links to each division's home page on its own Web site.

Standardize on Internet Explorer 5.0 as the browser client to be used throughout the company.

Understanding Host Header Names

IIS 5.0 allows multiple domain names to be mapped to a single IP address and TCP port number using a mechanism called *host header names*. This mechanism is a new feature of IIS 5.0 not available in previous versions of IIS and is a new feature of the HTTP 1.1 specification. To use host headers on an intranet or the Internet, the following must be configured:

- Multiple host names must be mapped to a single IP address using either a DNS server or a HOSTS file so the host names can be resolved to the IP address. For information on configuring Windows DNS server, see Appendix B.

- HTTP 1.1–compliant browsers must be used (MS Internet Explorer 3.0 or later, or Netscape Navigator 2.0 or later).

- Multiple host header names must be configured on the Web Site Property sheet for each virtual server.

Configuring Multiple Identities for a Virtual Server

To configure multiple identities for a virtual server, right-click the selected virtual server in the MMC and select Properties from the shortcut menu to open the Web Site Properties sheet. Select the Web Site tab and click the Advanced button to open the Advanced Multiple Web Site Configuration sheet (Figure 5-16). This sheet is used to add, remove, and edit identities for your Web site.

To specify an additional identity for your Web site, click the Add button and specify the IP address, port, and host header name (Figure 5-17). IIS 5.0 allows you to specify multiple host header names for the same IP/port combination.

Figure 5-16
The Advanced
Multiple Web Site
Properties sheet.

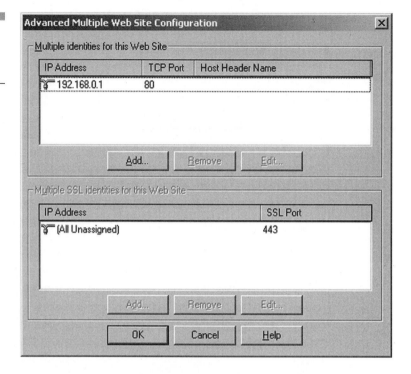

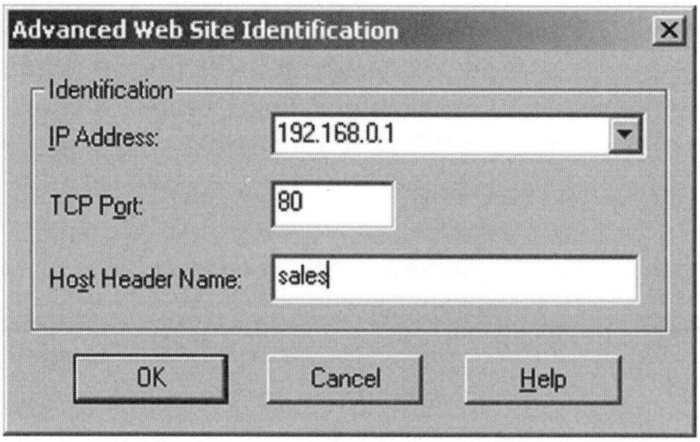

Figure 5-17
Specifying a Web
Site identity.

Why Use Host Header Names?

Suppose your company MTIT Ltd. has an IIS server with a Web site
accessed by the URL

    http://www.mtit.com

A merger takes place with another company. For a period of time your company has a dual identity, MTIT Ltd. and Santry Ltd. You register the new domain name `santry.com` using the same IP address because you want to access your MTIT Web site with the alternative URL

```
http://www.santry.com
```

To complete the process, you configure your Web server to respond to the additional identity as described in the previous section and access the site using an HTTP 1.1–compliant browser.

As another example, suppose you are an Internet service provider hosting several hundred Web sites each having its own domain name, but you only have a limited number of available IP addresses. To overcome this limitation, you could use host header names and assign all of the domain names to a single IP address. In this situation, you would need to enable users with older browsers that do not support host header names to reach the correct site. Refer to the IIS 5.0 online documentation for the topic "Supporting Host Header Names in Older Browsers" for more information on how to configure this.

SUMMARY

IIS 5.0 provides two mechanisms for mapping local and remote content to URLs: virtual servers (or Web sites) and virtual directories. By combining these two features, administrators can delegate management of Web sites to departmental Web site operators on intranets, or to Web site owners on a public Internet site, thus making their own job easier. These virtual servers and directories can be created and deleted without affecting the content on which they are based.

For More Information

TechNet has some useful information on virtual servers and virtual directories, although it refers to previous versions of IIS. Look in the following location for "Planning Your Content Directories and Virtual Servers:"

```
Internet, Server, MS Internet Information Server, Technical Notes,
Installation and Planning Guide, Chapter 6
```

Administering Content

Introduction

Creating and maintaining the content of your Web sites should not be the job of the administrator, but the responsibility of Web page developers, database developers, and programmers. The job of the administrator is to provide technical expertise, guidance, and support to these groups, and to establish rules, procedures, and mechanisms to facilitate the development and maintenance of Web sites. This chapter will cover issues relating to Web site development that are of importance to administrators, including

- Establishing policies and procedures for developing Web site content
- Selecting appropriate tools for Web content development
- Administering and utilizing Microsoft FrontPage for Web content development
- Administering and utilizing Microsoft Office for Web content development
- Publishing an Access database to the Web using Active Server Pages

Administering Content

Administering content is not the same as developing content, but it does include a basic understanding of the tools, procedures, and mechanisms for content development. In today's rapidly changing IT environment, as companies adjust to changes and reallocate resources to remain competitive, management often attempts to delegate to the overworked network or system administrator the additional task of planning, developing, and maintaining company Internet or intranet Web sites.

Resist their attempt to delegate this task to *you*.

The essence of Web site development is not formatting documents with HTML or writing scripts or programs. These are merely the underlying structure that support what Web sites really are—namely

- Vehicles for communicating company goals, policies, products, and services to employees, business partners, and the world.
- Tools for enabling collaborative business functions between departments and between clients and services.
- A reflection of management's understanding of where the company is coming from and where it is headed.

As a network or system administrator, you would normally not expect management to ask you to perform tasks such

- Designing a new company logo
- Producing a newsletter for customers
- Writing a company annual report or business plan
- Producing a TV commercial to market a service
- Writing a policy not directly relating to IT issues
- Deciding which company documents should be published and which shouldn't
- Designing a standard template for employee resumes
- Determining who should be allowed access to certain company files

Yet what those in management often do not understand is that by asking you as network administrator to create the company Web site or intranet site, they are in fact asking you to perform these kinds of tasks and make these kinds of decisions; tasks and decisions that really belong to the domain of executive and departmental management and are normally performed by clerical and middle-management staff.

As administrator, it is important that you raise these points to management, not just to release yourself from extra duties, but because you should not assume responsibility for tasks and decisions that rightly belong to others who are trained to do them. If you do, you will find yourself treading on other people's toes, often with painful results.

Establishing Content Development Policies and Procedures

Your response to management asking you to develop the company's Internet or intranet site should include taking the following steps:

1. Meet with management to determine the overall goals of the site, what the intended objectives are, and how to evaluate whether those objectives have been met—in other words, choose a project leadership team. Representatives of executive management, marketing, and IT should usually be involved in this.

2. Determine who will be responsible for making decisions about what specifically should be included in the site and what should not. Usually

this means assigning leadership of sections of the site to departmental middle managers.

3. Determine who will be responsible for soliciting and creating content, developing applications, and custom programming. Usually this involves teams of secretarial and clerical staff, applications developers, and IT support staff.

4. Establish a written policy indicating who is responsible for what regarding site development. For more information on this aspect, see the checklist of Chapter 1, *Installing IIS 5.0*.

5. Determine what resources will be required to complete the project, including hardware, software, and training for individuals. Develop a proposal that includes a cost analysis showing that it is cheaper to train and use existing people and to outsource programming needs than to utilize the costly time of an administrator or provide her with additional technical training. For example, training five secretarial people to use FrontPage and having them perform 100 hours of site development will be faster and cheaper than having a highly-paid network administrator perform 500 hours of site development. As another example, outsourcing database development or other programming needs for $5,000 will be considerably easier, cheaper, and faster than having an administrator take several weeks of advanced technical training courses in programming or database development.

6. Familiarize yourself with the basic tools that will be used to create the company Internet or intranet site. This way, you can assist content developers by making recommendations on designing site structure and navigation, giving advice on making use of advanced features of these tools, and providing other technical advice and support. If possible, try to have management budget for you or your IT staff to take Microsoft Official Curriculum courses for tools such as Internet Information Services 5.0, Internet Explorer 5.0, FrontPage, Visual InterDev, SQL Server, and so on.

7. Finally, develop procedures for content developers and programmers so they will know exactly how to

- Add, edit, and remove content on their portion of the site

- Create, test, and debug scripts, programs, and applications

- Conform to standards of style and navigation structure to give the whole Internet or intranet site a consistent look and feel

- Perform the limited administrative tasks assigned to Web site operators

- Request technical assistance from the IT department's Web site support people

Tools for Content Development

The decision on what tools will be used to build your company Internet or intranet site is one that you should not make yourself, but rather decide in close conjunction with management. The final choice of which tools to employ will depend upon a number of factors:

- Available software purchasing funds

- Available training funds

- Licensing requirements (another cost issue)

- Server and client capacity issues (for example, memory and HD requirements)

- Legacy document conversion issues

- Graphic design and layout costs

- Scripting and programming requirements

- Security restrictions and requirements

As an example, I've seen large companies with thousands of employees develop a functional intranet with Notepad as their main content development tool. The developers downloaded graphics from the Internet and processed scanned images with shareware image editing tools. The IT department and management worked together to establish policies to determine who would be responsible for what section of the intranet, and then handed out a few pages of instructions on basic HTML and some pointers to find more information on the Internet. It was amazing how much they accomplished with such a limited outlay of resources.

Then again, I've seen small companies use tools like Microsoft Front-Page, Access, and SQL Server to set up Web sites to enhance their business functionality. With a few days of technical training and a lot of wizards, these companies have set up online order systems, published interactive catalogs, established secure extranets, and so on.

In this book, we're obviously not going to consider how to use Notepad as a Web content development tool—although there are still real reasons for having content developers learn HTML. It's good for content developers to know the basics of HTML in order to make up for some of the WYSIWYG authoring application's deficiencies when laying out the underlying HTML code. Also, if your content developers are going to create dynamic Web applications using ASP, they should know the basics of HTML in order to develop something that is visually appealing to the user.

What we will consider in the rest of this chapter is how to implement, administer, and use two of the more popular and useful Microsoft Web publishing tools: Microsoft FrontPage 2000 and Microsoft Office 2000. As an administrator, you will need to know enough about the functionality of such tools to properly install them, assign appropriate permissions, and give technical advice to content developers on how to use them to create new Web content, convert legacy content to HTML, create connectivity to database content, and so on.

Despite everything I said about delegating content development to appropriate clerical and middle-management staff, the fact is that at first you will probably be responsible for designing the structure of the site, building a draft home page, and perhaps creating a demonstration Web-database application for test or pilot purposes. So it is to your advantage as an administrator to know enough about content development to get started —just don't let them make you do the whole thing!

Creating Web Content with Microsoft FrontPage

FrontPage is Microsoft's highly popular Web content creation tool. FrontPage 2000 is totally integrated into the Microsoft Office 2000 environment, giving you the same spell check, thesaurus, macros, and other editing tools found in other Office applications. These features make FrontPage 2000 well worth the upgrade price.

Here are some of the features of FrontPage 2000:

- A full-featured integrated WYSIWYG Web page editor
- A hierarchical Web site management environment that includes multiple views and link management capability
- Drag-and-drop frameset creation and management
- Wizards for easy creation of various types of Web sites
- Templates for Web page creation

- Themes for customizing the layout and graphic design of sites
- Automatic generation of navigation bars
- FrontPage components for automating tasks like indexing a site, adding search capability, activating forms, and scheduling
- Support for Dynamic HTML, Cascading Style Sheets, ActiveX controls, Java applets, JavaScript, and Visual Basic scripts
- Active Server Pages support and ODBC database connectivity wizards

End users who use FrontPage as their primary content development tool will need guidance and support to use FrontPage effectively. Any FrontPage training course will provide them with the skills necessary to produce simple FrontPage Webs and to design and edit Web pages, but either you, the administrator, or a member of your IT support team must be familiar enough with FrontPage to give technical advice on issues such as

- Creating and managing document templates
- Using includes for document headers and footers
- Designing pages that will load quickly and not waste bandwidth
- Incorporating ActiveX components or Java applets into their sites
- Importing Web content created with other tools into FrontPage Webs
- Generating logs and reports of site usage
- Incorporating Index Server for full text search capability
- Assigning FrontPage browsing, authoring, and administering permissions to users and groups
- Installing and configuring FrontPage extensions

Walkthrough: Creating a FrontPage Web

The following section takes you on a walkthrough on how to create and add content to a FrontPage Web on an IIS 5.0 server. Microsoft FrontPage uses the term *Web* to refer to a Web site or virtual server.

Before you implement FrontPage as a content development tool, some consideration has to be given to where and how to install FrontPage on the network. Typically, one of three scenarios are chosen (see Figure 6-1):

1. Install FrontPage on client machines (95/98, NT Workstation, or Windows 2000 Professional) *without* installing the Personal Web Server or IIS (Windows 2000 Professional) on the client machines.

Figure 6-1
Three ways of
publishing content
from clients to IIS
servers

Workstation
FrontPage

Production Server
IIS 5.0

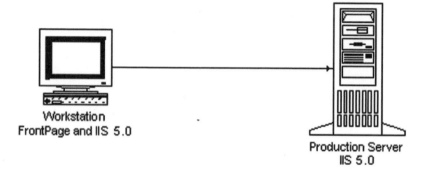

Workstation
FrontPage and IIS 5.0

Production Server
IIS 5.0

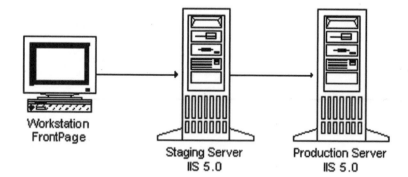

Workstation
FrontPage

Staging Server
IIS 5.0

Production Server
IIS 5.0

Have developers create and edit content *directly* on production servers running IIS. This is the simplest method and is suitable for low- to medium-security environments.

2. Install FrontPage on client machines along *with* IIS. Have developers create and edit content on their client machines, and then publish the

content to the production servers running IIS (or have an administrator copy the content to the production server). This method is suitable when Web sites do not involve complex scripts or applications that cannot be developed on Microsoft's Personal Web Server or Windows 2000 Professional with IIS.

3. Install FrontPage on client machines *without* installing the Personal Web Server on the client machines. Have developers create and edit content on an intermediate staging server running IIS. Have administrators copy the content from the staging servers to the production servers. This method is suitable for medium- to high-security environments, but it requires more administrative overhead.

Let's assume the first scenario above and install only the Web development portions of FrontPage 2000 on a client workstation, omitting the Personal Web Server and other administrative components. Log on to the client workstation as Administrator and install FrontPage 2000, choosing not to select the Personal Web Server or FrontPage Server Extensions.

An alternative would be to install FrontPage 2000 on the server itself, and log on to the server as Administrator to perform the steps below. The advantage of doing it this way is that you can create Webs and assign authoring permissions without having to go to the client machine to do so. This is the procedure we follow below.

If you are working with FrontPage in your networking environment, it is a good idea to visit the Microsoft Web site regularly to download and install the most current version of FrontPage server extensions, not only to eliminate bugs in earlier versions but to take advantage of exciting new features for Web developers.

After installing FrontPage, our next task will be to create a new virtual server (Web site) on the IIS server to contain the content created using FrontPage.

Using the Microsoft Management Console, connect to the IIS server, right-click the server icon, and select New, Web Site from the shortcut menu to open the New Web Site Wizard. Complete the steps of the wizard to create a new Web site by

- Assigning it a friendly name (in this case, MySite)
- Assigning it a fixed IP address (here, 192.16.0.54)
- Entering the path to the home directory for the site (here, C:\MySiteHome)
- Assigning appropriate permissions (leave Read and Script selected)

Figure 6-2
A newly created site call MySite

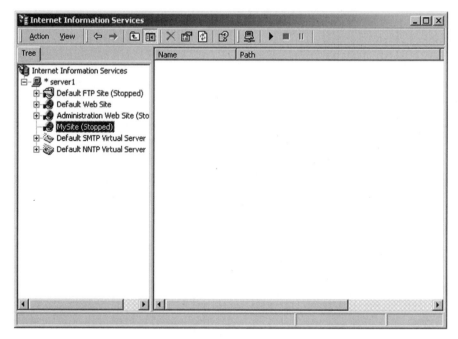

Note that the newly created Web site is in a stopped state and has no content yet because the site's home directory, C:\MySiteHome, is currently empty (see Figure 6-2).

At this point, if the home directory, C:\MySiteHome, is on an NTFS volume, you may want to check the permissions on the directory and make sure that those who will have the responsibility of creating and editing Web site content have the necessary permissions (for example, change or RWXD).

Now that we have created a new Web site, our next job will be to prepare it for receiving content from FrontPage. Select the MySite node and right-click. From the context menu, select All Tasks, Configure Server Extensions. This action starts the Server Extensions Configuration Wizard (see Figure 6-3). Click the Next button to begin the Wizard.

A dialog box (see Figure 6-4) for configuring the local groups for access to this site appears. These groups are where the browsers, authors, and administrators accounts will be contained. By default, the Web's IP address or name will be entered as a prefix for the account. In this example, MySite was entered as a group name prefix, in order to differentiate this Web from other Webs located on the server. Click the Next button to continue.

Figure 6-3
Starting the Server
Extensions
Configuration Wizard

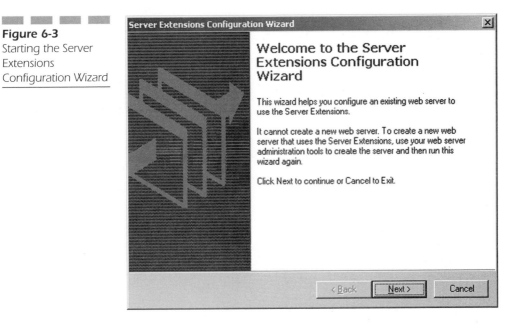

Figure 6-4
Specifying groups for
access to the
FrontPage Web

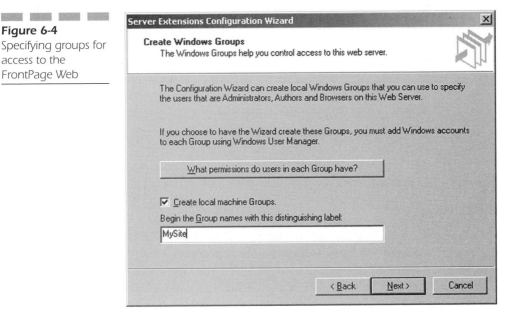

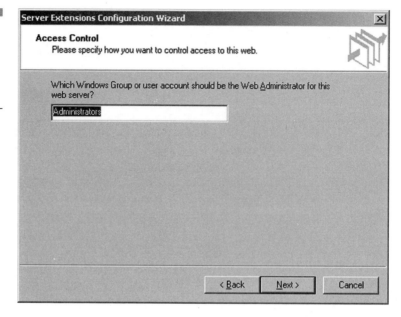

In this dialog box (see Figure 6-5), specify the group that will have access as an administrator of this FrontPage Web. This group will then be added to the new MySite Administrators group that will be created when this Wizard completes. Click the Next button to continue.

In this dialog box (see Figure 6-6), specify the local SMTP server's information and the email address to use when this Web sends email. This is used for the email component of the FrontPage extensions, which allows authors to send email from a Web page. Click the Next button to continue. This will bring up a summary of the Wizard. Click the Finish button to complete and close the Wizard dialog box.

Essentially, a new FrontPage root Web has been formed on the virtual server MySite. To see these virtual directories under MySite by using the MMC, you may need to click the Action button and select Refresh from the drop-down menu (see Figure 6-7). These virtual directories map to real subdirectories of the site's home directory, C:\MySiteHome. Many of these subdirectories are hidden and will not show up in Windows Explorer unless Show All Files is enabled on the Folder Options property sheet opened by Tools, Folder Options in Windows Explorer.

Some of these virtual directories are important for administrators, so here is a brief explanation of what they are used for (refer to books on FrontPage for more information regarding these virtual directories):

Figure 6-6
Specifying the local
SMTP server and
email settings

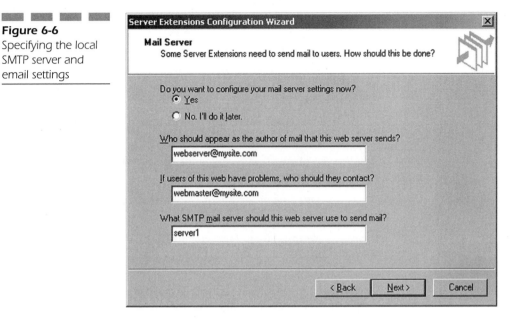

Figure 6-6
Specifying the local
SMTP server and
email settings

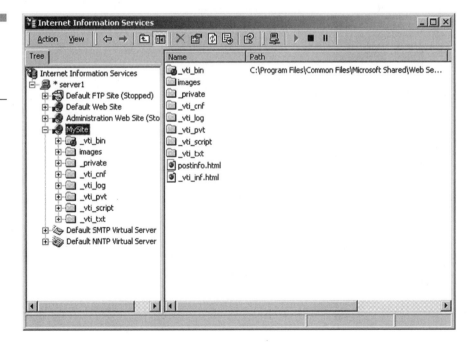

Figure 6-7
Virtual directories of
the FrontPage root
Web on the virtual
server MySite

_private/	Used for pages that should not be visible in browsers or indexed by search engines (for example, templates, headers, footers, includes).
_vti_cnf/	Looks as if it contains a duplicate of every page in the Web site. Actually, the duplicate pages only have the same name as the original and contain instead a series of name/value pairs specifying things like the date page was last modified, who modified, and so on.
_vti_txt/	Contains text indexes for the FrontPage Search WebBot component.
_vti_pvt/	Contains other FrontPage information, such as the list of dependencies and child Webs.
_vti_log/	Contains logs if authoring logging is enabled.
images/	You can store all your images for your site in this directory if you like.

A virtual directory called _vti_bin/ contains executables (DLLs) used by FrontPage for administration and authoring purposes. This directory points to a centralized directory that all FrontPage Webs use located in `C:\Program Files\Common Files\Microsoft Shared\Web Server Extensions\40\isapi`.

Now that the administrator has created a new virtual server with a FrontPage root Web on the IIS server, we use the MMC to Start the virtual server. We can then go to the client machine with FrontPage installed, connect to this new FrontPage Web we have created, and update it with new content.

Log on to the client machine as a user with author and browse permission and start FrontPage. From the File menu, select Open Web. A dialog box will appear (see Figure 6-8). Type in the IP address (or domain name if DNS is enabled) of the virtual server you want to connect to (in this case 192.168.0.54 for MySite) and click Open to open the FrontPage Web.

To create some content for this Web site, we will create a new Web using a wizard and add the resulting content to the existing Root Web. Select File, New, Web to open the New FrontPage Web dialog box (see Figure 6-9). Highlight the Corporate Presence Wizard, check the Add to Current Web checkbox, and click OK to start the Corporate Presence Web Wizard (see Figure 6-10). Follow through the steps of the wizard, making selections to customize the site as desired, and click Finish in the last step, and FrontPage will automatically create a basic corporate Web site.

Figure 6-8
Entering the IP address of the newly created FrontPage Web

Figure 6-9
Adding content to an existing Web by using a wizard

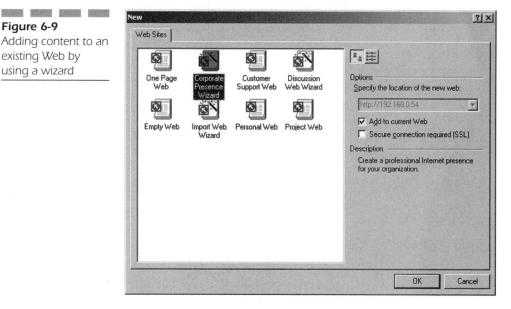

FrontPage shows the various pages that make up your newly created Web site. Explore the various views for your site by using the Views bar on the left. Figure 6-11 shows the site in Folder view, but other views allow you to examine the site's navigation structure, view the status of its hyperlinks, fix any broken links, and so on.

Figure 6-10
The Corporate
Presence Web Wizard
helps you build a
professional-looking
Web site

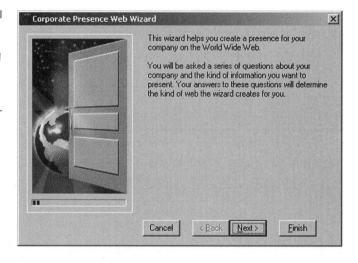

Figure 6-10
The Corporate
Presence Web Wizard
helps you build a
professional-looking
Web site

Figure 6-11
The MySite Web site
created using
FrontPage 2000

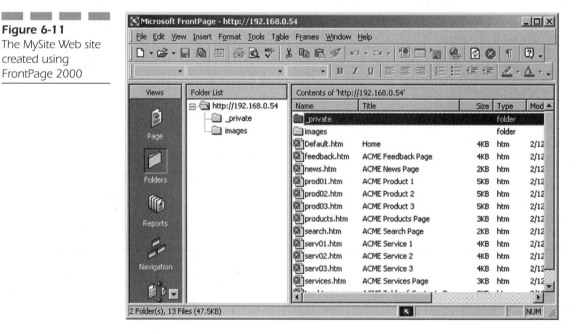

At this point, you may want to add graphics to your Web site by selecting and applying one of the available *themes*. These themes are design templates that specify the layout and graphic look of all pages in your site. A theme can be changed at any time with a few clicks of the mouse. Your Web site need never look old and boring, but may be updated any time.

From the Format menu, select Themes. Choose a theme from the Themes dialog box (a preview will be displayed for each theme you click on). Select whether you want to use vivid colors, add active graphics, or add a background image, and click OK (see Figure 6-12).

As a final step, view your new Web site using a browser such as Internet Explorer (see Figure 6-13). If the site is for intranet use, view its appearance in the browser you have chosen as a standard for your company. If it is an Internet Web site, view it in both Internet Explorer and Netscape Navigator, using both current and older versions of the software. This will ensure that whoever looks at your site sees what you expect them to see.

Creating Web Content with Microsoft Office

Microsoft Office is also a powerful content development platform for Web sites. Office 2000 comes with built-in HTML functionality, allowing you both to create new Web pages easily and to convert legacy documents to HTML for universal access.

Web pages represent a kind of universal document format because a Web page created on one machine can be viewed from any other machine

Figure 6-12
Applying a theme to your site to improve its appearance

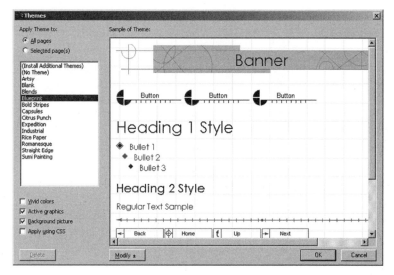

Figure 6-13
The final Web site for MySite. All it needs is for real content to be added!

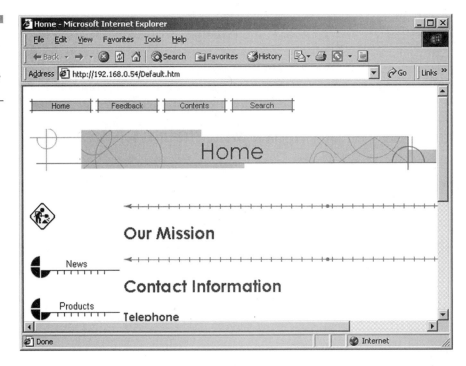

equipped with a browser. Browsers are available for all platforms and hence constitute a kind of *universal client software*.

Office suites such as Microsoft Office, on the other hand, constitute a kind of legacy publishing system. In order to view a Word or Excel document produced on one machine, the client machine must either have full versions of Microsoft Word or Excel installed *or* special read-only Word or Excel viewers installed.

If your Web site will contain quantities of legacy documents (Word, Excel, or PowerPoint documents), you have two options for displaying them:

- Convert the legacy documents to HTML using Office 2000.

- Ensure that client machines that need to browse your site have either Microsoft Office installed on them or at least the read-only Office viewers installed.

If you cannot control what software your client machines will have installed on them (which is usually the case with Internet sites), the first option may be the only viable one for you to follow. Using the option to save the document as a Web page allows Internet Explorer 5 users to see the document exactly as it was when created in Word. Office 2000 uses a combination of XML and Cascading Style Sheets to store the document information and allow it display in IE exactly the way it looked when created in Office 2000. Using this option of saving the document as a Web page allows an organization to take advantage of *Web Distributed Authoring and Versioning* (WebDAV), which is discussed later in this chapter.

Another option is to save the document in native format. If all client machines are equipped with Microsoft Office or Office viewers, they can open a read-only copy of the document. For intranet sites, such standards can be enforced companywide. For Internet sites, your best bet might be to save the documents as HTML or at least provide users with the ability to download the appropriate viewer.

Figure 6-14 shows the result of browsing the document personal.doc using Internet Explorer 5 when the client machine also has Office 2000 installed on it. The result is that the Word application opens within the browser window, allowing users to view and edit documents, all the while staying within the confines of the browser window.

Figure 6-14

Viewing a Word document using IE 3.02 on a machine with Office 2000 installed

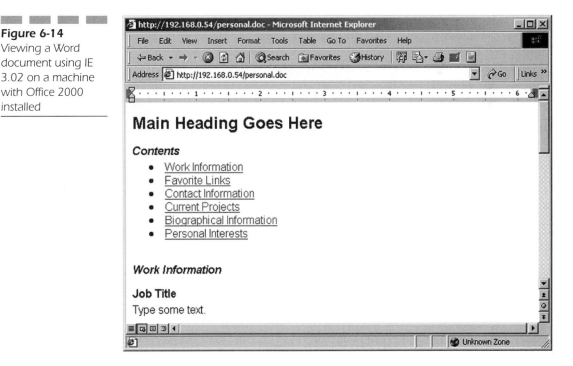

Web Distributed Authoring and Versioning (WebDAV)

Using Office 2000 and Internet Explorer 5.0, you can take advantage of WebDAV. WebDAV is a set of extensions to HTTP that allows for collaborative development and authoring to take place over the Web. WebDAV allows you to view folders and files on a Web server via Windows Explorer (see Figure 6-15) and edit documents directly as if they were on your system or network drive. The following requirements are needed to use WebDAV:

- Internet Explorer 5
- IIS 4 or Higher
- FrontPage Extensions

Figure 6-15 shows Windows Explorer. Under the My Network Places node are mappings to Web servers that were previously logged onto successfully. You can expand the root of the Web, in this case the IP address, and view documents and directories contained on the Web server. You can

Figure 6-15

Viewing a Web site's structure using Windows Explorer via WebDAV

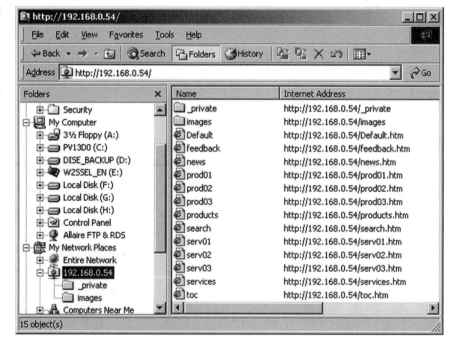

open documents directly, copy, move, and delete documents as if they were on a network or local drive.

WebDAV allows users to use the familiar tools of Office 2000 to edit content directly on the Web site using HTTP. An author can type in the URL of the document and then open it for editing by clicking the Edit icon in Internet Explorer. Internet Explorer is smart enough to open the document in the same application in which the document was created. IE will display the application's icon that created the document in the toolbar. Click the icon to open the document in the application for editing. The author can then save the changes to the document directly to its location.

For more on WebDAV, refer to the Windows 2000 Resource Kit.

Publishing to a Web Site from a Database

As another example of the power of Microsoft tools for creating Web content, the following walkthrough illustrates how easy it is to use Microsoft Access 2000 to create Active Server Pages that connect to and display content from an Access database.

Integrating relational databases into your Web site can be done in two basic ways:

■ The *push method* has the database engine automatically generate static HTML pages on a periodic basis or every time a certain amount of information in the database is updated. The push method is useful for databases that change infrequently. The static HTML pages generated can represent data in tables, results of queries, and so on. A good example of this method is the SQL Server Web Assistant, which is a tool for publishing static HTML content from an SQL database.

■ The *pull method* involves using Active Server Pages or some other mechanism to dynamically generate database content each time the page is accessed. This method is most useful when the database information frequently changes or the most current information must always be accessed. An example of the pull model is creating Active Server Pages to query an Access database by exporting the database to ASP.

Both of these methods make use of the *Open Database Connectivity (ODBC)* mechanism, which can be used to access data from almost any commercial relational database.

Walkthrough: Exporting an Access 2000 Database to Active Server Pages

The following walkthrough shows how to use Access 2000 to create dynamic Active Server Pages that publish information from an Access database to the previously created virtual server MySite. Access is suitable for the workgroup level when only a few dozen users are querying the database, whereas SQL Server is suitable for enterprise-level Web-database applications. Access 2000 allows you to export a database using either the push or the pull method. We will examine the pull method.

Start Microsoft Access 2000 and either use an existing database or create a new one using the New Database Wizard. The database shown in Figure 6-16 was created using the Ledger template in the New Database Wizard; it was populated with sample data created by the wizard. This database is called Ledger1.mdb and is located in the home directory of the

Figure 6-16

A database called Ledger1.mdb created using Access 2000

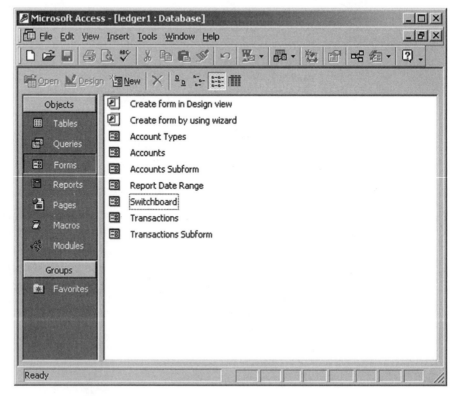

MySite Web site on the IIS server; that is, in the C:\MySiteHome directory, which is shared on the network as \\SERVER1\MySiteHome.

From the File menu, select Export to open the Export Table dialog box (see Figure 6-17). Next, we need to specify where we want to publish the database to; that is, which local directory or network share we want the generated Active Server Pages to be placed in. In this example, shown in Figure 6-17, we have chosen to publish the pages to the directory where the database itself is located: namely, the MySite Web site home directory located on the IIS server at C:\MySiteHome, which is shared on the network as \\SERVER1\MySiteHome.

From the Save as Type drop-down menu, select *Microsoft Active Server Pages* (.asp) option and click the Save button. This will bring up the Output Options dialog box (see Figure 6-18).

In this dialog box (see Figure 6-18), you can select a template that will be applied to your dynamically generated Web pages to add formatting and improve their appearance. If you decide to choose a template, you should first copy the template to where your database will be located (that is, copy the template to your Web site's home directory on the IIS server if this where the database will reside). In this walkthrough, no template is specified.

In order for your IIS server to connect with the Access database you wish to publish, you will need to specify a *data source name (DSN)* for *Open Database Connectivity* (ODBC).

Figure 6-17
Exporting the database table to an Active Server Page

Figure 6-18

Specifying options for
the Active Server
Page export

In this example, the database is called Ledger1.mdb and the data source
name selected to represent it on the network is `ledger` (see Figure 6-18).
The simplest option is to establish this as a System DSN (a user account
and password may be required) so the data source will be visible to all users
on the machine where the data source is defined (this will be done later).
Click on the OK button to close this dialog box and create the file.

Figure 6-19 now shows the contents of the MySite Web site in the
Microsoft Management Console (you may have to select Refresh from the
drop-down Action menu to get this view). Notice the following files:

- Ledger1.mdb (the database itself—the file Ledger1.ldb is an artifact of
  the database file being open under Access 2000)

- Accounts.asp (the Active Server Page that generates a Web page
  containing the current contents of the Accounts table)

Before we can actually browse the Active Server Page, we must first
define the System DSN for the database in ODBC. Open the ODBC Data
Source Administrator property sheets (see Figure 6-20) by selecting Start,
Programs, Administrative Tools, Data Sources (ODBC). Select the System
DSN tab and click Add. The Create New Data Source box appears. Select
the Microsoft Access Driver as the database driver to be used to connect to
your database and click Finish (see Figure 6-21). The ODBC Microsoft
Access 2000 Setup dialog box appears. Enter `member` as the Data Source

Figure 6-19
An Active Server Page has been added to the MySite Web site

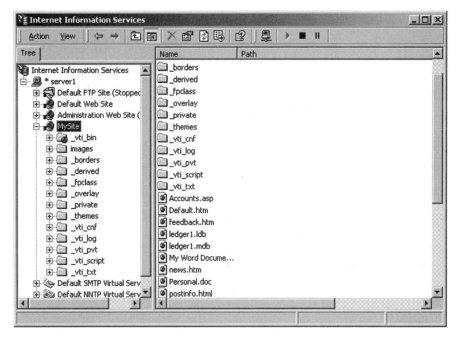

Figure 6-20
The System DSN tab in ODBC manager

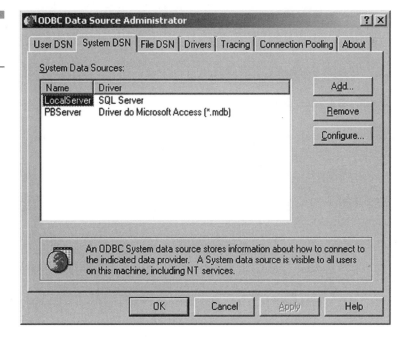

Figure 6-21
Select the Microsoft
Access Driver

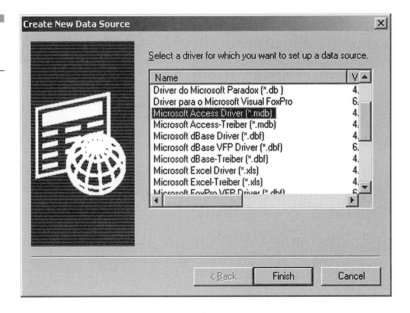

Figure 6-22
Assign a data source
name to your
database

Name (see Figure 6-22). Then click Select and browse to locate the Ledger1.mdb database in the home directory C:\MySiteHome.

You can also create a new database at this point, or compact or repair an existing one. For explanation of other options, see the ODBC help file.

When browsing to select your database, you can also specify the following options by clicking the appropriate checkbox:

- Read-only mode
- Exclusive mode

Select the Ledger1.mdb database and click OK to finish (see Figure 6-23).

You are finally ready to test the Active Server Page to see if it dynamically queries the database for its information. Make sure that the MySite home directory has both read and script permissions in IIS (check the MySite property sheet in the MMC) because these permissions are required for Active Server Pages to execute properly.

In the MMC, right-click the file Accounts.asp and select Browse from the shortcut menu. This will launch Internet Explorer and execute the script on the page, causing it to return the current contents of the Payments table to the Web browser (see Figure 6-24).

SUMMARY

In this chapter, we discussed managing content in an intranet and Internet environment. We also covered Microsoft Office's tools for editing documents and maintaining content. We discussed using WebDAV for extended remote authoring and document management capabilities. This chapter also contained information on FrontPage 2000 for those seeking more powerful site management and editing tools. Many more features of Office 2000 can enhance content management for organizations; refer to the Office 2000 documentation for complete coverage of what Office 2000 can provide.

Figure 6-23

Map the database file to the System DSN

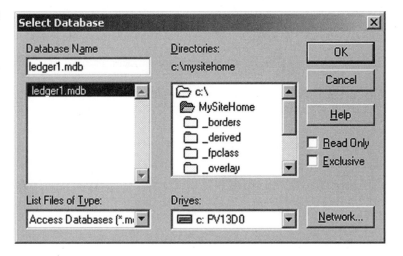

Figure 6-24
Results of executing
Accounts.asp

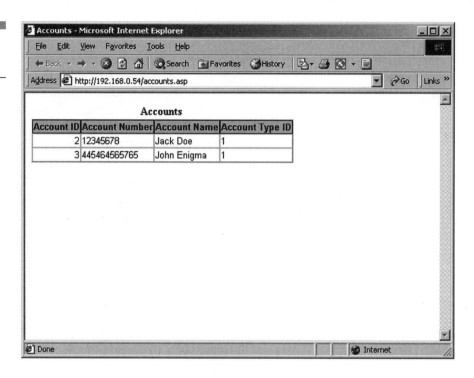

For More Information

For more information on administering Web site content, turn to the following Internet resources.

Microsoft Web Site

For an excellent source of information on all aspects of FrontPage 2000, visit

```
www.microsoft.com/frontpage
```

Microsoft Public Newsgroups

Microsoft FrontPage issues are discussed in the newsgroups

```
microsoft.public.frontpage.*
```

Microsoft Access has a large number of different newsgroups to browse:

`Microsoft.public.access.*`

Download and install the Microsoft Office 2000 60 Minute Intranet Kit. This provides support for Office Server Extensions for collaboration and targeted email.

`www.microsoft.com/office/intranet`

Microsoft TechNet

TechNet has FrontPage 2000 manuals located at

`Desktop Applications, MS FrontPage, FrontPage Manuals`

Also included is the FrontPage 2000 Server Extensions Resource Kit at

`Desktop Applications, MS FrontPage, Resource Kit`

Administering Clients

Introduction

Administering Internet Information Services 5.0 is only half the battle for the network administrator; the other half is administering the end-user client software. In Chapter 6, we considered administering end-user content creation tools; in this chapter, we look at administering the client browser software itself. After completing this chapter, you will have a basic understanding of how to install, configure, and manage *Microsoft Internet Explorer 5.0* (IE 5.0) using the *Internet Explorer Administration Kit* (IEAK). In particular, we will look at

- The basic features and functionality of Internet Explorer 5.0
- Configuring IE 5.0 security options
- The IE 5.0 Active Setup process
- Using the IEAK to create custom packages
- Distributing IEAK custom packages to clients

What Is Internet Explorer 5.0?

Internet Explorer 5.0 is Microsoft's newest version of its award-winning Internet browser client software. IE 5.0 includes a number of add-on components to further extend client functionality in both Internet and intranet environments:

- Communication add-ons: NetMeeting, Outlook Express, Chat
- Multimedia add-ons: NetShow, VRML Viewer, Media Player, and more
- Authoring add-ons: FrontPage Express, Web Publishing Wizard
- Additional enhancements: Microsoft Wallet, Task Scheduler, Web Fonts, support for Compressed HTML provided by IIS 5.0, Digested Security (IIS 5.0)
- Multiple language support

Why Use Internet Explorer 5.0?

In a corporate network, it is fairly straightforward to standardize on IE 5.0 for client machines. Internet Explorer 5.0 is installed by default on Windows 2000 machines. You can still use the Internet Explorer Administrative Kit to deploy a custom version of IE 5.0 on your Windows 2000 clients. Your custom IE 5.0 build will overwrite the settings that exist on the initial Windows 2000 installation. You can also use the custom IE 5.0 build to deploy on legacy NT and Windows 95/98 clients as well. Administration of client machines is further simplified by using the Microsoft Internet Explorer Administration Kit, described later in this chapter.

In a public Internet environment, users should be directed to upgrade to IE 5.0 to enhance their browsing experience and take full advantage of IIS 5.0 hosted sites.

Understanding and Configuring Internet Explorer 5.0 Security

In order to use Internet Explorer 5.0 within a corporate environment (and to use it effectively in an Internet environment), it is essential to understand Internet Explorer security. Internet Explorer 5.0 security can be controlled through

- Security zones
- Site certificates
- Security options settings

We will consider security zones and options settings in this chapter; site certificates are considered in Chapter 11.

Configuring IE 5.0 Security Zones

Internet Explorer 5.0 allows you to assign particular Web sites to specific zones. A *zone* is a security setting that controls access to a specific group of Web sites. When Internet Explorer 5.0 is installed, it creates four different security zones:

- *Local intranet zone,* which contains all Web sites on your company's intranet (LAN) and any specific sites you wish to add. Or from another angle, it contains all Web sites that don't require a proxy server to access them. Using the Internet Explorer Administration Kit, which is described later in this chapter, an administrator can define which sites are to be included in this zone.

■ *Trusted sites zone,* which contains any specific sites you trust that you wish to add.

■ *Internet zone,* which contains all Internet sites; that is, anything not on the local machine, not on the local network, and not assigned to any other zone.

■ *Restricted sites zone,* which contains any specific sites you don't trust that you wish to add.

These four zones can each be configured to one of the following security levels:

■ *High security.* All content that might damage the client system is excluded.

■ *Medium security.* The user is warned before content that might damage the client system is run. Unsigned controls will not be downloaded to the local machine.

■ *Medium-Low security.* Same a medium security, but without prompts. Unsigned controls will not be downloaded to the local machine.

■ *Low security.* All content is run without warning or notification to the user.

■ *Custom security.* The security setting for each form of active content is configured as prompt, disable, or enable.

The default security settings for the four zones when Internet Explorer 5.0 is installed are as follows:

Local intranet zone	Medium security
Trusted sites zone	Low security
Internet zone	Medium security
Restricted sites zone	High security

To configure security zones for IE 5.0, go to Control Panel, click Internet Options, and select the Security tab on the Internet Options property sheet that appears (see Fig. 7-1). From this property sheet you can add specific Web sites to any of the four zones except the Internet zone (which cannot be configured).

For example, let us add a new site to the local intranet zone (possibly an external site with the proxy server disabled for this site). On the Security tab, select Local Intranet and click on the Sites button. The Local intranet zone dialog box appears, asking whether you want to include in this zone the following:

Figure 7-1
Accessing the IE 5.0
security zone
configuration.

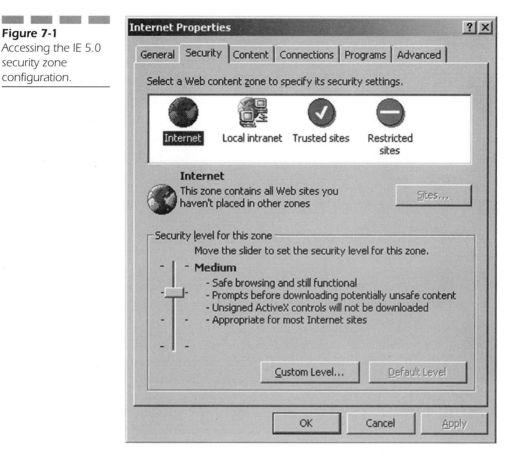

Figure 7-1
Accessing the IE 5.0
security zone
configuration.

- All local intranet sites not listed in other zones
- All sites that bypass the proxy server
- All network paths (using UNC paths)

  By default, each of the above three items is checked (see Fig. 7-2).
  Click Advanced to open another Local intranet zone dialog box (see Fig. 7-3). In this new box you can

- Specify which Web sites will be added to the local intranet zone
- Specify whether or not to require connection to sites in this zone using HTTPS

  Enter the Web sites you want to consider as part of the local intranet zone and click OK. Other zones are configured similarly.

Figure 7-2
Choosing what to
include in the local
intranet zone.

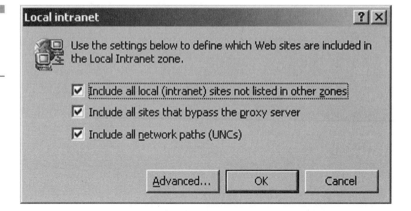

Figure 7-3
Adding a specific
Web site to the local
intranet zone.

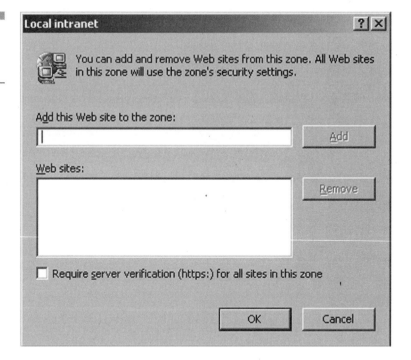

Configuring IE 5.0 Security Options Settings

The custom security setting described above allows you to enable, disable, or prompt regarding a number of security issues. To access these security options, go to Control Panel and open the Internet icon, select the Security tab, and click the Custom Level button. The following security options can be configured:

- *ActiveX controls and plug-ins settings:*
    - Download unsigned ActiveX controls
    - Script ActiveX controls marked safe for scripting
    - Initialize and script ActiveX controls not marked as safe
    - Download signed ActiveX controls
    - Run ActiveX controls and plug-ins
- *Cookie settings:*
    - All cookies to be stored on your machine
    - All session-level cookies
- *Download settings:*
    - File downloads
    - Font downloads
- *Java settings:*
    - Java permissions: high, medium, low, disabled, or custom
- *Miscellaneous settings:*
    - Access data sources across domains
    - Software channel permissions
    - Launching applications and files in an IFRAME
    - Navigate sub-frames across domains
    - Installation of desktop items
    - Submit nonencrypted form data
    - User data persistence
    - Drag and drop or copy and paste files
- *Scripting settings:*
    - Scripting of Java applets
    - Active scripting
- *User authentication settings (choose one of the following):*
    - Anonymous logon (disables HTTP authentication and uses guest account)
    - Prompt for username and password

- Automatic logon in intranet zone (prompts for username and password in other zones)

- Automatic logon with current username and password (Windows NT Challenge/Response and Windows Integrated Authentication)

Still other security options may be configured by using the Advanced tab on the Internet Options property sheet (Figure 7-4).

Understanding Internet Explorer 5.0 Active Setup

In order to administer Internet Explorer 5.0, we require a basic understanding of the Active Setup process. Internet Explorer 5.0 setup uses

Figure 7-4
Other security settings on the Advanced tab of the Internet Options property sheet.

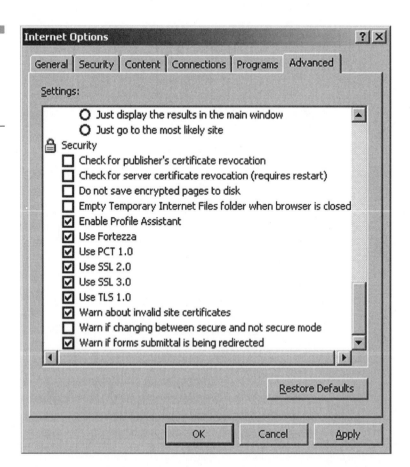

ActiveX technology running on the client computer to provide a faster, more efficient, modular setup process. Active Setup includes features such as the ability for setup to reconnect to the distribution source and resume setup where it was interrupted. It also provides detailed progress information about setup, including the estimated time to completion.

IE 5.0 Active Setup is initiated by running the self-extracting file IE5setup.exe. This file is 505KB in size and can be downloaded from the Internet, copied from a distribution server, supplied on an installation CD, or even distributed on a floppy.

IE5setup.exe gathers necessary information from the client and then downloads or copies to the local drive only those .cab files that are necessary to install or upgrade the selected components. When the necessary .cab files have been downloaded, Active Setup ends and the traditional ACME setup engine takes over.

Administering IE 5.0 Clients Using the Internet Explorer Administration Kit

The *Internet Explorer Administration Kit* (IEAK) is a tool for helping administrators deploy and support custom configurations of Internet Explorer 5.0. The IEAK is not included as a part of Windows 2000 operating system, but it is an essential tool for administrators rolling out IE 5.0 on corporate intranets, or ISPs wanting to provide customers with customized, preconfigured browser clients. In this section, we will examine how to plan, prepare for, create, and distribute customized IE 5.0 packages using the IEAK.

What Is the Internet Explorer Administration Kit?

The IEAK includes the following tools:

- *IEAK Wizard* allows administrators to create customized packages for IE 5.0 installations.
- *IEAK Profile Manager* allows administrators to maintain IE 5.0 clients by configuring user options from a centralized place.

■ *The Connection Manager Administration Kit* allows you to customize a users connection settings.

■ *IEAK Help* provides instructions on how to use IEAK effectively.

Uses of the Internet Explorer Administration Kit

The IEAK can be used in different ways, depending on whether you are a corporate intranet administrator, an Internet content provider, or an Internet service provider.

Corporate Intranet Administrators Corporate intranet administrators can use the IEAK to perform hands-free installations of IE 5.0, customized to meet the particular needs of their companies. Administrators can

■ Roll out IE 5.0 browsers with customized Search, Favorites, Start Page, title bar, and logo

■ Preconfigure IE 5.0 security settings including security zones, content ratings, proxy settings, and certificates

■ Customize setup to include optional components, including third-party custom components

■ Configure multiple distribution servers for load-balancing

■ Perform silent (unattended) installations

■ Apply system policies and other restrictions during installation

Internet Service Providers Internet service providers (ISPs) can use the IEAK to create custom IE 5.0 installation packages for Internet clients. ISPs can

■ Create installation packages that include bundled third-party software components

■ Designate which language version of IE 5.0 to install

■ Customize IE 5.0 with Search, Start, Favorites, support pages, logo, and title

■ Create sign-up packages for new customers and upgrade packages for existing customers

■ Use the IE 5.0 logo on their packaging materials, in accordance with the license agreement

Internet Content Providers *Internet content providers* (ICPs) can use the IEAK to create custom IE 5.0 installations packages similar to Internet service providers. In addition, ICPs can perform automatic software distribution via the Internet.

Obtaining and Installing the IEAK

The IEAK can be downloaded from the secure Web site

```
http://www.microsoft.com/windows/ieak/
```

To obtain the IEAK from this site, perform the following steps:

1. Register your name and company in the IEAK database. Click the Get the IEAK image on the left side of the page, select New Registration, and complete the registration form. Include your email address. When you complete your registration, a site password will be emailed to you within a few hours.

2. When you receive your site password, enter your email address and site password in the logon box. When you are admitted to the site, you will need to select one of the following options describing how you plan to distribute IE 5.0:

   ■ To customers outside your organization

   ■ To company employees within your organization

   ■ To meet special requirements (128-bit browser, dial-up networking)

   Select your distribution option and click Next to read your licensing agreement.

3. Read the licensing agreement carefully. If you agree, click on the link Sign a License and Distribution Agreement. When you click the link, email will be automatically sent to you containing another password, called a *customization keycode*. This keycode validates you as an authorized IEAK user. You will need it in order to run your copy of IEAK, so make sure you print it out and store it in a safe place. You should also print out and keep a copy of your licensing agreement.

4. Download the language version of IEAK of your choice by clicking the link Get Internet Explorer Administration Kit. You can also order it on CD at a nominal cost.

5. Per your licensing agreement, you must make quarterly reports to Microsoft of the licenses you distribute to customers.

Preparing to Use the IEAK in a Corporate Environment

Begin by being aware of the requirements for installing the IEAK:

- Windows NT 4.0 Server (version 3 or higher) or Windows NT 4.0 Workstation; Windows 95/98; or Windows 2000 (all versions).
- Disk space up to 100MB, depending on type of installation selected (standard, enhanced, or full). If you select several installation types (CD, Flat, or Download), you could need an additional 100 MB for each type.
- Internet Explorer 5.0 installed on the system to download the IEAK

In addition, you should gather all necessary information and additional custom files before running the IEAK. This should include the following:

- Create any custom bitmaps you wish to use to customize the browser and place them in a folder on the distribution server.
- Plan your distribution method for the IEAK custom package (from the Internet, from a distribution server, on a CD, or on a floppy).
- Obtain a digital certificate from a Certificate Authority and sign your cabinet files and custom files if necessary because of browser security settings.
- Collect URLs for users' Start page, Favorites, and support pages.
- Plan what kind of security settings you want implemented on the browsers.
- Plan how you want to configure the Windows Desktop Upgrade.

Walkthrough: Using the IEAK to Create a Package

The following walkthrough leads you through using the IEAK Wizard to create custom packages for the purposes of distributing and installing IE 5.0 on a corporate intranet environment. For use in an Internet service provider environment, consult the IEAK online documentation.

The IEAK Wizard runs through a series of five stages, each stage consisting of several steps. To start the IEAK Wizard, click on Start, Programs, Microsoft IEAK, IEAK Wizard.

Figure 7-5
Stage 1 of the IEAK Wizard is called Gathering Information.

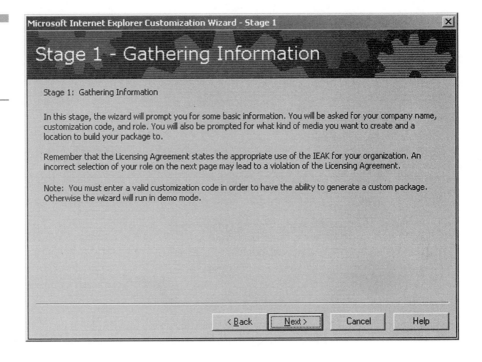

Stage 1: Gathering Information   Stage 1 of the IEAK Wizard is called *Gathering Information* (Figure 7-5). In stage 1, you will be prompted by the IEAK Wizard to enter the following information (Figure 7-6):

- Your company's name
- Your customization code (obtained during the IEAK registration process)

You will also need to provide the role you selected in your licensing agreement for using the IEAK:

- Content Provider/Developer
- Service Provider
- Corporate Administrator (we selected this option)

NOTE: *It is important that the selection you make on the screen shown in Figure 7-6 matches the selection you made when accepting your licensing agreement. If the two are different, you may be violating your licensing agreement.*

Figure 7-6
Enter your
customization code
in order to proceed
with the Wizard.

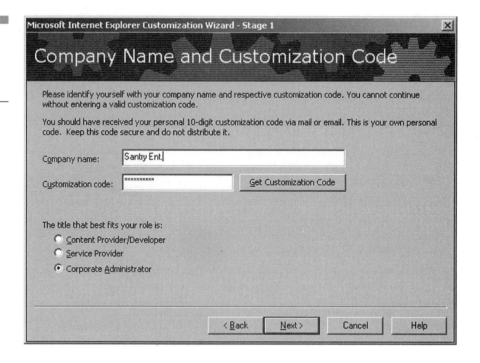

Next, select the platform that you are targeting for this IE package. You'll need to create a package for each platform that you want to create an IE installation for.

Now select or create the folder where your customized IE 5.0 packages will be placed when the wizard is finished (Figure 7-7). Your IE 5.0 installations will be performed from this download directory. In our example, we have chosen the directory C:\ieaktest. Click the Advanced button to specify a location for Automatic Version Syncronization files.

Next, select a language for the IE package. You will need to create a new package for each target language.

Next (Figure 7-8), select the installation media, such as CD or floppies, you wish to use for deploying IE 5.0 on your intranet. This completes stage 1, Gathering Information.

Next (Figure 7-9), select the installation options that you want to configure for your IE package.

Stage 2: Specifying Active Setup Parameters   Stage 2 of the IEAK Wizard is called *Specifying Setup Parameters* (Figure 7-10). In stage 2, you will need to connect with a Microsoft download site and download the IE

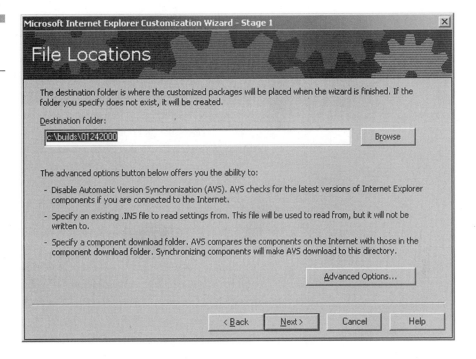

Figure 7-7
Choose an installation directory.

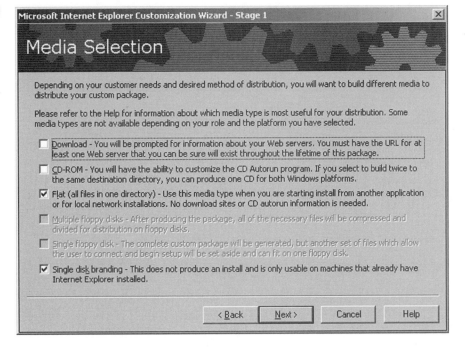

Figure 7-8
Selecting an installation media type for the IE 5 build.

Figure 7-9
Select the features to configure.

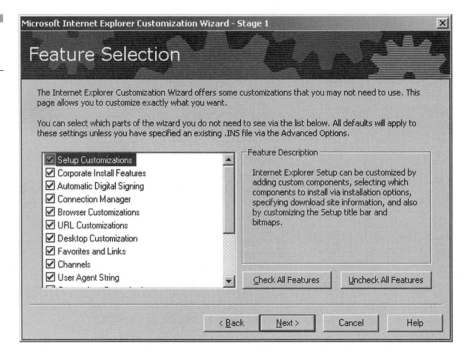

5.0 components you will use to create your custom installation packages, plus supply any additional third-party components that you want to bundle into your package.

First, you will be asked to select a Microsoft download site from which to download the newest versions of Internet Explorer 5.0 and its optional components.

Next, select which components you wish to download from the *Automatic Version Synchronization* (AVS) screen (Figure 7-11). This screen graphically shows you which components you have and don't have, and whether your components are up to date. The files that will be downloaded will be used to create the custom installation packages.

Select the components you wish to download and click on Synchronize, or click on Synchronize All to download all the components. Note: Only Internet Explorer 5.0 *must* be downloaded; all other components are optional.

Next, you will be given the opportunity to select up to 10 custom or third-party components to incorporate into your installation packages. These components should be in the form of self-extracting .exe files or cabinet (.cab) files. Any third-party custom components must be signed. This completes stage 2, Specifying Setup Parameters.

Figure 7-10
Stage 2 of the IEAK
Wizard is call
Specifying Setup
Parameters.

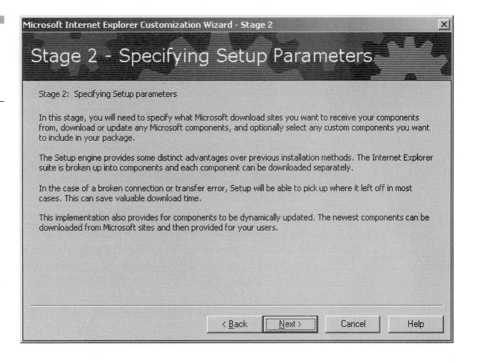

Figure 7-11
Select which
component to
download for
creating custom IE
5.0 installation
packages.

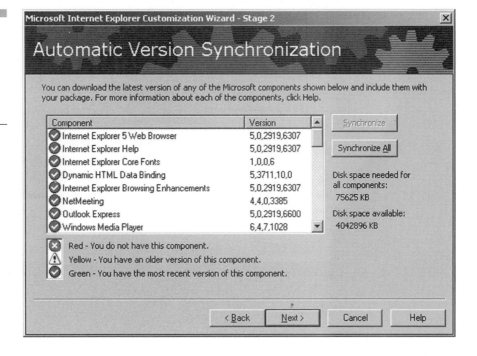

Figure 7-12
Stage 3 of the IEAK
Wizard is called
Customizing Setup.

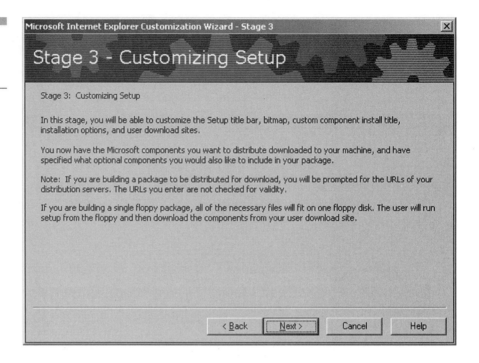

Stage 3: Customizing Setup   In stage 3 of the IEAK Wizard, you customize the Setup program that will be used to install your custom packages (Figure 7-12). Customization includes title bar, bitmap, user download sites, and more.

Begin this stage by choosing whether you want to customize the title bar and bitmap of the Active Setup screen for your customized package. If you choose to create a CD installation package, you can also customize the CD Autorun screen.

Next, decide whether you want to perform an *interactive*, *hands-free*, or *silent install* of your custom package. A silent install requires no input from the user on whose machine IE 5.0 is being installed, and the user will not even be aware that the installation is taking place (other than the increase in CPU and drive activity). A hands-free install is primarily the same as a silent install except that the user can see the progress of the installation. Silent installations have the following limitations:

- You may specify only one (not 10) installation option for different types of installs.

- You may specify only one (not 10) download site for downloading your package.

- You must decide whether to include the Active Desktop upgrade.

Figure 7-13
A silent install

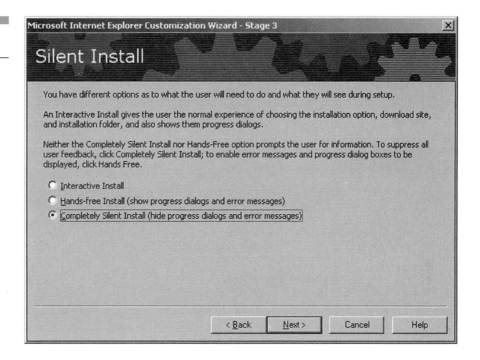

In Figure 7-13, we have selected to perform a silent install.

Next, create an installation option or configure an existing option and select which components to install when this option is selected (Figure 7-14).

Next, specify the download sites from which your custom package will be installed (Figure 7-15). For each download site, you must specify

- The site name
- The site URL
- The site region

Note that the URL specified here is *not checked* by the IEAK Wizard. You may specify up to 10 download sites. If you are performing a silent install, however, you may only specify one download site.

Next, you need to specify a unique version number for your custom packages to ensure that later versions are updated properly. You can also specify the URL to which the Internet Explorer Add a Component option points. Add a Component is accessed from the Internet icon in Control Panel.

Next, specify the target directory on the client computers on which the Internet Explorer program will be installed. You can specify

Figure 7-14
Create installation
options.

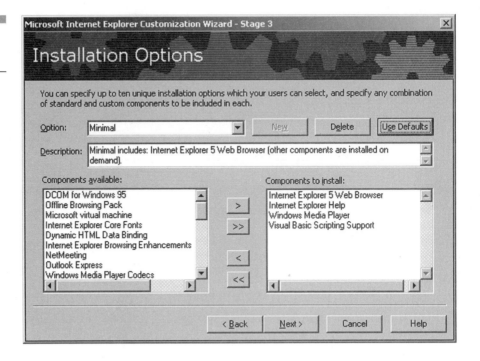

Figure 7-14
Create installation
options.

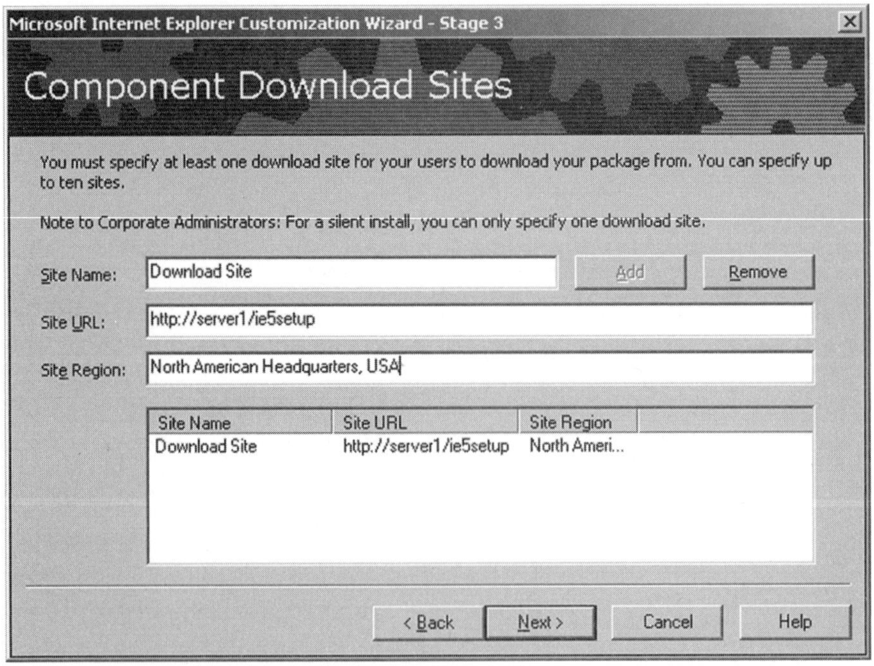

Figure 7-15
Specify download
sites for performing
custom installation
options.

- A subdirectory in the Windows directory
- A subdirectory in the Program Files directory
- The complete path for the destination directory

Next, specify whether the Windows Update should be installed along with IE 5.0 (Figure 7-16). Windows Update allows the user to make any updates to the Windows operating system or IE such as security patches. You can also specify a custom URL to point to the update site if you do not wish to use Microsoft's site.

Next, specify an installation directory for the IE package. You can allow the user to choose where to install Internet Explorer (unless you are performing a silent or hands-free install).

Next (Figure 7-17), specify whether you wish to allow uninstallation for the IE 5.0 package and whether to set IE 5.0 as the default browser for viewing Web files.

Next (Figure 7-18), you can specify whether to optimize the installation for Web download. Selecting this option will enable the installation to first check the user's machine to see if a recent version exists. If a version exists, it will not download and install the component; it will use the one already present.

Figure 7-16

Specify the Windows Update options.

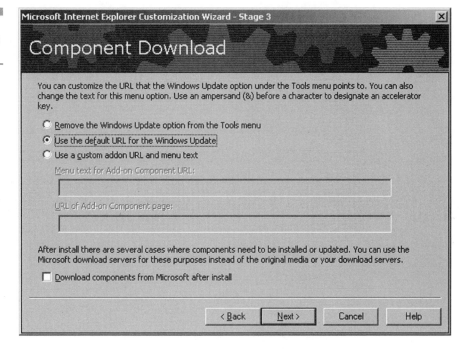

Figure 7-17
Specifying uninstall options and setting the default browser.

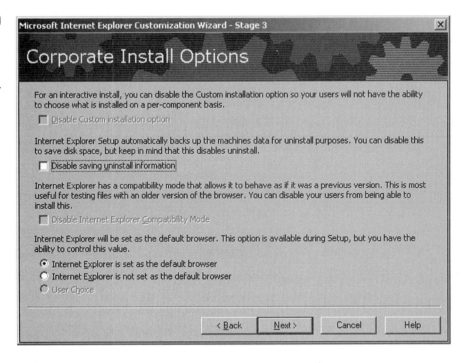

Figure 7-18
Optimizing your IE package for Web download.

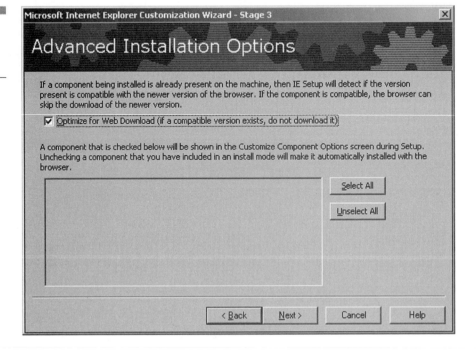

Next, the IEAK will present you with components that are available during AVS but were not selected as part of this install. You can select a component to make available on the media.

From this next screen (Figure 7-19), you can start the *Connection Manager Administration Kit* (CMAK). This kit allows you to configure connection information for your package. To start the CMAK, click on the Start CMAK button. For the purpose of this walkthrough, we will click the Next button to continue the IEAK. For more information on the CMAK, refer to the IEAK or Windows 2000 documentation.

Next, specify whether the Windows Desktop Update should be installed along with IE 5.0 (Figure 7-20).

Next, specify Certification Authority if you wish to sign your IE installation. This completes stage 3, Customizing Setup.

Stage 4: Customizing the Browser   In stage 4 of the IEAK Wizard, you will customize the IE 5.0 browser that will be installed on client machines (Figure 7-21). Customization options include title bar, bitmap, start page, search page, favorites, security zones, and more.

Begin by specifying any custom toolbar buttons you want to add to the IE 5.0 toolbar. Do this by clicking the Add button, which will bring up the

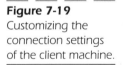

Figure 7-19
Customizing the
connection settings
of the client machine.

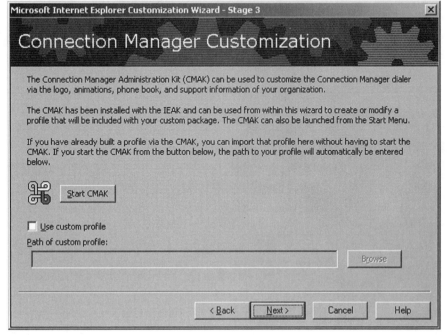

Figure 7-20
Specifying whether
to install the
Windows Desktop
Update.

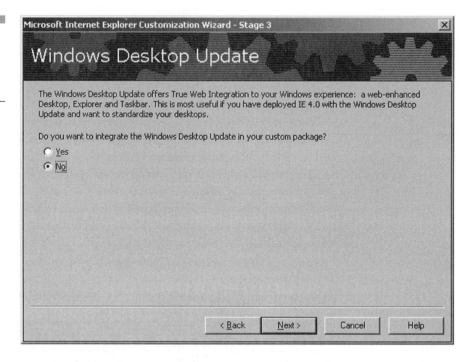

Figure 7-21
Stage 4 of the IEAK
Wizard is called
Customizing the
Browser.

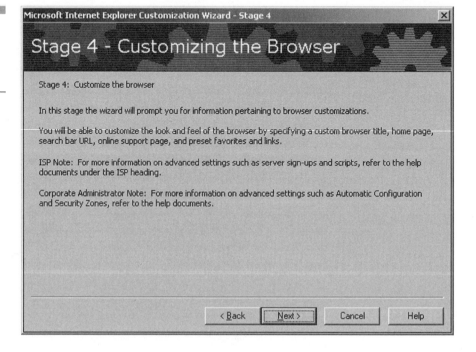

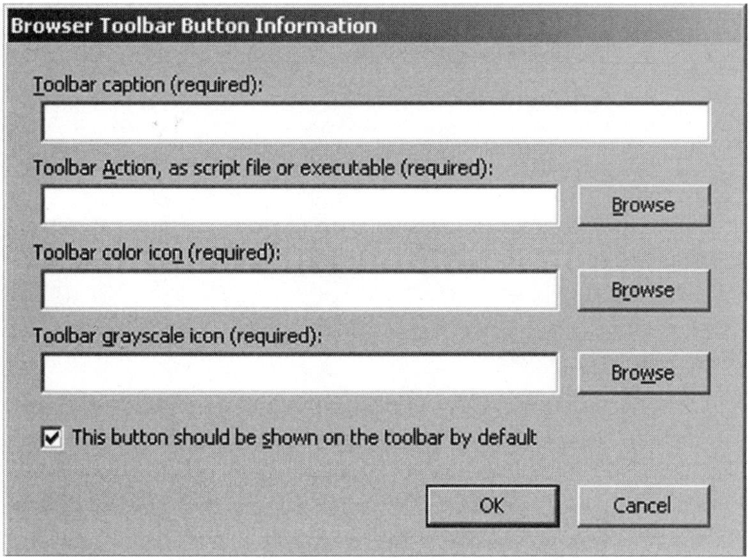

Figure 7-22
The Browser Toolbar
Button Information
dialog box.

Browser Toolbar Button Information

Toolbar caption (required):

Toolbar Action, as script file or executable (required):

Browse

Toolbar color icon (required):

Browse

Toolbar grayscale icon (required):

Browse

☑ This button should be shown on the toolbar by default

OK   Cancel

Browser Toolbar Button Information dialog box (Figure 7-22). Enter in the caption for the toolbar, the action to perform when the button is clicked, the color icon for when the mouse passes over it, and the grayscale icon for when it's disabled. Click the OK button to complete the addition of the button. It will then show up in the Wizard.

Next, you can specify custom images for the animated graphic to be displayed in the top right corner of IE 5.0. This will be displayed while the browser is making a request.

In this next screen, you can specify a static logo to be used in the top right corner for when the browser is not doing a process or request.

Next, customize the title bar and the toolbar background bitmap of Internet Explorer 5.0. Then, specify the following custom pages (Figure 7-23):

- Custom home page
- Custom search page
- Custom support page

Next, create a custom favorites list with URLs and folders to organize them (Figure 7-24). Click Add Folder to create a folder to organize your favorites and click Add URL to specify a favorite. You can also click Import to load an existing favorites list into your installation package.

Figure 7-23
Select your custom
start, search, and
support pages.

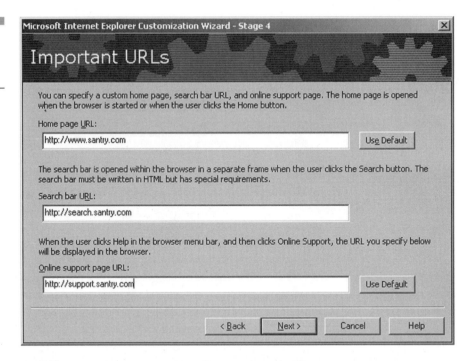

Figure 7-23
Select your custom
start, search, and
support pages.

Figure 7-24
Create a custom
favorites list.

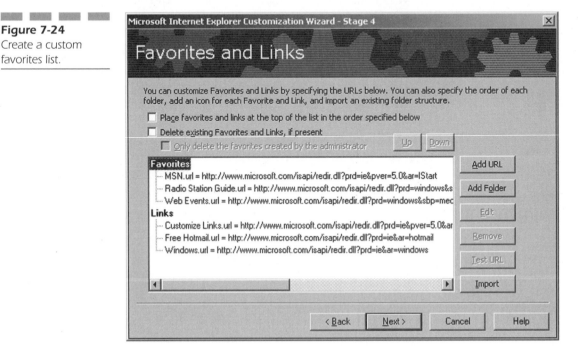

Next, configure the channel options for Internet Explorer. You can choose to delete existing channels, turn on desktop Channel Bar, and add additional channels and categories. You can also click Import to load existing channels into your installation package.

Next, choose whether to display the Microsoft Internet Explorer welcome page the first time the browser is started (Figure 7-25). You can also create a custom welcome page suitable for your corporate intranet.

Next, you can specify a custom user-agent string to be appended to the default user-agent string that the browser sends to the Web server during an HTTP request.

In the next screen, you can choose to import your existing connection settings. You can also choose to delete the user's existing connection settings on the target machine. After that, supply a path to the directory that contains the .ins file that automatically configures your browser (Figure 7-26). The .ins file can be modified and configured using the IEAK Profile Manager and is discussed later in this section.

Next, you can configure your proxy settings for each of the Internet protocols (HTTP, FTP, and so on) and select whether to use the proxy settings

Figure 7-25
Select the Welcome page.

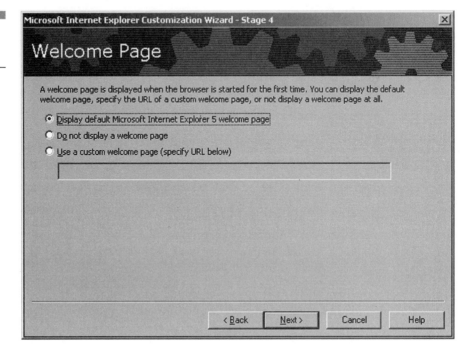

Figure 7-26
Enable automatic
browser
configuration using
an ins.file.

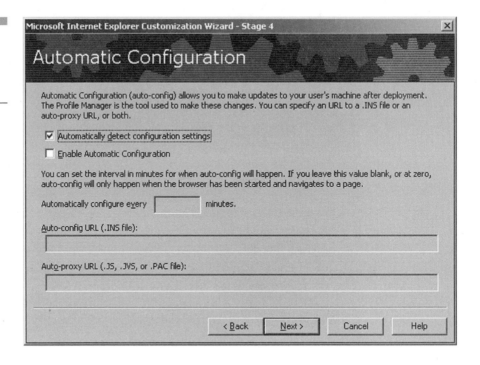

for the local intranet. Now, configure certificate settings for your IE 5.0 browser. Configuration options here include choosing to

- Import and modify Certificate Authorities (CAs) from the local machine
- Add a new root certificate
- Import and modify Authenticode settings

Next, you can configure security and content settings for your IE 5.0 browser. Configuration options here include customizing security zone and content ratings settings.

See Figures 7-27 and 7-28 for examples of the last two options. This completes stage 4, Customizing the Browser.

Stage 5: Customizing Components In stage 5 of the IEAK Wizard, you can customize available options for optional components and third-party components you have chosen to bundle with your installation package (Figure 7-29). Administrators can also configure system policies and various settings for users' machines.

Figure 7-27
Configuring
Certificate Authorities
and Authenticode
settings.

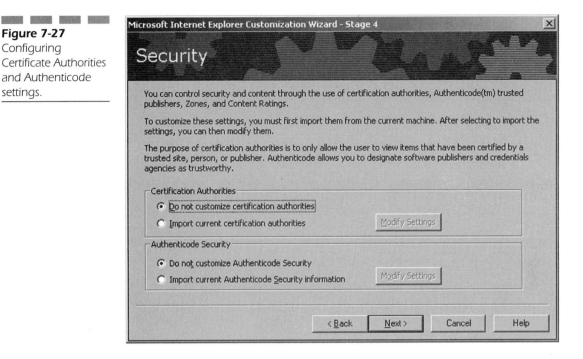

Figure 7-28
Configuring security
zones and content
ratings.

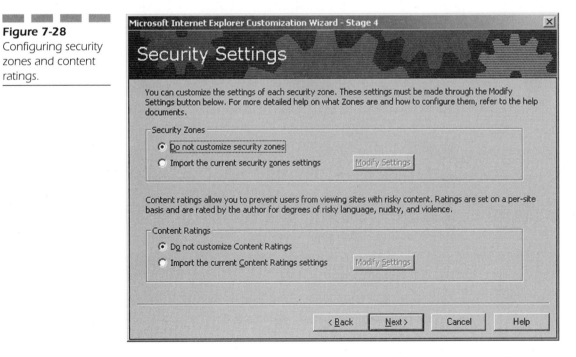

Figure 7-29
Stage 5 of the IEAK
Wizard is called
Customizing
Components.

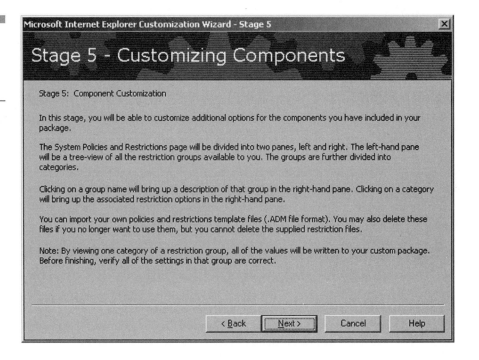

First, the Programs screen allows administrators to import their current program settings into the IE 5.0 browser build.

Next (Figure 7-30), you can configure email settings of Microsoft Outlook Express. You can specify the name of the SMTP and POP server and NNTP server. The next five screens allow an administrator to configure several options of Outlook Express. Among them are

- Custom welcome page or message.
- Configure default settings for Outlook Express (default for mail or news).
- Add newsgroups.
- Junk mail filtering.
- Customize the what elements to be displayed in the interface (toolbars and preview pane).
- Create custom signatures to be appended to outgoing email.
- Connect to a directory service or LDAP provider. This can connect to an Exchange server for example for address lookups.

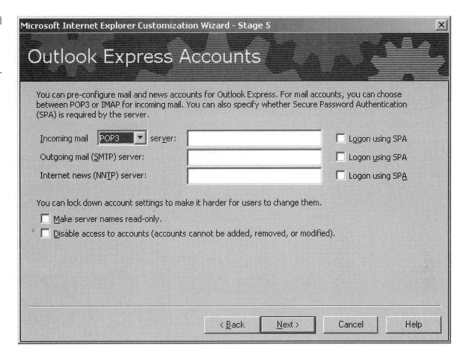

Figure 7-30
Configuring Outlook
Express settings.

First the System Policies and Restrictions screen allows administrators to configure settings and apply system policies for various applications and categories (Figure 7-31). These include

- Control Management (administrator-approved ActiveX controls)
- Microsoft NetMeeting settings
- Corporate Settings (for corporate license)
- Corporate Restrictions (for corporate license)
- Internet Settings (for example, autocompletion of form fields)
- Identity Manager (for shared access)
- Web Desktop settings (includes system policies)
- Offline Pages
- Microsoft Windows Media Player

Administrators can also import existing policy files at this point.

Finally, click Next and then Next again to close the IEAK Wizard. The Internet Explorer Administration Kit Wizard now has all the information it requires to create your custom installation package.

Figure 7-31
Customize settings
and system policies.

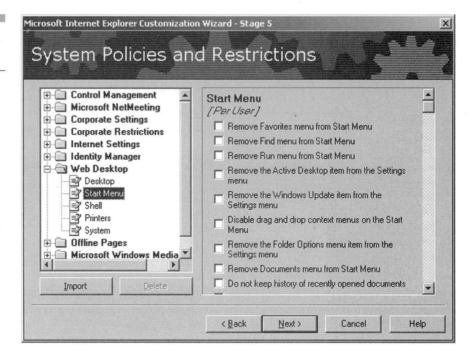

The IEAK Wizard then completes the following tasks (Figure 7-32):

- Preparing IE 5.0 customization files
- Creating the customized IE 5.0
- Building the custom redistributable folders

Finally, a message box will appear indicating that the package has been created and is located in the indicated path (Figure 7-33).

Distributing IE 5.0 Using IEAK Packages

To distribute your custom package to your corporate intranet client machines, create a Web site or virtual directory providing information on the download process and containing a link to the Active Setup installation engine file, IE5setup.exe. For more information on distributing IEAK packages, refer to the IEAK online documentation.

Figure 7-32
Completion of the
IEAK Wizard.

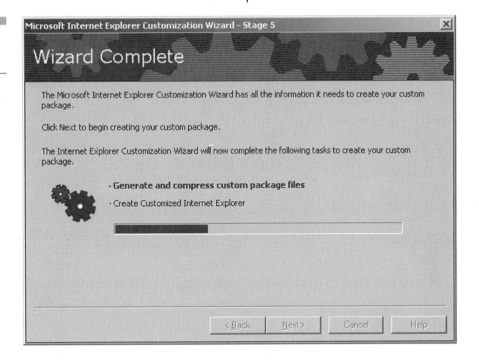

Figure 7-33
The IE 5.0 custom
installation package
has been successfully
created.

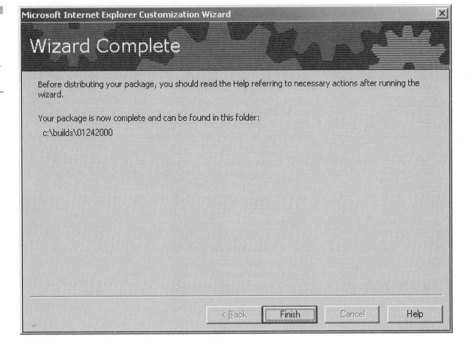

Maintaining Your IE 5.0 Package Using the IEAK Profile Manager

The IEAK Profile Manager allows administrators to create, edit, and save .ins files, which contain the configuration settings for IEAK installation packages.

The default .ins file is called Install.ins and in our walkthrough is located at

```
C:\ieaktest\Install.ins
```

See Figure 7-34 for the folder structure created in the package installation directory

```
C:\ieaktest
```

To edit the Install.ins file, start the IEAK Profile Manager by clicking Start, Programs, Microsoft IEAK, Profile Manager. The result is shown in

Figure 7-34
The install.ins file.

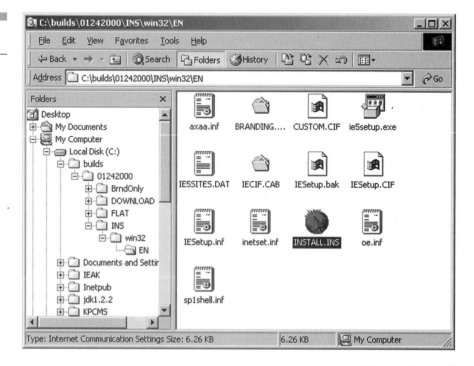

Figure 7-35
Starting the IEAK
Profile Manager.

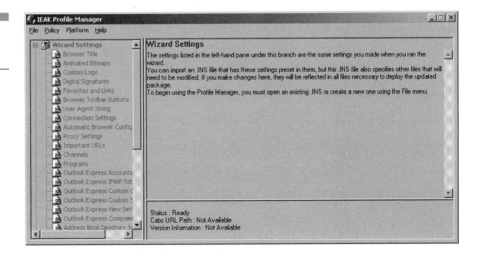

Figure 7-35. Now select File, Open and browse to open the Install.ins file for editing. In the left pane, select any item under

- *Wizard Settings* to modify settings selected during the running of the IEAK Wizard

or

- *System Policies and Restrictions* to modify system policy settings and restrictions

In Figure 7-35, the item Browser Title is selected under the Wizard Settings heading. In the right pane, you can now modify the title bar and bitmap just as if you had rerun a screen from the IEAK Wizard.

When all desired settings have been modified, choose File, Save to save the changes to the .ins file.

SUMMARY

Microsoft Internet Explorer 5.0 is the ideal browser client to complement Internet Information Server 5.0 in both intranet and Internet environments. To enable corporate administrators and ISPs to manage and configure customized IE 5.0 packages for clients, Microsoft supplies the additional tool, the Microsoft Internet Explorer Administration Kit.

For More Information

For more information on Internet Explorer and the IEAK, check out the following online resources.

Microsoft Web Site

For the latest information on Internet Explorer 5.0, see the Microsoft Web site at

```
www.microsoft.com/ie
```

To register and download the Internet Explorer Administration Kit, visit the Web site

```
www.microsoft.com/windows/ieak/
```

Microsoft Public Newsgroups

Microsoft Internet Explorer 5.0 issues are discussed in the newsgroups

```
microsoft.public.inetexplorer.ie5.*
```

Microsoft Internet Explorer Administration Kit is discussed in the newsgroup

```
microsoft.public.inetexplorer.ieak
```

Microsoft TechNet

You can find the Internet Explorer Deployment Guide on TechNet in the following location:

```
Internet, Client, MS Internet Explorer, Technical Notes,
Deployment Guide
```

Administering Indexing

Introduction

The ability to index a large corpus of documents is an important feature for any Internet or intranet server. Windows 2000 includes *Indexing Service 3.0*, a fully integrated indexing engine that can index HTML and legacy-format documents quickly and accurately. Although not a part of IIS 5.0, the importance of providing a search mechanism for your Web site is vital, so we will cover Indexing Service in this chapter. After completing this chapter, you will have a basic understanding of the capabilities, functions, and management of Indexing Service, including

- Basic capabilities of Indexing Service
- An understanding of the indexing process
- An understanding of the querying process
- Configuring indexing for various situations
- Managing indexing using the MMC
- Indexing a virtual server

What Can Indexing Service Do?

Indexing Service is integrated into Internet Information Services 5.0 and affords a means for Web server administrators to develop search tools for their sites. Indexing Service fully indexes both the content (text) and the properties of a variety of document formats, including

- HTML Web pages (.htm or .html)
- ASCII text files (.txt)
- Microsoft Word 95, Word 97, and Word 2000 documents (.doc)
- Microsoft Excel 95, Excel 97, Excel 2000 spreadsheets (.xls)
- Microsoft PowerPoint 95, 97, and 2000 presentations (.ppt)
- Internet Mail and news (with Internet Mail and News Services installed)

In addition, Indexing Service is extensible and can be configured to index other file formats, such as WordPerfect documents or Adobe PDF documents. The administrator simply has to obtain and install third-party *content filters* for the file formats required.

Indexing Service can index documents on multiple Web sites (virtual servers), multiple physical Web servers, and even file servers running Novell NetWare or any other server that can be accessed by a *Universal Naming Convention* (UNC) path. Indexing Service *catalogs* can be restricted in scope to a single virtual directory or a single virtual server or span many virtual or physical directories and servers.

Because catalog information is stored as Unicode characters, Indexing Service is capable of indexing and querying content in multiple languages, including

- English (US)
- English (international)
- Dutch
- French
- German
- Italian
- Japanese
- Spanish
- Swedish

Although Indexing Service is self-configuring and runs automatically in the background as a Windows 2000 service, using system resources when they are available, the administrator also has full control of the indexing process and can force a scan or a merge at any time to bring the index up to date. Indexing Service requires no maintenance and is self-correcting when errors occur.

Indexing Service includes a proprietary scripting language for constructing query engines using .htm, .idq, and .htx files. In addition, Active Server Pages may be used to construct queries.

Other advanced features of Indexing Service include hit highlighting, which is the ability to highlight word occurrences in queried documents, and the ability to index USENET news content.

Indexing Service is fully integrated with IIS 5.0 and supports all Windows 2000 security features. For example, by placing indexed content on an NTFS volume, a client performing a search query will only see returned documents that the client is allowed to read by NTFS permissions; the query will return no information concerning documents the client does not have read permission on, and the client will not even know of the existence of such documents.

NOTE: *Although content to be indexed can be placed on any server, including Windows 98 machines or Novell NetWare servers, it should be placed on NTFS volumes on Windows 2000 Servers. This enables Indexing Service to make use of Windows 2000 security features. Furthermore, the Windows NT file system automatically notifies Indexing Service when content is added, removed, or changed on the server, whereas Windows 98 or NetWare servers should be regularly polled for changes.*

How Does Indexing Service Work?

Indexing takes place automatically in the background when Indexing Service *Content Index* service is running. As documents are added or changed in the *corpus,* the body of documents to be indexed, the Content Index service incrementally adds these documents to the catalog when system resources are available so the overall performance of the IIS server will not degrade.

The following section explains the automatic indexing process in detail. Later sections will deal with how to manually administer the Indexing Service.

Understanding the Indexing Process

The basic process by which indexing takes place can be broken down into a series of steps:

1. *Scanning* inventorying virtual directories and servers for new documents to be indexed

2. *Filtering* using content filters to create word lists from documents scanned

3. *Merging* combining word lists and previous indexes to create more up-to-date indexes

Scanning takes place in two ways:

- *Full scan*   All documents in a directory are indexed.
- *Incremental scan*   Only documents that were modified are indexed.

   Scanning takes place whenever

- A new virtual directory or server is added that needs to be indexed. This triggers a full scan of the newly added directory or server.
- The system is booted and the Content Index service initializes. This triggers an incremental scan of all previously indexed directories to determine if any documents have been added, deleted, or changed and therefore need to be reindexed.
- The NTFS determines that a document has been added, removed, or changed in a directory that is configured to be indexed. The change notification is sent by NTFS to the Indexing Service, and an incremental scan of the directory takes place.
- A Windows 98 or Novell NetWare server is polled for changes to documents in an indexed directory. If changes are found, an incremental scan takes place.
- A full scan is forced by the administrator using the Indexing Service Manager snap-in of the Microsoft Management Console.

   When a scan takes place and a new or changed document is found, its content must be added to the index. Figure 8-1 outlines the content filtering process in detail. Documents in the corpus that have been scanned and require indexing are first sent to a *content filter,* whose main function is to extract text from the document. Content filters are associated with different document formats; for example, one content filter for Microsoft Word,

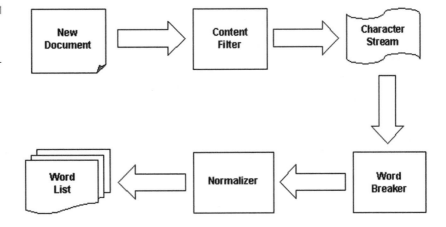

Figure 8-1
Outline of the
filtering process.

another content filter for Excel, and so on. The content filter mechanism is extensible so third-party filters may be added to the Indexing Service to enable it to index other document formats.

Content filters are also responsible for recognizing when embedded objects occur in documents and activating the appropriate content filter to handle these objects. Finally, content filters handle language shifts in documents: for example, from French to English and back again.

The stream of text characters produced by the content filter is then sent to a *word breaker*, a language-specific tool for recognizing words within the character stream. The words that are emitted from the word breaker are next sent to a *normalizer*, which performs a number of tasks including

- Removing noise words (*and, the, to,* and so on)
- Handling capitalization
- Removing punctuation

The final result produced by the normalizer in the content filtering process is a *word list,* which is a temporary index of the document that remains stored in the server's RAM in an uncompressed state. Word lists are the end result of the scanning and content filtering process and are the simplest kind of index produced by the Indexing Service. They act as a kind of temporary staging ground for the creation of *persistent indexes,* which are compressed multiple-document indexes stored on disk.

The final stage of indexing is the combining together, or *merging,* of word lists and persistent indexes to create a single master index. This merging process takes place in two stages, which are outlined in Figures 8-2 and 8-3.

Figure 8-2
Word lists and shadow indexes are combined into a new index by a shadow merge.

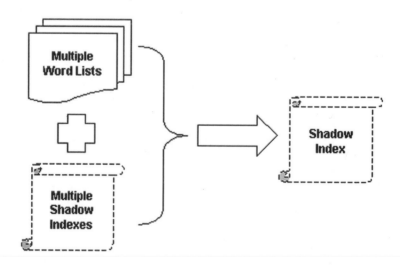

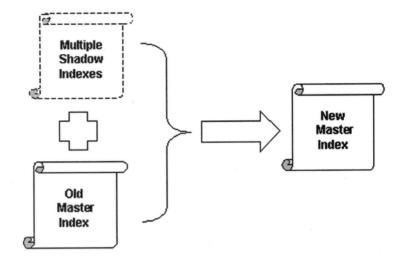

Figure 8-3
Shadow indexes and old master index are combined into a new master index by a master merge.

Shadow indexes are persistent indexes (indexes stored on disk) that are formed by merging volatile word lists and other shadow indexes. This process is called a *shadow merge,* and it frees up server memory and speeds up the resolution of queries. The merging process allows redundant data to be eliminated from the catalog, which increases the efficiency of the query process. Multiple shadow indexes can be, and usually are, in the catalog at any given time. Shadow indexes are also distinguished from word lists because the index data is stored in a compressed format. Shadow merges happen when certain conditions occur; these conditions are specified by settings in the Registry, but they can also be forced from the Indexing Service Manager.

If the system is relatively idle and resources are available, an *annealing merge* occurs. An annealing merge is a kind of shadow merge, and it results in fewer shadow indexes, thus freeing up disk space and speeding up queries.

The *master index* is the end product of the content indexing process. There is only one master index per catalog. This master index is kept up-to-date by merging it with shadow indexes to create a new master index by a process known as a *master merge,* which is very resource-intensive on the server. The master index is a persistent index whose data is stored in a highly compressed format. When indexing is complete for a corpus, no word lists or shadow indexes remain. Only a master index, making the querying process even more efficient, still exists. Master merges are triggered by conditions specified by settings in the Registry, but they can also be forced from the Indexing Service Manager.

The *catalog* is the top-level organizational structure in the Indexing Service, and contains the index, configuration information identifying the directories and shares being indexed, and other property information. Each catalog is a distinct, separate entity; queries may not cross multiple catalogs, but are instead restricted to a single catalog. When a typical installation of Windows 2000 is performed, a single *default catalog* is created for the server and the following virtual directories and virtual servers are indexed (assuming that IIS 5.0 is installed on C: drive):

Default Web site	`C:inetpub\wwwroot\`
IIS samples virtual directory	`C:\inetpub\iissamples\`
IIS administration Web site	`C:\<system root>\system32\inetsrv\iisadmin\`
IIS documentation	`C:\<system root>\help\`
Active data objects directory	`C:\program files\common files\system\ado\`
Remote data service directory	`C:\program files\common files\system\msdac\`
SMTP mail directory	`C:\inetpub\mail\`

The default catalog is stored in the following path:

`C:\inetpub\catalog.wci\`

The Catalog.wci directory is never indexed by Index Server, even if it is mapped to a virtual directory.

NOTE: *You may not see the Catalog.wci folder when you first look for it. Windows 2000 hides system files and folders from the user by default and the Catalog.wci is considered a system folder. Change your options in Windows 2000 Explorer to view hidden folders and files to view Catalog.wci.*

Additional catalogs can be created, and these can be assigned to documents stored in virtual directories, virtual servers, and even multiple physical servers. Catalogs that are created must be contained in locations whose ACLs allow administrators and system to have full control. A walkthrough of this is given later in this chapter.

NOTE: *Because queries cannot span multiple catalogs, creating new catalogs means that you will no longer be able to globally search your entire corpus of documents. This may or may not be desirable, depending on the function of your site.*

Understanding the Query Process

Indexing Services provides several ways to use idq or asp files. The following method describes the process used with idq and htx files:

- An HTML *query form,* which the user completes and submits (.htm file)
- An *Internet data query file,* which defines the basic parameters for the query, including its scope and restrictions (.idq file)
- An *HTML extension file,* which formats the result of the query and is used to generate an HTML response page (.htx file)

The .idq and .htx files must be in a virtual directory with read and script (or read and execute) permissions assigned.

The basic process of issuing a query and receiving a response from the Indexing Service can also be broken down into a series of steps (see Figure 8-4):

1. The user submitting the query completes and submits the query form (here called Query.htm).
2. The submitted query and the .idq file (here called Query.idq) are passed by IIS to Index Server, where they are processed against the catalog files.
3. Index Server then returns the raw results of the query and formats them using the .htx file (here called Query.htx).
4. The formatted results are returned to the user as a static HTML page (here called Result.htm).

To understand the .idq/.htx query process better, let's work through a simple example. First, here is the .htm file for a simple form requesting that the user enter keywords into the query textbox and press Submit to execute the query:

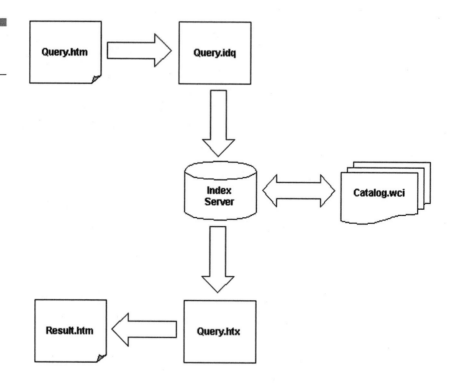

Figure 8-4
The .idq/.htx query process.

```
<HTML>
<HEAD><TITLE>Simple Query Form</TITLE></HEAD>
<BODY>
<FORM ACTION = "query.idq" METHOD = "GET">
<P>Search for the following:
<INPUT TYPE = "text" NAME = "CiRestriction">
<INPUT TYPE = "submit" VALUE = "Search now!">
<INPUT TYPE = "reset" VALUE = "Erase and start again!">
</FORM>
</BODY>
</HTML>
```

Notice in the previous HTML form that

- The file Query.idq takes the place of a regular form handler.
- The form sends its data using the GET method, which appends the query data to the URL of the handler and passes this as a text string to the server.
- The query words typed into the text box are assigned to the variable CiRestriction.

Next assume that the Internet query data (.idq) file has the following structure:

```
[Query]
CiCatalog=c:\iscatalogs
CiRestriction=%CiRestriction%
CiMaxRecordsInResultSet=50
CiMaxRecordsPerPage=10
CiScope=/
CiFlags=DEEP
CiTemplate=/Query.htx
```

The above Query.idq file can be explained as follows:

- The catalog to be searched is contained in the directory C:\iscatalogs.
- The query words searched for are contained in the variable %CiRestriction% that is passed from the query form.
- The maximum number of results returned is 50.
- The number of results returned per page is 10.
- The scope of the query begins at the root (/) of the corpus and includes all subdirectories (DEEP).
- The results generated by the query will be formatted by the file Query.htx.

Finally, assume that when Index Server processes the query, the results it returns are processed with the following .htx file:

```
<HTML>
<HEAD><TITLE>Results of Simple Query</TITLE></HEAD>
<BODY>
<%if CiMatchedRecordCount eq 0%>
No documents for the query "<%CiRestriction%>".
<%else%>
Documents <%CiFirstRecordNumber%> to <%CiLastRecordNumber%> of
     <%if CiMatchedRecordCount eq CiMaxRecordsInResultSet%>
     the first
     <%endif%>
<%CiMatchedRecordCount%>
matching the query "<%CiRestriction%>".
<%endif%>
</BODY>
</HTML>
```

If the query returns a total of 25 documents, the following results page will be presented to the user:

```
Documents 1 to 10 of 25 matching the query.
```

NOTE: *You can also create Indexing Services query forms using Active Server Pages (ASPs), but* .idq/.htx *queries are generally faster and more efficient in use of server resources than ASP queries. See the MSDN Online Library section on Indexing with Internet Information Services at* msdn.microsoft.com.

Indexing Service's Automatic Error Correction Features

When an error occurs in the indexing process, the Indexing Service is often able to correct the error without any user intervention. Examples include the following:

■ *Disconnected paths*   If the Indexing Service is indexing content on a remote network share and that share becomes disconnected, the Indexing Service will repeatedly poll the remote share until the connection returns and the catalog can be updated.

■ *Buffer overflows*   If content is stored on a local NTFS volume, the file system normally notifies Index Server when files are modified and should be reindexed. If the rate of file change is high, the number of file modification messages will be high and the notification buffer can overflow, resulting in lost messages. Index Server detects this condition and does an incremental scan to correct it.

■ *Disk full*   If the volume where the catalog is located is nearly full, indexing stops and an event log message is written to the application log. The administrator should then stop the Indexing Service, correct the problem by extending the volume or moving the catalog to a different volume, and then restart the Indexing Service (the steps for moving the catalog to another volume are outlined in the online documentation).

■ *Data corruption*   If catalog data becomes corrupt, the Indexing Service writes an event log message to the application log and automatically performs a recovery, refiltering the entire corpus if necessary. If refiltering is required, no queries are allowed. The administrator should stop and then restart the Content Index service so the recovery may be initiated.

NOTE: *Many of the events written to the application log by the Content Index (Ci) service are informational only. Administrators should monitor these logs regularly for warnings and stop events.*

Configuring the Indexing Service

Indexing Service and the indexing process can be managed several ways:

- By using the Indexing Service Manager snap-in for the Microsoft Management Console
- By creating a set of custom `.ida/.htx` files for remote administration through a browser (for user-created catalogs)
- By configuring certain Registry settings to manage the automatic scanning and merging processes

Before we implement the Indexing Service, however, certain planning issues should be addressed.

Planning Indexing

The following issues and system requirements should be considered before implementing Index Server (since the Indexing Service is automatically installed during a typical installation of Windows 2000 Server):

- Index Server program files can occupy 3 to 12MB, depending on language modules installed.
- Recommended RAM depends on the size of the corpus to be indexed. Microsoft's recommendations are as follows:

Number of Documents	RAM Required, MB
Less than 100,000	64
100,000–250,000	From 64 through 128
250,000–500,000	From 128 through 256
More than 500,000	256 or more

- The above RAM values are estimates only. Actual requirements will depend on the rate of queries and the rate of modification of files in the corpus. Monitor the performance of the Indexing Service to determine if more RAM will be required.

- The total size of the corpus to be indexed should be estimated beforehand. Approximately 40 percent of this value will be the disk space required by the `Catalog.wci` files for this corpus, so select a drive for the catalog that will have sufficient free space.

  For example, if the corpus of documents to be indexed occupies 500 MB of space on the hard drive, you will need an *additional* 40% × 500 MB = 200 MB of free space on the hard drive for the Index Server catalog and its associated files.

- The preferred location for your corpus and for the catalog is an NTFS volume on a Windows 2000 Server to take advantage of the security and file change notification features of NTFS volumes.

Administering the Indexing Service Using the MMC

As mentioned earlier, when IIS 5.0 is installed in a Typical install, Indexing Service is also installed. The default Web site is indexed immediately, creating a default catalog `Catalog.wci` located in

```
C:\inetpub\
```

To administer the default catalog on Indexing Service, select Start, Administrative Tools, Computer Management to open the Microsoft Management Console. Expand the Services and Applications node to display the Indexing Service Manager snap-in (see Figure 8-5).

Checking the Indexing Status

To check the indexing status of each catalog, select the Indexing Service icon in the scope pane (on the left). A list of catalogs will appear in the result pane on the right. In the case of Figure 8-5, the catalogs displayed will be the System catalog for searching the file system and the Web catalog for providing search functions for your Web site.

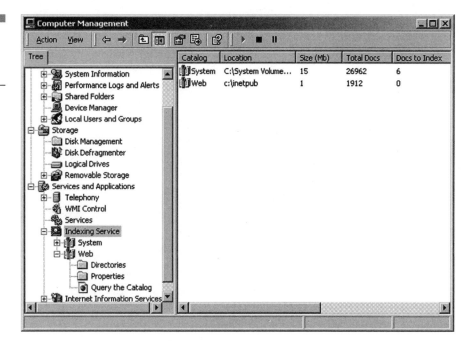

Figure 8-5
Managing Indexing
Services using the
MMC snap-in.

The columns that appear in the results frame when the Index Server icon is selected in the scope pane are as follows:

- *Catalog:* friendly name for catalog
- *Location:* physical location of `catalog.wci` directory
- *Size:* disk space occupied by persistent indexes
- *Total Docs:* size of corpus indexed so far
- *Docs to Index:* amount of corpus that remains to be indexed
- *Deferred for Indexing:* amount of documents set aside for indexing
- *Word lists:* number of word lists currently in RAM
- *Saved Indexes:* number of saved indexes on the hard drive
- *Status:* status of content indexing process

When *Saved Indexes* equals one and *Docs to Index* and *Word lists* equal zero, the corpus is fully indexed and fully optimized for queries.

The status field may take on the following values:

- Shadow merge
- Master merge

- Annealing merge
- Scan required
- Scanning
- Recovering

The only status message that requires the action of the administrator is "Scan required." When you see this message, you should force a scan (we will explain how to do this later).

Configuring the Indexing Service Global Properties

To configure global properties for the Indexing Service, right-click the Indexing Service icon in the scope pane and select Properties from the shortcut menu. The ,catalog_name. Properties sheet appears. This sheet has three tabs: General, Tracking, and Generation.

The General tab (see Figure 8-6) displays

- The friendly name of the catalog (the default catalog is called Web)
- The physical location of the catalog directory
- The current size of the master index in megabytes
- The current size of the property cache in megabytes

The Tracking tab (see Figure 8-7) allows you to

- Select whether to allow indexing of virtual directories for the selected catalog
- Select which virtual server (Web site) to associate with your selected catalog
- Select which news server to associate with your selected catalog

The Generation tab (see Figure 8-8) allows you to

- Choose whether files having unregistered file extensions will still be indexed
- Choose whether to have summaries (abstracts) displayed when a query is executed (default is yes)

Figure 8-6
The General Tab on
the property sheet for
the Indexing Services
catalog called Web.

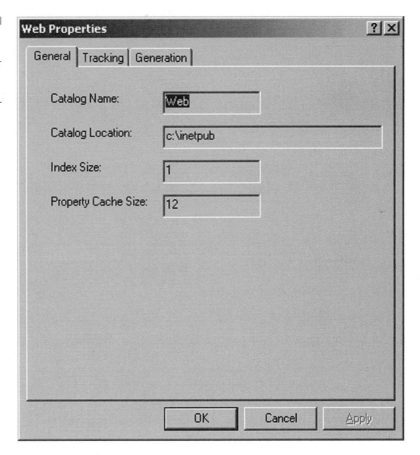

- Determine the maximum size in bytes of the summaries displayed when a query is executed (default is 320 bytes)
- Select whether to inherit these settings from the master service properties

Determining the Directories Currently Being Indexed

To determine which physical directories are currently being indexed, expand the selected catalog node in the scope pane to show the Directories

Figure 8-7
The Tracking tab on
the property sheet for
the Indexing Services
catalog called Web.

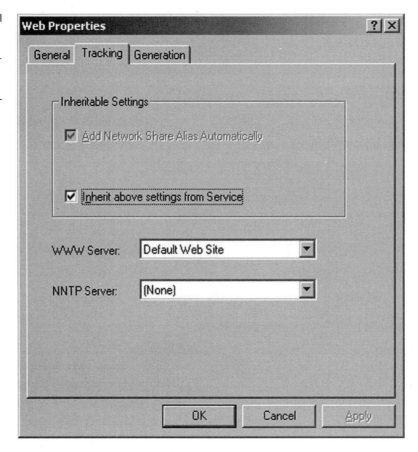

and Properties folder icons beneath it. Click the Directories folder icon to select it and view the virtual directories being indexed in this catalog in the results pane. (The physical directories mapped to the virtual directories in the site are actually displayed here—see Figure 8-9).

The columns displayed for each virtual directory being indexed include

- *Root,* which shows the physical path for each root being indexed
- *Alias,* a path that the user adds that is returned when a client submits a query from a remote computer (default is Not Applicable)
- *Include,* in which "Yes" means the directory has been included in the scope and is indexed

Figure 8-8

The Generation tab
on the property sheet
for the Indexing
Services catalog
called Web.

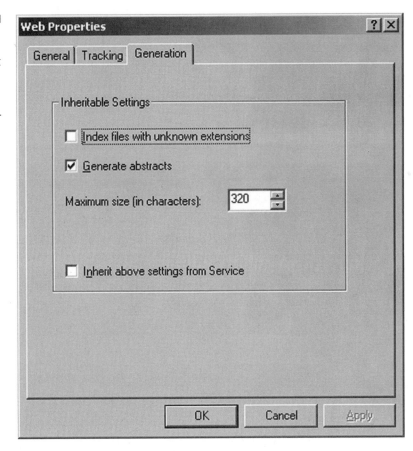

Determining the Properties Cached by a Catalog

To determine the properties cached by a catalog, click the *Properties* folder icon beneath the icon for the selected catalog in the scope pane and view the cached properties for the selected catalog in the results pane (see Figure 8-10).

Indexing Service indexes not only the text of documents but also their properties. Listed in the results pane are the various properties that can be indexed, some of which are described by friendly names. If a selected property has no entry in the Data Type and Cached Size columns, no instances of that property are currently cached. Information on individual properties can also be accessed by right-clicking a selected property and choosing

Figure 8-9
A list of virtual
directories being
indexed for the
catalog called Web,
shown by their
physical paths.

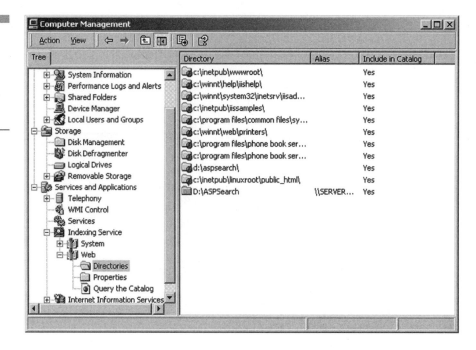

Figure 8-10
Viewing cached
properties for a
selected catalog.

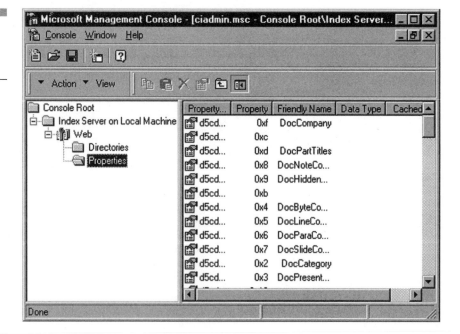

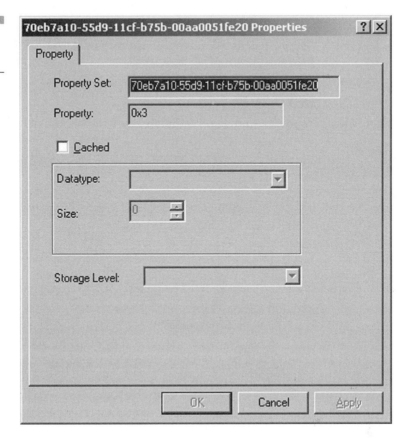

Figure 8-11
Property sheet for a
particular property.

Properties from the shortcut menu, which opens the Property sheet for the
selected property (see Figure 8-11).

For more information on properties that can be cached, refer to the Windows 2000 help file.

Forcing a Scan on a Virtual Directory

To force a scan on a virtual directory, expand the selected catalog node in
the scope pane to show the Directories and Properties folder icons beneath
it (see Figure 8-9). Click the Directories folder icon to select it. From the list
of virtual directories shown in the results pane, right-click the virtual directory you want to scan and select All Tasks, Rescan (Full) from the shortcut
menu. The Full Rescan dialog box will appear, prompting you to confirm
your decision by clicking Yes.

A scan should generally be forced when

- You have changed the characterization size on the property sheet for Indexing Services.
- You have added or removed a new word-breaker or filter (for example, for another language).
- You have changed the filtering on extensions that are not recognized.

Forcing a Merge

To force a merge of all persistent indexes in a catalog, right-click the catalog node in the scope pane and select All Tasks, Merge from the shortcut menu. The Merge catalog dialog box will appear, prompting you to confirm your decision by clicking Yes.

Merges should generally be forced when

- You add a large number of new documents to the corpus and they must be queried immediately.
- Queries to your catalog have slowed down due to the large number of persistent indexes. Forcing a merge will create one efficient master index, which will optimize the query process.

Stopping and Starting the Content Index Service

To stop or start the Content Index service, you can use one of two methods:

- In the Computer Management MMC snap-in, right-click the Indexing Services node in the scope pane and select Stop or Start from the shortcut menu.
- Select the Services node from the Computer Management MMC snap-in, select the Indexing service in the right pane, and select Stop or Start from the shortcut menu (see Figure 8-12).

Enabling Indexing on Virtual Directories

To cause a virtual directory to be indexed, right-click the virtual directory (or its parent virtual server, if you want to index all virtual directories that

Figure 8-12
Stopping and starting
the Indexing Services
from the Services
node in MMC.

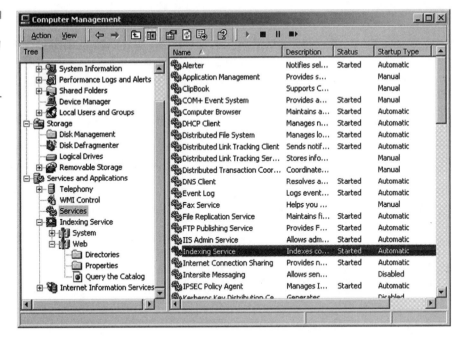

belong to a given virtual server) in the Internet Services Manager (MMC
with IIS snap-in installed). Select Properties to open the Directory Property
sheet, select the Directory tab, and, under the label Content Control, place
a checkmark in the Index This Directory checkbox. Index Server (if it is running) will now index your virtual directory.

An example of this procedure is shown in the walkthrough later in this
chapter.

Enabling Indexing on Nonvirtual (Physical) Directories

To cause a nonvirtual (physical) directory to be indexed, right-click the catalog in which you want the directory to be indexed in the Computer Management MMC snap-in and select New, Directory from the shortcut menu
(note that this does not create a physical directory, but simply makes an
existing physical directory available for indexing). The Add Directory dialog
box now appears (see Figure 8-13).

Enter the local path to the physical directory you want to index, type in
a UNC alias that will be the path returned to the client when the client

Figure 8-13
Enabling indexing on
a nonvirtual (physical
directory).

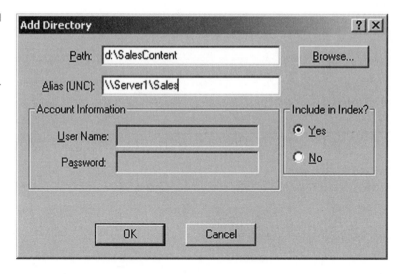

queries the directory (typically this is the UNC of the share created on the directory), and click OK.

Index Server Registry Settings

Administrators can also configure certain Registry settings of Index Server to control how the automatic scanning and merging processes take place. The following is a list of some of the more important Registry settings. These Registry settings are stored under

```
\HKEY_LOCAL_MACHINE
        System
                CurrentControlSet
                        Control
                                ContentIndex
```

Registry settings associated with *word lists* and *shadow merges*:

- *MaxWordLists*   The maximum number of word lists that can exist at any time. When this number is exceeded, a shadow merge occurs.
- *MaxWordlistSize*   The maximum amount of memory occupied by a word list in increments of 128KB.
- *MinWordlistMemory*   The minimum amount of free memory needed to create word lists.

- *MinSizemergeWordlists*   The minimum aggregate size of word lists that forces a shadow merge.

Registry settings associated with *master merges:*

- *MasterMergeTime*   The default time for master merge is each night at midnight. You can change this to the time when server load is least.

- *MinDiskFreeForceMerge*   A master merge will be initiated if the free disk space is less than this parameter and the aggregate shadow index space is greater than MaxShadowFreeForceMerge.

- *MaxShadowIndexSize*   A master merge will be initiated if the aggregate shadow index space exceeds this value.

- *MaxFreshCount*   If the number of documents modified since the previous master merge exceeds this value, a new master merge is done.

Walkthrough: Indexing a Virtual Server

In the following walkthrough, we will use Indexing Services to index a new virtual server whose Web content resides both on the local machine and on a network share. In the process, we will also create a new catalog exclusively for this virtual server and modify an existing set of .idq/.htx query files to support a search page for our Web site. You'll need some mixed content (Word and HTML files, for instance) for the new site if you want to follow along.

First, we will modify the MMC to allow us to administer both IIS and Indexing Services. Click Start, Run, type MMC and click OK to open the MMC.

From the MMC menu bar, click Console, Add/Remove Snap-In. In the Add/Remove Snap-in dialog box, click Add, select Indexing Service, and click OK. At this point, the Connect to Computer dialog box appears to ask you if the Indexing Service you want to manage is local or remote (see Figure 8-14). Select Local Computer and click Finish. Select Internet Information Service, click OK, and then click OK to return to the MMC.

Next, we will create a new Web with a local home directory and two content directories, one local and one remote. But before we do this, we will create the directories needed. We create the following directories and add the content described to them:

Figure 8-14
Adding Indexing
Service to the MMC.

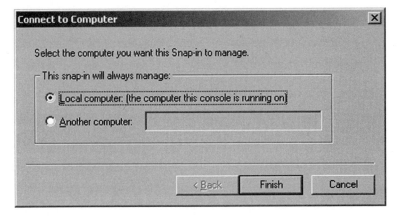

■ On server1 (local machine):

Create `D:\litroot`.

Directory contains default.htm.

Create `D:\lit`.

Directory contains HTML documents.

■ On server2 (remote machine):

Create `C:\lit2`.

Share as `MORELIT`.

Directory contains Word documents.

To create the new virtual server, open the Internet Information Services node in the MMC, select the local server's node (here, server1), right-click, and select New, Web Site from the shortcut menu.

The New Web Site Wizard appears. Enter a name for the Web site (for example, MyLitWeb), select an IP address (here, `192.168.0.54`, which is one of two IP addresses bound to the network adapter card on server1), choose `D:\litroot` as the home directory, accept the remaining defaults, and click Finish to create the new virtual server.

To create the two virtual directories for content, right-click the newly created MyLitWeb node and select New, Virtual Directory to run the New Virtual Directory Wizard. Map aliases to physical directories as follows:

Alias: `lit1`

Map to: `D:\lit on SERVER1`

Alias: `lit2`

Map to: `\\SERVER2\MORELIT`

Note than when you map the second alias to the UNC share, a dialog box appears asking for the security credentials that should be used to access the share from the Web site. We previously created a user called `lituser` on the domain controller and assigned this user read permission to the `MORELIT` share on server2. This is the user whose credentials are now entered into the wizard.

Finally, we need to start the new virtual server by right-clicking the MyLitWeb node and selecting Start from the shortcut menu (or select the node and click the Start button on the rebar). Figure 8-15 shows the newly created virtual server and its virtual directories.

Now we will create a new Indexing Service catalog specifically for our new Web site. In the MMC, right-click the Indexing Service node and select Stop from the shortcut menu to stop the Indexing Service.

On the local server, create a folder to contain the new catalog (for example, `D:\litcat`).

Figure 8-15
The new virtual server MyLitWeb is created.

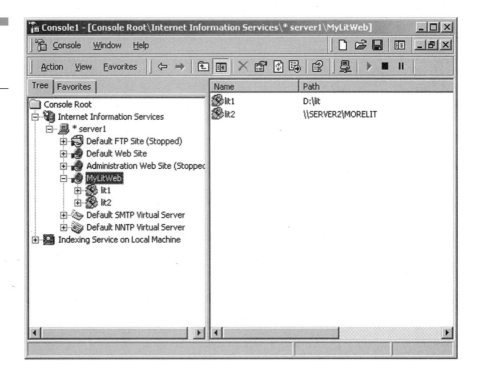

Figure 8-16
Creating a new
catalog for the new
virtual server.

Figure 8-17
The new catalog is
offline until the
Indexing Service is
restarted.

Right-click the Indexing Service node and select New, Catalog from the shortcut menu. The Add Catalog dialog box appears. Give the new catalog a name and enter its location (see Figure 8-16). Click OK. A dialog box warns you that the newly created catalog will remain offline until you restart the Content Index service (see Figure 8-17).

Note that under the Indexing Service node, you now have three child nodes (see Figure 8-18):

- *System,* which is the default catalog for searching the local file system
- *Web,* which is the default Web catalog
- *Literature Catalog,* which is the newly created catalog

Fields for catalog size, number of documents, and so on contain no values in the MMC results pane. This is because the Content Index service has not yet been restarted.

If you use Windows Explorer to look at the contents of D:\litcat at this point, you will see that it now contains a Catalog.wci folder within it.

Before we restart Indexing Service, we will configure the new catalog we have created. Right-click the Literature Catalog node (or whatever you have called it) and select Properties from the shortcut menu to bring up the Literature Catalog Properties sheet.

The General tab on this property sheet indicates the following information for the new catalog:

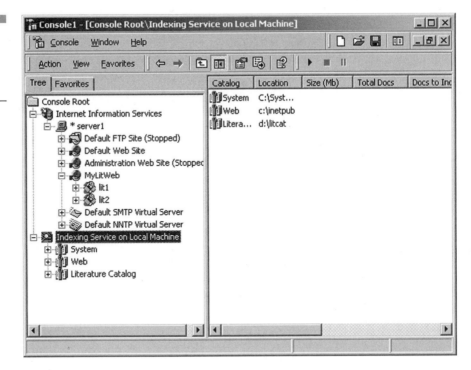

Figure 8-18
A new catalog is
created to index the
virtual server
MyLitWeb.

- Name of catalog
- Location of catalog
- Size of catalog

The Tracking tab specifies

- Whether to index virtual directories (the default is checked)
- What virtual server to map to the catalog
- Whether to index news directories and map a news server to the catalog

From the Virtual Server drop-down box, select MyLitWeb. This action associates the new catalog with the new virtual server (see Figure 8-19). The Generation tab specifies

- Whether to index files that have unrecognized extensions.
- Whether to return abstracts or summaries of documents when a query is performed

Figure 8-19
Mapping a virtual
server to a new
catalog.

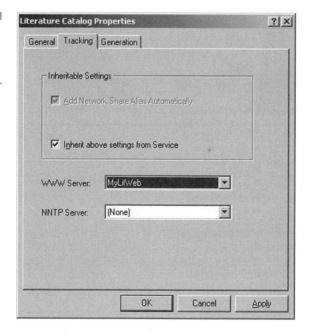

- The size in characters of the file abstracts returned by the query
- Whether to inherit settings from the Service settings (default is checked)

At this point we should enable our new virtual server for indexing. In the MMC under the Internet Information Services node, right-click MyLitWeb to bring up its property sheet (see Figure 8-20). Select the Home Directory tab, place a checkmark beside *Index this resource,* and click OK. The whole site, including both its home directory and any virtual directories, are now enabled for indexing and automatically starts being indexed by Indexing Service.

Now select the Indexing Service node in the MMC and click the Start button on the rebar to restart Indexing Service.

NOTE: *If you don't want to wait for automatic indexing to begin, you can force a scan of virtual directories to begin the indexing process. If this fails to start the indexing process, reboot the machine to get indexing going again.*

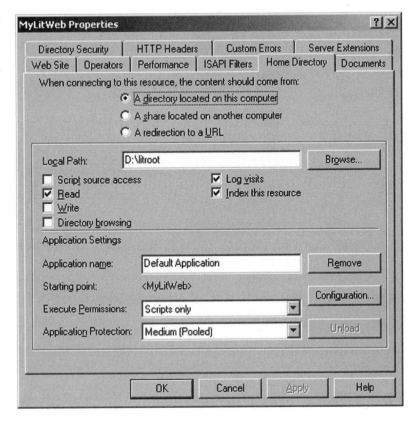

Figure 8-20
Enabling indexing on
a virtual server.

The result so far is shown in Figure 8-21. Notice the following in this figure:

- Under the catalog node (MyLitWeb) are two folders: Directories and Properties.
- Under the Directories node are the home folder and the two virtual directory nodes.

If the corpus to be indexed is sufficiently large, you will be able to watch indexing taking place for the new virtual server. Select the Index Server node in the scope pane of the MMC and then hide the scope pane using the Show/Hide Scope button on the rebar. Figure 8-22 shows indexing of MyLitWeb taking place. Virtual roots are being scanned, and at this point there are

- Three of four documents remaining to be filtered
- There are no word lists residing in memory

Figure 8-21
New nodes under
the new catalog
node in the MMC
nameplace.

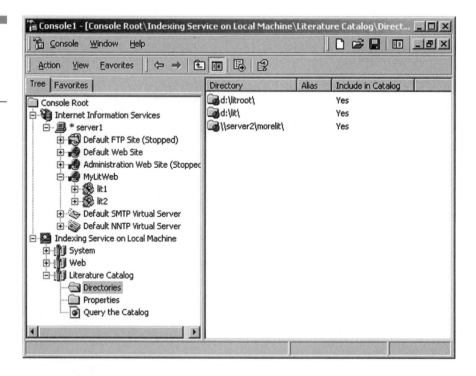

Figure 8-21
New nodes under
the new catalog
node in the MMC
nameplace.

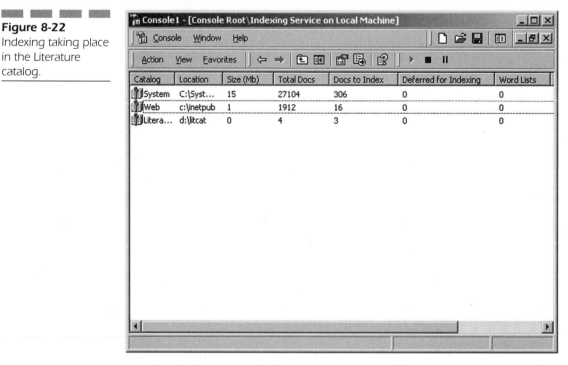

Figure 8-22
Indexing taking place
in the Literature
catalog.

A short time later, scanning (filtering) of documents is complete. Figure 8-23 shows the following:

■ All documents have now been filtered.

■ One word list resides in memory.

At this point, we can right-click the Literature Catalog node and select All Tasks, Merge from the shortcut menu. The Merge Catalog dialog box appears (see Figure 8-24). Click Yes to force a shadow merge and then a master merge. The final result is shown in Figure 8-25.

Finally, we can test the index and search the documents by selecting the Query Catalog node under the Literature Catalog node. This will present a

Figure 8-23
All documents are now filtered and virtual roots scanned.

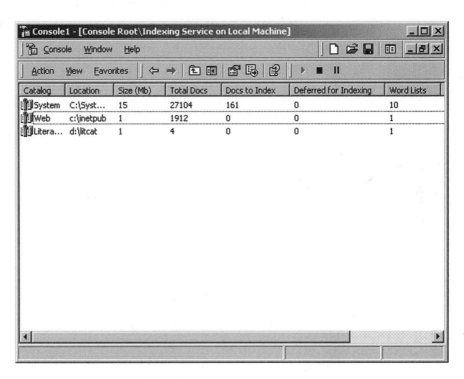

Catalog	Location	Size (Mb)	Total Docs	Docs to Index	Deferred for Indexing	Word Lists
System	C:\Syst...	15	27104	161	0	10
Web	c:\inetpub	1	1912	0	0	1
Litera...	d:\litcat	1	4	0	0	1

Figure 8-24
The Merge catalog dialog box.

Figure 8-25
The indexing process
is now complete.

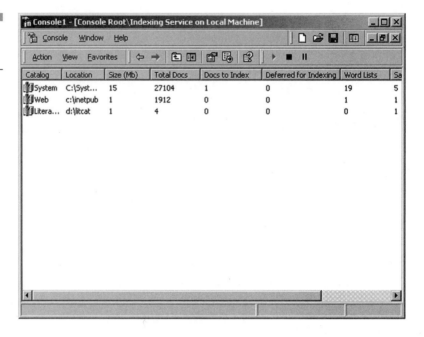

Catalog	Location	Size (Mb)	Total Docs	Docs to Index	Deferred for Indexing	Word Lists	Sa
System	C:\Syst...	15	27104	1	0	19	5
Web	c:\inetpub	1	1912	0	0	1	1
Litera...	d:\litcat	1	4	0	0	0	1

search form in the right pane of the MMC (see Figure 8-26). Type in search criteria and click the Search button to test the index and display any results that match.

SUMMARY

Indexing Service 3.0 is integrated into IIS 5.0 and provides administrators with a mechanism for indexing HTML and legacy content on virtual servers. Complex queries may be performed by suitably building `.idq/.htx` files or Active Server Pages. Indexing Service runs automatically in the background as a Windows 2000 service, but it can also be manually administered using the Microsoft Management Console.

For More Information

For more information on indexing services, try the following online resources.

Figure 8-26
Searching the newly
created catalog.

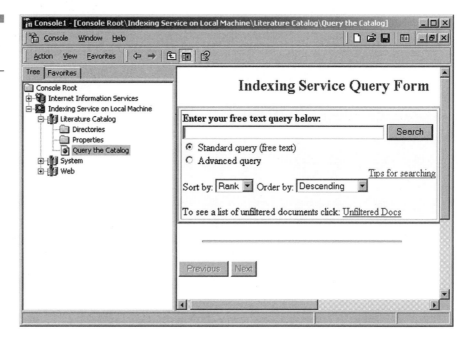

Microsoft Web Site

For general information about Indexing Services, visit the Windows 2000 Web site at

    www.microsoft.com/windows2000

Microsoft Newsgroup

The following newsgroup is devoted to discussions of Indexing Service:

    microsoft.public.inetserver.indexserver

Administering the FTP Service

Introduction

The *File Transfer Protocol* (FTP) Publishing Service is another core component of Internet Information Services 5.0, enabling users to transfer files to and from Internet and intranet sites. After completing this chapter, you will be able to administer the FTP service on IIS 5.0 and be able to

- Explain the underlying mechanism of FTP
- Understand the security implications of using FTP
- Configure various property settings for FTP sites
- Create and manage an FTP site
- Access an FTP site from both Internet Explorer and the command line

Understanding the File Transfer Protocol

File Transfer Protocol, or FTP, is one of the oldest Internet protocols. It specifies a mechanism whereby files can be transferred from one host to another. Although the HTTP protocol has taken over some of the functions of FTP, FTP continues to be popular for tasks such as

- Providing high-speed dedicated sites for downloading applications and for software upgrades and patches
- Providing anonymous write-only drop boxes for uploading files to servers
- Enabling file transfers in heterogeneous (mixed) networking configurations (for example, between Windows 2000 and UNIX)

One reason for the continued popularity of FTP is its simple administration, which we will learn more of shortly.

FTP is a client/server protocol. In order for files to be transferred between two hosts, one of them must be running FTP *server* software (such as IIS 5.0) and the other must be running FTP *client* software (such as IE 5.0 or the command line FTP utility that is part of Windows 98 and 2000). File transfers can be either ASCII or binary and take one of two forms:

- *Uploading* or *putting*—transferring files from the client to the server
- *Downloading* or *getting*—transferring files from the server to the client

How an FTP Session Works

Like HTTP, FTP uses TCP as a transport protocol, which provides for reliable connection-oriented file transfers. When an FTP client connects with an FTP server such as IIS 5.0, a TCP connection is established, and the connection remains open until the session is terminated or until the server issues a timeout.

The following outline explains the basic process of establishing an FTP session and transferring a file (see Figure 9-1).

1. The FTP client forms a TCP connection with the FTP server using a TCP three-way handshake.

2. In order for a TCP connection to be formed, both the client and the server must open a TCP port. FTP servers have two preassigned port numbers.

   - Port 21 is used for sending and receiving FTP control information. This port is continuously monitored by the FTP server, which listens for an FTP client that wants to connect to it. After an FTP session is established, the connection to port 21 remains open for the entire session.

   - Port 20 is used for sending and receiving FTP data (ASCII or binary files). The data port is open only when data is being transferred and is closed when the transfer is complete.

3. FTP clients have their port numbers dynamically assigned when the FTP client service is invoked. These client port numbers are chosen from the range 1024 to 65,535. Ports 0 through 1023 are known as *Well-Known Port Numbers* and have uses preassigned to them by the Internet Assigned Numbers Authority (IANA). For a listing of Well-Known Port Numbers used by Windows 2000, open the text file

   `C:\winnt\system32\drivers\etc\services`

4. When an FTP session is started, the client opens a control port that connects to port 21 on the server.

5. When data needs to be transferred, the client opens a second port to connect to port 20 on the server. Each time a file is transferred, a new data port is opened by the client and then released.

Figure 9-1
How an FTP Session
works.

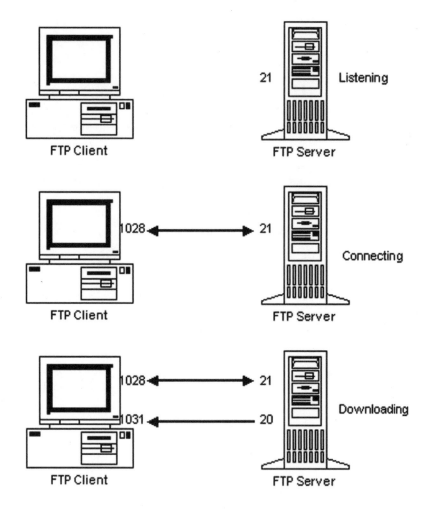

The Netstat Utility

The netstat command-line utility, available for both Windows 2000 and Windows 98, may be used to monitor and troubleshoot FTP connections. By typing

```
netstat -p tcp
```

an administrator can view the connection statistics for the TCP protocol on either the client or the server.

As an example of using the netstat utility, the following are the results of running the command netstat -p tcp on the server during the various stages of a typical FTP session. The client is a Windows 98 host called SUPER running the command-line FTP utility, and the server is an FTP site on IIS 5.0.

Protocol	Local Address	Foreign Address	State
TCP	Server1:1025	Localhost:1026	ESTABLISHED
TCP	Server1:1026	Localhost:1025	ESTABLISHED
TCP	Server1:1027	Localhost:1029	ESTABLISHED
TCP	Server1:1029	Localhost:1027	ESTABLISHED
TCP	Server1:1041	Localhost:1043	ESTABLISHED
TCP	Server1:1043	Localhost:1041	ESTABLISHED

1. Prior to the client establishing an FTP session, there are only local TCP connections.
2. After an FTP session has been opened from the client by typing ftp 172.16.8.101 and logging on as anonymous, the client machine is dynamically assigned the port number 1040 as its FTP control port connecting to port 21 on the server (port 21 on the server is called port ftp here). Note that from here on the localhost TCP connections are omitted.

Protocol	Local Address	Foreign Address	State
TCP	Server1:ftp	SUPER:1040	ESTABLISHED

3. After dir is typed on the client to get a directory listing from the FTP server, data port 1047 is assigned to the client to connect to port 20 on the server (port 20 on the server is called port ftp-data here). After the data has been transferred, the server port goes into a TIME_WAIT state and is unavailable for further use until the server causes the port to time out.

Protocol	Local Address	Foreign Address	State
TCP	Server1:ftp-data	SUPER:1047	TIME_WAIT
TCP	Server1:ftp	SUPER:1045	ESTABLISHED

4. After `get test.txt` is typed to download a file called test.txt from the server, a second data port (1048) is opened on the client for the new data transfer.

Protocol	Local Address	Foreign Address	State
TCP	Server1:ftp-data	SUPER:1047	TIME_WAIT
TCP	Server1:ftp-data	SUPER:1048	TIME_WAIT
TCP	Server1:ftp	SUPER:1045	ESTABLISHED

5. After the connection with the server is closed by typing `bye`, all the ports opened on the server are placed in the TIME_WAIT state until they time out.

Protocol	Local Address	Foreign Address	State
TCP	Server1:ftp-data	SUPER:1047	TIME_WAIT
TCP	Server1:ftp-data	SUPER:1048	TIME_WAIT
TCP	Server1:ftp	SUPER:1045	TIME_WAIT

Understanding FTP Site Security

FTP sites should generally be accessed using *anonymous access*. With anonymous access, a user trying to connect to an FTP site uses the IUSR_*SERVERNAME* account created when IIS is installed. When anonymous access is enabled,

- Users connecting with the Windows 2000 command-line FTP utility will have to actually log on to the FTP site using the username anonymous and anything for a password (it is traditional to use your email address for your password, which allows the sitemaster to determine who is logged on to the FTP site at any given time).

■ Users connecting with browsers such as Internet Explorer are automatically authenticated using the IUSR_*SERVERNAME* account. No username or password needs to be entered from the browser.

With FTP, the only alternative to anonymous access is for the user to access the site using a valid Windows 2000 user account. The problem is that with FTP authentication, the username and password are transmitted as clear text (that is, unencrypted). Anyone running Network Monitor or some other protocol analyzer on your network would be able to trap user credentials, resulting in a security breach. For this reason, FTP sites should generally be set for anonymous access, and this should be the *only* authentication scheme allowed. This will prevent users from trying to use their domain credentials to try to gain access to the site. The procedure for doing this will be explained later in this chapter.

Additional security methods should be employed when necessary, especially when your FTP site is connected to the Internet. Be sure to consider the following options:

■ Denying access to all users except those from certain blocks of IP network numbers or Internet domains

■ Checking that NTFS permissions are set properly on home directories, which includes changing the permission on the Everyone group to *change* (RWXD) instead of *full control* (RWXDPO), or removing the Everyone group and adding the IUSR_*SERVERNAME* account with *change* (RWXD) permission

■ Changing the default FTP control port 21 to some other value

■ Logging all FTP connections and reviewing them regularly to check for evidence of hacking

■ Setting up a proxy server and firewall to filter packets and control FTP access (Microsoft Proxy Server 2 can fulfill this role)

Configuring FTP Site Properties

Like the WWW service, IIS 5.0 can be configured to have an unlimited number of FTP servers running on it simultaneously, each responding to its own unique IP address and *fully qualified domain name* (FQDN). Each of these *virtual* FTP servers (or FTP sites) behaves as if it were a distinct machine.

Each can be configured separately and can be stopped, started, and paused independently.

Also like the WWW service, the property sheets for the FTP service on IIS 5.0 can be configured at several levels: *Master, Site,* and *Directory* levels.

Finally, again like the WWW service, when a new FTP site is created, it automatically inherits the Master FTP property settings of the IIS server on which it is created. Likewise, when a new FTP virtual directory is created, it automatically inherits the Site property settings of the FTP site on which it is created. When a Master FTP property setting is changed, you are given the option of passing this change along to all existing FTP sites on the IIS server. Similarly, when a property setting is changed on an FTP site, you are given the option of passing this change along to all existing virtual directories on the FTP site.

You can access and configure property settings for each of the three levels as follows:

- *Master* properties can be configured for all FTP sites running on the IIS server. To access Master properties, right-click the IIS server node in the *Microsoft Management Console* (MMC) and select Properties from the shortcut menu (or select the IIS server node in the MMC, click the Action button on the rebar, and select Properties from the drop-down menu).

- *Site* properties (or Virtual Server properties) can be configured individually for each FTP site running on the IIS server, including the default FTP site created when IIS is installed. To access Site properties, right-click the FTP site node in the MMC and select Properties from the shortcut menu.

- *Directory* properties (or Virtual Directory properties) can be configured individually for each virtual directory defined within an FTP site on the server. All files will inherit the property settings of the virtual directory that contains them. To access Directory properties, right-click the virtual directory within the FTP site and select Properties from the shortcut menu.

FTP property sheets have different options available depending on whether they configure Master, Site, or Directory settings. Here are the property sheet tabs available for each level and the function they provide:

- *FTP Site* tab (Master and Site levels): configure site identification, limit connections, enable logging, view current sessions
- *Security Accounts* tab (Master and Site levels): configure anonymous access, grant operator privileges

- *Messages* tab (Master and Site levels): configure welcome, exit, and busy messages

- *Home (or Virtual) Directory* tab (Master, Site, and Directory levels): configure content location and access permissions, choose directory listing style

- *Directory Security* tab (Master, Site, and Directory levels): grant or deny access to hosts

- *Service* tab (Master level only): designate which FTP site is to be administered by IIS 3.0 Internet Information Services Manager

In addition to these functions, the IIS Server Properties sheet can be used to throttle FTP bandwidth and configure the global MIME mappings. These features are covered in Chapter 3 and function the same for both the WWW and FTP services.

Configuring FTP Site Identification

To give the FTP site a friendly description that will appear beside the node in the MMC, type a name in the Description textbox (see Figure 9-2).

Use the IP Address drop-down box to assign a particular IP address to the FTP site. If you leave the setting here at All Unassigned, the FTP site will respond to all IP addresses that are not specifically assigned to other FTP sites, in effect making this the new default FTP site. Only IP addresses that have been previously configured in the Network application of Control Panel will appear in the drop-down box here.

The default TCP port for FTP control messages is port 21. To change this value, enter a new number in the TCP Port box. *Note that the IIS server will need to be rebooted for the new port number to come into effect.* Users will need to be notified of the change in port numbers because when they try to access this FTP site, they will have to include the port number.

For example, if the port is changed to 1253 and users are using the command-line FTP utility in Windows 2000 to connect to an FTP site with the address 164.43.25.8, they will have to type the following at the command prompt to open a session:

```
ftp 164.43.25.8:1253
```

If they try to access the same server using Internet Explorer, they must use the URL

```
ftp://164.43.25.8:1253
```

Figure 9-2
Configuring site
identification, limiting
connections,
enabling logging,
and viewing
connections.

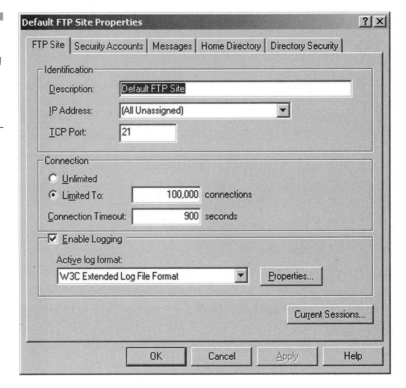

NOTE: *Do not use any of the Well-Known Port Numbers for the FTP control port number, other than port 21. Otherwise, conflicts may occur with other TCP services.*

Configuring FTP Connection Limits and Timeouts

Selecting Unlimited (see Figure 9-2) will allow the FTP site to service an unlimited number of connections simultaneously. To limit the number of simultaneous FTP connections allowed to your site (or to the server, if this is a Master property setting), choose Limited To and enter a value in the textbox (the default is 100,000).

To configure the amount of time an FTP connection remains in a TIME_WAIT state before timing out and freeing the port for other use, enter a value in the Connection Timeout textbox (the default is 900 seconds, or 15 minutes).

Configuring FTP Logging

By default, the Enable Logging checkbox is selected (refer to Figure 9-2), and logs are recorded in W3C Extended Log File Format. FTP sites may be logged in one of three formats:

- Microsoft IIS Log File Format
- ODBC Logging
- W3C Extended Log File Format

To configure logging for any of these formats, select the format using the Active log format drop-down box and click the Properties button. Configuring logging formats is covered in Chapter 3.

Viewing and Terminating FTP User Sessions

To view the currently open FTP sessions, click the Current Sessions button on the FTP Site tab of the Site (or Master) property sheet. This opens the FTP User Sessions box (see Figure 9-3), with which you can view three kinds of information concerning connected users.

Figure 9-3
Viewing currently open FTP sessions.

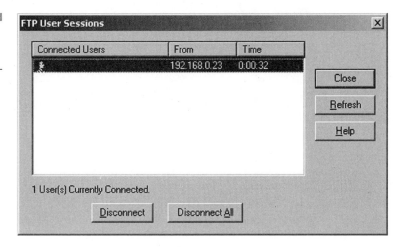

- The password used to log on to the FTP site (with anonymous access, users generally log on with the username anonymous and use their email address for a password, although they may use anything for a password)
- The IP address of the user's machine
- The amount of time since the session started

To disconnect a particular user, select the user and click Disconnect. To terminate all sessions, click Disconnect All. Click Refresh to refresh the list of sessions currently open.

Configuring FTP Authentication Methods

To allow anonymous access to your FTP site, use the Security Accounts tab in the Default FTP Site Properties sheet and select the Allow Anonymous Connections checkbox (this is selected by default; see Figure 9-4). To limit

Figure 9-4
Configuring anonymous access and granting operator privileges.

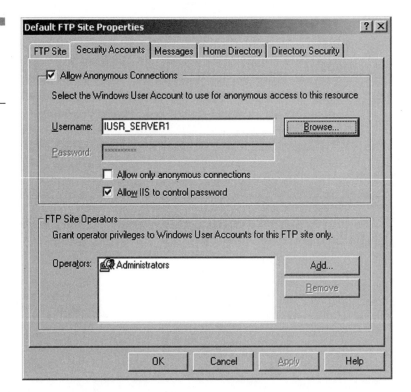

access to *only* anonymous connections, select the Allow Only Anonymous Connections checkbox (this is cleared by default). As discussed previously, *both* checkboxes should normally be selected so users do not try to access the FTP site using their domain credentials. Because these credentials would be passed to the server as clear text, they can be viewed by any protocol analyzer connected to the network, creating the risk of a security breach.

Anonymous access to an FTP site makes use of the IUSR_*SERVERNAME* account that is created when IIS is installed. If you want to change this account, create a new user account in the Local Users and Groups MMC snap-in and enter the username and password of this account in the Username and Password textboxes on this property sheet (you can also select Browse to locate the new account on in the directory). Make sure this account is assigned the right to log on locally in Local User and Groups snap-in (anonymous access requires this right). Instead of entering the account password in the Password textbox, you can select the Enable Automatic Password Synchronization checkbox to synchronize the passwords between this property sheet and User Manager; however, you can do this only if the IUSR_*SERVERNAME* account is an account *local* to the machine on which IIS is installed.

Enabling anonymous access to your FTP site means that users *must* log on with the username anonymous but can use anything for a password.

For more on the security implications of enabling or not enabling anonymous access to your FTP site or server, see the section *Understanding FTP Site Security* earlier in this chapter.

Configuring FTP Site Operators

Grant operator privileges for your FTP site or server to Windows 2000 user accounts and groups by clicking the Add button (see Figure 9-4) and browsing the accounts list. By default, the Administrators local group is assigned operator privileges, but FTP site operators do not *have* to be members of the Administrators local group.

FTP site operators have the right to administer *only* the FTP site to which they are assigned. Operators have limited administration rights and are able to perform simple administrative tasks such as

- Setting access permissions
- Enabling and configuring logging

- Limiting connections to the site
- Enabling/disabling anonymous access
- Creating welcome and exit messages
- Configuring IP level security
- Choosing a directory listing style

Operators cannot perform the following tasks unless they are also members of the Administrators local group:

- Configuring a new anonymous account
- Creating new virtual directories
- Viewing connected users and disconnecting them
- Changing the IP address or TCP port number of the site
- Granting operator privileges to users
- Changing the home directory

Typically, FTP site operators will consist of the Administrators local group and the company or departmental person responsible for managing the particular FTP site.

Configuring FTP Messages

Use the Messages tab to configure welcome, exit, and busy messages for your site or server (see Figure 9-5). *Welcome* messages may include such information as

- The purpose of the FTP site
- Who owns and manages the site and the sitemaster's email address
- A brief description of the top-level directory or the location of an index.txt file cataloging the site
- Names and locations of mirror sites
- Rules on uploading or downloading files

Exit messages are typically short and sweet. *Maximum connections* messages indicate that the FTP site is currently too busy to respond to the user's request for a session. They may also include a list of mirror sites that may be tried.

Figure 9-5
Configuring
welcome, exit, and
busy messages.

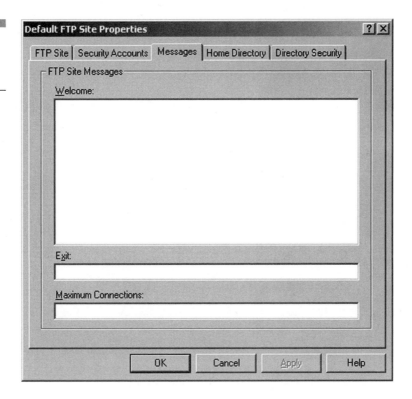

Configuring FTP Home Directory Location

The actual content for an FTP site may be a folder in

■ The local computer (IIS server)
■ A remote network share

The default FTP site created when IIS is installed is located at

```
C:\inetpub\ftproot
```

but this is a purely arbitrary location.

For FTP Site properties, the Home Directory tab (see Figure 9-6) can be used to configure the location of the home content for the FTP site. For FTP Directory properties, the Virtual Directory tab can be used to configure the location of the content mapped to the virtual directory on the FTP site.

Figure 9-6

Configuring content location, access permissions, and directory listing style.

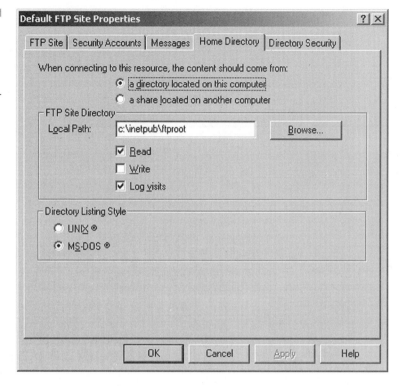

- To specify *local* content, select Directory Located on This Computer and type the full path to the folder in the Local Path textbox or use the Browse button to locate it.

- To specify *remote* content, select A Share Located on Another Computer and type the UNC path to the share in the Network Share textbox. You *must* then specify a valid Windows 2000 account that has access permissions to the network share. Click Connect As and enter an appropriate account in the Network Directory Security Credentials dialog box. If anonymous access is enabled on the FTP site, the anonymous account IUSR_*SERVERNAME* can be assigned NTFS or share-level permissions on the shared folder and can be entered in the Network Directory Security Credentials box.

NOTE: *Do not enter an Administrator account in this dialog box; this may lead to a security breach.*

Configuring FTP Access Permissions

Access permissions to FTP home and virtual directories are best controlled by locating the content folder on an NTFS volume and assigning NTFS permissions. Typical NTFS permissions for FTP content directories are read (RX), add (WX), and change (RWXD). If the volume is also located on a remote host, shared folder permissions will also have to be assigned (usually read or change).

The permissions assigned on this property sheet (see Figure 9-6) combine with NTFS and shared permissions on the content folder so those permissions that explicitly deny access take precedence over those that explicitly grant access. Typically you should select

- Read for FTP sites and directories that allow users to download files (for example, the download directory)
- Write for FTP sites and directories that allow users to upload files (for example, the incoming directory)

The third checkbox, Log Visits, logs all visits to the home or virtual directory in the FTP site.

NOTE: *Log Visits allows you to selectively log some FTP virtual directories but not others, reducing server overhead due to the cost of logging.*

Configuring FTP Directory Listing Style

When a GUI client such as Internet Explorer accesses an FTP site, it is presented with a directory listing. This directory listing can be configured to be either of two styles (see Figure 9-6):

- MS-DOS style
- UNIX style

Generally, UNIX style is preferred for Internet sites, as some older browsers understand only this format. MS-DOS style is easier to navigate and is preferred for intranet sites that have standardized on Internet Explorer.

Note that this option can be configured only at the FTP site level, and not at the level of individual virtual directories on a site.

Configuring FTP Site IP Level Security

Using the Directory Security tab (Figure 9-7), you can grant or deny access to your FTP site or virtual directory on a

- *Global* basis (either grant all computers access or deny all computers access)
- *Per-host* basis, according to IP address
- *Per-Network* basis, according to IP network number and subnet mask
- *Per-fully-qualified-domain-name* basis, using DNS Lookup (if available)

Note that using DNS Lookup may slow down site access because of the extra overhead related to the name resolution process.

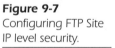

Figure 9-7
Configuring FTP Site
IP level security.

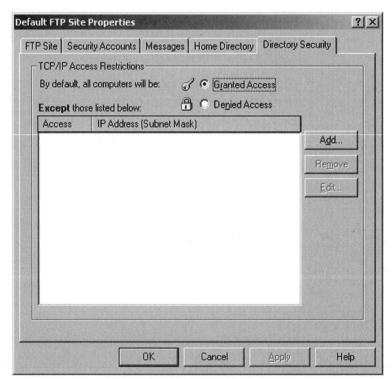

Configuring FTP for Administration by IIS 3.0

If your network contains a mix of IIS 5.0 and IIS 3.0 servers, you can configure one and only one FTP site on each IIS 5.0 server to be administered by the IIS 3.0 version of Internet Services Manager by using the Service tab on the FTP Service Master Properties sheet for your server (Figure 9-8).

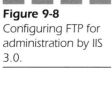

Walkthrough: Creating an FTP Site

FTP sites can be created and managed on IIS 5.0 using any of the following tools:

- The *Internet Services manager* (ISM) snap-in of the *Microsoft Management Console* (MMC)
- The HTML version of the Internet Service Manager
- The Windows Scripting Host

Figure 9-8
Configuring FTP for administration by IIS 3.0.

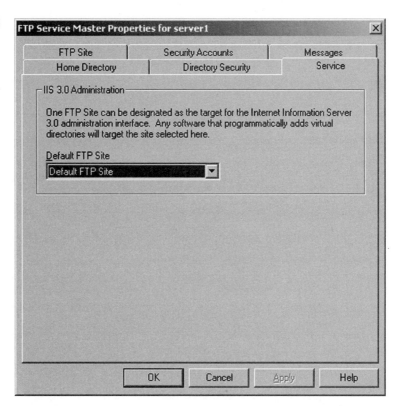

This walkthrough will cover use of the MMC with the ISM snap-in to create, configure, and test a new FTP site with virtual directories.

Create the following local folders on your IIS server to host the content for the FTP site:

- `C:\MyFtpHome`

- `C:\MyFtpDownload`

- `C:\MyFtpUpload`

Create a file called downtest.txt and place it in the MyFtpDownload folder. Create a second file called uptest.txt and place it in the root of the machine you are using to connect to the FTP site. If these content folders are on an NTFS volume, make sure they have at least change (RWXD) permission assigned to them for the Everyone group.

From the MMC, right-click the IIS server node and select New, FTP Site from the shortcut menu. The New FTP Site Wizard appears. Click Next to proceed to configure your FTP site. Enter a friendly name for your new FTP site (here MyFtpSite has been selected as the name; see Figure 9-9). This name may also be defined in a host record on a DNS server if the site will be accessed through domain names, so avoid spaces and non-alphanumeric characters in your site name.

Figure 9-9

Giving your FTP site a friendly name.

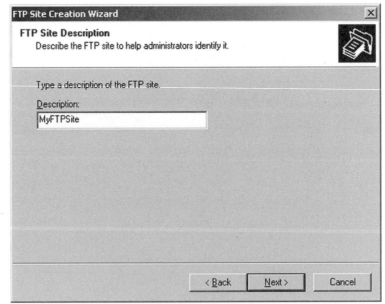

Figure 9-10

Assign an IP address and port number.

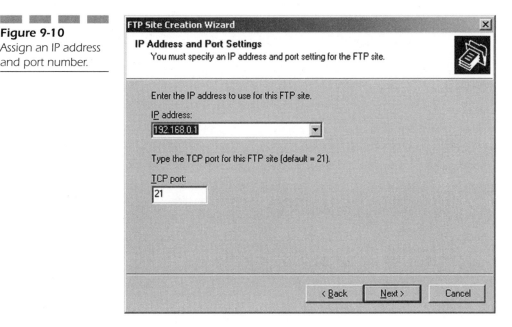

Figure 9-10

Assign an IP address and port number.

Next select an IP address and port number for your new FTP site (see Figure 9-10). Typically, the IP address should be unique to the site, and the port should be the default port 21.

Next, specify the local or network path to the home directory for the FTP site (Figure 9-11). Here we have chosen the local folder

```
C:\MyFtpHome
```

as the home directory for the site.

Read access is now assigned to the home directory of the new site (see Figure 9-12). This is a typical choice, as the home directory usually contains only read-only top-level documents such as the site index or list or readme.txt file.

Click Next. In the next dialog box, click Finish to create the new FTP site on the server. The newly created site is in a stopped state, so use the Start button on the rebar to start the new site.

Now that we have created a new FTP site called MyFtpSite, we will create two new virtual directories within this site:

■ Downloads will be used for storing files that users can download.

■ Incoming will be used as a drop box for users who need to upload files to the site.

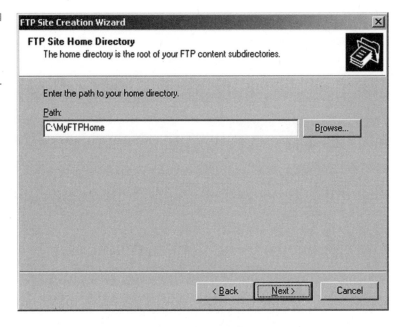

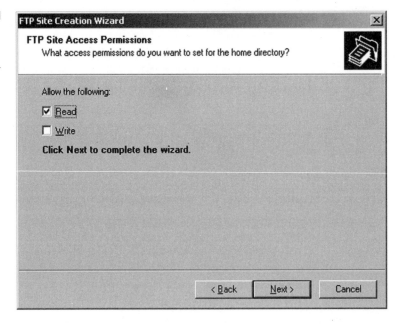

Create the Incoming virtual directory by right-clicking the MyFtpSite
icon in the MMC and selecting New, Virtual Directory from the shortcut
menu. This starts the New Virtual Directory Wizard. Click Next to begin

Figure 9-13
Specifying the name
of your virtual
directory.

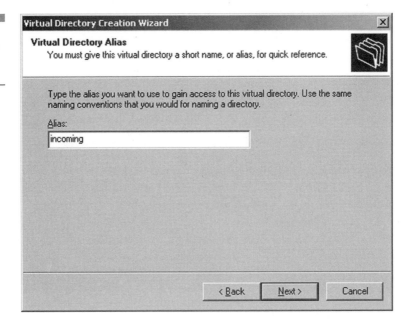

configuring your directory. Enter the name incoming as the alias for the new virtual directory (see Figure 9-13).

Next, enter the path to the folder that the incoming virtual directory will be mapped to (see Figure 9-14), namely

```
C:\MyFtpUpload
```

Finally, assign Write access *only* to the new virtual directory (see Figure 9-15). This will allow anonymous users to upload files to the incoming directory, but will not allow them to see what files other users have uploaded. This is a typical setup, called an *FTP drop box,* which protects the privacy of users uploading their files. This is also called a location for *blind uploads.*

Click Next. In the next dialog box, click Finish to create the virtual directory. Create the download virtual directory similarly, assigning it read access only.

We can now view the results in the Internet Services Manager (see Figure 9-16). Note the new icons in the scope pane (left side) for the FTP site and virtual directories. If you want to view the contents of a virtual directory, right-click the virtual directory and choose Open or Explore from the shortcut menu.

We can try connecting to the new site using the command-line FTP utility on a Windows 2000 host, either the local host or a remote one. Just open

Figure 9-14
Map the new virtual
directory to a content
folder.

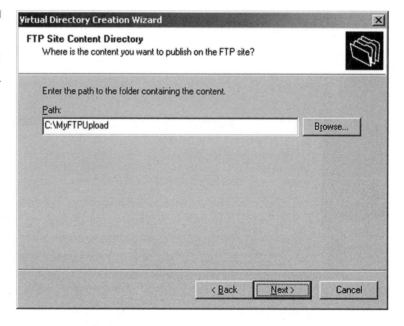

Figure 9-15
Creating an FTP drop
box having write
access only.

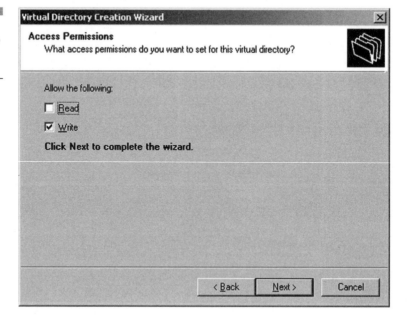

a Command Prompt session, type `ftp` to start the utility, and then type
`open` to open the site (Figure 9-17).

Figure 9-16
Viewing the new FTP
site in the Internet
Services Manager.

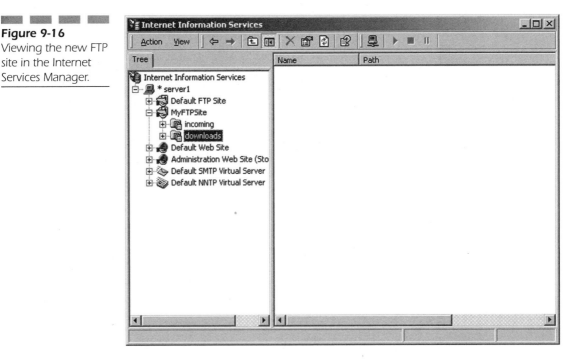

Figure 9-17
Testing the new FTP
site from a command
prompt.

Following is a transcript of a session where we have connected to the new FTP site from a command prompt. In it, we download the file download.txt from the /downloads directory and upload the file upload.txt to the /incoming directory.

```
C:\.ftp 192.168.0.1
Connected to 192.168.0.1.
220 server1 Microsoft FTP Service (Version 5.0).
User (192.168.0.1:(none)): anonymous
```

```
331 Anonymous access allowed, send identity (e-mail name) as
password.
Password:
230-Welcome to my FTP site!
230-=============================
230-put uploads into /incoming
230-get downloads from /downloads
230-=============================
230 Anonymous user logged in.
ftp. cd downloads
250 CWD command successful.
ftp. dir
200 PORT command successful.
150 Opening ASCII mode data connection for /bin/ls.
-r-xr-xr-x   1 owner     group     87 Jan   2 16:50
downtest.txt
226 Transfer complete.
73 bytes received in 0.02 seconds (3.65 kbps)
ftp. get downtest.txt
200 PORT command successful.
150 Opening ASCII mode data connection for downtest.txt(87 bytes).
226 Transfer complete.
ftp. cd ../incoming
250 CWD command successful.
ftp. dir
200 PORT command successful.
150 Opening ASCII mode data connection for /bin/ls.
550 .: Access is denied.
ftp. put uptest.txt
200 PORT command successful.
150 Opening ASCII mode data connection for uptest.txt.
226 Transfer complete.
ftp. bye
221 Thanks for visiting!
```

This session listing illustrates how to use basic FTP command-line commands such as open, close, get, and put. For a listing of all available FTP
command-line commands, type the following at the command prompt:

```
C:\. ftp
fpt. ?
```

A list of all FTP commands will appear. To get a brief explanation about a
specific command—for example, the command put—simply type

```
ftp. ? put
putsend one file
```

The three-digit number at the start of each line returned by the FTP
server is called an *FTP return code*. For example, the return code 200
always means that the command was successfully executed.

Another way of testing the new FTP site is to use Internet Explorer as an FTP client program. Start Internet Explorer and open the following URL:

`ftp://172.16.8.101/download`

The result is the directory listing shown in Figure 9-18. This is an example of the MS-DOS style of directory listing.

With Internet Explorer 5.0, if the browser tries to access an FTP site that is either stopped or has read access disabled, the error message in Figure 9-19 appears. FTP error messages are not configurable with IIS 5.0.

Figure 9-18
Accessing an FTP site using Internet Explorer.

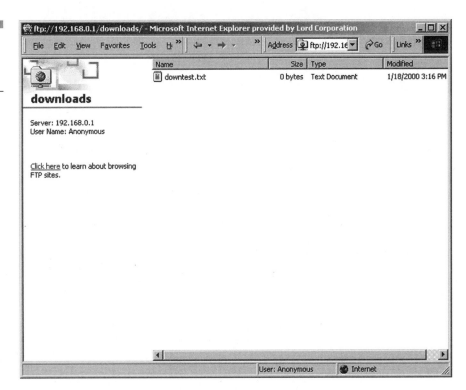

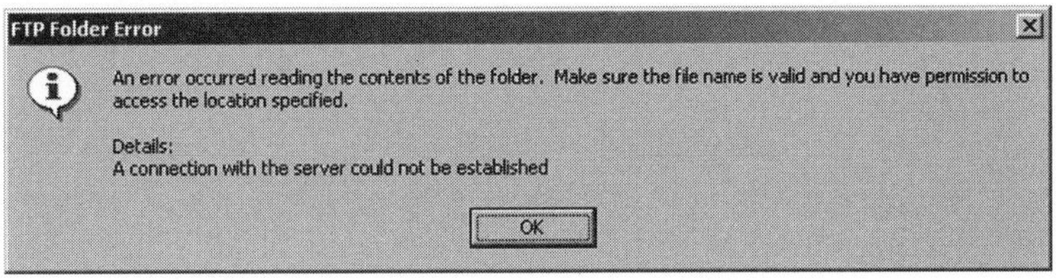

Figure 9-19
Message indicating inaccessible FTP site.

SUMMARY

IIS 5.0 has a fully configurable FTP service with the capability of hosting multiple FTP sites (virtual servers) on a single machine. Content for FTP sites may be hosted on either the local IIS server or on a remote network share. FTP sites are a useful complement to Web sites, providing a centralized location for downloads and making blind uploads possible.

For More Information

To learn more about administering the FTP service, try the following online resources.

Microsoft Web Site

Visit a really large FTP site:

```
ftp.microsoft.com
```

View how it is organized and laid out by opening the site in Internet Explorer.

Microsoft Newsgroups

You can post questions about the Microsoft FTP service on IIS 5.0 to the group

```
microsoft.public.inetserver.iis
```

Administering Performance

Monitoring and optimizing the performance of servers is an important task for any administrator. Ensuring that Web, FTP, and other Internet servers can handle peak loads effectively is critical for any company using the Internet for business purposes. This chapter looks at Windows 2000 monitoring and diagnostic tools as they apply to Internet Information Services 5.0, including

- Performance Monitor
- Task Manager
- Command-line TCP/IP utilities
- IIS logs
- Event Viewer
- Network Monitor
- IIS *Web Capacity Analysis Tool* (WCAT)

Also discussed are various techniques for tuning and optimizing the performance of IIS services, including

- Optimizing hardware components
- Relocating resource-consuming applications
- Stopping unnecessary services
- Restricting the use of logging
- Restricting the use of SSL
- Throttling bandwidth
- Limiting the number of connections
- Maximizing processor time for services
- Adjusting cache size to optimize memory usage
- Optimizing content type
- Best practices for ASP coding
- Enabling HTTP Keep-Alives

IIS Performance Monitoring

Monitoring the performance of IIS servers can provide the administrator with information about

- Bottlenecks affecting server performance
- Unbalanced loads resulting from frequently accessed sites
- Inability of users to form connections because of high traffic
- Average and peak resource usage
- Long-term trends in resource usage
- Server errors due to hardware or software failures

This performance information can be used to

- Plan hardware and software upgrades to meet expected capacity.
- Isolate and correct hardware and software problems affecting performance.
- Tune and optimize services to meet average and peak loads.
- Report site access statistics for billing purposes.
- Minimize overspending related to the purchase of unnecessary hardware upgrades.

The tools used to monitor IIS performance are the basic monitoring and troubleshooting tools that come with the Windows 2000 Server operating system, plus additional tools developed specifically for IIS.

Performance Monitor

Windows 2000 Performance Monitor is the primary tool for monitoring and evaluating IIS performance (see Figure 10-1). With Performance Monitor, administrators can

- Monitor various aspects of IIS services in real time.
- Log performance data over time to identify baselines and evaluate trends.
- Create charts and reports to display performance data.
- Set alert conditions to notify administrators when performance criteria are exceeded.
- Identify bottlenecks in processor, memory, disk, and network subsystems.
- Observe how performance changes in response to hardware/software configuration changes.
- Calculate system capacity and forecast future needs.

Figure 10-1

Using Performance
Monitor to chart
server activity.

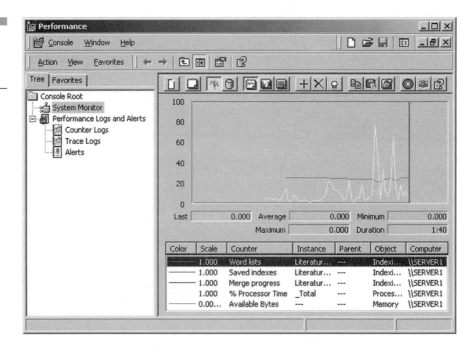

Performance Monitor can display or log the activity of *instances* of *counters* belonging to various kinds of server *objects*. Objects are hardware and software processes that make use of server resources. Examples of objects are

- Memory
- LogicalDisk
- PagingFile
- Redirector

Counters are grouped according to the type of object to which they belong and specify the particular form of hardware or software activity to be monitored. Examples of counters for the object PhysicalDisk are

- % Disk Read Time
- % Free Space
- Disk Bytes/Transfer
- Free Megabytes

When Performance Monitor is monitoring a particular object, it collects all instances of all counters for that object.

Instances are multiple occurrences of particular counters, depending on the hardware and software involved. For example, the % Disk Time counter might have the instances

- 0 C: D:
- 1 F: G: H:
- _Total

meaning the instance "Partitions C: and D: on Physical Disk 0" the instance "Partitions F, G, and H on Physical Disk 1" and the instance "Total of all Disks," respectively.

Figure 10-2 shows an Add to Chart dialog box illustrating the preceding example. To see a description of what type of information the selected counter collects, click the EXPLAIN button in the Add to Chart box, and a Counter Definition section will appear at the bottom of the dialog box.

When various components of IIS are installed on a system, new Performance Monitor objects are also installed to enable administrators to monitor these services. These new objects, in addition to standard Windows 2000 Performance Monitor objects, provide administrators with a wide range of tools for monitoring the performance of IIS servers. To review the functions monitored by standard Windows 2000 Performance Monitor objects, refer to

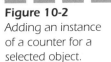

Figure 10-2
Adding an instance of a counter for a selected object.

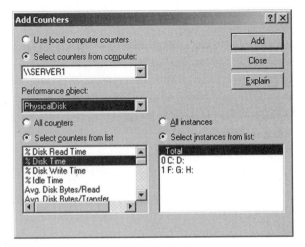

the Windows 2000 Server Resource Kit and the Windows 2000 Professional Resource Kit available on the TechNet CD.

Following is a detailed list of the counters available for IIS and related services, along with the counter definitions that can be viewed by clicking the EXPLAIN button on the Add to Chart dialog box:

- Internet Information Services Global
- Web Service
- Active Server Pages
- FTP Service
- Content Index
- Content Index Filter
- HTTP Content Index

The counters can be classified into four main categories, depending on how they are collected:

- *Instantaneous* counters give moment-by-moment readings.
- *Average* counters give average values over a recent time interval (usually one minute).
- *Cumulative* counters give total values since the associated service was last started.
- *Maximum* counters give peak values since the associated service was last started.

In addition to monitoring the objects in the following list, administrators should also monitor the basic counters for detecting bottlenecks in processor, memory, disk drive, and network usage, because these are the four basic hardware elements that most affect server performance.

1. Recommended counters for monitoring the *processor* include

   - *Processor* % Processor Time (should be less than 75 percent most of the time)
   - *System* Processor Queue Length (should be less than 2 most of the time)
   - *Processor* Interrupts/sec (a drastic increase here could indicate a device failure)

   Failure to satisfy one or more of these criteria indicates that your processor could be a bottleneck. The solution is to upgrade the processor, add another processor, or offload some of the server load to another machine.

2. Recommended counters for monitoring *memory* include

   - *Memory*   Available Bytes (should be above 4 MB most of the time)
   - *Memory*   Committed Bytes (should be less than the amount of physical RAM)
   - *Memory*   Pages/sec (should be less than 5 most of the time)

   Failure to satisfy one or more of these criteria indicates that your physical memory (RAM) could be a bottleneck. The solution is to add more RAM.

3. Recommended counters for monitoring the *disk subsystem* include

   - *PhysicalDisk*   % Disk Time (should not be close to 100 percent for frequent, extended periods)
   - *PhysicalDisk*   Disk Queue Length (should be less than 2 most of the time)
   - The same two counters for the LogicalDisk object

   Failure to satisfy one or more of these criteria indicates that your disk subsystem could be a bottleneck. The solution is to upgrade to a better controller, a faster spindle, or a RAID 0 stripe set.

4. Recommended counters for monitoring the *network subsystem* include

   - *Network Segment*   % Network Utilization (a sustained value of 60–80 percent is considered saturated)
   - *Network Interface*   Bytes Total/sec (the higher the value, the better the network card)

   Failure to satisfy one or more of these criteria indicates that your network subsystem could be a bottleneck. Upgrade to a faster network card, add another network card, or segment the network to reduce broadcast traffic.

NOTE: *The PhysicalDisk and LogicalDisk objects require enabling to be monitored. To enable these objects from the command prompt, type*

```
diskperf -y (for a regular hard drive)
```

or

```
diskperf -ye (for a RAID stripe set)
```

The Network Segment object is available in Performance Monitor only when the Network Monitor Agent service is installed on the server.

The Network Interface object is available in Performance Monitor only when the SNMP service is installed on the server.

Internet Information Services Global Counters   Counters for the object Internet Information Services Global provide performance information regarding all IIS services running (i.e., WWW, FTP, NNTP, SMTP, etc.). The following counters may be monitored for this object; the descriptions are taken verbatim from the explanation offered when you click on the EXPLAIN button after selecting a counter to add.

Cache Flushes   The number of times a portion of the memory cache has been expired due to file or directory changes in an Internet Information Services directory tree

Cache Hits   The total number of times a file open, directory listing, or service-specific object request was found in the cache

Cache Hits %   The ratio of cache hits to all cache requests

Cache Misses   The total number of times a file open, directory listing, or service-specific object request was not found in the cache

Cached File Handles   The number of open file handles cached by all of the Internet Information Services

Current Blocked Async I/O Requests   Current requests temporarily blocked due to bandwidth throttling settings

Directory Listings   The number of directory listings cached by all of the Internet Information Services

Measured Async I/O Bandwidth Usage   Measured bandwidth of asynchronous I/O averaged over a minute

Objects (the default counter)   The number of objects cached by all of the Internet Information Services (including file handle tracking objects, directory listing objects, and service-specific objects)

Total Allowed Async I/O Requests   Total requests allowed by bandwidth throttling settings (counted since service startup)

Total Blocked Async I/O Requests   Total requests temporarily blocked due to bandwidth throttling settings (counted since service startup)

Total Rejected Async I/O Request   Total requests rejected due to bandwidth throttling settings (counted since service startup)

Web Service Counters   Counters for the object Web Service provide performance information specifically related to the WWW service on IIS. The following counters may be monitored for this object:

Anonymous Users/sec   The rate at which users are making anonymous connections using the Web service

Bytes Received/sec   The rate at which data bytes are received by the Web service

Bytes Sent/sec   The rate at which data bytes are sent by the Web service

Bytes Total/sec (the default counter)   The sum of Bytes Sent/sec and Bytes Received/sec (i.e., the total rate of bytes) transferred by the Web service

CGI Requests/sec   The rate of CGI requests being simultaneously processed by the Web service

Connection Attempts/sec   The rate at which connections using the Web service are being attempted

Current Anonymous Users   The number of users who currently have anonymous connections using the Web service

Current Blocked Async I/O Requests   Current requests temporarily blocked due to bandwidth throttling settings

Current CGI Requests   The current number of CGI requests simultaneously being processed by the Web service

Current Connections   The current number of connections established with the Web service

Current ISAPI Extension Requests   The current number of extension requests simultaneously being processed by the Web service

Current Nonanonymous Users   The number of users who currently have a nonanonymous connection using the Web service

Delete Requests/sec   The rate at which HTTP requests using the Delete method are made (such requests are generally used for file removals)

Files Received/sec   The rate at which files are received by the Web service

Files Sent/sec   The rate at which files are sent by the Web service

Files/sec   The rate at which files are transferred (i.e., sent and received) by the Web service

Get Requests / sec   The rate at which HTTP requests using the Get method are made (such requests are generally used for basic file retrievals or image maps, although they can also be used with forms)

Head Requests / sec   The rate at which HTTP requests using the Head method are made (such requests generally indicate that a client is querying the state of a document to see whether it needs to be refreshed)

ISAPI Extension Requests / sec   The rate of ISAPI extension requests that are simultaneously being processed by the Web service

Logon Attempts / sec   The rate at which logons using the Web service are being attempted

Maximum Anonymous Users   The maximum number of users establishing concurrent anonymous connections using the Web service (counted since system startup)

Maximum CGI Requests   The maximum number of CGI requests simultaneously processed by the Web service

Maximum Connections   The maximum number of simultaneous connections established with the Web service

Maximum ISAPI Extension Requests   The maximum number of extension requests simultaneously processed by the Web service

Maximum Nonanonymous Users   The maximum number of users establishing concurrent nonanonymous connections using the Web service (counted since service startup)

Measured Async I / O Bandwidth Usage   The measured bandwidth of asynchronous I/O averaged over a minute

Nonanonymous Users / sec   The rate at which users are making nonanonymous connections using the Web service

Not Found Errors / sec   The rate of errors due to requests that couldn't be satisfied by the server because the requested documents could not be found (generally reported as an HTTP 404 error code to the client)

Other Request Methods / sec   The rate at which HTTP requests are made that do not use the Get, Post, Put, Delete, Trace, or Head method (these may include Link or other methods supported by gateway applications)

Post Requests / sec   The rate at which HTTP requests using the Post method are made (post requests are generally used for forms or gateway requests)

Put Requests / sec   The rate at which HTTP requests using the Put method are made

System Code Resident Bytes   System code resident bytes (!)

Total Allowed Async I / O Requests   Total requests allowed by bandwidth throttling settings (counted since system startup)

Total Anonymous Users   The total number of users establishing an anonymous connection with the Web service (counted since service startup)

Total Blocked Async I / O Requests   Total requests temporarily blocked due to bandwidth throttling settings (counted since service startup)

Total CGI Requests   *Total Common Gateway Interface* (CGI) requests—custom gateway executables (.exe) that the administrator can install to add forms processing or other dynamic data sources; CGI requests spawn a process on the server that can be a large drain on server resources (counted since service startup)

Total Connection Attempts   The number of connections that have been attempted using the Web service (counted since service startup)

Total Delete Requests   The number of HTTP requests using the Delete method (generally used for file removals; counted since service startup)

Total Files Received   The total number of files received by the Web service (counted since service startup)

Total Files Sent   The total number of files sent by the Web service (counted since service startup)

Total Files Transferred   The sum of Total Files Sent and Total Files Received, the total number of files transferred by the Web service (counted since service startup)

Total Get Requests   The number of HTTP requests using the Get method (generally used for basic file retrievals or image maps, although they can be used with forms, counted since service startup)

Total Head Requests   The number of HTTP requests using the Head method (such requests generally indicate that a client is querying the state of a document to see whether it needs to be refreshed; counted since service startup)

Total ISAPI Extension Requests   Total custom gateway dynamic link libraries (.dll) the administrator can install to add forms processing or other dynamic data sources; unlike CGI requests, ISAPI requests are simple calls to a DLL library routine and thus are better suited to high-performance gateway applications (counted since service startup)

Total Logon Attempts   The number of logons that have been attempted using the Web service (counted since service startup)

Total Method Requests   The number of HTTP Get, Post, Put, Delete, Trace, Head, and other method requests (counted since service startup)

Total Method Requests/sec   The rate at which HTTP requests using Get, Post, Put, Delete, Trace, or Head methods are made

Total Nonanonymous Users   The total number of users establishing a nonanonymous connection with the Web service (counted since service startup)

Total Not Found Errors   The number of requests that couldn't be satisfied by the server because the requested document could not be found (generally reported as an HTTP 404 error code to the client; counted since service startup)

Total Other Request Methods   The number of HTTP requests that do not use the Get, Post, Put, Delete, Trace, or Head methods (may include Link or other methods supported by gateway applications; counted since system startup)

Total Post Requests   The number of HTTP requests using the Post method (generally used for forms or gateway requests; counted since service startup)

Total Put Requests   The number of HTTP requests using the Put method (counted since service startup)

Total Rejected Async I/O Requests   Total requests rejected due to bandwidth throttling settings (counted since service startup)

Total Trace Requests   The number of HTTP requests using the Trace method; such requests allow the client to see what is being received at the end of the request chain and to use the information for diagnostic purposes (counted since service startup)

Active Server Pages Counters for Active Server Pages provide performance information specifically related to ASP scripts running on IIS. The following counters may be monitored for this object:

Debugging Requests The number of documents being debugged.

Errors during script runtime The number of page requests that failed due to runtime errors in the script (Monitor this counter to gauge how ASP scripts are written by developers. A high number of errors can mean poorly written scripts or problems connecting to resources, which can have a huge effect on performance and client satisfaction.)

Errors from ASP Preprocessor The number of page requests that failed due to preprocessing errors

Errors from Script Compilers The number of page requests that failed due to compilation errors

Errors / Sec The number of errors encountered per second

Request Bytes In Total The total number of bytes for all requests

Request Bytes Out Total The total number of bytes sent out to clients, excluding HTTP headers

Request Execution Time The number of milliseconds it took to execute the most recent request (another indicator of poorly written scripts or problems connecting to resources)

Request Wait Time The number of milliseconds the request was waiting in the queue

Requests Disconnected The number of request that were disconnected due to failure

Requests Executing The number of requests currently executing

Requests Failed Total The total number of failed requests due to authorization failures, errors, and rejections.

Requests Not Authorized Authorization failures (use this counter to see requests to resources that shouldn't be made)

Requests Not Found The total number of HTTP 404 errors (an indicator of broken links in your Web site)

Requests Queued The number of requests waiting

Requests Rejected   The number of requests rejected due to insufficient resources available to them (keep an eye on this to spot problems with the system)

Requests Succeeded   The number of requests that were processed successfully

Requests Timed Out   The number of requests that did not complete due to time out errors (another indicator of problem scripts, possible problems with the script not connecting to resources)

Requests Total   The total number of all requests including successful and nonsuccessful requests

Request/Sec   The number of requests per second

Script Engines Cached   The number of script engines in cache (i.e., VBScript, Jscript, ActivePerl, used for script interpretation)

Session Duratio   The number of miliseconds that the most recent session lasted (sessions are established when the developers of the ASP scripts uses the session variable in their ASP code. The more session variables used, the more resources are being allocated by the Web server for the script. Avoid using session variables whenever possible.)

Sessions Current   The current number of sessions

Sessions Timed Out   The number of sessions that have timed out

Sessions Total   Total number of sessions since IIS has started

Template Cache Hit Rate   Percentage of hits in the template cache

Template Notifications   The number of template invalidated due to changes

Templates Cached   The number of templates currently in cache

Transactions Aborted   Monitors COM+ transactions that have been aborted, which could indicate possible errors with application

Transactions Commited   The number of successful transactions

Transactions Pending   The number of transactions in progress

Transactions Total   The total number of transactions

Transactions/Sec   Transactions started per second

FTP Service Counters   Counters for the object FTP Service provide performance information specifically relating to the FTP service on IIS. The following counters may be monitored for this object:

Bytes Received/sec   The rate at which that data bytes are received by the FTP service

Bytes Sent/sec   The rate at which data bytes are sent by the FTP service

Bytes Total/sec (the default counter)   The sum of Bytes Sent/sec and Byte Received/sec; the total rate at which bytes are transferred by the FTP service

Current Anonymous Users   The number of users who currently have an anonymous connection using the FTP service

Current Connections   The current number of connections established with the FTP service

Current Nonanonymous Users   The number of users who currently have a nonanonymous connection with the FTP service

Maximum Anonymous Users   The maximum number of users establishing concurrent anonymous connections with the FTP service (counted since system startup)

Maximum Connections   The maximum number of simultaneous connections established with the FTP service

Maximum Nonanonymous Users   The maximum number of users establishing concurrent nonanonymous connections with the FTP service

Total Anonymous Users   The total number of users establishing an anonymous connection with the FTP service (since service startup)

Total Connection Attempts (all instances)   The number of connections that have been attempted using the FTP service (since service startup), for all instances listed

Total Files Received   The total number of files received by the FTP service

Total Files Sent   The total number of files sent by the FTP service since service startup

Total Files Transferred   The sum of Total Files Sent and Total Files Received, the total number of files transferred by the FTP service since service startup

Total Logon Attempts   The number of logons that have been attempted using the FTP service (since service startup)

Total Nonanonymous Users   The total number of users establishing a nonanonymous connection with the FTP service (since service startup)

Indexing Service Counters   Counters for the object Indexing Service provide performance information specifically relating to the Indexing Service. The following counters may be monitored for this object:

 # documents indexed   The number of documents indexed since the index was mounted

Deffered for Indexing   Files not available and deferred for indexing

Files to be indexed   Files to be indexed

Index size (MB)   Size of the content index in megabytes

Merge progress   Percentage of current merge completed

Running queries   Number of running queries

Saved Indexes   Number of saved indexes

Total # documents   Total number of documents in the index

Total # queries   Total number of queries since index was mounted

Unique keys   Number of unique keys (words, etc.) in the index

Wordlists (the default counter)   Number of wordlists

Indexing Service Filter Counters   Counters for the object Indexing Service Filters provide additional performance information relating to the Indexing Service filtering of documents. The following counters may be monitored for this object:

Binding time (ms)   Average time spent binding to indexing filters

Indexing speed (Mbph)   Speed of filtering contents of files, in megabytes per hour

Total indexing speed (Mbph)   Speed of filtering file contents and properties, in megabytes per hour

Http Indexing Counters   Counters for the object Http Indexing provide performance information relating to running queries and caching results on Indexing Sevice. The following counters may be monitored for this object:

% Cache hits   Percentage of queries found in the query cache

% Cache misses   Percentage of queries not found in the query cache

Active queries   Current number of running queries

Cache items   Number of completed queries in cache

Current requests queued   Current number of query requests queued

Queries per minute   Number of queries per minute

Total queries   Total number of queries run since service startup

Total requests rejected   Total number of query requests rejected

Task Manager

Windows 2000 Task Manager is a useful tool for monitoring performance and detecting problems with IIS services (see Figure 10-3). With Task Manager, administrators can

- Monitor the instantaneous CPU and memory usage of `inetinfo.exe`, the global IIS process.

- Monitor the instantaneous CPU and memory usage of related services such as `cisrv.exe` and `cidaemon.exe` (Index Server), `certsrv.exe` (Certificate Server), and so on.

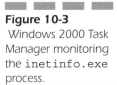

Figure 10-3
Windows 2000 Task Manager monitoring the `inetinfo.exe` process.

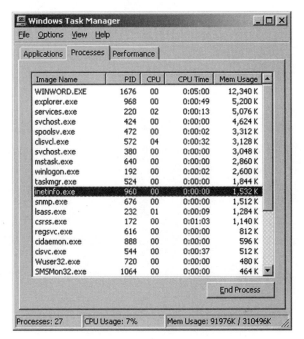

- Graphically view the running CPU and memory usage for all processes combined.

- Detect and terminate runaway processes and applications.

Command-Line TCP/IP Utilities

Several TCP/IP command-line utilities are useful to administrators for monitoring and troubleshooting IIS services. These utilities include

- The general TCP/IP troubleshooting utilities ipconfig and ping (see Appendix A).

- telnet, which enables you to impersonate a client and send commands one line at a time to each IIS service. For example, if you are having problems with NNTP clients connecting to the NNTP service on IIS, try connecting with telnet instead by using the default NNTP port 119 on the server (see Figure 10-4). When a connection is made, the NNTP server should return a 200 NNTP status message. Respond to this message by typing list and then pressing Enter (you must enter set local_echo in your telnet session to be able to see what you type in telnet). If telnet replies with a list of newsgroups, your news server is probably functioning properly, and the problem likely resides with the news client (see Figure 10-5). To obtain a list of commands understood by the NNTP service, type help and press Enter.

- netstat, which displays the current state of TCP/IP connections and various TCP/IP protocol statistics for the server. Type netstat /? at

Figure 10-4

Connecting to the NNTP server using telnet.

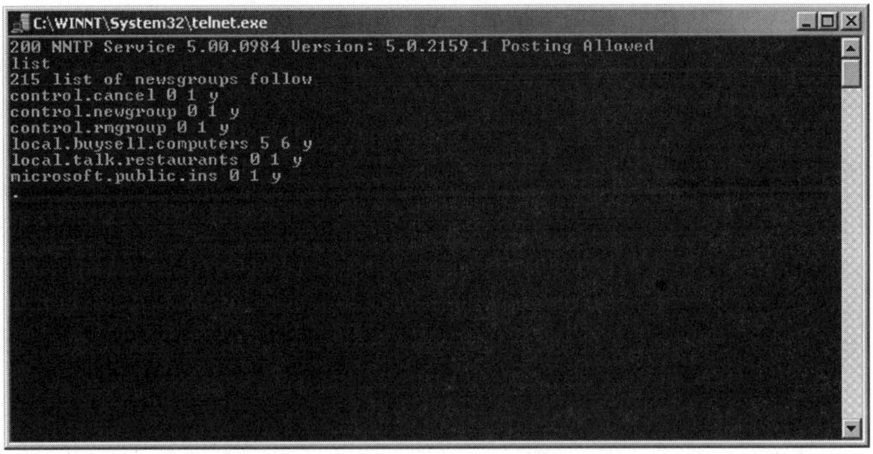

Figure 10-5
Obtaining a listing of
newsgroups on the
NNTP service of IIS.

Figure 10-5
Obtaining a listing of
newsgroups on the
NNTP service of IIS.

the command prompt for usage information about this command. Some of the more important parameters are as follows:

```
netstat -a
```

displays all connections and listening ports (server-side connections are normally not shown).

```
netstat -n
```

displays addresses and port numbers in numerical form.

```
netstat -s
```

displays per-protocol statistics.

```
netstat -p tcp
```

shows connections for the TCP protocol; this may be used with the -s option to display per-protocol statistics.

- nslookup, a command-line utility for examining records in the DNS server database, generally used to troubleshoot DNS-related problems (see Appendix B).

IIS Logs

The IIS logging capability enables administrators to determine how many clients are connecting to the server, when they connect, what they are viewing, and so on. This information is useful for

- Determining which sites or services are most popular so that these sites can be tuned for maximum responsiveness
- Determining which sites have problems such as broken links or failed applications

Logged information can be viewed directly in text files, exported from an ODBC-compliant database, or imported into a log analysis program.

Event Viewer

Event Viewer provides administrators with information regarding system errors, warnings, and significant events related to Windows 2000 services. Event Viewer records three kinds of logs:

- *System* log: contains events related to Windows 2000 services and device drivers
- *Security* log: contains the Windows 2000 audit log
- *Application* log: contains events related to applications running on Windows 2000

Events related to IIS and other Internet services are logged in the System log (see Figure 10-6). The keywords in the *Source* column may be filtered to focus in on particular IIS and related services, such as

- W3SVC: the WWW service
- MSFTPSVC: the FTP service
- SMTPSVC: the SMTP service
- NNTPSVC: the NNTP service

Events related to Internet services are logged in the Application log. Keywords in the *Source* column include

- Ci: the Indexing Services
- CERTSVC: Certificate Services
- MSDTC: Microsoft COM+
- Active Server Pages
- FrontPage 4.0

Figure 10-6
Events are logged in
the System log.

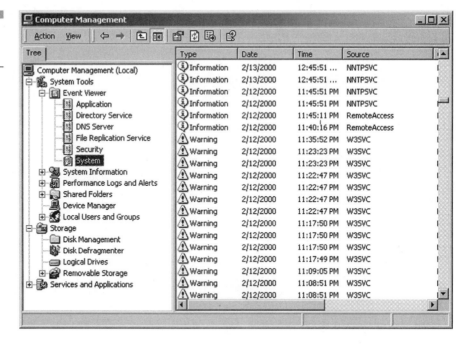

Network Monitor

Network Monitor can be used by administrators to capture and analyze
network traffic at the packet level. (Figure 10-7 shows a Network Monitor
trace of an HTTP Get request.) Network Monitor is more a diagnostic tool
than a performance tool, enabling administrators to examine

- Packet traffic *from* the server to troubleshoot connection problems,
  addressing problems, and protocol problems
- Packet traffic *to* the server to detect attempts to hack IIS servers, plus
  the problems mentioned previously

IIS Web Capacity Analysis Tool (WCAT)

Another tool in the administrator's arsenal is Microsoft's WCAT, which is
included with the Windows 2000 Resource Kit from Microsoft. The WCAT
is designed to simulate workloads on IIS servers and to test their responses

Figure 10-7
Network Monitor
trace of an HTTP Get
request.

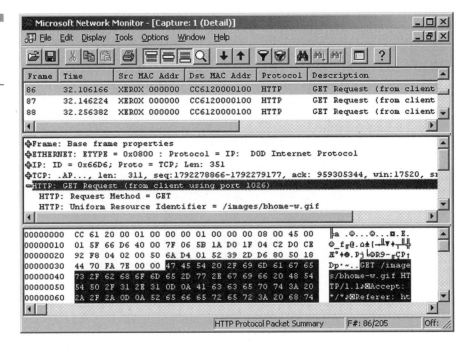

to a variety of client requests, including HTTP methods, FTP, SSL, ASP, ISAPI, and CGI. By studying the response of your IIS server under different kinds of simulated loads, you can identify bottlenecks and determine how best to optimize IIS performance through hardware upgrades and software performance tuning.

Running WCAT requires three machines, all of which have to be running Windows 2000 or Windows NT 4.0 (see Figure 10-8).

- *The WCAT server.* This is the machine being tested and has IIS installed on it. Installing the WCAT server components on an IIS server simply adds a number of test files that can later be deleted from the server.

- *The WCAT client* This machine runs the virtual clients that make connections to and request pages from the WCAT server. Each virtual client is a thread running within a single WCAT process. WCAT supports up to 200 virtual clients per machine, and because most browsers typically use four separate connections for downloading Web content, this translates into simulating up to 50 browser clients. To exceed this limit, you can use several machines as WCAT clients.

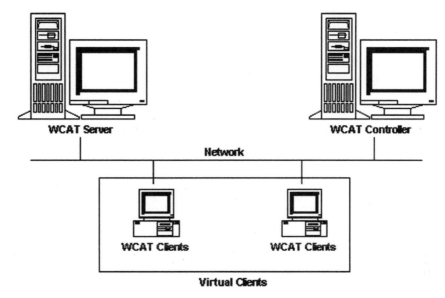

Figure 10-8
Using the Web
Capacity Analysis Tool
(WCAT)

■ *The WCAT controller*   This machine administers and monitors the WCAT testing procedure and controls the nature of the test being administered through controller input files. The output of a WCAT test can be a log file or a Performance Monitor file, which allows a variety of methods to be used for analyzing and interpreting the test results.

WCAT comes with more than 40 prepackaged tests that administrators can run to determine server performance under different workloads. For each test, the administrator can vary parameters to adjust the load on the server. These parameters include

■ Number of clients in the test
■ Rate of requests by clients
■ Size and type of page requested by clients
■ Frequency of requests for each page
■ Total length of time of the test

Administrators can also customize server load by writing their own client controller scripts.

For more information on WCAT, refer to the Windows 2000 Resource Kit.

IIS Performance Tuning

In this section we examine various strategies, tips, and tricks that administrators can use for tuning the performance of IIS servers. These are listed in no special order.

Removing Unnecessary Applications

Running other resource-intensive applications (e.g., Microsoft Exchange Server, File and Print services) on an IIS server will severely impact the resources available to IIS services. It's a good idea to move such applications to a separate server so that IIS has full control of the machine's hardware resources.

Stopping Unnecessary Services

Every service running on Windows 2000 Server uses valuable system resources. Services that are not necessary to the functioning of your machine should either be stopped and set to start manually or disabled entirely.

Administrators should be fully aware of service dependencies before they begin to disable unnecessary services. A good practice is to disable services one at a time and to monitor the effect on system performance and integrity for a period of time before disabling the next service. To stop or disable a service, use the Services node in Computer Manager MMC snap-in. To view dependencies between services, double-click on the service you are studying and select the Dependencies tab on the service Property sheet.

The following services are *not required* on a dedicated IIS server.

- Alerter
- ClipBook Server
- DHCP Client
- Messenger
- Net Logon
- Network DDE
- Network DDE DSDM
- Network Monitor Agent

- NWLink NetBIOS
- NWLink IPX/SPX Compatible Transport
- Spooler
- TCP/IP NetBIOS Helper
- UPS

The following services may be required for *specific purposes.*

- RPC Locator (required for remote administration)
- Server (required for use of User Manager)
- Workstation (required if you are using remote UNC virtual roots)

Optimizing Use of IIS Logging

IIS logging slows server performance. It is a good idea to enable logging only on sites, virtual directories, and individual files that need to be logged for billing or performance monitoring purposes.

To disable logging on a site's home directory, a particular virtual directory, or an individual file, access the Property sheet for the object, select the Home Directory, Virtual Directory, or File tab, and clear the Log Access checkbox under Content Control.

To disable logging entirely for a Web site, access the site Property sheet, select the Web Site tab, and clear the Enable Logging checkbox.

Optimizing Use of SSL

SSL slows IIS performance significantly. SSL should be enabled only on sites and portions of sites where it is needed. For example, on a shopping site SSL could be enabled only for those Web pages that contain Web forms for users to submit their credit card information and disabled everywhere else on the site.

To disable SSL on a particular virtual directory or an individual file, access the Property sheet for the object, select the Directory Security or File Security tab, click Edit under Secure Communications, and clear the Require Secure Channel When Accessing This Resource Checkbox (this assumes that SSL has already been enabled on the server).

To disable SSL entirely for a Web site, access the site Property sheet, select the Directory Security tab, click Edit under Secure Communications, and clear the Require Secure Channel When Accessing This Resource checkbox.

Restricting Use of Bandwidth

If other network-intensive applications must run together with IIS on a single machine, you may need to restrict the total bandwidth used by IIS on the machine's network subsystem. To restrict bandwidth for all IIS services running on a machine, access the server Property sheet and check the Enable Bandwidth Throttling checkbox. Specify the limit for the network bandwidth that should be made available to all IIS Web and FTP sites on the machine.

Another situation that calls for restricted bandwidth is when an IIS server hosts several sites, one of which is extremely popular. To ensure that the other sites can be easily accessed under heavy load, you can restrict the bandwidth available to the popular site. To restrict the bandwidth for a particular site on an IIS server, access the site Property sheet, select the Performance tab, and check the Enable Bandwidth Throttling checkbox. Specify the limit for the network bandwidth that should be made available to the particular site.

If your IIS server is using more than 50 percent of its network bandwidth on a regular basis, you need to upgrade your network subsystem. Consider adding a second network card, upgrading to a faster card, or off-loading some of the server content to another server.

Restricting Processor Usage

If several out-of-process applications are running on the machine, you may need to restrict the processor usage of the applications running on IIS. To restrict processor usage for all IIS out-of-process applications running on a machine, access the server Property sheet and check the Enable Process Throttling checkbox. Specify the limit for the maximum CPU usage in percentage. If enforce limits is not checked, the only action that gets performed here is an event written to the Event Log when the limit is exceeded.

If your IIS server has several applications running on the machine causing high CPU utilization, you need to install additional CPUs, install load balancing, or upgrade the server.

Limiting Connections

Limiting connections to your IIS server is another method of conserving and managing network bandwidth. Limiting connections can be done only at the Web site (virtual server) level, not at the virtual directory or file level. To limit connections to a particular site on an IIS server, access the site Property sheet, select the Web Site tab, and under Connections select Limited To and specify the maximum number of simultaneous connections allowed as well as the Connection Timeout value. Because browsers typically form up to four simultaneous connections with a Web server when they connect to download files, the value specified in the Limited To textbox represents four times the maximum number of client browsers that can simultaneously connect to the server.

If a browser tries to connect to the server and then breaks off in midstream (for example, if the user waits five seconds for the connection and then clicks the Stop button on the browser—a typical occurrence), the server continues processing the connection request until the timeout occurs. A lower value of Connection Timeout will ensure that these broken connections are terminated more quickly, freeing resources for more connections to occur. Too low a value of Connection Timeout may terminate client connections before the client has completed downloading, resulting in a slower response at the client end.

Enabling HTTP Keep-Alives

HTTP Keep-Alives are enabled by default on all sites on an IIS server. This performance-enhancing function of IIS should be left enabled by administrators; only advanced developers might consider temporarily disabling this feature under certain specialized circumstances.

Optimizing Memory Usage Against Response Speed

IIS allows administrators to control how IIS uses memory in order to optimize the server's response speed to client requests. To optimize memory usage for response speed for a particular site on an IIS server, access the site Property sheet, select the Performance tab, and under Performance

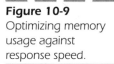

Figure 10-9
Optimizing memory
usage against
response speed.

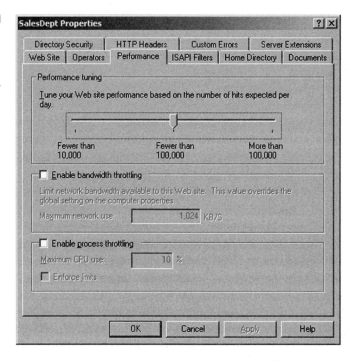

Tuning adjust the slide control so that the setting is *slightly higher* than the observed number of connections per day (see Figure 10-9). If the slide control is set *much higher* than the observed number of connections per day, the result will be an unnecessary expenditure of the server's memory resources and an overall drop in performance.

Optimizing Content Type

Response speed is dependent on the type of content residing on the Web server. Server performance can be improved by using the following content types *only when necessary:*

- Active Server Pages
- CGI scripts
- ISAPI applications
- Database queries
- Video files
- High-resolution JPEG image files

Optimizing Processor Usage

IIS services run in the background like other Windows 2000 services. Windows 2000 usually gives foreground applications a boost to ensure that they receive a large share of processor time so that they will be responsive to the user. IIS performance can be enhanced by disabling this boost.

To disable the processor boost for foreground applications on Windows 2000, access the System program in Control Panel to open the System Properties sheet, select the Advanced tab, click on the Performance Options button, and select the Background Services option in the *Application response* section (see Figure 10-10). This setting optimizes the server for running background services like IIS.

Use High-Performance Applications

Although not the administrator's job to write ASP code, a main culprit for performance problems on IIS is poorly written ASP code. Some key things to keep in mind when developing ASP pages are

- Reduced the amount of connections to network resources
- Avoid nesting HTML with ASP code. This causes IIS to have to parse out the logic from the ASP. It's best to develop the ASP to build a string and assign it to a varible, and at the end of the script processing, to do a write of the string.

Figure 10-10
Disabling the processor boost for foreground applications.

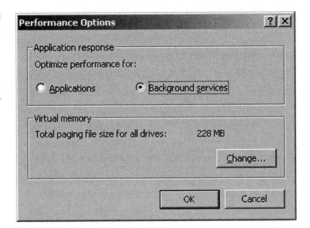

- Keep logic in objects rather than ASP script. Objects are compiled code and execute faster than interpreted ASP scripts.

- When obtaining information from databases, get all the data using one SQL statement if possible. Avoid using nested queries, which cause creating several recordsets per page and creating several connections over the network to SQL Server. Use disconnected recordset whenever possible.

- Avoid using session and application variables when possible. These variables are stored on IIS and require resources.

- Consider dividing applications into multiple tiers on several servers. For example, place your database on one server, COM+ services on another, do client-side data validation on the browser, and ASP scripting on another server.

- If the application uses extensive database activity consider ODBC connection pooling.

- Use the Performance monitor to find execessive errors for potential problems with ASP Scripts on IIS and notify the developers.

SUMMARY

The performance of IIS servers can be monitored using a variety of standard Windows 2000 tools. A variety of techniques can be used to enhance the performance of IIS servers under various conditions. An important part of the administrator's job is to monitor, maintain, and enhance the operation of IIS servers for both intranet and Internet use.

FOR MORE INFORMATION

Microsoft Web Site

Download the Web Capacity Analysis Tool from the following site

`www.microsoft.com/TechNet/download/wccat.asp`

Microsoft Newsgroups are a good place to hold discussions about such things as IIS 5.0 performance. Post an article to or lurk around the following newsgroup:

```
microsoft.public.inetserver.iis
```

Refer to the Microsoft TechNet article on ASP Best Practices for high performance scripting:

```
Windows Product Family | MS Windows 2000 | Resource Kit | Windows
2000 Internet Information Services Resource Guide | Appendix A -
ASP Best Practices
```

Refer to the Microsoft TechNet article on load balancing for distributing network load like IIS servers across multiple servers:

```
Windows Product Family | MS Windows 2000 | Resource Kit | Windows
2000 Server Distributed Systems Guide | Part 3 - Enterprise
Technologies | Chapter 19 - Network Load Balancing
```

Administering SSL with Certificate Services

Administrators concerned about IIS security have an additional option from those described in Chapter 4, "Administering Security." That option is to enable the *Secure Sockets Layer* (SSL) protocol for encrypted transfer of data between servers and clients. To simplify setting up and maintaining SSL, the Windows 2000 includes an additional tool called Certificate Services that provides administrators with the ability to issue, install, and revoke X.509 digital certificates. After completing this chapter, you will be able to

- Understand how SSL enables secure transactions between Web servers and clients
- Install and configure Certificate Services for issuing X.509 digital certificates
- Generate a certificate request and public/private key pair
- Submit the certificate request to a Certificate Authority and install the received certificate on the server
- Use HTML tools to request a certificate
- Enable SSL on virtual servers and virtual directories
- Install a Certificate Authority certificate on a browser's root store

Understanding Secure Sockets Layer

Secure Sockets Layer version 3.0 (SSL 3.0) is a protocol that enables encrypted sessions between browser clients and Web servers. SSL makes use of *public key cryptography,* a mechanism that uses two encryption keys to ensure that the session is secure:

- A *public key,* which can be given to any application or user that requests it
- A *private key,* which is known only to its owner

In addition to the public/private key pair, SSL makes use of *digital certificates,* which are files issued by Certificate Authorities, which act as a kind of identity card for the application or user. Digital certificates are text files that contain information that identifies an application or user. The certificate also contains the public key of the application or user.

A *Certificate Authority* (CA) is a trusted agency responsible for confirming the identity of the application or user and issuing a digital certificate for identity purposes. An example of a third-party Certificate Authority is *VeriSign:*

`www.verisign.com`

Alternatively, Internet Information Services administrators can use Microsoft Certificate Services to act as their own Certificate Authority, issuing and revoking digital certificates within their organization as required.

Certificates installed on IIS servers to provide proof of identity for the servers are called *server certificates.* Those installed on client browsers are called *client certificates.* Both server and client certificates have to be signed (verified to be authentic) by a Certificate Authority. The certificate used to identify the Certificate Authority as being who it says it is is called a *site certificate,* or *CA certificate,* and is signed by the CA itself.

Certificates can expire and can be *revoked* if necessary. The CA keeps a list of revoked certificates called the *Certificate Revocation List,* which may be used to check the identity of digital certificate holders.

How SSL Works

In SSL sessions all data passing between the client and the server is encrypted. An SSL session is established by a series of steps outlined in the following series of diagrams. In Figure 11-1, a client establishes a connection to a server. After a connection is established, the server sends the browser its public key and server certificate (see Figure 11-2). At this point,

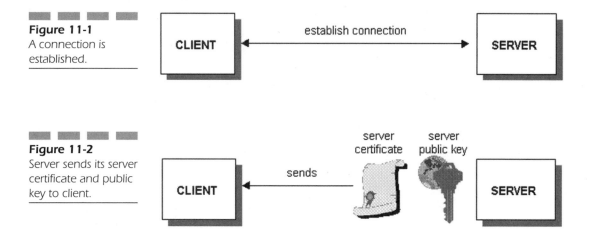

Figure 11-1
A connection is established.

Figure 11-2
Server sends its server certificate and public key to client.

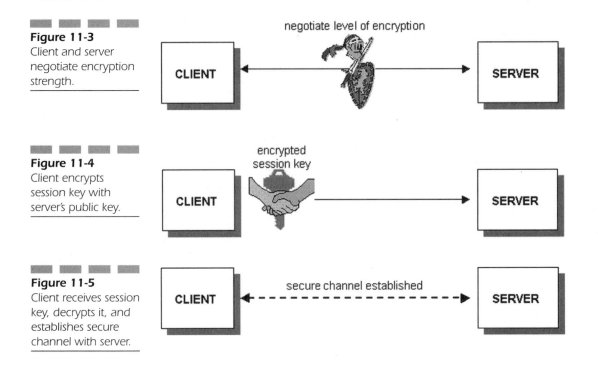

Figure 11-3
Client and server
negotiate encryption
strength.

Figure 11-4
Client encrypts
session key with
server's public key.

Figure 11-5
Client receives session
key, decrypts it, and
establishes secure
channel with server.

the server and client discuss and decide on the level of encryption to be used in encrypting the transmitted data (see Figure 11-3).

When an encryption strength has been decided on, the client creates a session key, which will be used to encrypt data during the current SSL session. The client takes the session key it created and encrypts it using the server's public key. The client then sends the encrypted session key to the server (see Figure 11-4). If anyone were to capture the session key at this stage, they would not be able to use it, because it can be decrypted by only the server's private key, which only the server possesses.

The server receives the encrypted session key and uses its private key to decrypt it. Both the client and the server now possess the session key, and they use this to establish a secure channel for sending data to one another (see Figure 11-5).

Finally, the client and server exchange data with each other, first encrypting then decrypting the data with their session keys (see Figure 11-6).

Implementing SSL on IIS 5.0

In order to enable an SSL session between a client browser and an IIS server, the following is required:

Figure 11-6
Secure channel for
transmitting data is
now established.

- The Web server requires a server certificate from a trusted CA.

- The server certificate must be installed on the server.

- SSL must be enabled on the selected virtual server (or virtual directory on the server) using the Directory Security tab on the virtual server's Property sheet.

- The client browser must add the CA certificate to its root store so that it can verify the authenticity of the server's certificate.

- The client must access the SSL-enabled server using a secure URL beginning with `https://`.

This process will be illustrated in the walkthrough later on in this chapter.

Understanding Certificate Services

Microsoft Certificate Services provides administrators with the ability to issue, install, and revoke standard X.509 digital certificates. These certificates can be used to provide trusted verification of the identity of users of your corporate intranet, extranet, or Internet storefront.

Certificate Server can process standard *Public-Key Cryptography Standards* (PKCS) 10 certificate requests and issue standard X.509 certificates in response. Certificate Server is also extensible and can support other certificate formats by using third-party extensions.

Certificate Services includes tools for administering, logging, and revoking digital certificates for servers, clients, and other CAs. Clients supported include Internet Explorer 2.0 and higher and Netscape Navigator 3.0 and higher. A server log (database) contains a record of all certificates requested, issued, and revoked by Certificate Server.

Certificate Services is a Windows 2000 service that runs continually in the background and takes full advantage of Windows 2000 stability, security features, and reliability.

Installing Certificate Services

Prior to installing Certificate Services, you need to create a shared folder for Certificate Services to use to store its Certificate Authority certificates and various configuration files (for example, C:\CA shared with read permission for everyone). It must be shared so that clients can access and install CA certificates from it. The shared folder must be stored on the local machine where Certificate Services is installed.

To install Certificate services, click Start, Programs, Add/Remove Programs and click on Add/Remove Windows Components. When the Windows Components Wizard (see Figure 11-7) comes up, select Certificate Services. A dialog will appear warning you that the computer cannot be added or removed from a domain after installing Certificate Services (see Figure 11-8). Click Yes and click Next.

In the next screen (see Figure 11-9), you need to specify the type of authority that this server will be. In this example the server is not a member of an Active Directory domain, so the Enterprise options are disabled. The available options are

Figure 11-7
Selecting Certificate Services in the Windows Components Wizard.

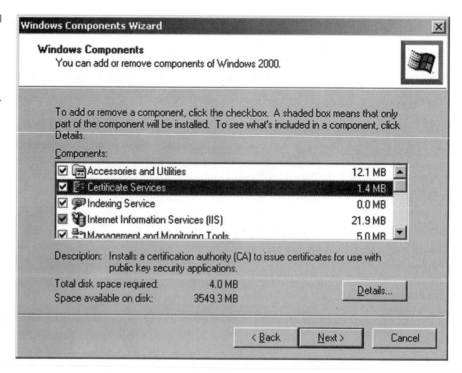

Figure 11-8
Dialog informing that
the computer cannot
be renamed after
installing Certificate
Services.

Figure 11-8
Dialog informing that
the computer cannot
be renamed after
installing Certificate
Services.

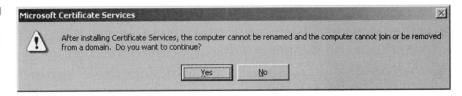

Figure 11-9
Specifying the
Certificate Authority
type.

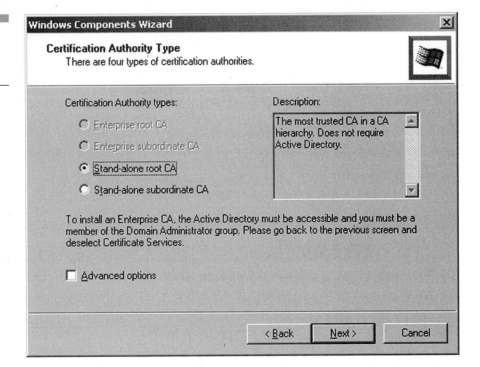

- *Enterprise root CA*   Integrated with Active Directory to determine
  identity of requestor. Used commonly with intranets where users will
  be members of the Active Directory domain.

- *Enterprise subordinate CA*   Subordinate authority to an existing root
  authority. Must obtain a CA from a root authority.

- *Stand-alone root CA*   By default requests will be sent to a pending
  queue and then on to an administrator who can approve or deny. This
  option does not require Active Directory services to be present and can
  be used with third-party directory services.

■ *Stand-alone subordinate CA*   Subordinate authority to an existing root authority; must obtain a CA from a root authority. This option does not require Active Directory.

The Advanced Options checkbox allows selection of hashing algorithms and cryptographic service providers and configuration of Certificate Authority hierarchies.

In this example, Stand-alone root CA is selected for a stand-alone Web server. Click Next to continue.

Click Next and specify identification information for the Certificate Server (see Figure 11-10). Click next to continue.

In the next screen, you need to specify the shared folder you created earlier as the Configuration Data Storage Location for Certificate Service (see Figure 11-11). You can also change the locations of the certificate store database and log locations, which by default are in

```
C:\winnt\System32\CertLog
```

Click Next, and the Completing Installation screen appears. Certificate server now installs on the local machine, and the following tasks are automatically performed:

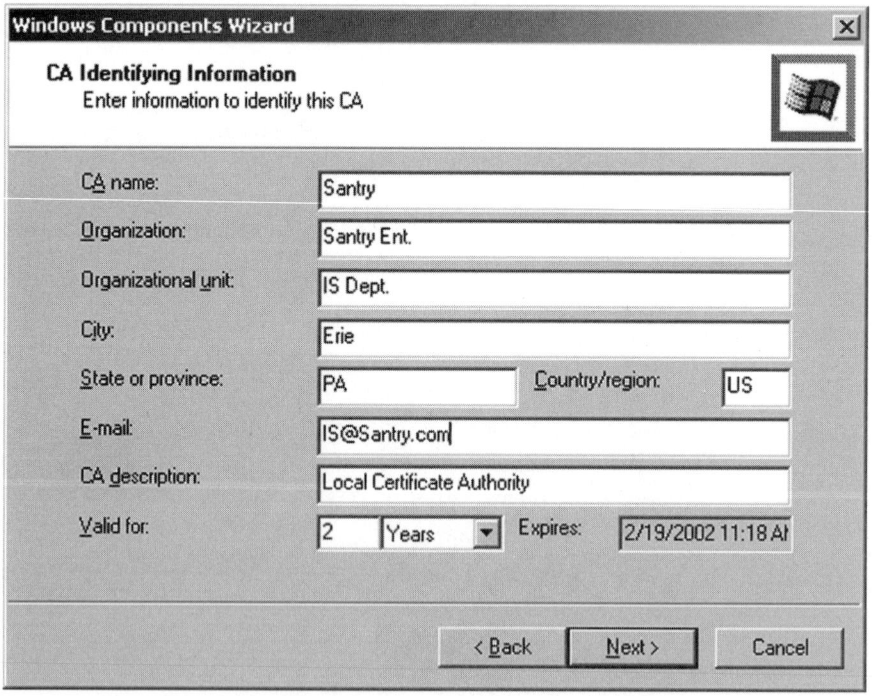

Figure 11-10
Specify identification information for Certificate Services.

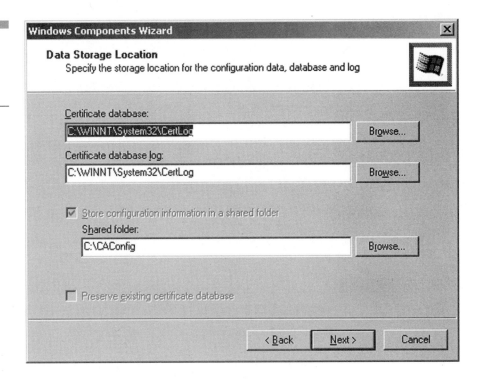

- Certificate Server program files are installed in

  `C:\winnt\System32`

- HTML tools for Web-based certificate requests are installed in

  `C:\winnt\System32\CertSrv`

  and this physical directory is mapped to a new virtual root:

  `/CertSrv`

- A self-signed root certificate is created and installed in the certificate storage location. A *root certificate* is one that identifies the *Certificate Authority* (CA) and is signed by the CA itself or by a root authority (also a CA) higher up in the CA hierarchy.

- A public/private key pair is created and saved in the key repository.

- Certificate Server is added to the Certificate Authority Certificate List Web page, stored in

  `C:\winnt\System32\CertSrv\CertEnroll\cacerts.htm`

  and also in the shared folder.

- The following three files are saved in the shared location (C:\CAConfig):

Certificate Server's configuration file, `CertSrv.txt`

Certificate Server's signature certificate,
`<servername>_<CA_name>.crt`

Certificate Server's key exchange certificate,
`<servername>_<CA_name>_Exchange.crt`

- The Certificate Authority service is installed in the list of system services. The Certificate Authority service is set to start automatically using the System account on Windows 2000 startup.

Click Finish, and the Certificate Services will start. Later in this chapter we will go through the process of approving certificate requests using the Certificate Services Manager MMC snap-in.

Walkthrough: Creating and Installing a Site Certificate

In order to manage certificate requests we will first create a request for our certificate server. The following walkthrough takes us through the process of

- Generating a certificate request file for a server. A *certificate request file* is an ASCII text file that contains encrypted information used to obtain a digital certificate.

- Submitting the request file and generating a server certificate. A *server certificate* identifies the server (or virtual server) to browser clients and enables these clients to connect to the server through SSL.

- Installing the server certificate and enabling SSL on a Web site.

- Enabling the client to recognize the server's Certificate Authority so that SSL communication can take place.

The process illustrated in the following section will work both with a local CA like Microsoft Certificate Services and a trusted third-party CA like VeriSign.

Begin by creating a new Web site on the IIS 5.0 server and placing some Web content in the site's home directory (we created the site `SalesDept` and assigned it the IP address `192.168.0.54`).

Creating a Key Pair and Certificate Request

Open the Internet Services Manager (MMC), select the virtual root (here SalesDept), right-click on the Web and select Properties, click on the Directory Security tab, and click the Server Certificate button (see Figure 11-12). This will start the Web Server Certificate Wizard; click Next to begin the Wizard.

In the first screen (see Figure 11-13), select the *Create a new certificate* option. Click next to continue.

Administrators have a choice of two ways (see Figure 11-14) of creating keys:

Figure 11-12

The Directory Security tab in the IIS Web site properties sheet.

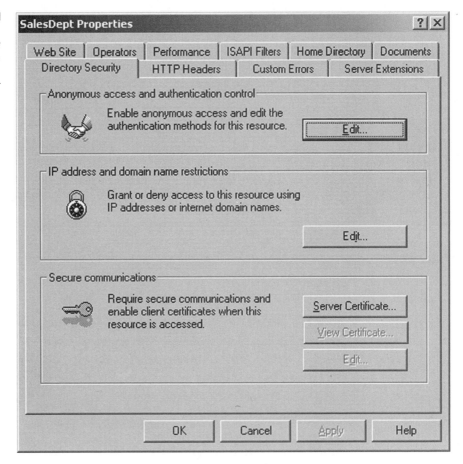

Figure 11-13
Creating a new
certificate request in
the Web Server
Certificate Wizard.

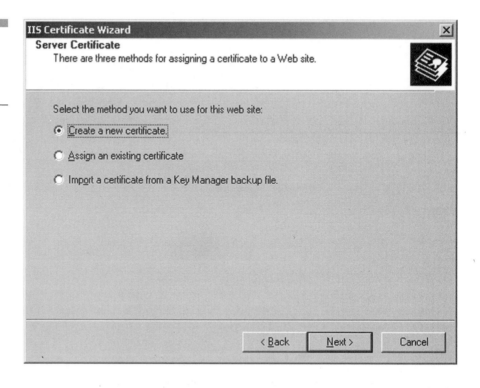

Figure 11-13
Creating a new
certificate request in
the Web Server
Certificate Wizard.

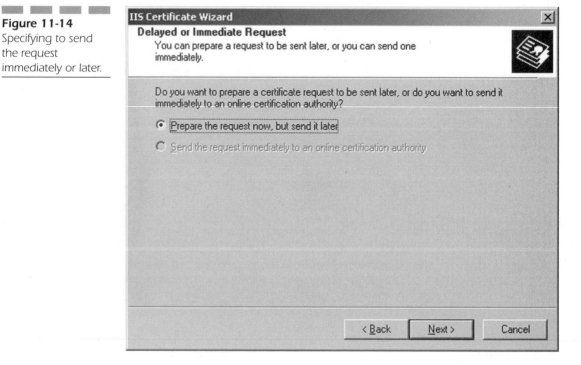

Figure 11-14
Specifying to send
the request
immediately or later.

- Select *Put the Request in a File That You Will Send to an Authority* if the Certificate Authority is a trusted third-party company like VeriSign.
- Select *Automatically Send the Request to an Online Authority* if you have Microsoft Certificate Server or some other CA server installed on your network.

We will select the first option because it works in both cases and illustrates how to send a certificate request to a remote authority like VeriSign. Click Next to continue.

The next screen of the wizard (see Figure 11-15) requests you to

- Assign the key a name (here SalesDept)
- Assign the key a bit length (Longer bit lengths are more secure but take longer to authenticate.)

The next few screens of the Wizard ask for the following information (in parentheses is what we submitted):

- *Organization*   The legal name of your company (Santry Ent.).
- *Organizational Unit*   The division in your company responsible for digital certificate security (Sales Dept).

Figure 11-15
Specifying a name for the certificate request and bit value.

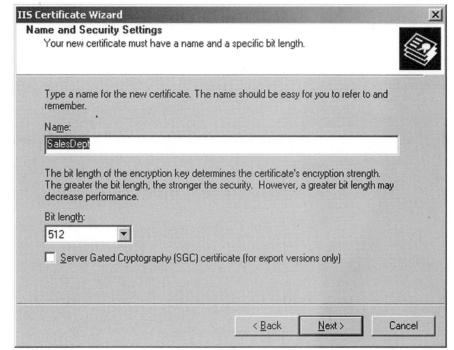

- *Common Name* The fully qualified domain name (FQDN) for the server (here being `server1.santry.com`). Note that using the FQDN here for the Common Name implies that DNS is being used on your network for name resolution (see the Note later in this section on common names and FQDNs)

- *Country* here United States (US).

- *State/Province* here Pennsylvania (PA).

- *City* (Erie).

Specify the location for the new certificate request.

A new directory called `C:\CertTest` was first created to hold the generated certificate request file. The default name, `NewKeyRq.txt`, is used for the certificate request file to be generated.

Next you are informed that

- A certificate request will now be created.

- The key will be installed in Key Manager but requires a valid certificate to be activated.

Click Finish to generate the key pair and request file. The next screen will inform you that the request file has been generated and is stored in the location you earlier specified (see Figure 11-16). It will also provide you with a link to various certificate authorities with which you can complete your certificate request.

The newly created certificate request file, `C:\CertTest\NewKeyRq.txt`, contains the new encrypted certificate request string (see Figure 11-17). This file conforms to the standard PKCS 10 certificate request format. Open the certificate request file using Notepad, select all the text, and choose Edit, Copy to copy this highlighted text to the clipboard.

Submitting a Certificate Request File to a Certificate Authority

At this point, if we were going to request our server certificate from a trusted third-party organization like VeriSign, we would access a certificate request HTML form on a Web page, paste the clipboard text into the HTML form, and submit it. An alternative would be to email the clipboard text to the appropriate email address. See VeriSign's Web site:

`www.verisign.com`

Figure 11-16
Completing the
Wizard to create the
certificate request.

Figure 11-17
The certificate
request file, which
will be used to
request a certificate.

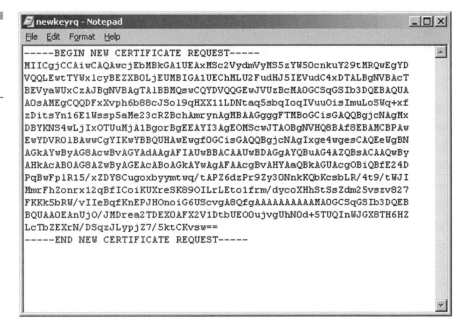

Instead, we will use our HTML-based Certificate Web site to submit the certificate request to Certificate Services.

Open the Certificate Services HTML page using Internet Explorer on the machine where Certificate Services is installed by opening the following URL:

```
http://localhost/certsrv
```

Select the Request a Certificate option (see Figure 11-18) and then click the Next button to continue.

In this screen (see Figure 11-19) select the Advanced option and click the Next button to continue.

In this screen (see Figure 11-20) select how to submit your certificate request. To use the key you just generated in IIS, select the second option to submit the key file. Click Next to continue.

Click in the text area, paste the clipboard contents into the HTML form, and click Submit to submit your certificate request to Certificate Services (Figure 11-21).

In this last screen (see Figure 11-22), you will be notified that your request has been received and is pending approval by the certificate authority.

Figure 11-18
The HTML Certificate Request page.

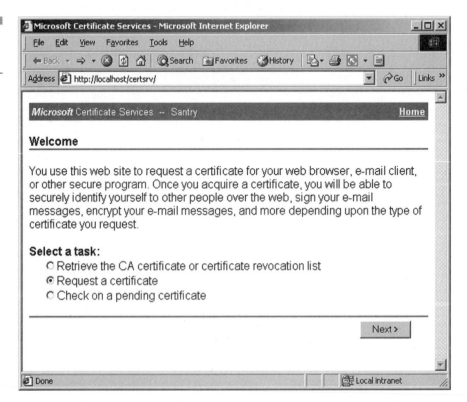

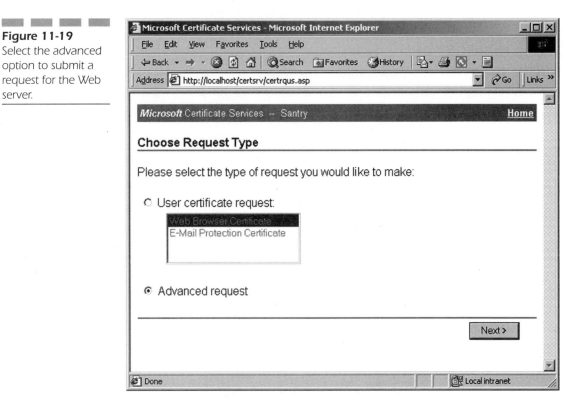

Figure 11-19
Select the advanced
option to submit a
request for the Web
server.

Certificate Server Tools

Microsoft Certificate Services is administered using the MMC administration by going to start, programs, administrative tools, Certification Authority.

The Certification Authority MMC snap-in is shown in (see Figure 11-23) and has the following four nodes under the root authority:

- *Revoked Certificates*   This node contains all certificates that have been issued and then revoked.
- *Issued Certificates*   This node contains all certificates that have been approved and issued by the certificate services administrator.
- *Pending Requests*   This node contains all pending certificate requests to your root authority. To approve requests right click on the certificate.
- *Failed Requests*   This node contains any declined requests.

To approve the recent request submitted to Certificate Services, select the Pending Requests node in the MMC. In the right pane of the MMC, you

Figure 11-20
Specifying how to
submit the certificate
request.

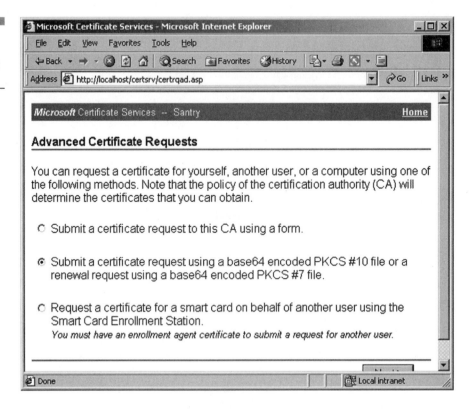

will see the information that you provided when creating the request. Right-click on the request and select All Tasks, Issue from the context menu.

Now select the Issued Certificates node from the left pane of the MMC and see that the request has been placed in this folder and is a certificate. If you were to deny the request, it would have been placed in the Failed Requests node. You can also revoke certificates, which then will be placed in the Revoked Certificates node. In the next section we will install the newly approved certificate on a virtual server in IIS.

Installing a Server Certificate

Open the Certificate Services HTML (see Figure 11-18) page using Internet Explorer on the machine where Certificate Services is installed by opening the following URL:

```
http://localhost/certsrv
```

Figure 11-21
Paste the certificate request key into the form.

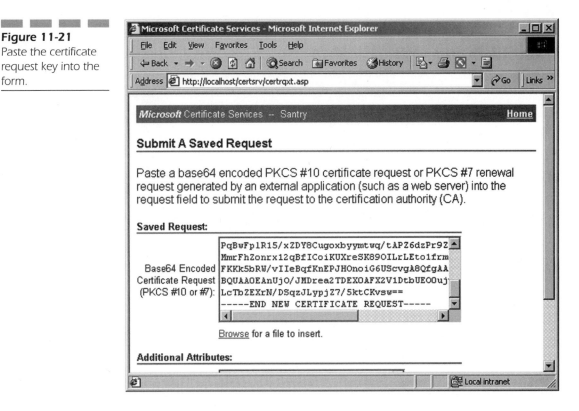

Select the Check On A Pending Certificate option and click on the Next button.

Select the pending request from the select box (see Figure 11-24) and click on the Next button to continue.

In the screen shown in Figure 11-25, select base64 encoding for the file download and then click on the Download CA Certificate link to begin the download process. A dialog will appear; select to save the file and place it in the `c:\CertTest\` directory.

Now that we have received the server certificate file from the certificate authority, the next step is to install the new server certificate on our virtual server so that we can enable SSL for accessing it.

If it is not still running, open the IIS Manager MMC snap-in and expand the server node. Select the SalesDept virtual server. Right-click and select Properties from the context menu to open the SalesDept Properties dialog. Select the Directory Security tab (see Figure 11-12) and click on the Server Certificate button to start the Web Server Certificate Wizard. Click on the Next button to begin installing the certificate.

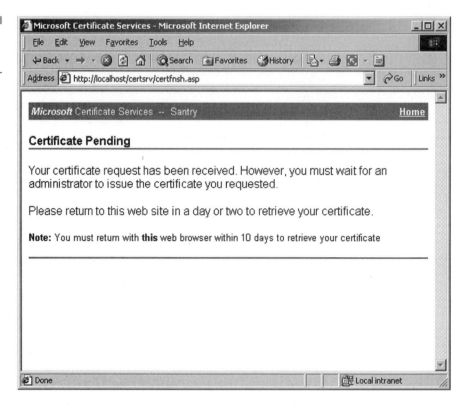

In this screen (Figure 11-26), select the Process A Pending Request and Install Certificate option. Click on the Next button to continue.

In this screen (see Figure 11-27), select the newly created certificate, C:\CertTest\newcert.cer, and click the Next button to view a summary of the certificate. Click Next and then Finish to complete the installation of the certificate on this virtual server.

Enabling SSL on a Virtual Server

Next we will enable SSL on the virtual server SalesDept. In the MMC, right-click on the SalesDept node and select Properties to open up the SalesDept Properties sheet. With the Web site tab selected, assign the number 443 as the SSL Port number. This is the default port for secure communications (see Figure 11-28).

Next select the Directory Security tab. Under Secure Communications, select the Edit button to open the Secure Communications dialog box. Place

Figure 11-23
The Certificate
Services Manager
MMC snap-in.

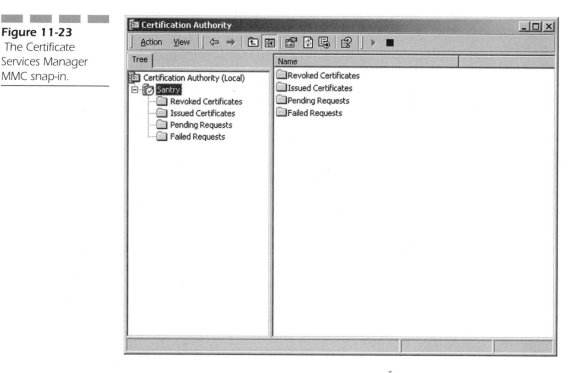

a checkmark in the checkbox labeled *Require Secure Channel When Accessing This Resource*. This action enables SSL for the selected virtual server (see Figure 11-29). This dialog box can also be used to determine what happens if the browser accessing the secure Web site has a client certificate installed. The three options are

- *Do Not Accept Client Certificates* (default)   If the client browser has a client certificate installed, an `Access Denied` message will be returned.

- *Accept Certificates*   It makes no difference to the server whether the client browser has a client certificate installed or not; access is granted in either case.

- *Require Client Certificates*   Unless a client has a valid certificate granted by the root CA (here Certificate Server), access will be denied.

This dialog box may also be used to map client certificates to users' Windows 2000 accounts and creating a trust list. Leave the default setting here and click ok twice.

Figure 11-24
Selecting the
processed request
from the CA.

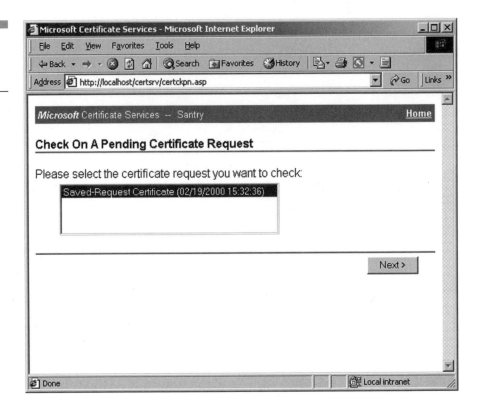

Adding the CA Certificate to the Root Store of the Client Browser

Finally, before SSL communication can take place between the client browser and the Web site, the client must be able to recognize the server's certificate as valid. To do this, the client must contact the server's Certificate Authority, which in this case is the local Certificate Server. In this example, note that our client is Internet Explorer 5.0.

If you fail to perform the preceding step and instead try to connect directly to the SSL Web site using the secure HTTPS URL, `https://server1.santry.com`, you will first receive the normal and expected Security Alert message (see Figure 11-30). Click ok. A message saying that the certificate issuer is untrusted will appear (see Figure 11-31). This occurs because the client cannot verify the server's certificate because it does not yet recognize the CA's root certificate. Click Yes to proceed and enable SSL for this connection.

Figure 11-25
Specifying download options.

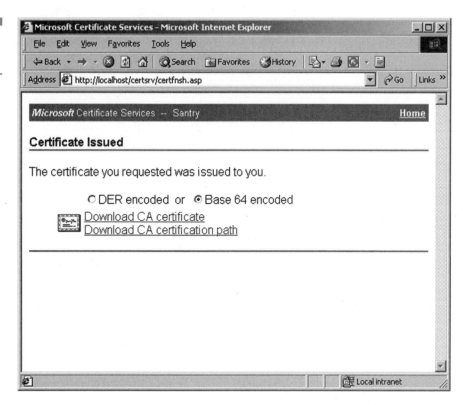

To avoid having a notice come up every time you access the site, the client browser needs to acquire and install the root CA certificate for the CA that issued a certificate to the server. Once this root CA certificate is loaded into the browser, the browser is able to verify the server's certificate and form an SSL connection to the server.

NOTE: *Note that we are trying here to connect to the SSL-enabled virtual server using the* fully qualified domain name *(FQDN) of the virtual server. In other words, on the corporate DNS server, there is a host record mapping the FQDN,* server1.santry.com, *to the virtual server's IP address,* 192.168.0.54.

This is important because at the beginning of this walkthrough to generate the certificate request, we defined the Common Name of the server as server1.santry.com.

Figure 11-26
Installing a new
certificate using the
IIS Certificate Wizard.

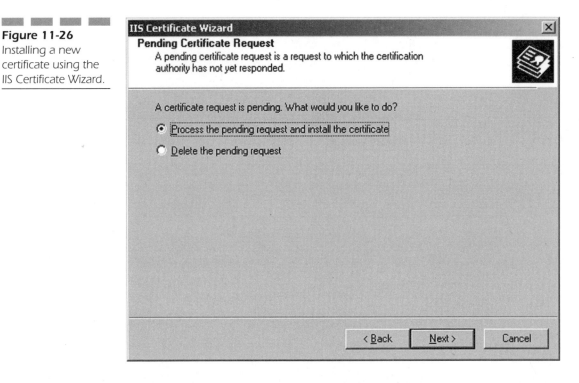

Figure 11-27
Specifying a path to
the certificate.

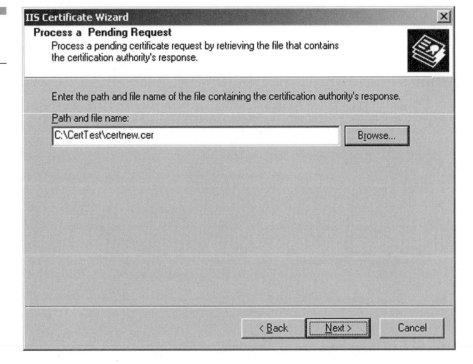

Figure 11-28
Assign the default
port number 443 to
SSL.

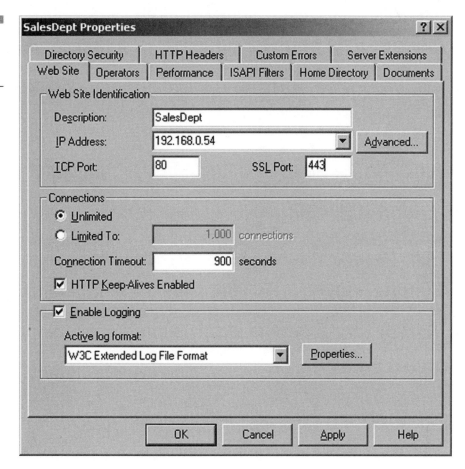

Entering this as the Common Name assumes that we are using DNS to resolve FQDNs in all URLs. Had we wanted to be able to access the secure site by its IP address alone, e.g., `http://192.168.0.54,` *we would have had to define* `192.168.0.54` *as the common name when we created the key pair and certificate request.*

To accomplish verification, the client browser needs to install the certificate in the Trusted Root Store of the browser. To install the the certificate click the View Certificate button (see Figure 11-31) when the security alert dialog is presented when accessing the virtual server via Internet Explorer. This will bring up a dialog (see Figure 11-32) containing information for the certificate. Click the Install Certificate button to start the Certificate Import Wizard. Click next to begin the Wizard.

Figure 11-29
Check the checkbox
to enable SSL on the
virtual server.

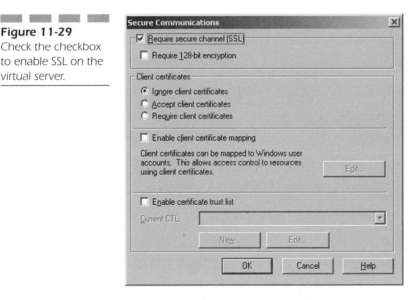

Figure 11-30
Security alert
message seen when
you are accessing a
secure site.

Figure 11-31
The certificate issuer
is untrusted.

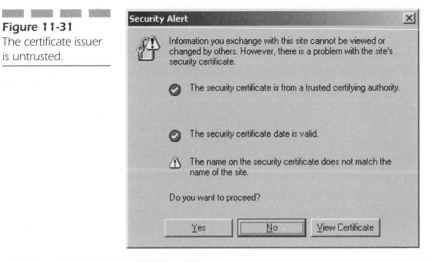

Figure 11-32
Viewing certificate
information.

In this screen (Figure 11-33) select the default option to automatically place the certificate in the appropriate store. Click Next and then Finish to complete the Wizard (see Fig 11-34) and add the certificate as a trusted root.

You can confirm that the certificate has been added to the root store by selecting Tools, Internet Options (for IE 5.0), selecting the Content tab, clicking the Certificates button, and selecting the Intermediate Certification Authorities tab (see Figure 11-35).

Figure 11-33
The Certificate Import
Wizard of Internet
Explorer 5.0.

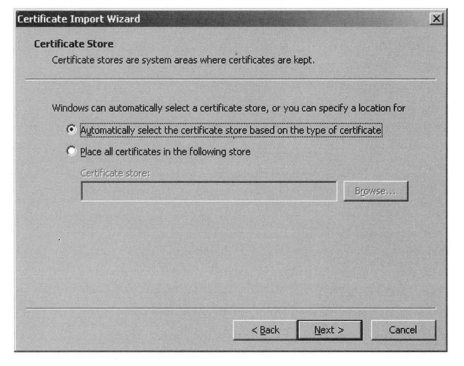

Figure 11-33
The Certificate Import
Wizard of Internet
Explorer 5.0.

Figure 11-34
Completing the
installation of the CA
Root.

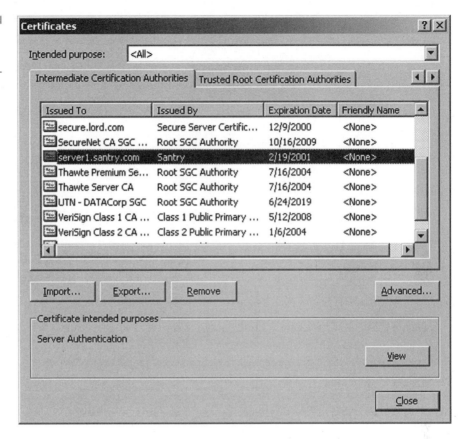

Figure 11-35
Viewing Root CAs in
Internet Explorer 5.0.

Finally, test the SSL-enabled site SalesDept with the CA-enabled browser by opening the secure HTTPS URL:

```
https://server1.santry.com
```

The home page of the SSL-enabled site should load without any security alerts.

SUMMARY

By using Microsoft Certificate Services and IIS 5.0 SSL capabilities, clients and servers can establish secure channels to encrypt all data transmissions between them. This chapter has illustrated the steps involved in enabling an SSL session between clients and servers.

FOR MORE INFORMATION

Search the following Microsoft Web site for the topics "SSL" and "Certificate" for more information on these topics:

```
www.microsoft.com
```

The best newsgroup to post questions relating to SSL and Certificate Server is

```
microsoft.public.inetserver.iis
```

More on Certificate Services can be found on the TechNet CD at

```
Windows Product Family | MS Windows 2000 | MS Windows 2000 Server
| Resource Kit | Windows 2000 Server Distributed Systems Guide |
Part 2 - Distributed Security | Chapter 16
```

Other WWW Sites

Be sure to visit VeriSign's site at

```
www.verisign.com
```

Administering the SMTP Service

Introduction

The SMTP service running on Microsoft Internet Information Services 5.0 allows administrators to set up, maintain, and administer an SMTP service for sending and receiving messages over the Internet. After completing this chapter, you will be able to

- Understand how the SMTP service on IIS 5.0 works
- Install the SMTP service on IIS 5.0
- Administer the SMTP service using the MMC
- Configure the various SMTP service properties
- Create new local and remote SMTP domains
- Create a message and send it using the SMTP service
- Monitor and tune the performance of the SMTP service

Understanding the SMTP Service

The Microsoft SMTP service on IIS 5.0 fully supports the *Simple Mail Transfer Protocol (SMTP)* and is compatible with most SMTP servers and clients. It is ideally suited for building Internet applications that use SMTP. For example, you could use it for an Active Server Pages application that mails a response to a user who submits a form. In general, its purpose in being included in IIS is to provide an outbound mail service for applications that are designed to be mail-aware. It is *not* intended for use as a general-purpose Internet mail server for corporate or ISP use.

The SMTP service on IIS 5.0 can

- Support hundreds of simultaneous connections
- Support multiple domains on one server
- Receive mail from other applications or SMTP servers
- Send mail to other SMTP servers
- Support encrypted SSL security
- Restrict unsolicited commercial email

The SMTP service does *not* include

- Support for POP3 or IMAP
- Support for personal mailboxes for users

How the SMTP Service Works

When the SMTP service is installed as part of IIS, it creates a default folder structure that it uses to send and receive messages. This structure is shown in Figure 12-1.

The folder located at

```
C:\Inetpub\Mailroot
```

contains the various subfolders used by the SMTP service for sending and receiving messages. The Mailroot folder has five subfolders in addition to two undocumented subfolders. These subfolders are used by the SMTP service as follows:

- *Badmail*   This folder is used to store messages that are undeliverable and cannot be returned to the sender.

- *Drop*   This folder is the drop box for all incoming messages to the SMTP service on IIS.

Figure 12-1
The default folder structure created when SMTP service is installed on Windows 2000.

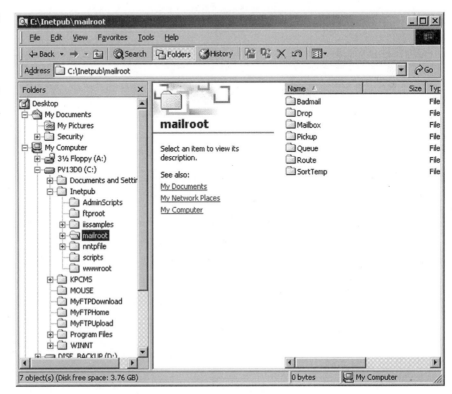

- *Pickup* This folder is monitored continuously by the SMTP service, which will send any messages that are placed in it. If a message is placed here, it is immediately moved to the Queue folder for further processing.

- *Queue* This folder holds messages that SMTP is unable to send because of bad connections or busy servers. Messages held here are monitored at intervals until they can be sent; otherwise, they are reported as undeliverable and moved to the Badmail folder.

- *SortTemp* This folder is created during setup to hold temporary files.

- *Route* This folder is not covered in the IIS 5.0 documentation, but seems to be involved in the process of configuring a *route domain,* which is a specific delivery path for a selected domain.

- *Mailbox* This folder is also undocumented. It is not clear what it is used for—in this release, the SMTP service for IIS 5.0 does *not* support mailboxes. Its functionality will probably be enabled in a future release.

SMTP is a protocol for delivering mail from server to server. To understand how the SMTP service on IIS 5.0 works, we will separately examine what happens to incoming mail and outgoing mail.

How the SMTP Service Processes Mail

The following is a somewhat simplified presentation of how the SMTP service is used to deliver mail. Mail messages can originate from two sources (see Figure 12-2):

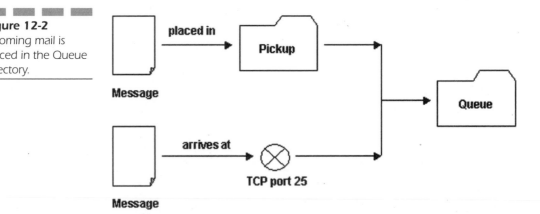

Figure 12-2
Incoming mail is placed in the Queue directory.

1. Messages can be manually created using a text editor and then copied to the directory.

   `C:\Mailroot\pickup`

   When the SMTP service detects that a message has been placed in its Pickup directory, it forwards the message to the Queue directory, where it is automatically processed for delivery to its final destination, which may be either local or remote.

2. Messages may also enter the SMTP service using TCP port number 25 (the default port for SMTP) and be forwarded to the Queue directory, where they are processed and forwarded to another mail server along the route to the final destination.

What happens next to the mail depends on whether its destination is the local SMTP service running on IIS 5.0 or whether it needs to be relayed to another SMTP server to reach its remote destination (see Figure 12-3).

If the message's destination is local, the SMTP service moves the message from the Queue directory to the Drop directory. At that point, the SMTP has finished the message delivery. There is no support in this release

Figure 12-3
How the SMTP
service delivers mail.

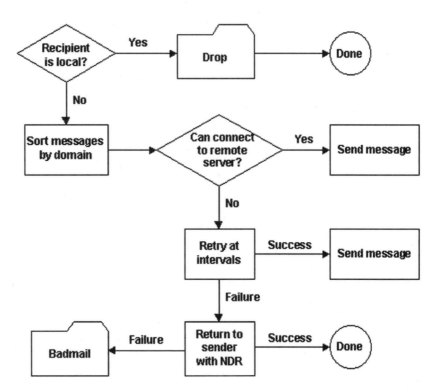

of Microsoft's SMTP service for delivering messages to personal mailboxes, or for creating and configuring such mailboxes.

If the message's destination is remote, the SMTP service sorts the message according to its destination domain. This is done so the service can pipeline messages by sending multiple messages to a single destination domain using only one connection, which enhances the performance of the SMTP service.

After the message is sorted, the SMTP service tries to connect to the destination mail server. If the mail server fails to respond or indicates that it is not ready to receive the message, the message stays in the Queue folder and the SMTP service attempts to deliver the message at predefined intervals.

If after a predetermined number of tries the SMTP service fails to deliver the message, the service attempts to connect to the SMTP server that sent the message to return it to its sender. If it is successful in forming this connection, the message is returned to the sender along with a *nondelivery report* (NDR) outlining the reasons for the failure.

If the SMTP service can neither deliver the message nor return it to its sender, it moves the message to the Badmail directory. At that point, the SMTP service has finished its job.

Installing the SMTP Service

The SMTP service is automatically installed on Windows 2000 as part of the IIS 5.0 installation. However, if you performed a *custom* installation of Windows 2000 and did not install the SMTP service, you can install it later by running the Add/Remove Programs application and installing Windows Components.

The hardware and software requirements for installing the Microsoft SMTP service are the same as those for installing IIS 5.0: Windows 2000 Server.

In addition, it is recommended that you install your Mailroot directory on an NTFS partition and make sure there is enough free space to hold your SMTP message queue.

To install the SMTP service, click Start, Settings, Control Panel, Add/Remove Programs. When the initial screen appears, click Add/Remove Windows Components on the left side of the dialog box. The Windows Components Wizard will appear. Select *Internet Information Services* (IIS) and

Figure 12-4
Select the SMTP
Service for
installation.

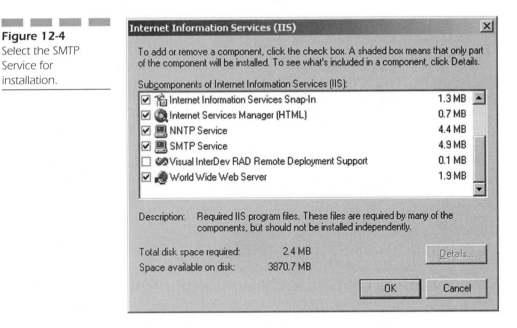

click the Details button to open the *Internet Information Services* (IIS) component box (Figure 12-4). Check the SMTP Service checkbox and click OK and then Next to continue with the setup.

The result of installing the SMTP service is a new node under the server node in the *Microsoft Management Console* (MMC) (see Figure 12-5). This new node is called *Default SMTP Virtual Server* and has two subnodes:

- *Domains* access property sheets for creating and configuring domains for the SMTP service.
- *Current Sessions* status information concerning current users, location of message source, and connection time since start of session.

Tools for Administering the SMTP Service

Windows 2000 provides three tools for administering and managing the SMTP service on IIS 5.0:

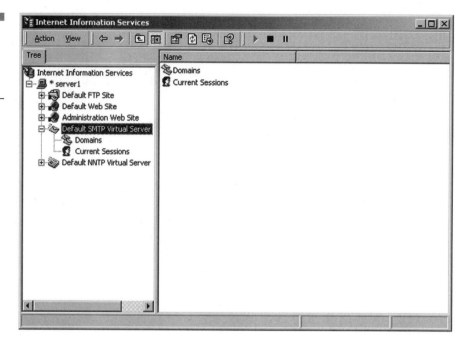

- *Internet Service Manager* The SMTP snap-in extension in the MMC allows full administration of any SMTP server on the local LAN.

- *Windows 2000 Terminal Services* Terminal Services is integrated into the Windows 2000 operating system. Terminal Services allow you to remotely administer your Windows 2000 services from a client running the Terminal Services client as if you were physically connected to the machine.

- *Windows Scripting Host (WSH)* This tool allows VBScript administration scripts to be run either from the graphical WSH utility (Wscript.exe) or from the command line (Cscript.exe).

This chapter deals only with using the MMC version of Internet Services Manager to administer the NNTP service. The Terminal Services session works identically to the MMC version except instead of using the actual MMC, your connection is being conducted via the terminal session. For information on administering SMTP through the WSH, refer to the Windows 2000 online documentation.

Various administrative tasks can be initiated and performed using the MMC version of the Internet Services Manager (see Figure 12-5). Most of these actions can be performed by selecting the Default SMTP Virtual Server node in the scope pane (left pane) and then either using the rebar buttons, accessing the Action drop-down menu, or right-clicking on the node and using the context menu.

- The default SMTP Virtual Server can be stopped, started, and paused.
  - *Stopping* the virtual server disconnects all currently connected users and allows no new connections to be established.
  - *Pausing* the virtual server allows no new connections to be established, but does not disconnect current connections.
  - *Starting* the virtual server allows new connections to be established with the server.
- Property sheets can be opened for the default SMTP site. These property sheets can be used to configure various aspects of the SMTP service and are described in the next section.
- Create a new domain. Domains in SMTP are different from Windows 2000 domains or DNS domains and are administrative objects for organizing mail for delivery.
- View current connections and domain information.
- Terminate all current connections.
- Connect to and administer SMTP Virtual Servers on other IIS 5.0 servers on the local LAN.

To verify that the SMTP service is running on an IIS 5.0 server, use the Services program in the Computer Manager.

NOTE: *Be careful when stopping the SMTP service, as it will close all connections, and mail being processed may fail to be delivered. If the SMTP service needs to be configured, it is better to pause the service, which doesn't affect current connections.*

Configuring the SMTP Service

The default SMTP Virtual Server is configured through property sheets, similar to the WWW and FTP sites running on IIS 5.0. The Default STMP

Virtual Server Properties sheet is opened by right-clicking the Default SMTP Virtual Server node in the Internet Services Manager and selecting Properties from the shortcut menu; it can also be opened using the Properties button on the rebar or the Action drop-down menu on the rebar.

The Default SMTP Virtual Server Properties sheet has six tabs that perform the following administrative functions:

- *General*   Configure site identification, IP address, TCP ports, maximum connections, and connections timeout, and enable logging.
- *Access*   Select anonymous user and grant operator privileges, configuring SSL, and IP restrictions.
- *Messages*   Limit message size and session size, limit number of messages per session and recipients per message, cc nondelivery report, specify Badmail directory.
- *Delivery*   Limit number of retries and retry interval for local and remote queue; limit maximum hop count; specify masquerade domain, fully qualified domain name, and smart host; perform reverse DNS lookup; configure authentication method for outgoing security.
- *LDAP Routing*   Configure a related *Lightweight Directory Access Protocol* (LDAP) server that will be used for this SMTP Virtual Server.
- *Security*   Grant operator privileges.

Configuring SMTP Virtual Server Identification

Using the SMTP General tab, specify the following information (see Figure 12-6):

- *Description*   This will appear beside the SMTP node in the MMC.
- *IP address*   Specify the IP address for the site. Click the Advanced button to open the Advanced Multiple SMTP Identities Configuration dialog box, where you can specify additional IP addresses and TCP port numbers for the SMTP site. These IP addresses must have already been bound to the network adapter by going to Start, Settings, Network and Dial-Up Connections.

Figure 12-6

The General tab on the Default SMTP Virtual Server Properties sheet.

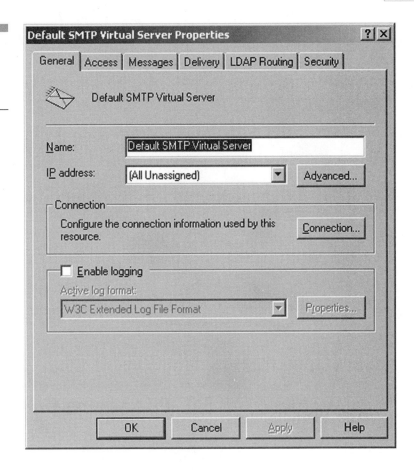

Configuring SMTP Incoming Connections

Incoming connections are made by remote SMTP servers connecting to the default SMTP site running on IIS in order to send mail. For these incoming connections, click the Connection button in the Default SMTP Virtual Server Properties dialog box (see Figure 12-6) to open the Connections dialog box, where you have two options (see Figure 12-7):

- *Limited to (number)* Simultaneous incoming connections may be unlimited or may be limited to a specified number (1,000 connections are suggested).

- *Connection time-out* The time-out for inactive connections can be specified (the default is 600 seconds or 10 minutes).

Figure 12-7
The Connections
dialog box.

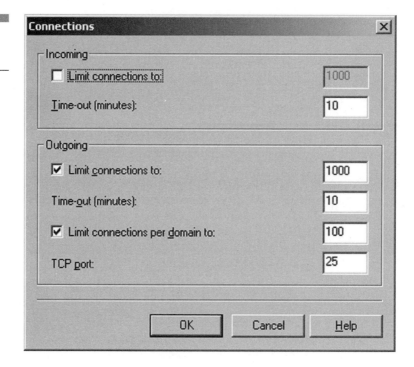

Configuring SMTP Outgoing Connections

Outgoing connections are made by the default SMTP Virtual Server running on IIS in order to connect and send mail to remote SMTP servers. For these outgoing connections, you can specify (see Figure 12-7)

- *TCP port number*   This is the TCP port that the default SMTP Virtual Server uses to connect to remote SMTP servers. The default SMTP port for outgoing connections is TCP port 25.

- *Limited to (number)*   Simultaneous outgoing connections can be unlimited or can be limited to a specific number (1000 connections are suggested).

- *Connection time-out*   The time-out for inactive connections can be specified (the default is 600 seconds or 10 minutes).

- *Limit connections per domain*   The number of simultaneous outgoing connections made to specific domain can be unlimited or can be limited to a specific number (100 connections are suggested). This number cannot be greater than the maximum number of simultaneous outgoing connections allowed.

Configuring SMTP Logging

Logging may be enabled or disabled for SMTP. Any of the four standard logging formats described in Chapter 3 may be selected and enabled here (see Figure 12-6).

NOTE: *If you enable logging on SMTP and select the default settings, the SMTP events logged will be added to those of the WWW and other services running on IIS. You may want to configure a separate log file for each service running on IIS to keep separate and easily interpreted records. Do this by logging SMTP logs to a separate directory from the other service log files.*

Configuring SMTP Virtual Server Access

The Access tab (see Figure 12-8) lets you specify the following information:

Access Control   Click on the Authentication button in the Access Control section of the Access tab to bring up the Authentication Methods dialog box (Figure 12-9). The Authentication Methods dialog box is where you specify the Password Authentication Methods for incoming messages to the SMTP Virtual Server:

- *Anonymous Access*   No username or password is required to access the mail server.
- *Basic Authentication*   Users must input a valid username and password to access the server. These credentials are sent as clear text (actually unencoded text) over the network.
- *Requires TLS Encryption*   Check this box to enable *Transport Layer Security* (TLS) encryption. The client must support TLS encryption for this option to work.
- *Default Domain*   Specify the default domain that you want to authenticate users against.
- *Windows security package*   Encrypted transmission of valid Windows 2000 account credentials is used. This requires *Microsoft Outlook Express (IE 5.0)* as the news client.

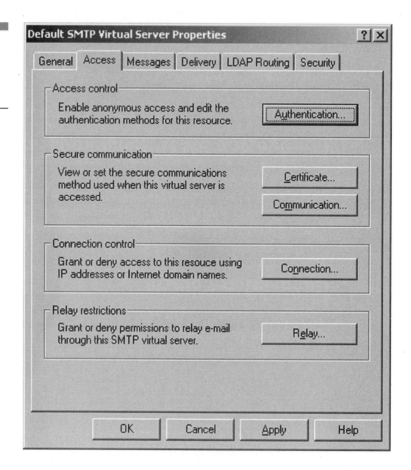

Secure Communication

Click the Certificate button in the Secure Communication section of the Access tab (refer to Figure 12-8) to start the Web Server Certificate Wizard. Refer to Chapter 11 for information on creating certificate requests for your Web server and installation of certificates. Clicking on the Communication

Figure 12-9
Configuring
authentication for the
SMTP Virtual Server.

button brings up a dialog box that specifies whether to require a secure channel to access the SMTP Virtual Server.

Connection Control

Use the Connection Control to grant or deny access to your Default SMTP Virtual Server by IP address or by domain name (see Figure 12-10). This is done in the usual way, similar to the process for the WWW service described in Chapter 3 *Administering the WWW Service*.

Configuring SMTP Relay Restrictions

You can enable or disable relay of incoming mail to remote addresses by clicking the Edit button on the Relay Restrictions section of the Access tab on the Default SMTP Virtual Server Properties sheet to open the Relay

Figure 12-10
Specifying IP address
and domain name
restrictions.

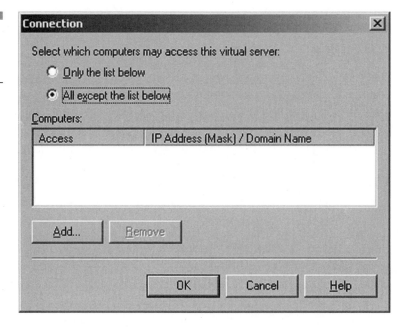

Restrictions dialog box (see Figure 12-11). The default setting is All Computers Are Not Allowed to Relay.

You can also allow any computer that successfully authenticates to relay by selecting this checkbox.

NOTE: *Be aware that if you are connected to the Internet and you enable relay restrictions without requiring authentication, you may be targeted by distributors of unsolicited commercial email, which can adversely affect the performance of your server.*

Configuring SMTP Message Limits

Using the Messages tab (Figure 12-12), the maximum message size and maximum session size (bytes transferred per session) may be unlimited or limited to values specified. The default settings are

Figure 12-11

Enable or disable
relaying of the SMTP
service.

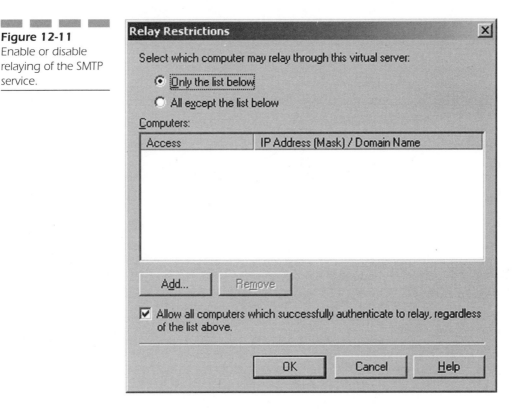

- Maximum message size: 2048KB or 2MB
- Maximum session size: 10240KB or 10MB
- Maximum messages per connection: can be unlimited or limited to the
  value specified. The default setting is 20 messages per connection (see
  Figure 12-12). Sending multiple messages using a single connection
  improves the performance of the SMTP service. Determining the best
  value for this setting is discussed later in this chapter.
- Maximum number of recipients per message: 100 recipients per
  message

You can also use this tab to specify that the SMTP service *send a copy of
nondelivery reports to* a specified email address.

Finally, specify the location of the Badmail *directory*. This folder contains
messages that can neither be delivered nor returned to sender (*dead letters*)
and must be located on a local drive.

Figure 12-12
The Messages tab on
the Default SMTP
Virtual Server
Properties sheet.

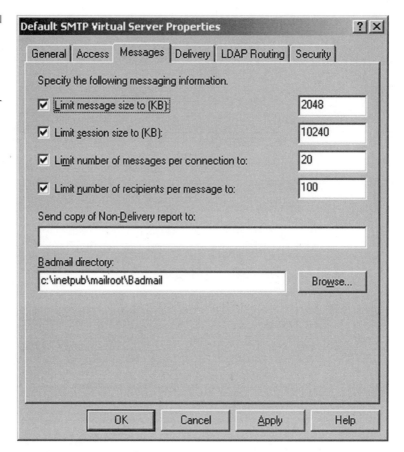

Figure 12-12
The Messages tab on
the Default SMTP
Virtual Server
Properties sheet.

NOTE: *If a message is larger than the maximum message size, it will still be processed. But if an incoming message is larger than the maximum session size, the socket will close and the message will not be processed. In this case, the message transfer agent of the sending SMTP server will continue to resend the message until it times out, adding extra overhead on your server. To avoid this problem, do not set the maximum session size to too small a value.*

Configuring SMTP Retry Settings

Using the Delivery tab (Figure 12-13), specify the *retry intervals* (time between retries) for when the SMTP attempts to deliver a message and

Figure 12-13
The Delivery tab on
the Default SMTP
Virtual Server
Properties sheet.

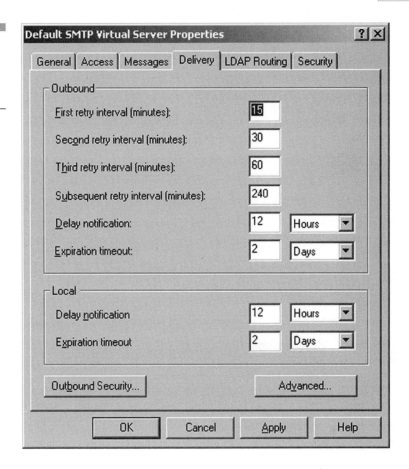

fails. The default value for the first retry is 15 minutes, the second retry is 30 minutes, the third retry is 60 minutes, and any subsequent retries after that are 240 minutes.

Specify the delay notification. This is how long before the server will send a notification on delayed delivery. The default value is 12 hours. This setting can be configured separately for messages in the local and remote message queues.

Specify the *expiration timeout* (how long the server will retry) before the SMTP will return the message to the sender together with a *nondelivery report* (NDR). The default value is 2 days. This setting can be configured separately for messages in the local and remote message queues.

Configuring SMTP Advanced Delivery Settings

The *maximum hop count* (see Figure 12-14) is the maximum number of SMTP servers to which the message may be routed along its delivery route. The default value is 15 hops. If this value is exceeded as the message travels along a route, the message is returned to sender with an NDR.

Specify a *masquerade domain* to replace the local domain name in the From field of messages sent from the default SMTP site. This replacement is only in effect on the first hop.

Specify a *fully qualified domain name* (FQDN) for the default SMTP site. Use the domain name specified on the DNS tab of the TCP/IP Properties sheet *or* specify a new, unique domain name.

By default, the name specified on the DNS tab of the TCP/IP Properties sheet is used. If you change the domain name, you must stop and restart the SMTP service before the new name will take effect.

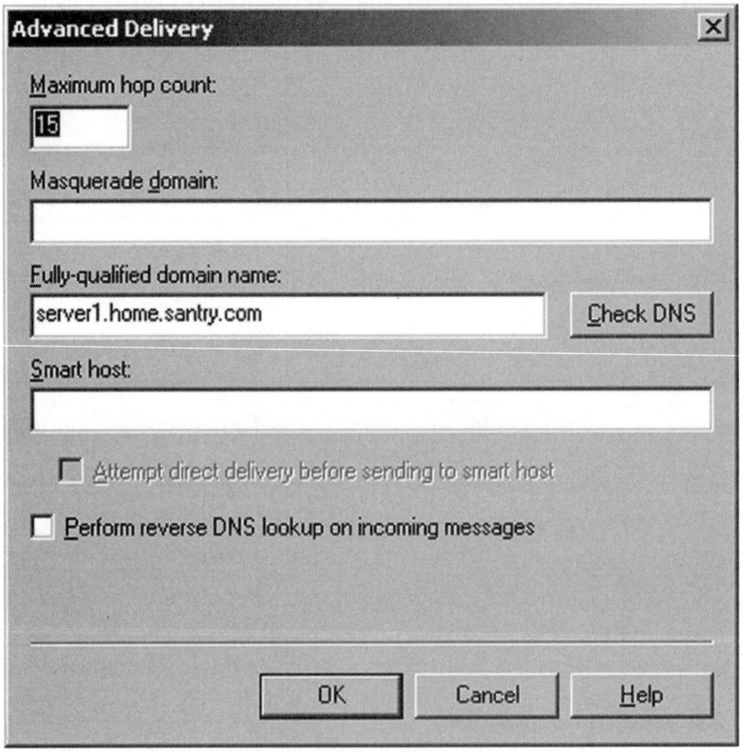

Figure 12-14

Configuring the advanced delivery settings for the server.

Specify a *smart host,* which is an SMTP server to which all outgoing messages are routed. The name of the smart host can be

- The FQDN of the smart host
- The IP address of the smart host (enclose this value in parentheses)

You can choose to *attempt direct delivery before sending to smart host.* This will cause the SMTP service to try to deliver remote messages locally before sending them to the smart host. This option is available only if a smart host has been specified, and by default is disabled.

You can choose to *perform reverse DNS lookup on incoming messages* to configure the SMTP service to check that the IP address in the From field of the message matches the originating IP address in the message header. This option can slow performance if enabled, and is disabled by default.

Configuring SMTP Authentication Method for Outgoing Messages

For outgoing mail, you can specify what authentication method will be required by the receiving SMTP server. To do this, click the Outbound Security button on the Delivery tab of the Default SMTP Virtual Server Properties sheet to open the Outbound Security dialog box (Figure 12-15). The three options you can choose from are

- *No authentication* This is the default setting because choosing an authentication method for all receiving SMTP servers on a global level (that is, for all remote domains) is unlikely to be required; most SMTP servers will accept connections without requiring any credentials. Therefore, you will probably want to leave this as the default setting.
- *Clear text authentication* The account name and password recognized by the remote SMTP server are sent unencrypted.
- *Windows security package* Encrypted transmission of valid Windows 2000 account credentials is used.

In addition, you can enable or disable *Transport Layer Security (TLS)* encryption globally for outgoing mail to all remote domains. In this case, all receiving SMTP servers must support TLS.

Figure 12-15
Configuring
outbound security.

Outbound Security   ☒

◉ Anonymous access
No user name or password required.

○ Basic authentication
The password will be sent over the network in clear text using standard
commands.

User name: [   ]   [Browse...]

Password: [   ]

○ Windows security package

The client and server negotiate the Windows Security Support Provider
Interface.

Account: [   ]   [Modify...]

Password: [   ]

☐ TLS encryption

                    [OK]   [Cancel]   [Help]

NOTE: *When you create remote domains, you can specify a different
authentication method for delivering mail to these domains to override the
one globally specified. Creating remote domains is explained later in this
chapter.*

Configuring LDAP Routing

Specify LDAP connection information by using the LDAP Routing (see Figure 12-16) tab of this property sheet. You can use an LDAP provider to map
email recipients and senders to the values contained in the LDAP Directory.
If you want to connect your SMTP Virtual Server to an LDAP provider like
Exchange Server, Windows 2000 Active Directory, or Microsoft Site Server,
specify

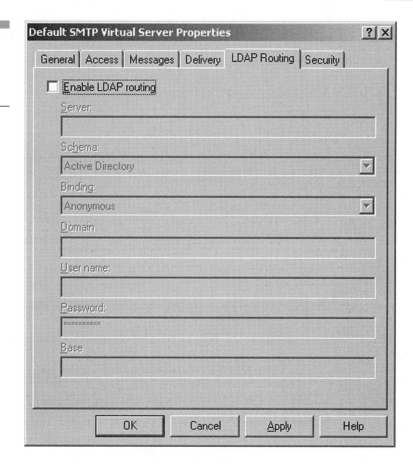

Figure 12-16
The LDAP Routing tab on the Default SMTP Virtual Server Properties sheet.

- The *server name* of the LDAP provider

- The directory *schema* to connect to; the possible options are Exchange Server, Active Directory, or Site Server

- The *binding* used to specify how the virtual server will identify itself to the LDAP provider. The options are similar to authentication options for WWW services: anonymous, basic clear text, Windows SSPI, or as a Service Account that the SMTP service is running under.

- The *domain* specify the domain that contains the account you wish to use to connect to the LDAP provider. This option will only be enabled if you are using Plain Text or Windows SSPI as your binding.

- The *user name* is the account you want to use to bind to the LDAP Directory. For example, if your directory were structured with the organization as MTIT Inc., a unit of Members, and the container or account of Charlie_Smith, a potential *Distinguished Name* (DN) of the account you could pass here is `cn=Charlie_Smith,ou=Members, o=MTITInc`. This option will only be enabled if you are using Plain Text or Windows SSPI as your binding.

- Enter the user account's *password*. This option will only be enabled if you are using Plain Text or Windows SSPI as your binding.

- Enter the *base* used for where you want the SMTP to start searching in the LDAP Directory.

Configuring SMTP Site Operators

Grant and revoke operator privileges for administering the default SMTP site using the Security tab of this property sheet (Figure 12-17). By default, everyone in the Administrators local group on the IIS server is granted operator status for SMTP.

Understanding SMTP Service Domains

SMTP service domains can be either *local* or *remote*.

- *Local SMTP service domains* (also called *service domains* or *supported domains*) are DNS domains that are serviced by the SMTP service running on IIS. Arriving messages addressed to a local domain are delivered to the Drop directory. When SMTP is installed on IIS, it creates a *default domain,* which is usually the domain name specified in the DNS tab of the TCP/IP properties sheet for the server. Configuring the default SMTP virtual server as described in the previous section configures the default domain. If you create a new local domain, it will be an *alias* of the default domain and will have the same properties as the default domain.

- *Remote SMTP service domains* (also called *remote domains* or *nonlocal domains*) are DNS domains of remote servers that are not local and that the SMTP must look up using DNS in order to deliver mail. Delivery settings can be configured individually for remote domains,

Figure 12-17
The Security tab of
the SMTP Virtual
Server Properties
sheet.

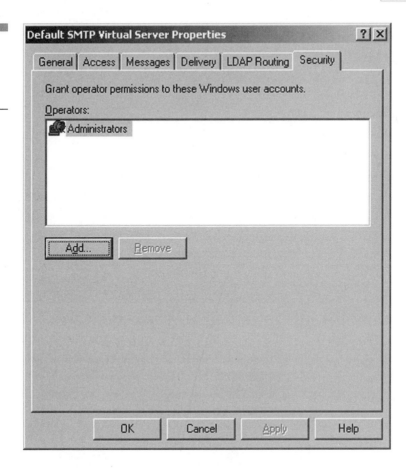

and these settings override global settings configured using the Default
SMTP Virtual Server Properties sheet.

Creating a New SMTP Service Domain

To create a new SMTP service domain using the MMC, right-click the
Domains node under Default SMTP Virtual Server node and select New,
Domain from the shortcut menu to open the New Domain Wizard (Figure
12-18). Select the type of domain you want to create:

- *Remote* for delivery to a remote SMTP server
- *Alias* an alias for the default domain and the end point for mail
delivery

Figure 12-18
The New SMTP Domain Wizard for creating new SMTP domains.

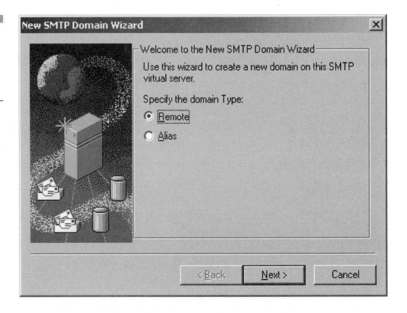

Figure 12-19
Specifying the name for a remote domain.

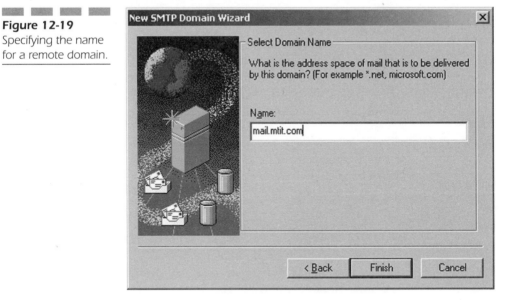

If you choose the *remote* option, click Next and specify a name for the new domain (`mail.mtit.com` has been used in Figure 12-19, but you can also use wildcards, for example, `*.mtit.com`). The procedure is similar for creating an alias domain. Figure 12-20 shows the MMC when two new domains have been created, one alias and one remote.

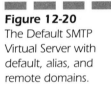

Figure 12-20
The Default SMTP
Virtual Server with
default, alias, and
remote domains.

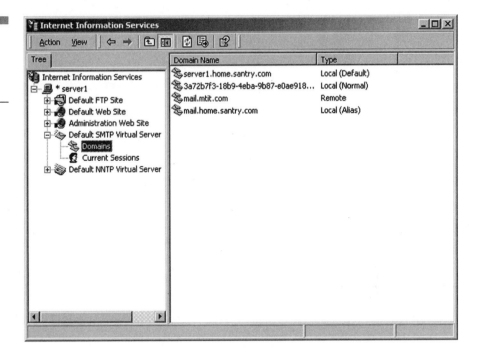

Walkthrough: Sending a Message Using the Pickup Directory

To send a message using the SMTP service on IIS, use an ASCII text editor to create a simple text file similar to the one shown in Figure 12-21.

Note the blank line (CR1LF) that must be included between the header and the message body. There is a similar blank line (CR1LF) at the end of the body of the message. Save the message as message.txt in the folder C:\tempmail.

Configure the settings on the Delivery tab of the Default SMTP Virtual Server Properties sheet as follows:

- Enter one minute for all retry intervals
- Expiration timeout: five minutes

Now use Windows Explorer to move the message from the C:\tempmail directory to the C:\Mailroot\Pickup directory. Click immediately on the Pickup directory to view its contents, and note that it is empty. The SMTP service continually monitors the Pickup directory for mail to deliver, and when it finds a message, it moves it to the Queue directory.

Figure 12-21

An example of an SMTP message composed using Notepad.

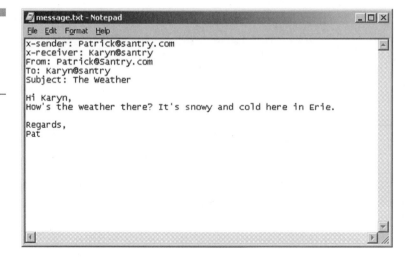

Figure 12-22 shows the contents of the Queue directory immediately after the message.txt file has been moved into it. Note the mail message waiting to be delivered. Notice that the message has been renamed using a message ID number with the extension *.eml, which stands for "email." If you double-click this message, it will open in Outlook Express. Figure 12-23 shows the .eml file opened in Notepad. Note the headers added by the SMTP service.

After four minutes has expired (the total retry intervals), the contents of the Queue directory change; the directory now includes a *.rtr file, which indicates that SMTP service could not deliver the message and is attempting to return the message to the sender (see Figure 12-24). The .rtr remote transcript file is a text file that explains why the message cannot be delivered. You can open and read this file if you like.

Finally, after two minutes, the maximum retries value is exceeded, the *.rtr file is deleted, and the message *.eml file is moved to the Badmail directory. If you explore the Badmail directory and open the *.eml file in it using Notepad, you can view the *nondelivery report* (NDR).

As another exercise, try modifying the recipient headers to send the message to the destination address `ingrid@server1.santry.com` (or your equivalent), which will send the message to the local default SMTP domain. Move the message to the Pickup directory, and SMTP transfers it to the Queue directory and from there to the Drop directory, where incoming mail is stored.

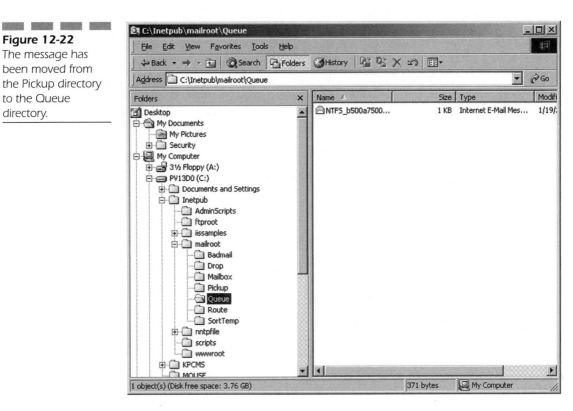

Figure 12-22
The message has been moved from the Pickup directory to the Queue directory.

Figure 12-23
A formatted message in the Queue directory waiting to be delivered.

Figure 12-24
The message
cannot be returned
to the sender.

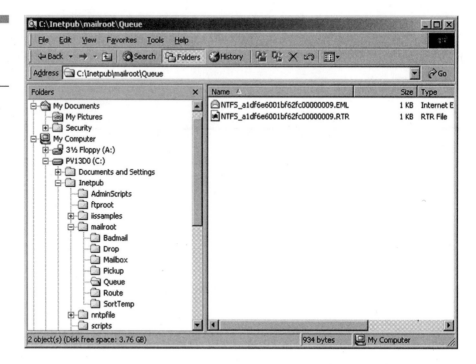

Monitoring and Tuning SMTP Service Performance

The performance of the SMTP service on IIS 5.0 can be monitored using the following tools:

- *Event Viewer* The SMTP service logs significant events to the Windows 2000 security log. Look for events whose source is SMTPSVC.

- *IIS Logs* View the IIS logs in a text editor or import them into a log analysis program to generate reports of SMTP site usage.

- *Performance Monitor* The SMTP service includes the Performance Monitor SMTP Server object with a number of counters that may be monitored for that object.

You should monitor standard counters to detect memory, processor, disk, and network bottlenecks in addition to specific SMTP counters. In particular, you should set a Performance Monitor alert for low disk space on the volume where the mailroot directory is located because low disk space conditions can lead to messages becoming corrupted.

Some of the more important SMTP Server Performance Monitor counters to watch are

Local Queue Length	Number of messages in the local queue. This should normally read zero. If it is greater than zero, the SMTP service may be receiving more messages than it can handle. If it steadily increases, something may be interfering with your SMTP process, causing a delay in message processing.
Remote Queue Length	Number of messages in the remote queue. The same concerns apply as for the Local Queue Length Counter.
Inbound Connections Current	The total number of connections currently inbound. This should normally be greater than zero. If it remains zero for an extended period, you may have a network problem that is preventing mail from entering your server.

Following are some things you can do to enhance the performance of the SMTP service on IIS 5.0:

- Apply general enhancements, such as adding more memory, a faster processor, a stripe set, and a faster network connection to your server.
- Disable IIS logging for the SMTP service.
- Regularly clear the Badmail directory.
- Disable reverse DNS lookup.
- Optimally configure the *Maximum number of outbound messages per connection* setting on the Messages tab of the Default SMTP Site Properties sheet. Do this by monitoring the counter *SMTP Server: Messages Sent/sec,* and make sure that the setting on the property sheet is *less* than the average value of the Performance Monitor counter. This will ensure that the SMTP service opens simultaneous connections with remote servers to speed the processing of remotely destined mail.

SUMMARY

The Microsoft SMTP service is a fully functioning SMTP delivery service that can be configured to send mail to remote SMTP servers. The administration of the service is integrated into the MMC together with other IIS 5.0 services. Remote administration using a browser can also be performed.

For More Information

Search the Microsoft Web site for the keyword SMTP to find more information about this service.

Search the TechNet knowledge base for articles relating to the SMTP service. The SMTP help file is located in `c:\winnt\help\mail.chm`.

Administering the NNTP Service

Introduction

Using the NNTP service running on Microsoft Internet Information Services 5.0, administrators can set up, maintain, and administer a news server for hosting USENET-style discussion groups on a corporate intranet/extranet. After completing this chapter, you will be able to

- Understand how the NNTP service works on IIS 5.0
- Install and configure the NNTP service on IIS 5.0
- Create and maintain newsgroups on IIS 5.0
- View and post to newsgroups using Outlook Express
- Set an expiration policy for a newsgroup
- Map a newsgroup directory to a virtual directory

Understanding the NNTP Service

The Microsoft NNTP service on IIS 5.0 fully supports the standard *Network News Transfer Protocol (NNTP)* and is compatible with most NNTP servers and clients. Some of its features include

- *Integration with standard Windows 2000 services such as Performance Monitor and Event Viewer*   The NNTP service installs a collection of performance counters for monitoring it with Performance Monitor. Error conditions are written to the Windows 2000 System Log viewable from Event Viewer.

- *Integration with Windows 2000 security, including access control lists (ACLs) on NTFS volumes*   Access to a particular newsgroup may be controlled by assigning NTFS permissions to the newsgroup's content directory.

- *Several forms of authentication*   Users may be authenticated through Basic authentication, Windows 2000 integrated authentication, or as anonymous users.

- *Support for a variety of content formats*   In addition to plain ASCII text, other supported formats include MIME, HTML, GIF, and JPEG formats.

- *A variety of administration tools*   The NNTP service may be administered from the Microsoft Management Console, through a Terminal Services session, and through the Windows Scripting Host.

- *Integration with Index Server*   Both text and properties of news messages can be fully indexed.
- *Integration with SSL*   Newsgroup sessions may be encrypted using the Secure Sockets Layer protocol version 3.0.

How the Network News Transfer Protocol Works

NNTP is both a client/server protocol and a server/server protocol. In the client/server scenario an NNTP client connects to an NNTP server to receive a list of available newsgroups on the server (see Figure 13-1). The default TCP port on the server for client connections is port 119 (the default TCP port for an SSL connection is 563).

Figure 13-1
Interaction between
NNTP clients and
servers.

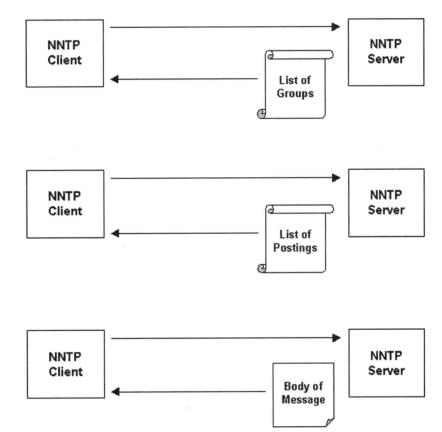

■ The client selects an available newsgroup, and the server returns a list of headings of postings made to the newsgroup.

■ The client selects a posting in the newsgroup, and the server returns the body of the message for the client to read.

In the server/server scenario, one NNTP server receives a news feed from another NNTP server to replicate newsgroup content between servers. This is the basis of the worldwide USENET news server network.

NOTE: *This release of the Microsoft NNTP service does not support receiving newsfeeds from USENET news servers.*

Installing the NNTP Service

The NNTP service is not installed during installation of Windows 2000. Instead, it can be installed by doing a Custom setup or can be installed afterwards by running setup in maintenance mode.

The hardware and software requirements for installing Microsoft NNTP service are the same as those for installing IIS 5.0; namely, Windows 2000 Server on Advanced Server.

To install the NNTP service on a Windows 2000 Server, click Start, Setting, Control Panel, and click Add/Remove programs. When the initial dialog box appears, click Add/Remove Windows Components to open the Select Components screen. Select *Internet Information Services* (IIS) and click the Details button to open the *Internet Information Services* (IIS) component box (Figure 13-2). Check the NNTP Service checkbox, click OK and Next. Click Next to continue with the setup.

The result of running the setup is a new node under the server node in the Microsoft Management Console (see Figure 13-3). This new node is called *Default NNTP Virtual Server* and has four subnodes under it:

■ *Newsgroups*   You can create any number of newsgroups that will be made available on your news server using the Newsgroup Wizard. Under this node, any newsgroups you create will be listed.

Figure 13-2
Select NNTP Server
component for
installation.

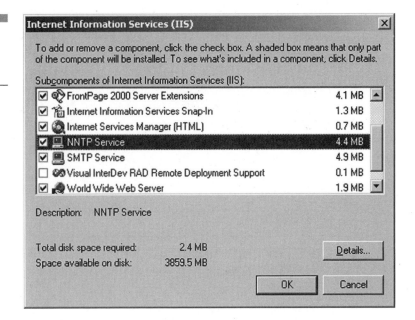

Figure 13-2
Select NNTP Server
component for
installation.

Figure 13-3
The Internet Services
Manager after the
NNTP service has
been installed.

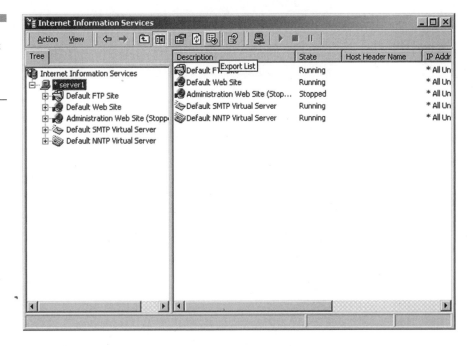

■ *Expiration policies*   Newsgroup articles can be configured to expire when a certain number of postings or a certain quantity (in megabytes) of postings occurs. Under this node, any configured expiration policies are listed.

■ *Virtual Directories*   Newsgroup content directories can be mapped to virtual directories, both local and remote. Under this node, any configured virtual directories are listed.

■ *Current sessions*   This shows the sessions still open, who is connected, and for how long.

The NNTP service installation process also creates the directory structure shown in Figure 13-4. Included in this directory structure are

■ InetPub\nntpfile, which contains all content directories, header files, hash files, and group list files

■ InetPub\nntpfile_temp.files_, which contains temporary files

■ InetPub\nntpfile\root, which contains all newsgroups created by administrator, plus demo and system groups

Figure 13-4
The directory structure created by the NNTP services installation.

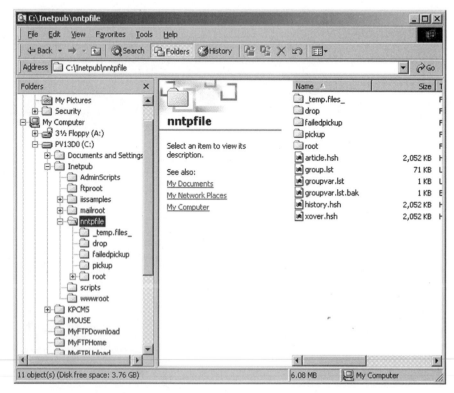

Individual newsgroups are stored as a series of nested folders under InetPub\nntpfile\root.

For example, creating the newsgroup local.music.tribal would create the following three folders to contain it:

- InetPub\nntpfile\root\local
- InetPub\nntpfile\root\local\music
- InetPub\nntpfile\root\local\music\tribal

The actual newsgroup content is stored in the last of the three folders listed previously and consists of a number of .nws files, each containing an individual newsgroup message. These files are plain ASCII files and can be viewed with Notepad.

Administering the NNTP Service

Windows 2000 provides three tools for administering and managing the NNTP service:

- *Internet Service Manager* The NNTP snap-in extension in the *Microsoft Management Console* (MMC) allows full administration of any NNTP server on the local LAN.

- *Microsoft Terminal Services* Terminal Services is integrated into the Windows 2000 operating system. Terminal Services allow you to remotely administer your Windows 2000 services from a client running the Terminal Services client as if you were physically connected to the machine.

- *Windows Scripting Host (WSH)* This allows VBScript administration scripts to be run either from the graphical WSH utility (Wscript.exe) or from the command line (Cscript.exe). Included in the Option Pack are several examples of VBScripts to perform common administrative tasks like modifying expiration policies, adding and deleting newsgroups and NNTP sites, and managing user sessions.

This chapter deals only with using the MMC version of Internet Services Manager to administer the NNTP service. The Terminal Services sessions work identically to the MMC version except, instead of using the actual MMC, your connection is being conducted via the terminal session. For information on administering NNTP through the WSH, refer to the Windows 2000 online documentation.

A variety of administrative tasks can be initiated and performed with the MMC version of the Internet Services Manager (see Figure 13-3). Most of these actions can be performed by selecting the Default NNTP Virtual Server node in the scope pane (left pane) and then either using the rebar buttons, accessing the Action drop-down menu, or right-clicking the node and using the context menu.

- The Default NNTP Virtual Server can be stopped, paused, and started.
  - *Stopping* the site disconnects all currently connected users and allows no new connections to be established.
  - *Pausing* the site allows no new connections to be established, but leaves currently connected users connected.
  - *Starting* the site allows new connections to be established with the server.
- Property sheets can be opened for the Default NNTP Virtual Server. These property sheets can be used to configure various aspects of the NNTP service and are described in the next section.
- A new expiration policy can be created. This will be demonstrated in the walkthrough later on in this chapter.
- Local and remote virtual directories for hosting newsgroup content can be created. This will also be demonstrated in the walkthrough.
- Current expiration policies, virtual directories, and connected user sessions can be viewed.
- NNTP sites on other IIS 5.0 servers on the local LAN can be connected to and administered.

NOTE: *Stopping the Default NNTP Virtual Server does not stop the NNTP service, but only prevents users from connecting to the news server. To actually stop the NNTP Service, select Start, Programs, Administrative Tools, Component Services, and select the local services node from the Component Services Manager. Stop the Network News Transport Protocol (NNTP). After the NNTP is stopped like this, it cannot be restarted using the Internet Services Manager. Instead, it must be restarted using the Local Services node in Component Services Manager.*

Configuring NNTP Virtual Server Properties

The Default NNTP Virtual Server is configured through property sheets, similar to the WWW and FTP sites running on IIS 5.0. The Default NNTP Virtual Server Properties sheet is opened by right-clicking the Default NNTP Virtual Server node in the Microsoft Management Console and selecting Properties from the shortcut menu (it can also be opened using the Properties button on the rebar or the Action drop-down menu on the rebar).

The Default NNTP Virtual Server Properties sheet has six tabs that perform the following administrative functions:

- *General* Configure site identification, IP addresses, TCP ports, maximum connections, and enable logging.
- *Access* Select anonymous user and grant operator privileges, configuring SSL, and IP restrictions.
- *Settings* Allow and disallow client posting, limit posting size, allow interaction with other servers, specify moderator.
- *Directory Security* Specify groups for administering the NNTP Virtual Server.

Configuring NNTP Virtual Server Identification

The General tab enables you to specify the following information (Figure 13-5):

- *Name* This will appear beside the NNTP node in the MMC.
- *IP Address* Specify the IP address for the site. Click the Advanced button to open the Advanced Multiple News Site Configuration dialog box to specify additional IP addresses for the news server. These additional IP addresses must have already been bound to the network adapter by using the Control Panel, Network program.
- *Path Header* The string specified here will be used for the Path heading in new postings (see Figure 13-22 for an example).

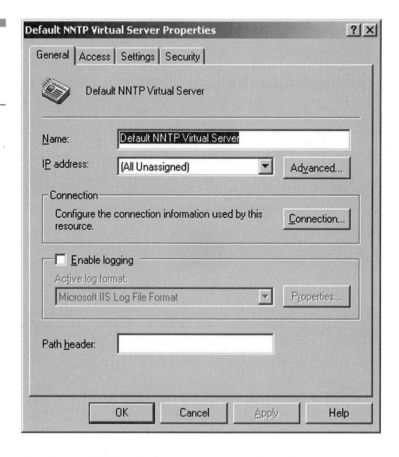

Configuring NNTP Connections

Click on the Connection button in the General settings of the dialog box
in Figure 13-5 to open the Connection dialog box (see Figure 13-6). Client
connections may be specified as either Unlimited or Limited To a number
the administrator may specify (the default setting is Limited to 5,000

connections). *Connection timeout* specifies the period of inactivity after which a client's connection is terminated (the default is 600 seconds, or 10 minutes).

Configuring NNTP Logging

Logging may be enabled or disabled in Figure 13-5. Any of the four standard logging formats described in Chapter 3, *Administering the WWW Service,* may be selected and enabled here.

Configuring NNTP Virtual Server Access

The Access tab (see Figure 13-7) enables you to specify the following information:

Access Control   Click the Authentication button in the Access Control section of the Access tab to bring up the Authentication Methods dialog box (Figure 13-8).
    The Authentication Methods dialog box is where you specify the Password Authentication Methods for the NNTP Virtual Server:

- *Anonymous Access*   No username or password is required to access the news server.
- *Basic Authentication*   Users must input a valid username and password to enter the site. These credentials are sent as clear text (actually unencoded text) over the network. This method makes use of the AUTHINFO standard NNTP extension.
- *Windows Security Package*   Encrypted transmission of valid Windows 2000 account credentials is used. This requires *Microsoft Outlook Express (IE 5.0)* as the news client.
- *Enable SSL Client Authentication*   Refer to Chapter 11 for more information on enabling SSL. SSL is usually used together with Basic Authentication to provide secure encrypted authentication and data transmission.

Specifying the Anonymous Access Account

Click the Authentication button in the Access Control section of the Access tab (refer to Figure 13-7) to bring up the Authentication Methods dialog box

Figure 13-7

Configuring access to
the NNTP Virtual
Server.

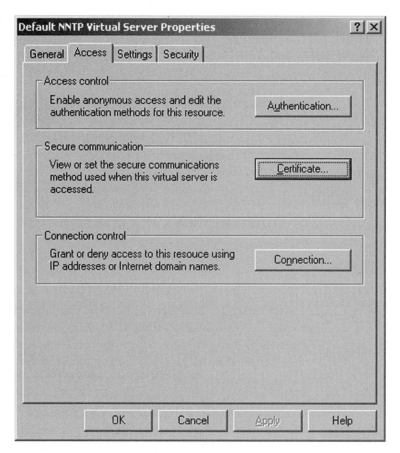

(refer to Figure 13-8). From this dialog box, click the Anonymous button to
bring up the Anonymous Account dialog box, which you use to specify the
Windows 2000 account used to allow anonymous access to the news site
(see Figure 13-9). Refer to Chapter 4, *Administering Security*, for further
information regarding configuring an Anonymous Access account and
enabling or disabling automatic password synchronization between this
property sheet and User Manager.

Secure Communication

Click the Certificate button in the Secure Communication section of the
Access tab (see Figure 13-7) to start the Web Server Certificate Wizard.
Refer to Chapter 11 for information on creating certificate requests for your
Web server and installation of certificates.

Figure 13-8
Configuring
authentication for the
NNTP Virtual Server.

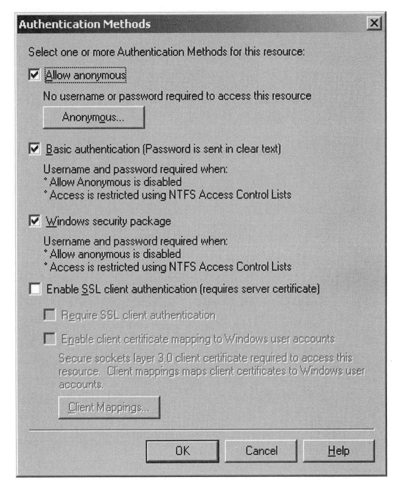

IP Address and Domain Name Restrictions

Use the IP Address and Domain Name Restrictions option to grant or deny access to your Default NNTP Site by IP address or by domain name (see Figure 13-10). See Chapter 3 for more information on how to accomplish this.

Configuring NNTP Posting Restrictions

Clearing the Allow Client Posting checkbox in the Settings tab (see Figure 13-11) prevents users from posting to the NNTP Virtual Server. Limit Post Size specifies the maximum size of any individual posting submitted to the

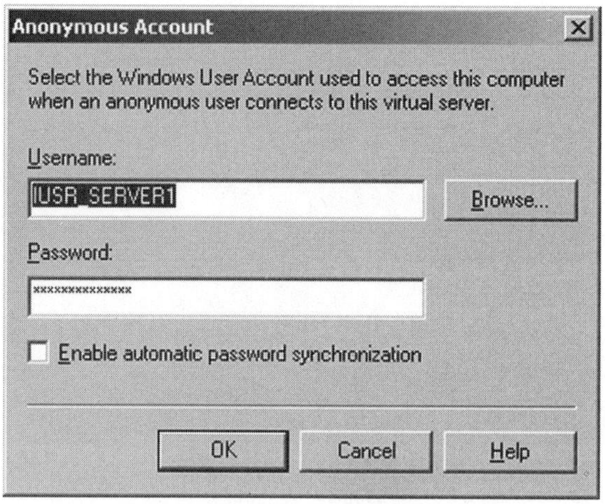

Figure 13-9
Specifying the
Anonymous Access
account.

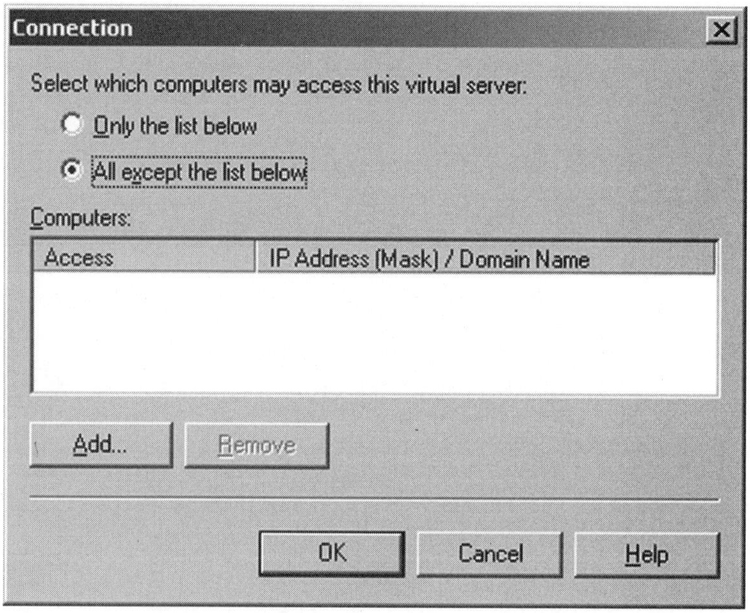

Figure 13-10
Specifying IP address
and domain name
restrictions.

news server (the default limit is 1000KB, or 1MB, per posting). Limit Connection Size specifies the maximum amount of posting a client may perform during a single connection (the default limit is 20MB per connection).

Clearing the Allow Feed Posting checkbox in the Settings tab prevents newsfeeds from posting to the NNTP Virtual Server. (Refer to Figure 13-11.)

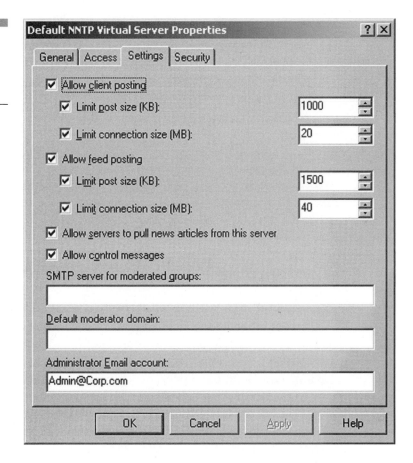

Limit Post Size specifies the maximum size of any individual posting submitted to the news server (the default limit is 1500KB, or 1.5MB, per posting). Limit Connection Size specifies the maximum amount of posting a client may perform during a single connection (the default limit is 40MB per connection).

Configuring NNTP Server Pulls and Control Messages

Checking the Allow Servers to Pull News Articles From This Server box permits other news servers to pull news feeds from this server. Checking Allow Control Messages permits both clients and servers to send control messages to the news server. *Control messages* direct the NNTP service to perform specific actions such as

- Deleting an article from a newsgroup
- Creating a new newsgroup
- Deleting an existing newsgroup

These messages are typically sent by other news servers, but can also be used by hackers to target the news server. Refer to the Windows 2000 online documentation for further information about how to secure your news server against attack through use of control messages.

Configuring NNTP Moderated Newsgroups

Moderated newsgroups are groups where articles that are submitted are not posted immediately, but are first sent to a newsgroup moderator, who either approves (and posts) them or rejects (and discards) them. Enabling moderated newsgroups requires an SMTP server for sending submitted articles directly to the moderator of the group. The SMTP server for moderated groups must be specified on this property sheet (refer to Figure 13-11) by using its DNS name; that is, `mail.mtit.com`.

The Default moderator domain specifies the email address to which postings to a moderated news group are sent if there is no specific moderator assigned to the newsgroup. For example, if the name of the moderated newsgroup is

`alt.talk.canola.moderated`

and the default moderator domain is specified as

`canolacorp.com`

then submitted messages will be forwarded to the following email address:

`alt.talk.canola.moderated@canolacorp.com`

If, for any reason, a submission cannot be delivered to the moderator of the newsgroup, a *Non-Delivery Report* (NDR) will be sent to the Default NNTP Virtual Server administrator as specified by the Administrator Email account field.

Configuring NNTP Virtual Server Operators

Grant and revoke operator privileges for administering the Default NNTP Site on the News Site Operators section of the Security tab (see Figure 13-12). By default, everyone in the Administrators group on the IIS server is granted operator status for NNTP.

Configuring NNTP Newsgroups

Select the newsgroups node under the NNTP Virtual Server node in the MMC. This will display the current existing newsgroups for the NNTP Virtual Server in the right pane of the MMC (see Figure 13-13). To edit an

Figure 13-12
Specifying the administrative account for the NNTP Virtual Server.

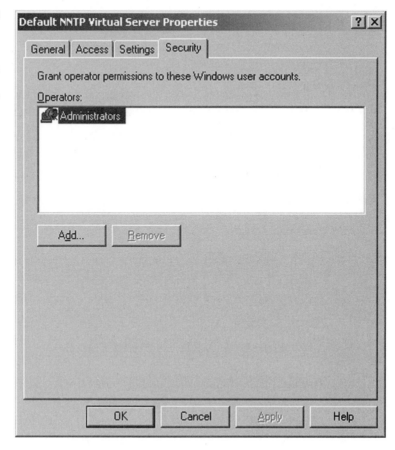

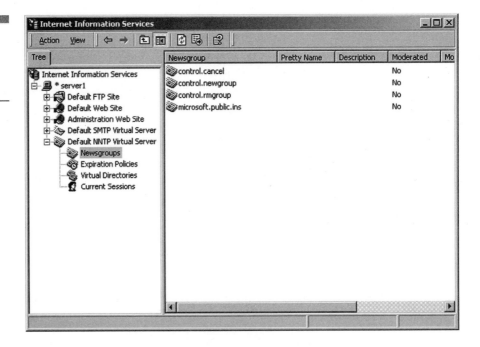

existing newsgroup, select the group in the right pane, and then select
Action, Properties from the rebar. Creating a new newsgroup is demonstrated in the following section.

Walkthrough: Creating and Administering a Newsgroup

The following walkthrough will take you through the creation, testing, and
administration of a newsgroup. Modify settings as needed to match the particular configuration of your IIS setup.

Creating a New Newsgroup

Right-click the Newsgroups node under the NNTP Virtual Server node in
the MMC and select New, Newsgroups to open the New Newsgroups Wizard (see Figure 13-14).

Figure 13-14
Specifying a name for
a newsgroup in the
New Newsgroups
Wizard.

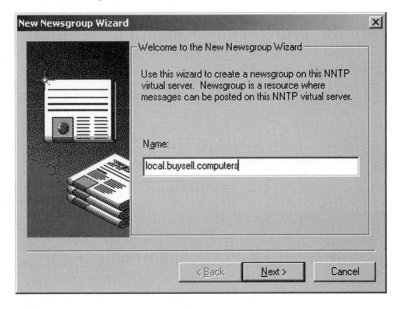

Specify a name for your new newsgroup. The name we have chosen is

```
local.buysell.computers
```

because this will be a newsgroup on a local intranet news server.

Click Next to specify a description for the newsgroup and a pretty name for display (see Figure 13-15). Click Finish to close the wizard.

Notice that the new newsgroup is now listed in the right pane of the MMC under the Newsgroups node of the Default NNTP Virtual Server.

The NNTP service has now created the following directory structure to store messages posted to the new newsgroup (see Figure 13-16):

- `C:\InetPub\nntpfile\root\local\`
- `C:\InetPub\nntpfile\root\local\buysell\`
- `C:\InetPub\nntpfile\root\local\buysell\computers\`

Figure 13-16 shows us that there is no content yet in the newsgroup. Our next job will be to post a message to the group.

Figure 13-15
Adding a description
and pretty name for
a newsgroup.

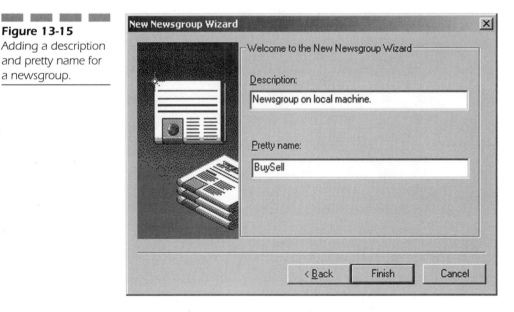

Figure 13-15
Adding a description
and pretty name for
a newsgroup.

Figure 13-16
Local directory
structure after
creating a
newsgroup.

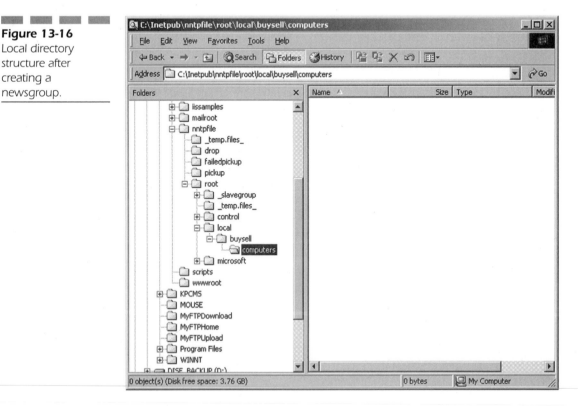

Posting to a Newsgroup Using Outlook Express

Outlook Express is the Internet mail and news client that comes with Internet Explorer 5.0. We will assume that Outlook Express has already been configured for SMTP/POP3 mail and only needs to be configured for accessing newsgroups.

Open Outlook Express on the local machine (the news server) by double-clicking its icon on your desktop. Select Tools, Accounts from the menu bar to open the Internet Accounts dialog box.

Select Add, News to open the Internet Connection Wizard (see Figure 13-17). This wizard will lead us through the steps of configuring our news client to connect to the default NNTP site on our local news server.

Begin by entering your name (we used Charlie Smith).

Click Next and enter your email address (we used `charlie@mtit.com`). Click Next. The next screen is called Internet News Server Name. Enter your news server's name in the textbox (we entered `server1`). Click Finish to finish configuring Outlook Express to connect to your news server.

Figure 13-17
The Internet
Connection Wizard.

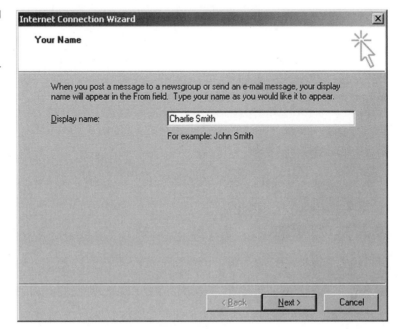

Figure 13-18
Caption required.

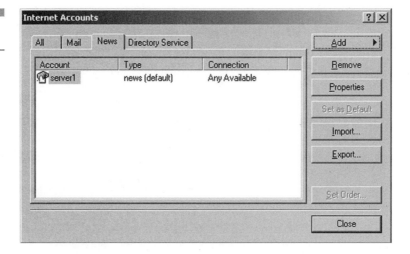

Figure 13-19
Downloading a list of
newsgroups to your
newsreader.

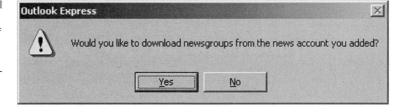

Figure 13-18 shows the News tab on the Internet Accounts dialog box, showing that the new news server account has been created. To modify news server account settings, select server1 and click Properties to open the server1 Properties sheet. Accessing the four tabs on this sheet allows us to modify settings selected through the wizard, plus additional settings on the Advanced tab such as

- Requiring SSL for logging onto the news server
- Modifying the SSL port number to match that of the server
- Configuring server timeouts
- Using newsgroup descriptions
- Breaking apart messages longer than a given length

Close the Internet Accounts dialog box. You are now prompted to download a list of newsgroups from the news server (see Figure 13-19). Click Yes and a message will appear indicating that a list of newsgroups from server1 is being downloaded.

A dialog box called Newsgroup Subscriptions will now appear listing all the newsgroups on server1 that can be downloaded (see Figure 13-20). Double-click on the group

```
local.buysell.computers
```

to subscribe to the new group.

Note the other groups already there. The group

```
microsoft.public.ins
```

contains a welcome message. The other groups are control groups that handle control messages sent to the server by other news servers.

Select the newly created group and click Go To in order to open the group in Outlook Express. Post a test message to your new newsgroup and then open it for reading in Outlook Express (see Figure 13-21). Continue making a few additional postings, replying to existing postings, or starting new threads.

Open Windows Explorer and view the folder containing the posted messages for the new newsgroup (see Figure 13-22). This folder is located at

```
C:InetPub\nntpfile\root\local\buysell\computers\
```

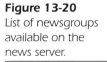

Figure 13-20
List of newsgroups available on the news server.

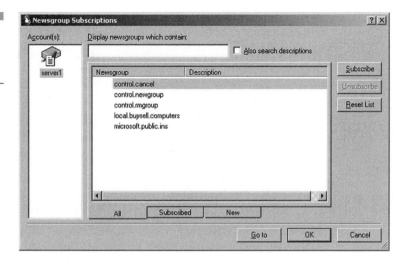

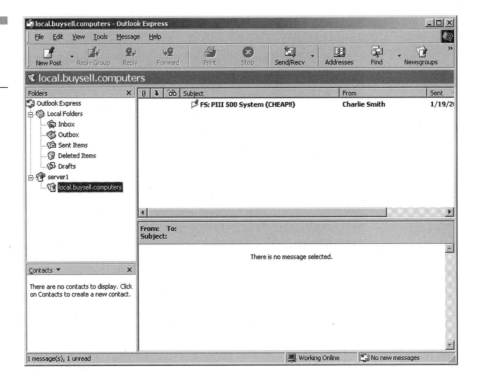

Notice the new files in this folder: 1000000.nws is an individual message posted to the news server.

These .nws files are plain ASCII text files that can be opened and examined using Notepad (see Figure 13-23 for an example). The .nws files consist of a group of headers followed by the body of the message.

Setting a Newsgroup Expiration Policy

We will next configure an expiration policy for the newly created newsgroup. Return to the Microsoft Management Console, expand the Default NNTP Virtual Server node in the scope pane, and select the Expiration Policies icon in the scope pane. Right-click the Expiration Policies node and select New, Expiration Policy. This will start the New Expiration Policy Wizard (Figure 13-24).

Enter a description for the new expiration policy.

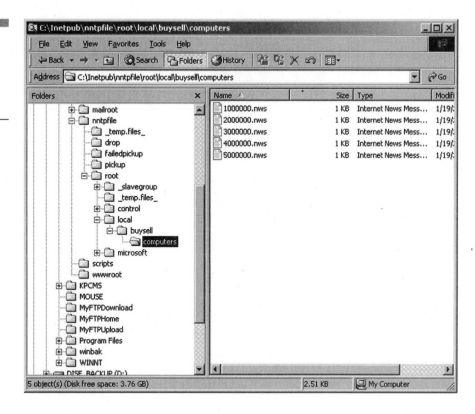

Figure 13-22
News files created in the content directory for `local.buysell.computers`.

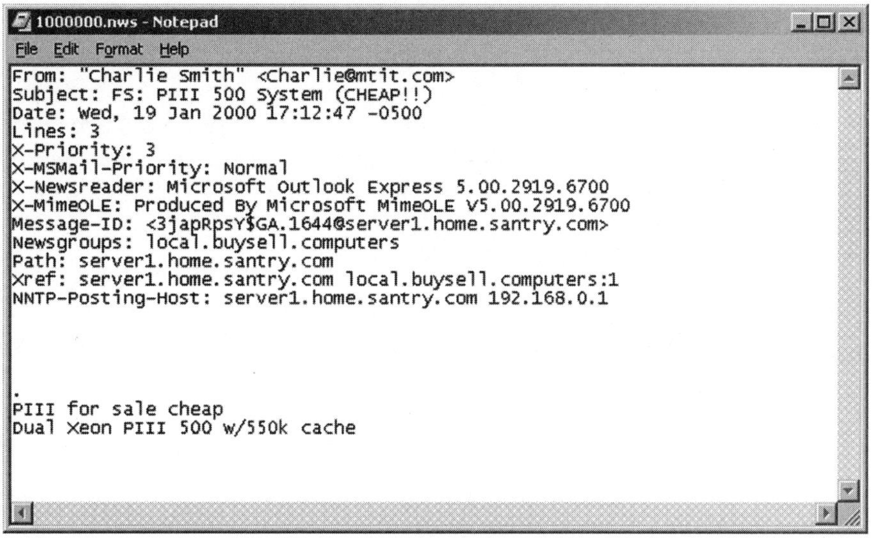

Figure 13-23
Inside a newsgroup posting .nws file.

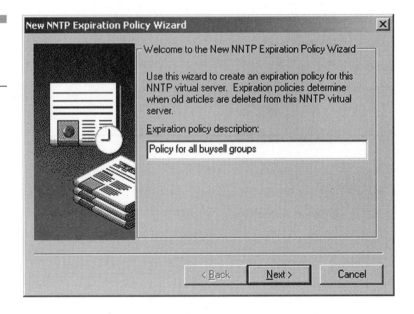

Click Next and select the Only Selected Newsgroups on this Virtual Server option (see Figure 13-25).

Click Next and then the Add button (see Figure 13-26) to specify the name of the newsgroups that will be affected.

Click Next and configure when articles should be deleted (see Figure 13-27). Enter an age after which given articles are retired from the news server's store.

The result of creating this expiration policy is shown in the results pane of the MMC (see Figure 13-28). If we need to edit the properties of the expiration policy we have created, simply double-click the Policy for all buysell groups node in the results pane, and the Policy for all buysell groups Properties sheet appears (see Figure 13-29). Use this property sheet to reconfigure settings entered during running of the wizard.

Mapping a Newsgroup's Home Directory to a Virtual Directory

Finally, we will conclude by creating a new newsgroup and mapping its home directory to the local path

```
D:\talkstuff
```

Figure 13-25
Selecting the
newsgroups on the
NNTP Virtual Server.

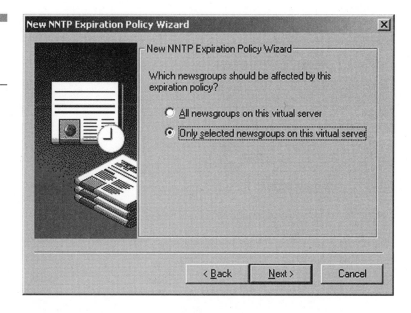

Figure 13-25
Selecting the
newsgroups on the
NNTP Virtual Server.

Figure 13-26
Specifying the
newsgroups that will
be affected by the
expiration policy.

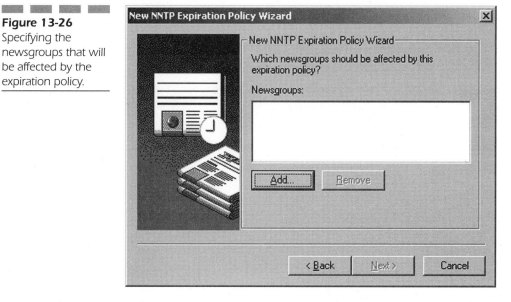

Begin by creating a new newsgroup called

```
local.talk.restaurants
```

Right-click the Virtual Directories node under the Default NNTP Virtual Server node in the scope pane of the MMC and select New, Virtual

Figure 13-27
Configuring deletion
time for a
newsgroup.

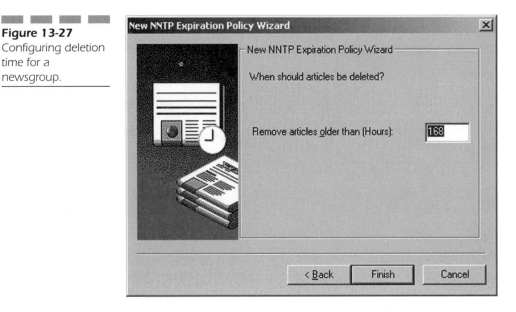

Figure 13-28
A new expiration
policy has been
created.

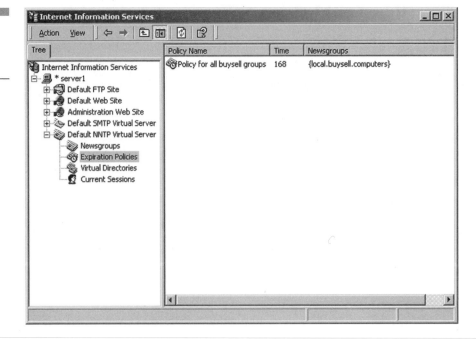

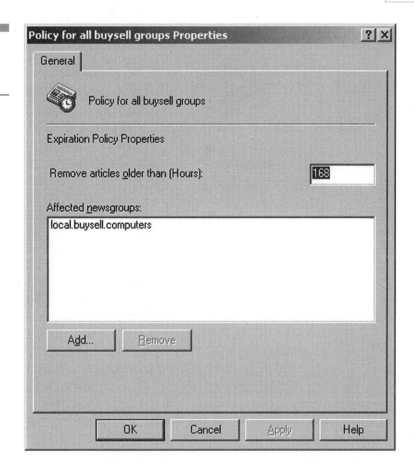

Directory to open the New NNTP Virtual Directory Wizard (see Figure 13-30).

Enter `local.talk.restaurants` in the text field.

Click Next and select the option of File System to specify that you want the directory to be on the local machine. Click Next. Enter the physical path to the folder where the newsgroup content will be stored (see Figure 13-31). If this was to be a remote virtual directory (instead of a local one), you would enter the UNC path to the folder here. Then, in the next screen, you would be required to specify a Windows 2000 user account that can be used to grant access to the newsgroup's content. Because we are doing a local virtual directory, no user account is necessary.

Click finish to create the new virtual directory.

Figure 13-30
Creating a new
virtual directory for
newsgroup
container.

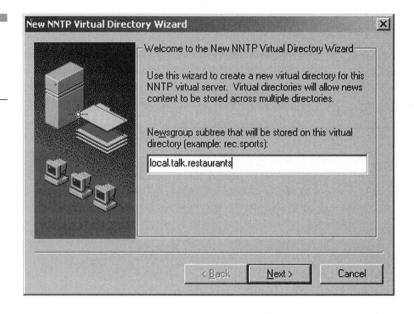

Figure 13-30
Creating a new
virtual directory for
newsgroup
container.

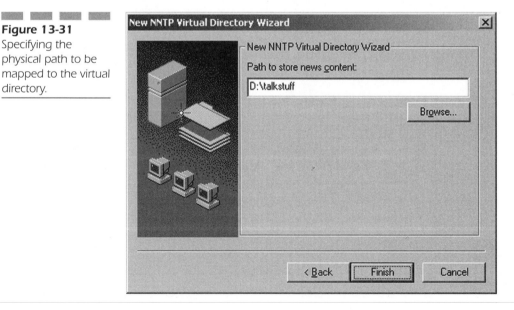

Figure 13-31
Specifying the
physical path to be
mapped to the virtual
directory.

Figure 13-32
The new virtual
directory is listed in
the results pane.

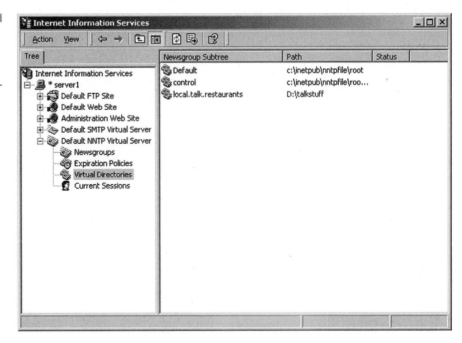

Select the Directories node under the Default NNTP Site node in the
scope pane of the MMC, and you can view the new virtual directory in the
results pane (see Figure 13-32). To make changes to the virtual directory
settings, simply double-click the local.talk node in the results pane and the
Local.talk Properties sheet will appear (see Figure 13-33).

Configuring the Virtual Directory Properties

Double-clicking the Virtual Directory that you created allows you to modify the properties of your newsgroup (see Figure 13-33). If you double-click
the Default Newsgroup subtree, the Properties dialog box will be displayed
for that newsgroup. Click the Contents button to view the location of the
selected virtual directory. The Default Newsgroup will display the following path:

```
C:\InetPub\nntpfile\root\
```

Figure 13-33
Editing the virtual
directory properties.

If a remote directory is selected, it must be specified as a valid UNC path.
User credentials must also be specified to allow access to the share. Click
OK to accept any changes and close this dialog box.

Click the Secure button to configure the encryption options for this newsgroup. Click OK to accept any changes and close this dialog box.

At the bottom of the Properties dialog box (see Figure 13-33), you'll see
options for access restrictions for the selected newsgroup.

The following access restrictions may be specified regarding the NNTP
home directory:

■ Allow Posting permits clients to post to newsgroups stored in this
directory.

■ Restrict Newsgroup Visibility allows only users who have proper
access permissions to view newsgroups located in this directory.
This means that

If Restrict Newsgroup Visibility is *checked* but the client does not have access permissions on the newsgroups, the client will *not* be able to retrieve the list of newsgroups from this server.

If Restrict Newsgroup Visibility is *unchecked* and the client does not have access permissions on the newsgroups, the client *will* be able to retrieve the list of newsgroups from this server but will *not* be able to obtain any lists of articles for the newsgroups or read any of the articles.

NOTE: *If the Restrict Newsgroup Visibility option is checked, a performance drop will occur on the news server. This option should not be checked if anonymous access is allowed to your news server.*

In addition, the following Content control settings may be configured for this directory:

■ Log Access enables the NNTP service to log access by individual clients to the newsgroups. Enable Logging must first be selected on the News Site tab.

■ Index News Content allows message properties and content to be indexed by Index Server for full-text searching of newsgroup articles.

Monitoring and Tuning NNTP Service Performance

The performance of the NNTP service on IIS 5.0 can be monitored using the following tools:

■ *Event Viewer*   The NNTP service logs significant events to the Windows 2000 System Log. Look for events with a source of NNTPSVC.

■ *IIS Logs*   View the IIS logs in a text editor or import them into Site Server to generate reports of NNTP site usage.

■ *Performance Monitor*   The NNTP service includes the performance monitor *NNTP Server* and *NNTP Commands* objects with a number of counters that may be monitored for these objects.

You should monitor the standard counters for detecting memory, processor, disk, and network bottlenecks in addition to specific NNTP counters. In particular, you should set a performance monitor alert for low disk space on the volume where the nntpfile directory is located.

Some of the more important NNTP performance counters to watch are

NNTP Server: Bytes Total/sec, the total rate of bytes transferred by the NNTP service.

NNTP Server: Current Connections, the number of connections to the NNTP server.

NNTP Commands: Logon Failures/sec, the number of logons per second that have failed. If your server is connected to the Internet, a high value for this counter could indicate a possible attempt to hack into your system.

NNTP Server: Maximum Connections, the maximum number of simultaneous connections to the NNTP server. This counter should be *much less* than the setting for Limited To on the News Site tab of the Default NNTP Site Properties sheet.

The NNTP service may require the maintenance action of *rebuilding the NNTP service* under the following circumstances:

- A disk fails, causing a portion of the news files to be lost.
- You manually delete portions of the news files in order to free up resources.
- Access to messages in newsgroups becomes erratic.
- An error message is written to the System log indicating that you should rebuild the NNTP service.

Rebuilding the NNTP service reconstructs the index and hash files and can be accomplished by the following steps: stop the Default NNTP Virtual Server using the MMC. Then right-click the Default NNTP Virtual Server node and select Task, Rebuild Server from the shortcut menu to open the Rebuild NNTP Virtual Server dialog box (Figure 13-34). Select the rebuild mode:

- *Standard* mode rebuilds only group.lst.
- *Medium* mode rebuilds files that are found to have errors.
- *Thorough* mode rebuilds all files including the .xix files.

When rebuilding is complete, start the Default NNTP Site again.

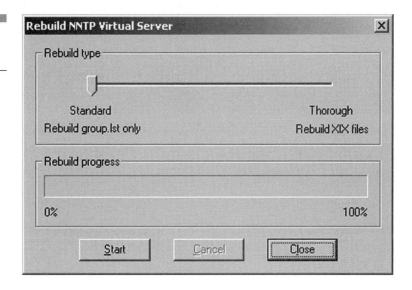

Figure 13-34
The Rebuild NNTP
Virtual Server

SUMMARY

Microsoft NNTP Service may be administered and configured using the Internet Services Manager, the Microsoft Terminal Services, and the Windows Scripting Host. Simple wizards guide administrators through the process of creating and managing newsgroups, expiration policies, and virtual directories for storing newsgroup content.

For More Information

For more information on administering the NNTP service, check out the following resources.

Microsoft Web Site

Search the Microsoft Web site for the keyword "NNTP" to find more information about this service.

TechNet

Search the TechNet knowledge base for articles relating to the NNTP service.

Administering Active Server Pages

Introduction

Using *Active Server Pages* (ASPs), developers can create dynamic Web applications incorporating HTML, scripts, and ActiveX components. *Data Source Names* (DSN) can be set up on the server so the Active Server Pages can display and modify databases contained in databases. Microsoft COM+ Services add transactional functionality to Active Server Pages, enabling developers to build transactional client/server Web applications that are reliable and scaleable. After completing this chapter, administrators will be able to

- Understand the Active Server Pages model compared to CGI
- Create simple Active Server Pages using VBScript
- Create a *Data Source Name* (DSN) on the Web server to connect to back-end databases
- Understand the basic concept of a transaction
- Know the features of COM+ Services
- Explain how Active Server Pages integrate with COM+

This chapter provides only a brief introduction to Web application development using Active Server Pages, databases, and COM+. A full treatment of the subject would require a book of its own, and would be targeted more at a developer audience than network and system administrators.

Understanding Active Server Pages

Traditionally, the usual way of extending the functionality of Web servers has been to use the *Common Gateway Interface* (CGI). CGI is a specification describing how a Web server communicates with gateway applications, which are server-side programs that can receive data from a client browser, process it, and return it to the client. Gateway programs can be written in high-level programming languages like C++ but are more often written in interpreted scripting languages like Practical Extraction and Report Language (Perl). The CGI specification defines how data can be passed from the client browser to the Web server using URL query strings, extra URL path information, or HTTP POST method. Similarly, the CGI specification defines how data is passed from the server to the gateway application using command-line arguments, standard input, or environment variables.

CGI is widely implemented in the Web server community, primarily because Perl is a relatively easy scripting language to learn. Many Webmasters earned their stripes by learning how to write Perl scripts to handle HTML forms, monitor hit counts, perform simple search functions, query databases, and so on. CGI suffers from an inherent defect, however: The gateway program must be started as a separate process every time it is referenced by the server. The result is that CGI tends to be slow and has high server overhead: Every time a CGI form handler is invoked, the Perl interpreter has to be loaded into memory, the Perl script receives the data through the CGI and processes it, and the Perl interpreter is unloaded again.

A method that overcomes some of the weaknesses of CGI is to use custom gateway *application programming interfaces* (APIs) such as Microsoft's ISAPI and Netscape's NSAPI. Gateway applications written using these APIs tend to be much faster than CGI using Perl scripts, primarily because the processing is performed by compiled executables, or DLLs, written in C++ programming language. However, the negative side of using these APIs is that it requires the developer to know a high-level programming language like C++, and the binary executable is not portable across different server platforms, but must be recompiled for each Web server.

To overcome these problems, Microsoft developed the Active Server Pages model, which incorporates the flexibility of scripts, the ease of Visual Basic, and the power of compiled ActiveX server components for the creation of powerful, dynamic Web-based applications.

What Are Active Server Pages?

Active Server Pages (ASPs) are a methodology for combining together HTML with the following three additional elements:

- *ASP scripts:* VBScript, JScript, and other scripts executed on the server
- *ASP objects,* built-in and installable server-side programming objects with methods and properties
- *ASP components,* written in any programming language to extend server functionality

Active Server Pages are ASCII text files saved with the extension .asp and stored on the Web server in a virtual directory that must have both read and script (or execute) access enabled.

The implementation of Active Server Pages on IIS 5.0 provide developers with tools for

■ Creating dynamic Web content that responds to user input.

■ Database connectivity for integrating an HTML front end with a back-end relational ODBC-compliant database.

■ Building scaleable Web applications using a component-based programming architecture.

■ Optionally running Web applications in a separate address space, thus minimizing the impact on the server should the application fail.

Using Active Server Page Scripts

Active Server Page scripts are scripts written in any ActiveX scripting language and contained on an Active Server Page. The IIS 5.0 implementation of Active Server Pages includes a scripting engine that supports the following scripting languages out of the box:

■ *Visual Basic Script (VBScript),* a subset of the Microsoft Visual Basic programming language. This is the default ASP scripting language.

■ *Java Script (JScript),* supported by most browsers. JScript is not a subset of the Java programming language, but is a separate scripting language.

In addition, ActiveX scripting engines may be installed on IIS 5.0 for other scripting languages such as Perl and REXX.

ASP scripts run on the server, not the client. Typically, an ASP will be invoked as follows (Figure 14-1):

■ A client browser tries to access an ASP directly or accesses an HTML page that invokes the ASP as a form or event handler.

■ The ASP is executed on the server and generates a plain HTML response page that is returned to the client.

■ The client displays the HTML response page returned from the server.

The advantages of running scripts on the server include

■ Harnessing the processing power of the server

■ Making use of application libraries and DLLs on the server

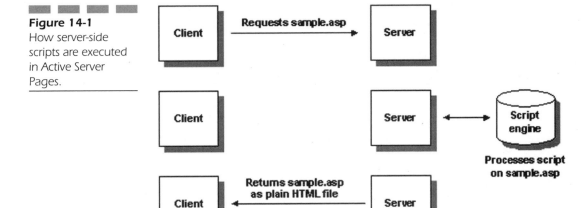

Figure 14-1
How server-side
scripts are executed
in Active Server
Pages.

- Returning to the client a plain HTML file that is equally acceptable to all clients (hence no worries about client compatibility)
- Centralized development and management of applications
- The ability to split an application into multiple *tiers* for processing distribution.

A few simple examples will illustrate the power and simplicity of the Active Server Pages methodology. For the following examples, a virtual directory named aspstuff was created on the Default Web site to contain the ASPs and corresponding HTML files.

Example 1: A Simple HTML Form With an ASP Form Handler

The first example is a simple Web page, one.htm, that creates an HTML form asking the user to submit the user's name. When the user clicks the submit button on the page, the data submitted is passed to the Active Server Page one.asp that serves as a form handler for the HTML form. The script on one.asp is executed on the server, and the server returns the file one.asp as a plain HTML response, greeting the user.

Here is the code for one.htm:

```
<html>
<head><title>ASP Sample 1</title></head>
<body bgcolor=white>

<h1>ASP Sample 1</h1>
<hr>
Please enter your name and I will greet you!
<form method=post action=one.asp>
<input type=text name="person">
<input type=submit>
</form>

</body>
</html>
```

Figure 14-2 shows the client accessing the page one.htm in his browser and entering his name in the form.

Here is the code for the ASP one.asp that acts as a form handler for one.htm:

Figure 14-2

A simple HTML form with an ASP handler.

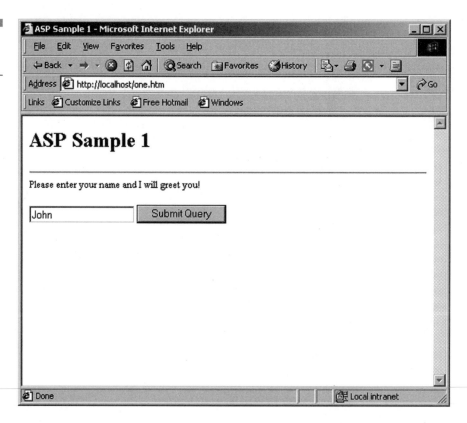

```
<html>
<head><title>ASP Sample 1 Response</title>
</head>
<body bgcolor=white>
<p>Hello

<%
name=request.form("person")
response.write(name)
%>

</p>

<p>
Goodbye <%= name %>
</p>

</body>
</html>
```

Figure 14-3 shows the response page returned to the client's browser.

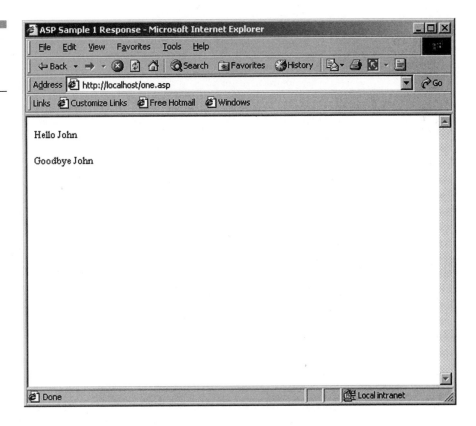

Figure 14-3
The response page returned by the ASP handler.

Here is the actual HTML code returned to the browser, which can be viewed by selecting View, Source in Internet Explorer. Note that the page `one.asp` is returned to the browser, but the script on the page has been executed on the server and the resulting page has only plain HTML on it:

```
<html>
<head><title>ASP Sample 1 Response</title>
</head>
<body bgcolor=white>
<p>Hello

John

</p>

<p>
Goodbye John
</p>

</body>
</html>
```

Here's how it works:

1. The entire script on the `one.asp` ASP is enclosed in script delimiters `<%...%>`.

2. The form `one.htm` uses the HTTP POST method to invoke one.asp as its form handler.

3. The name that the client enters in the textbox in the form is passed to the server as the variable person.

4. The statement

   ```
   name=request.form("person")
   ```

   uses the form collection of the built-in object request to retrieve the contents of the variable person and assign it to the variable name. Built-in objects are discussed later in this chapter.

5. The statement

   ```
   response.write(name)
   ```

   uses the write method of the built-in object response to write the contents of the variable name to the HTTP output stream, displaying the name John on the browser.

6. The expression

   ```
   <%= name %>
   ```

   sends the contents of the variable name to the HTTP output stream, displaying the name John a second time on the browser. Note that this expression does not need to be part of the script on the ASP.

Example 2: A Simple ASP Mileage Converter

The second example is a simple Web application for converting miles to kilometers. The page `two.htm` has an HTML form for the user to enter the number of miles. Pressing the Convert button sends the data to the ASP `two.asp`, which calculates the equivalent number of kilometers and returns the result to the user.

Here is the code for `two.htm`:

```
<html>
<Head><title>ASP Sample 2</title></head>
<body bgcolor=white>

<h1>ASP Sample 2</h1>
<hr>
<p>Conversion Utility</p>
<p>
<form method=post action=two.asp>
<input type=text name="miles"> miles=? kms
</p>
<p><input type=submit name=Convert value="Convert!"></p>
</form>

</body>
</html>
```

Figure 14-4 shows the client accessing the page `two.htm` in a browser and entering the number of miles in the textbox on the form.

Here is the code for the ASP `two.asp` that performs the calculation request by one.htm:

```
<html>
<head><title>ASP Sample 2 Response</title></head>
<body bgcolor=white>

<%
dim sMiles, sKms
const sConv = 1.6
sMiles = request.form("miles")
sKms = sConv * sMiles
response.write sMiles & " Miles5" & sKms & " kms"
%>

</body>
</html>
```

Figure 14-5 shows the resulting page returned to the client's browser.

Here is the HTML code returned to the browser, which can be viewed by selecting View, Source in Internet Explorer:

Figure 14-4
A simple Web application for converting mileage.

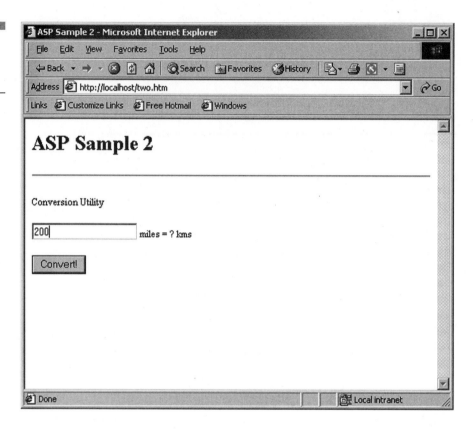

```
<html>
<head><title>ASP Sample 2 Response</title></head>
<body bgcolor=white>

200 Miles = 320 kms

</body>
</html>
```

If you are familiar with Visual Basic (or any other form of BASIC for that matter), you will recognize statements such as

■ dim sMiles, sKms (declares two variables)

■ const sConv51.6 (declares a constant and assigns it a value)

■ sKms5sConv * sMiles (an arithmetic expression converting miles to kilometers)

Active Server Page scripts use *Visual Basic script (VBScript)* by default, which is a subset of the Visual Basic programming language. So if you know

Figure 14-5
The result of
performing a mileage
conversion.

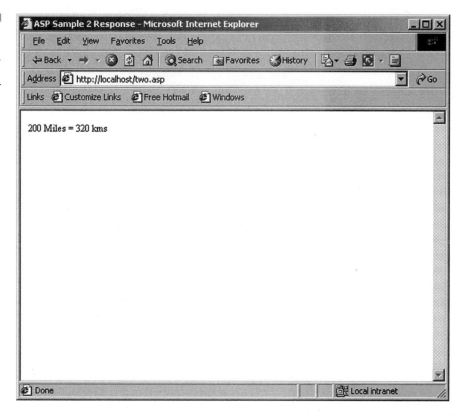

any Visual Basic, you can leverage your knowledge for building Web applications on IIS 5.0.

Example 3: Another ASP Mileage Converter

The third example is a Web application that generates a conversion table for converting one unit of distance to another. The page three.htm has an HTML form for the user to select which unit to convert to which. Pressing the Generate button causes the ASP three.asp to create and return a sample conversion table to the user.

Here is the code for three.htm:

```
<html>
<head><title>ASP Sample 3</title></head>
<body bgcolor=white>

<h1>ASP Sample 3</h1>
<p>Generate table to convert: </p>

<form method=post action=three.asp>
     <p>from <select name="unit1" size="1">
             <option selected value=0>miles</option>
             <option value=1>kilometers</option>
             <option value=2>furlongs</option>
             </select> to <select name="unit2" size="1">
                     <option value=0>miles</option>
                     <option selected value=1>kilometers</option>
                     <option value=2>furlongs</option>
             </select></p>
             <p><input type="submit" name="Generate"
value="Generate!"></p>
</form>

</body>
</html>
```

Figure 14-6 shows the client accessing the page three.htm in a browser and choosing to create a conversion table from kilometers into furlongs. Here is the code for the ASP three.asp that generates the table:

```
<html>
<head><title>ASP Sample 3 Response</title></head>
<body bgcolor=white>

<h1>Conversion Table</h1>
<hr>
<%
dim sConv(2,2), sLabel(2)
sConv(0,0)=1
sConv(0,1)=1.6
sConv(0,2)=8
sConv(1,0)=.625
sConv(1,1)=1
sConv(1,2)=5
sConv(2,0)=.125
sConv(2,1)=5
sConv(2,2)=1
sLabel(0)="miles"
sLabel(1)="kms"
sLabel(2)="furlongs"
sUnit1=request.form("unit1")
sUnit2=request.form("unit2")
response.write "<table border=1 cellpadding=5>"
for k = 1 to 5 step 1
     var1=k
     var2=var1 * sConv(sUnit1,sUnit2)
     response.write "<tr>"
     response.write "<td>" & var1 & " " & sLabel(sUnit1) & "</td>"
     response.write "<td>" & var2 & " " & sLabel(sUnit2) & "</td>"
     response.write "</tr>"
```

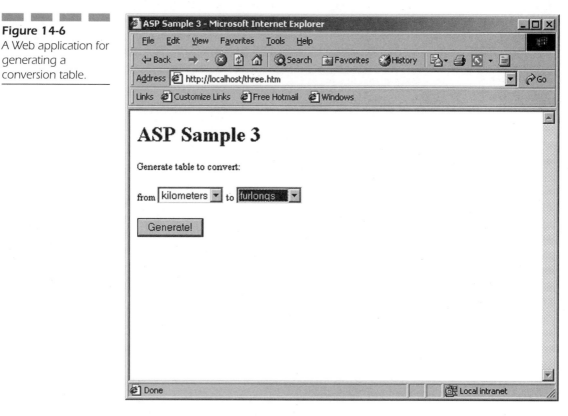

Figure 14-6
A Web application for generating a conversion table.

```
next
response.write "</table>"
%>

</body>
</html>
```

Figure 14-7 shows the resulting page returned to the client's browser.

A simple For . . . Next loop is used to create the table. The three-by-three matrix sConv holds the conversion factors, whereas the three-element vector sLabel holds the names of the units.

Example 4: Using ASP To Send Email Via the SMTP Service

The fourth example of using Active Server Pages is a simple Web application that allows users to send email from an HTML form, four.htm, by

Figure 14-7
A conversion table
generated by an
Active Server Page.

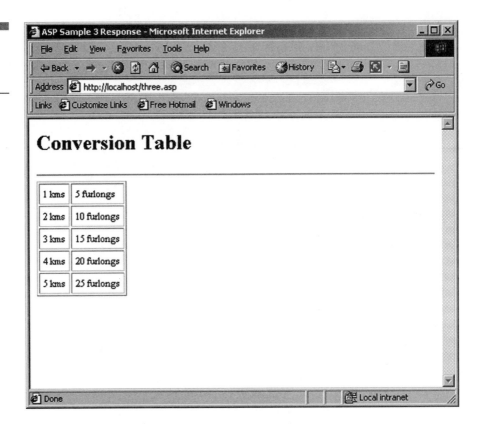

using the SMTP service on IIS 5.0. Refer to Chapter 12, *Administering the SMTP Service*, to understand how to configure this service. Here, the Active Server Page four.asp is the email form handler for the Web page four.htm.

Here is the code for four.htm:

```html
<html>
<head><title>ASP Sample 4</title></head>
<body bgcolor=white>

<h1>ASP Sample 4</h1>
<hr>
<h2>Send email using the SMTP service</h2>
<form method=post action=four.asp>
<br>Sender's address:
<input type=text name="sSender" size=30>
<br>Receiver's address:
<input type=text name="sReceiver" size=30>
<br>Subject or message:
<input type=text name="sSubject" size=30>
<br>Body of message:<br>
<textarea cols=40 rows=4 name="sBody"></textarea>
<br><input type=submit value="Send mail now!">
```

```
</form>
</body>
</html>
```

Figure 14-8 shows the client accessing the page `four.htm` in her browser and using it to send mail.

Here is the code for the ASP `four.asp` that sends the email using the SMTP service on IIS 5.0:

```
<html>
<head><title>ASP Sample 4 Response</title></head>
<body bgcolor=white>
<%
Set fs = CreateObject("Scripting.FileSystemObject")
Set msg =
fs.CreateTextFile("c:\InetPub\mailroot\pickup\message.txt", True)
msg.WriteLine("x-sender: " & Request.Form("sSender"))
msg.WriteLine("x-receiver: " & Request.Form("sReceiver"))
msg.WriteLine("From: " & Request.Form("sSender"))
msg.WriteLine("To: " & Request.Form("sReceiver"))
msg.WriteLine("Subject: " & Request.Form("sSubject"))
msg.WriteBlankLines(1)
msg.WriteLine(Request.Form("sBody"))
```

Figure 14-8

A simple form to send email using an ASP form handler.

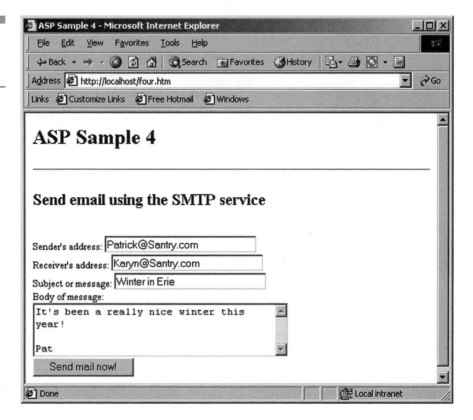

```
msg.Close
Response.Write("<html><body>")
Response.Write("<h1>Message sent!</h1>")
Response.Write("</html></body>")
Set fs = Nothing
Set msg = Nothing
%>
```

```
</body></html>
```

Here's how it works:

1. The user completes the form and passes the variables to the server using the HTTP POST method.

2. The statement

   ```
   Set fs  = CreateObject("Scripting.FileSystemObject")
   ```

   creates a file system object and assigns it to the variable fs.

3. The statement

   ```
   Set msg = fs.CreateTextFile("c:\InetPub\mailroot\pickup\
   message.txt", True)
   ```

   creates a TextStream object and assigns it to the variable msg. In effect, it creates and opens the text file message.txt for writing.

4. The lines with msg.WriteLine use the WriteLine method of the TextStream object msg to write lines of text to the file message.txt.

5. The line msg.Close uses the Close method of the msg object to close the text file message.txt.

6. Because the file message.txt has been created in the Pickup subdirectory of the Mailroot directory, the SMTP service immediately moves it to the Queue subdirectory and processes it for delivery. See Chapter 13 for more information on various subdirectories of Mailroot.

Using Active Server Page Objects

Another element of Active Server Pages is ASP objects. These programming objects come in two forms: built-in objects and installable objects. ASP objects can have forms, methods, and collections just like VB objects.

Using Built-in ASP Objects

There are six built-in objects in the ASP methodology. These objects can be used in ASP scripts. They include the following:

- *Application*   This object can be used to share information between users of an application. In IIS 5.0, an application consists of all .asp files contained in a virtual directory and its subdirectories.
- *ObjectContext*   This object can be invoked to start or end a transaction.
- *Request*   This object retrieves the contents of variables passed from clients to servers during HTTP request messages. An example of using this object is the collection request.form used in Example 1 to pass a value from the HTML form to the ASP application.
- *Response*   This object is used to send a text stream to the requesting client. An example is the response.write method in Example 1.
- *Server*   This object can provide the developer with properties and methods on the IIS server.
- *Session*   This object stores values from page to page in an ASP application.

Using Installable ASP Objects

In addition to the above, the ASP framework is extensible and allows the installation of ActiveX components to generate useful objects. These five installable objects include

- *Browser capabilities,* which allow the server to determine the characteristics of the client browser connecting to it
- *Content linking,* which automatically generates a table of contents and navigational hyperlinks
- *Content rotator,* which can rotate a banner ad every time a page is viewed
- *Database connectivity,* which allows the ASPs to interact with various database systems
- *File access,* which allows you to use ASPs to interact with the local file system

For more information on the methods, properties, and collection of ASP objects, refer to the IIS online documentation.

Using Active Server Page Components

ASP components are ActiveX server components conforming to the COM standard and written in any programming language that provide more speed and responsiveness than can be afforded by ActiveX scripts. The development language for ActiveX components can be

- C++
- Java
- Visual Basic

For more information on creating and using ASP components, refer to the IIS documentation.

Walkthough: Establishing a Database Connection to SQL Server

Most Web applications today do more than just simple calculations. Many of these Web applications are front-ends to databases. In order to be able to connect to these back-end databases via Active Server Pages, you as an administrator will need to set up a *data source name* (DSN) on the Web server. This DSN is what ASP developers will refer to in their code in order to connect to a back-end database. The DSN contains a reference to all the information needed to connect to a database. In this walkthrough, we will create a connection to a SQL Server database on the Web server so ASP scripts can connect to the database located on SQL Server.

First, select Start, Programs, Administrative Tools, Data Sources (ODBC) to start the ODBC Data Source Administrator (Figure 14-9). Select the System tab to create a System DSN. A System DSN will be available for all users of the machine including the system. Other options are User DSNs, which are available to just the user who created it, and File DSNs.

Click the Add button to open the Create New Data Source dialog box (Figure 14-10), which contains listings of all available *Open Database Connectivity* (ODBC) drivers available on the system. Select SQL Server and click the Finish button.

Next, the Create a New Data Source to SQL Server dialog box (Figure 14-11) will appear. Enter in a name for your DSN—in this example, we used `dsnSQLServer`. This is the name that ASP developers will refer to in their code to connect to the database. In the Description field, enter a description to describe what this connection is. In the drop-down box, select your SQL Server. By default, the ODBC connector will list all SQL Servers that are available on your network. You can also type a server in manually if it does not appear in this list. Click the Next button to continue.

Figure 14-9
Creating a system
DSN on the Web
server.

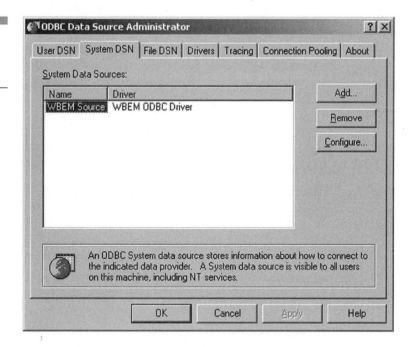

Figure 14-10
The Create New Data
Source dialog box.

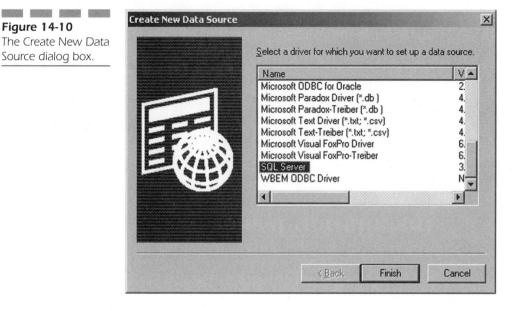

Figure 14-11
Specifying
connection
information.

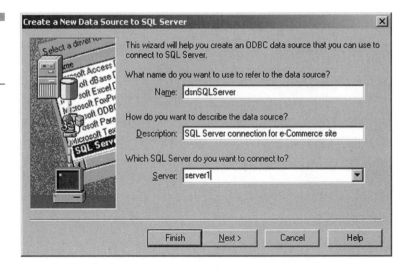

Figure 14-11
Specifying
connection
information.

Figure 14-12
Specify how you
wish to connect to
the database.

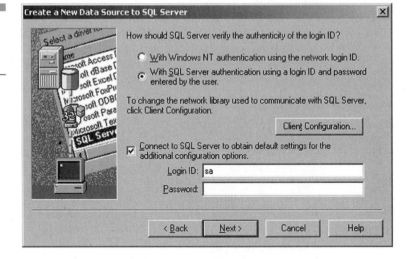

In this dialog box, specify how you wish to connect to the database (see Figure 14-12). You can use either Windows NT authentication or SQL Server's built-in security. Refer to the SQL Server documentation on SQL Server security. In this example, use the built-in *sa* (system administrator) account to authenticate to the database. Click the Next button to continue.

14-13
Setting a default database.

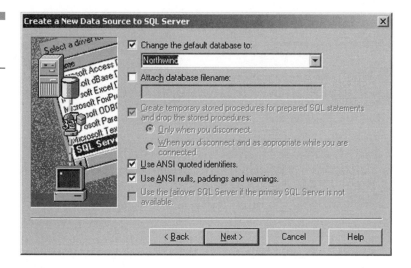

Figure 14-14
Specifying locale and character type information.

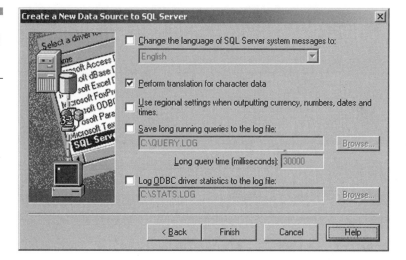

Next, specify which database you want to be the default database for this connection. In this example (Figure 14-13), the Northwind database is selected. Keep the default values and click on the Next button to continue.

In the next dialog box (Figure 14-14), you can specify language information, data type information, and logging. Keep the default values and click

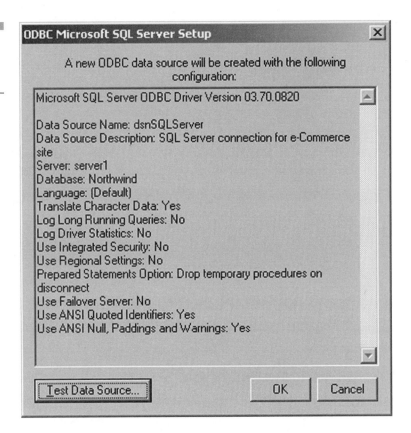

the Finish button to bring up a summary of your connection (Figure 14-15). Click the Test button to bring up a dialog box (Figure 14-16) that confirms the connection test was successful. Click on OK three times to close the underlying dialog boxes and to complete your ODBC entry.

For more thorough coverage of SQL Server, refer to Microsoft's Web site at

```
http://www.microsoft.com/SQL/
```

NOTE: *When connecting to a database via ASP scripts, remember the security context under which the scripts run. If you are trying to connect to a SQL Server database over a network, make sure that you use either a domain account as your anonymous IIS user account or duplicate IIS account on the SQL Server. Also, in the case of Access databases, Access creates a temporary file when you access the database. Be sure that the IIS account has the permissions to write to the directory that the database is in to create the temporary file. This is just one of the common errors that can*

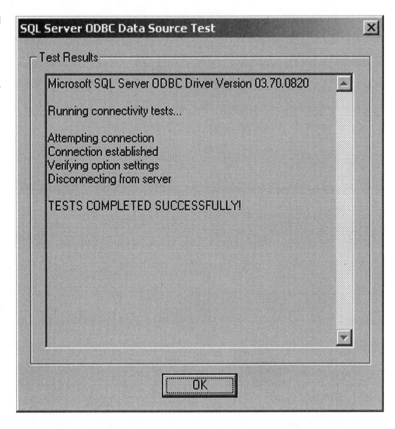

Figure 14-16
A successful test of
connecting to the
SQL Server database.

*occur when trying to establishing database connectivity with IIS. Refer to
Microsoft's Web site for a complete listing of ODBC error codes and their
meaning.*

        msdn.microsoft.com/library/psdk/dasdk/odap1v77.htm

Example 4: Connecting to a Database Via Asp

This next example is an ASP script that connects to the DSN that was created in the previous walkthrough and displays data from a table contained
in the database.

```
<html>
<head><title>ASP Sample Database Display</title></head>
<body bgcolor=white>
```

```
<H1>Customer Names</H1>
<%
Set Conn = CreateObject("ADODB.Connection")
Conn.open "DSN=dsnSQLServer;UID=sa;PWD="
sSQL = "SELECT * FROM Customer"
Set rs = Conn.Execute(sSQL)
If Not rs.EOF Then
       Do Until rs.EOF
              Response.Write rs("CompanyName") & "<BR>"
       Rs.MoveNext
Loop
End If
rs.Close
Conn.Close
Set rs = Nothing
Set Conn = Nothing
%>

</body></html>
```

Here's how it works:

1. First, an instance of the Active Database Connection Object is assigned to the variable Conn.

2. Then the DSN and database logon information that was created in the walkthrough is passed to the connection object.

3. Then the SQL statement is assigned to the variable sSQL, which is then passed to the Execute method of the connection object. This in turn creates a recordset.

4. The recordset is then checked to see whether any records match. If records are returned, it loops through the recordset and displays the value of the CompanyName field in the browser using the response.write method of ASP.

5. All objects are then closed and set back to nothing to clean the allocated memory space.

We could continue creating more complex Active Server Page scripts and testing them, but the subject is so wide that it really demands a book of its own. For more information about writing Active Server Page scripts, consult the online documentation for IIS on an item called the Scripter's Reference.

Understanding COM+ Services

COM+ is a developer tool for building three-tiered transaction-oriented Web applications using components that integrate and manage the functions of clients, servers, and data sources. COM+ can be used to

- Package components into integrated applications
- Manage threads and processes in distributed applications
- Manage ODBC connections to provide high-performance database access
- Share data sources among users while managing states and synchronization
- Instantiate objects when needed on a just-in-time basis
- Manage distributed transactions and provide recovery features in case of failure
- Isolate application processes to provide a robust fail-over environment
- Use DCOM for component integration and communications across the network

Understanding Transactions

The core of the COM+ services is the Microsoft Distributed Transaction Coordinator (MS DTC), which was first introduced with SQL Server 6.5. The MS DTC manages transactions, which are collections of business processes that must either all succeed or all fail together as a group. The MS DTC runs as a Windows 2000 service and can be stopped and started using the Services program in Administrative Tools.

A good example of a transaction is a credit card purchase at a restaurant. The parties involved in the transaction are the customer, the restaurant owner, and the credit agency. The following business processes must either all succeed or all fail in any given transaction:

- The customer's credit account must be debited by the amount of the meal.
- The restaurant owner's merchant account must be credited by the amount of the meal minus the transaction fee.
- The credit agency's account must be credited by the amount of the transaction fee.

If any one portion of this transaction fails, the whole transaction must fail and any completed portions must be rolled back; otherwise, someone will lose money somewhere and will certainly complain.

Microsoft Component Services are designed to handle the underlying architecture to support such distributed transactions using Web applications as the front-end interface.

Active Server Pages and COM+

In IIS 5.0, Active Server Pages are grouped together into applications. An application is a tree of directories and files (Active Server Pages), usually starting with a virtual server or virtual directory and extending downward into all subdirectories or until another application is defined.

Applications can be run in two different ways on IIS 5.0:

■ They can be run *in-process* in the same address space as the main IIS process inetinfo.exe. (This is the default method and was the only option in earlier versions of IIS.)

■ They can be run *out-of-process and pooled.* this allows the application to be pooled with other applications, but still outside of the IIS.

■ They can be run *out-of-process* as an isolated process in their own address space, being managed by the COM+.

The second preceding option provides *process isolation,* which has the following advantages:

■ The inetinfo.exe process and all other processes on the IIS server are protected against failure of the application.

■ If the application does fail, the COM+ service can restart it automatically without requiring the server to be stopped and started again.

■ ActiveX components can be loaded and unloaded without requiring that other processes and services be stopped first.

In effect, the server code responsible for managing Active Server Pages and ISAPI applications has been moved from the main inetinfo.exe process to a new module, called the *Web Application Manager (WAM),* that is managed by Microsoft COM+. Applications are assigned *globally unique identifiers (GUIDs)* by the WAM and are registered by COM+ as *packages.* Even the default IIS process inetinfo.exe is managed by COM+ as an *in-process package.* Because of this management by COM+, each application can be started and stopped independently of other applications on IIS 5.0.

NOTE: *MTS packages that were running under Microsoft Transaction Services in IIS 4.0 will automatically be upgraded to COM+ when upgrading NT 4 to Windows 2000.*

Walkthrough: Configuring an Application

By default, when you create a virtual directory in IIS, it will be configured as an application that runs outside of the process of IIS. Applications are designated with by icon that has a package with an object in it. Figure 14-17 shows a virtual directory called aspstuff that is designated as an application.

To define the process that this application will run, select the application icon in the right pane (in this example ASPStuff) and click the Properties button on the rebar to open the ASPStuff Properties sheet (see Figure 14-18). Note the name of the application is the same as the name of the virtual directory.

By default, when the virtual directory is created, the application is set up as Medium pooled. This means that the application will run outside of the process of IIS, but with other applications that are also running outside of the IIS process. In this example, the setting is changed to High (isolated); meaning that this application will run in an isolated process outside of the IIS process and separate from other applications running on IIS.

Figure 14-17

A virtual directory configured as an application.

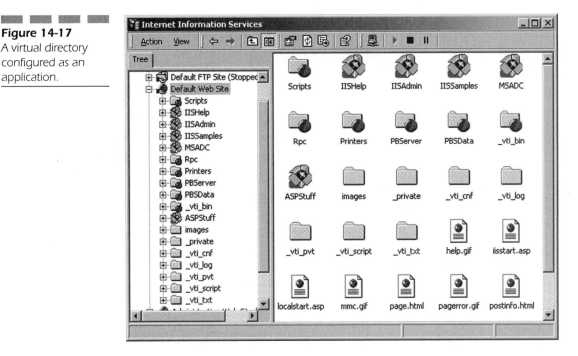

Figure 14-18
Changing the
application's runtime
process.

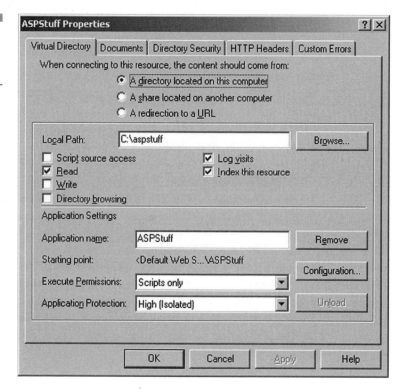

Configuring Component Services

To see the effect on COM+ when an IIS application's process is changed to isolated, select Start, Programs, Administrative Tools, Component Services. This will start the Component Services MMC snap-in (Figure 14-19). Expand the Component Services node, and then expand the Computers node, My Computer node, and then Com+ node. This will display all the COM+ applications currently configured on the server. Listed here are IIS In-Process Applications and IIS Out-of-Process Pooled Applications. Below these IIS applications in Figure 14-19 is an IIS-—{default web site//root/asp-stuff}. This package is created when the virtual directory is set up to run in an isolated process. You can further configure the COM+ package to run under certain security roles and configure it to run as a transaction.

Component Services includes a number of wizards for creating custom business solutions by assembling packages and components together. Using Component Services requires extensive knowledge of technologies like ActiveX and DCOM, plus understanding of the methods and APIs of com-

Figure 14-19
The Component
Services Manager
MMC snap-in.

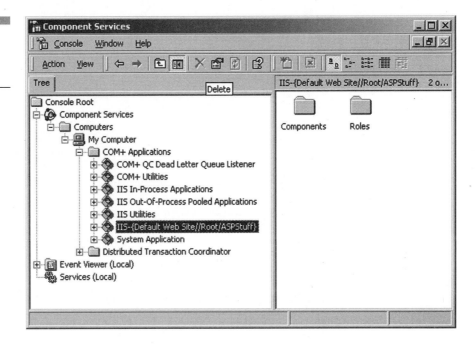

ponents created with high-level programming languages, all of which are beyond the scope of this book. For more information on configuring COM+ applications, refer to the COM+ Technical Series Guide available on MSDN online:

```
msdn.microsoft.com
```

SUMMARY

Active Server Pages are a methodology that combines server-side scripts, ASP objects, and server components to create Web applications that extend the functionality of a Web server. You can create DSNs on the Web server to connect to back-end database management systems. In IIS 5.0, Active Server Pages are managed by the Application Manager, a component of Component Services, which allows them to run either in-process or out-of-process, depending on your need for security and stability.

For More Information

For information on Microsoft's plan for using COM+ in the Enterprise, read

```
www.microsoft.com/com/tech/complus.asp
```

View the ASP FAQ on Microsoft's Web site:

```
msdn.microsoft.com/library/backgrnd/html/msdn_aspfaq.htm
```

For a complete reference on Microsoft scripting technologies, check out

```
msdn.microsoft.com/scripting/
```

For information on database access technologies, refer to

```
www.microsoft.com/data/
```

Some other WWW sites on ASP include

```
www.activeserverpages.com
www.aspin.com
www.15seconds.com
www.actionjackson.com
www.asptoday.com
www.santry.com
www.asp101.com
www.4guysfromrolla.com
```

Troubleshooting

Successful troubleshooting of a product is largely the result of three factors:

- Experience (you have seen something like this before)
- Training (you have read something about this before)
- Research (find someone else who has seen this before)

In addition, the following factors also help:

- Imagination (intuition)
- Methodical reasoning (the process of elimination)
- Risk-taking (try something new)
- Luck (you'll need it!)

This book has been designed to enhance your abilities to troubleshoot IIS 5.0 configurations by providing walkthroughs of basic tasks to enable you to gain experience, by clearly explaining configuration options to train you in the product and make you knowledgeable in it, and by listing additional resources you can consult for further research.

Nevertheless, from the author's own experience and that of many other administrators and Web masters, Internet Information Services 5.0 is a complex product that sometimes behaves in unexpected and highly frustrating ways.

The author has worked with the product extensively and has communicated with and listened to other administrators who have worked with it, and one result of this process is this final chapter called "Troubleshooting." Not simply a rehash of concepts from previous chapters, nor intended to replace a thorough study of the previous chapters and of the IIS online documentation, this chapter instead describes many problems from *real life* that administrators have wrestled with in their attempts to implement IIS 5.0 in their corporate and ISP environments, while other scenarios have been *contrived* to simulate known problems you might encounter as you implement IIS 5.0 in your network.

The result is not a cookbook of official solutions but rather a grab-bag of tips, tricks, workarounds, and warnings covering all of the areas dealt with in this book. Instead of telling you what the product should ideally be doing, we will look instead at what it really does in various situations and contexts, in combination with different hardware and software, and under different needs and demands.

In addition to reading this chapter, you can find information about troubleshooting IIS 5.0 in the following places:

- There are "Troubleshooting" chapters in the online documentation.
- The release notes for each component should be consulted.
- The IIS 5.0 Resource Kit.
- You should browse the Microsoft public newsgroups.
- Consult Support Online on Microsoft's Web site to search the Knowledge Base.
- Search for mailing lists (list servers) dealing with IIS 5.
- Read current issues of *Windows 2000 Magazine* and other magazines.
- Visit other relevant Web sites.
- Have a beer with colleagues from other companies using IIS (my favorite!).

I encourage you as you gain expertise with Internet Information Services 5.0 to take the time to document your stories of frustration and success and share them with the online community through your personal Web site, online newsletter, mailing lists, and newsgroups. I also encourage you to be patient with and give clear advice to those who are still struggling with issues that now seem clear to you.

Finally, I ask you not to be frustrated or disappointed if your particular problem is not described here. Please remember that at the time of this writing, this product has been in release version for only one month, and that is barely time to become familiarized with its wealth of new features, let alone discover, document, and fix all of its bugs. This chapter is in no way intended to be the final word on troubleshooting IIS 5.0.

So let's look now at some examples of real problems and how administrators have tried to solve them and contrived scenarios of problems you are likely to encounter as you work with IIS 5.0. All situations have been fictionalized to try to emphasize the key issues involved. The suggestions and workarounds are presented "as-is" by the author, who accepts no liability for the effects of implementing them but nevertheless presents them in good faith.

Good luck!

Installation Issues

Install or Upgrade?

"Hi, I have an existing IIS 4 machine with NT installed. What do you recommend? Should I do a fresh install or upgrade my OS to Windows 2000?"

This is not an official answer, but the consensus out there with administrators and Web masters seems to be that an upgrade is more likely to succeed when upgrading your Web server. Existing settings for your Web applications will be ported over to IIS 5, and any legacy MTS components will be automatically upgraded to the new COM+ archetecture.

SQL Server and IIS 5.0

"I want to install IIS 5.0 on a machine with an SQL database on it as well. In what order should I install things?"

Although it's recommended to distribute your SQL Server and IIS on different machines, the following installation steps are recommended by some administrators:

- Windows 2000 Server
- SQL Server 7
- SQL Service Pack 3
- IIS 5.0

One Hundred Percent CPU Usage

"I installed IIS 5.0 on a server with a huge number of documents to be scanned, filtered, and merged into a catalog. The problem is, I have just installed IIS 5.0, and for the last two hours my CPU usage has hovered close to 100 percent."

This is normal behavior on a fresh system when there is a great deal of preinstalled content (including the online documentation). When IIS boots, Indexing Services starts indexing the corpus, driving CPU usage high for a time of anywhere from a few minutes to many hours. Use Task Manager to observe the activity of the `cidaemon.exe` process.

Documentation Problems

Cannot Access Online Documentation from Any Machine Except the IIS Server

"I can access the online documentation from the IIS server console using the Start menu, but when I try to access it from any other machine by opening the URL, `http://server1/iishelp`, it doesn't work. I get a 403.6 Forbidden IP Address status message. Why?"

Using the MMC, open the Properties sheet for the IISHELP virtual directory under the server node. Select the Directory Security tab, click Edit for IP Address and Domain Name Restrictions, and grant access to the IP address of the machine(s) from which you want to be able to access the documentation.

Remote Administration

Cannot Access Remote Administration Tools (HTML) Except on IIS Server

"I can open the Internet Service Manager (HTML) on the IIS server using the Start menu, but I can't open it from another computer using the URL, `http://<server_ name>:<TCP_port>` What's wrong?"

The Administration Web Site in the MMC has IP address restrictions in place, granting access only to `127.0.0.1` and localhost. Access the Directory Security tab on the Administration Web Site Properties sheet and Edit the IP address restrictions to include the machine(s) from which you want to be able to access the site.

If this is already set properly, check to see whether the RPC Locator service is running.

The WWW Service

No Logging Formats Available in WWW Properties Sheet

You try to enable logging on IIS by accessing the Web Site tab of the server Properties sheet, but no logging formats are listed in the Active log format drop-down list.

Open a command prompt and type

```
cd \winnt\system32\inetsrv
regsvr32 iislog.dll
regsvr32 iscomlog.dll
regsvr32 logui.ocx
```

Exit the command prompt and enable logging. This will register the log files with IIS. Stop and start IIS after making these changes.

Access and Authentication Issues

Users Cannot Access Web Site

You create a Web site for your corporate intranet, place content in the appropriate home directory, and access the site with your browser as Administrator. Users complain that they cannot access the Web site you have created. What should you do?

Try checking the following:

- Is IIS read permission assigned to the home directory of the site? (Check the Home Directory tab of the WWW Properties sheet.)
- Is NTFS read permission assigned to the Users group?
- Are any applicable IP address restrictions in effect on this site? (Check the Directory Security tab of the WWW Properties sheet.)
- Is at least one authentication method (anonymous, basic, challenge/response) enabled for the site? (Check the Directory Security tab of the WWW Properties sheet.)

Anonymous Users Cannot Access Web Site

You create a Web site for an Internet server, place content in the appropriate home directory, and can access the site with your browser as Administrator. People complain that they cannot access the Web site you have created. What should you do?

Try checking the following:

- Is anonymous access enabled for your site? (Check the Directory Security tab of the WWW Properties sheet.)
- Is the anonymous user account IUSR_SERVERNAME synchronized with User Manager? (Check the Directory Security tab of the WWW Properties sheet.)
- Does the anonymous user account IUSR_SERVERNAME have the right to log on locally? (Select Policies, User Rights on the User Manager menu.)

Users Cannot Access Web Site Using Basic Authentication

You create a Web site, place content in the appropriate home directory, and can access the site with your browser as Administrator. Basic Authentication is enabled on the site, but users complain that they cannot access the Web site you have created. What should you do?

- Has a default domain been specified for Basic Authentication? (Check the Directory Security tab of the WWW Properties sheet.)
- Does the user have the right to log on locally? (Select Policies, User Rights on the User Manager menu.)

Netscape User on UNIX Workstation Cannot Access Web Site

"I'm using Netscape Navigator on a UNIX workstation, and I can't connect to a Web site on an IIS 5.0 server. I get a logon box, but when I enter a valid Windows 2000 account, logon fails."

Make sure that Basic Authentication is enabled for the Web site. Netscape Navigator does not support Windows 2000 Integrated Authentication.

Third-Party Authentication Tools

If you want remote users to be authenticated, do not want to use Basic Authentication because it is insecure, and do not want to use Windows 2000 Integrated Authentication because some users are running Netscape Navigator or because you want to maintain a Web user database separate from your Windows 2000 user database, you may want to consider installing a third-party ISAPI filter authentication tool. A number of administrators have recommended AuthentiX from Flicks Software, at

`www.flicks.com/flicks/authx.htm`

Virtual Directories and Servers

Cannot Create Virtual Servers with IIS 5.0 on Windows 2000 Professional

"I have IIS 5.0 installed on Windows 2000 Professional and Internet Explorer 5. I have a default Web site, but I can't create any additional ones. What's wrong?"

Nothing is wrong. IIS 5.0 on Windows 2000 Professional does not support virtual servers.

Missing IP Addresses

"I have installed Windows 2000 on a machine and created 200 IP addresses for the Network Adapter Card in Control Panel, Network, TCP Properties. Then I went to the Web Site tab on my Web site Properties sheet and tried to select an IP address from the drop-down list. Unfortunately, it is blank (or maybe incomplete)."

The workaround is to type the IP address directly into the IP Address box on this property sheet. Make sure that you use one of the IP addresses you created on the server.

Content Development Issues

Error "Server error: cannot access the server configuration files"

You have FrontPage extensions installed on your server, and you enable a site as a FrontPage Web using the Home Directory tab of your Web site Properties sheet. You start FrontPage and try to connect to the Web site but get the error, "Server error: cannot access the server configuration files."

From the IIS MMC snap-in, right-click on the Web and use the Check Server Extensions option from the context menu.

Unable to Save Active Content in the FrontPage Web

"Content authors are complaining that they cannot save their scripts in a FrontPage Web. How can I fix this?"

Some people have noticed this behavior with FrontPage 2000 extensions. The fix appears to be selecting the server node in the IIS Manager and selecting Properties from the context menu. In the Server Properties dialog, check the *Allow authors to upload executables* option.

Users Cannot Log On to IIS Using FrontPage

"As Administrator, I can connect to a Web running FrontPage on the local IIS server, but remote users cannot log on and connect to the Web using FrontPage. They have been given Authoring permission on the Web and have the correct ACLs on the NTFS partition that contains the content. What's wrong?"

You need to give the user the right to log on locally to the IIS server as well.

Site Server and Site Server Commerce Edition

Site Server Express

"Having moved to Windows 2000 Server, we can no longer find Site Server Express to analyze our log files. Where is it?"

Site Server Express is no longer part of Windows 2000 Server. You can opt to install the full version of Site Server, which includes a reporting and analysis program like the one in Site Server Express.

Can't Install Site Server or Site Server Commerce Edition

"While upgrading to Windows 2000, the installation informed me that I cannot use Site Server under Windows 2000."

You need to download and install Site Server Serice Pack 3 and the Windows 2000 fix located on Microsoft's Web site at

```
http://www.microsoft.com/siteserver
```

Proxy Server 2.0 and Windows 2000

"While upgrading to Windows 2000, the installation informed me that I cannot use Microsoft Proxy Server under Windows 2000. What do I need to do to get it to work?"

Download the Microsoft Proxy Server 2.0 Update Wizard to install Microsoft Proxy Server on Windows 2000. Refer to Microsoft's Web site to download the Wizard

```
http://www.microsoft.com/proxy/Support
```

Indexing Services

Documents to Filter Does Not Zero after Master Merge

"I forced a scan of all my virtual directories and forced a master merge, and I still have a few documents that are unfiltered. What's wrong?"

The documents are probably open or in use by an application that locks files in use, like Microsoft Word. The documents have been scheduled for filtering by the *Content Indexing* (CI) service and will be filtered at the first available opportunity.

Master Merge Halts before Completion

"I forced a Master Merge and was watching the CI statistics by selecting the Index Server node in the MMC, and I noticed that indexing was half completed and then stopped. I still have six persistent indexes, and nothing more is happening. What do I do?"

Check Event Viewer—your disk that holds the catalog is probably full. Free up disk space and stop and start the CI service.

Documents on Remote UNC Share Are Not Indexed

You create a new virtual directory mapped to a remote UNC share. You force a scan of the new virtual directory, but the documents are not filtered.

Check the domain\user and password you used to enable access to the UNC share.

Indexing Services Indexes Hidden FrontPage Directories

How do I stop Index Server from indexing the `hidden` `_vti` directories created by FrontPage?

Access the Properties sheets for these hidden directories in the MMC, and on the Directory tab, clear the Index This Directory checkbox.

Query Does Not Return Expected Result

"I tried a query, and several pages came up in the result set, but a page I know has the query keywords didn't come up. Why?"

Check out the following:

- Do you have NTFS permission to read the page?
- Has the page been filtered yet?
- Is the page in the same language as the query?

Message "Query too expensive"

"I have a large corpus indexed by Index Server, and I submitted a complex query on the corpus and got the message `Query too expensive' instead of a result set."

Increase the value of the registry setting MaxRestrictionNodes.

The FTP Service

Cannot Upload to FTP Site When Anonymous Access Is Disabled

"I have an FTP site that I want my users to access. The site does not have anonymous access enabled. Why can't my users log on and upload files?"

If anonymous access is disabled for an FTP site, a user has to enter a valid Windows NT user account and password to log on to the site. This account must be assigned the right to log on locally on the ISS server.

Performance Issues

Error "Winsock error: no bufferspace is supported"

"I have been adding more virtual servers to my server, and when I reached about 600 virtual servers I began to get intermittent error messages saying, 'Winsock error: no bufferspace is supported.' What do I do?"

Your server is reaching its capacity for hits. You will need to limit the number of hits per day to fewer than 10,000 for your busier sites or offload some sites to another server. You can also try upgrading your server's hardware.

Limit hits per day by accessing the Performance tab of the Web site Properties sheet.

SSL and Certificate Server

Cannot Use Host Header Names with SSL Enabled

You have SSL enabled for the default Web site on an IIS 5.0 server, and you create a virtual server on the same IP address using Host Header Names. You try to access the virtual server and get the default Web site instead.

Host Header Names cannot be used with SSL.

The SMTP Service

Messages Are Corrupted

"I've noticed that lately some of my SMTP messages are corrupted. What do I do?"

You have low disk space on the volume where the mailroot directory is located. Free more space.

Queue Directory Filling Up

"My queue directory is gradually filling up, and users complain that some of their messages are not getting through to their intended recipients."

A remote SMTP server may be down, or some other problem may be occurring. Use Notepad to view the .rtr and .ltr transcript files in the queue directory to try to determine why the messages are not remaining in the queue.

Also check that the route domain path to the remote host is correct.

.bad Files in the Queue Directory

"I noticed there are some .bad files in the queue. What are these?"

Your badmail directory is full. Clear it.

The NNTP Service

Configuring the NNTP Service To Pull USENET Newsfeeds

"I want to configure my default NNTP site to pull newsfeeds from a USENET server. How do I configure this?"

This release of Microsoft NNTP Service cannot pull newsfeeds from other NNTP servers.

Using Telnet To Verify That NNTP Service Is Accepting Connections

"I can't post messages to my NNTP service on IIS from Outlook Express on a client machine. I'm not sure if the problem is with the server or with the client."

Start Telnet on the client machine, set the preferences for local echo, and open the remote system, ,news_server.:119

- If the result is "200 NNTP Service," then the NNTP service is accepting client connections.
- If the result is "502 Connection refused," then the NNTP service may be paused or may have reached its connection limit.
- If the result is "Connect Failed," then the service may be stopped. If it is not stopped, then it is not accepting connections. Try rebuilding the NNTP service.

If you can connect to the service, enter the command

List

- If the result is a list of newsgroups, then the NNTP service is running well, and the problem must be with the client.
- If the result is the message "480 Logon required," then anonymous access is not enabled on the Default NNTP Site.

Active Server Pages

Application Errors

"I created a virtual Web in Visual InterDev, but now the ASP will not work correctly."

Ensure that the Web is set up as an application. Right-click on the virtual Web and select Properties from the context menu. Under the Application Settings section, click the Create button to make this Web an application.

ODBC Errors

```
Microsoft OLE DB Provider for ODBC Drivers error '80004005'
[Microsoft][ODBC Microsoft Access 2000 Driver]
The Microsoft Jet database engine cannot open the file '(unknown)'.
It is already opened exclusively by another user, or you need
permission to view its data.
```

This error occurs when the database is open in design mode. Exit out of design mode and rerun the ASP script.

Another cause for this error is when the IUSR_MACHINENAME (the account used for IIS anonymous access) account doesn't have permissions on the folder in order to create the temporary .idb file used by Microsoft Access.

```
Microsoft OLE DB Provider for ODBC Drivers error '80004005'
[Microsoft][ODBC Driver Manager] Data source name not found and no
default driver specified
```

This error occurs when there is problem locating a system DSN, or the DSN is defined incorrectly in the ASP code.

```
Microsoft OLE DB Provider for ODBC Drivers error '80004005'
[Microsoft][ODBC SQL Server Driver][dbnmpntw]ConnectionOpen
(CreateFile()).
```

This can happen when there are Named Pipe connection problems to SQL Server. Create duplicate accounts (IUSR_MACHINENAME) on the IIS box and the SQL Server or use a domain user account as the anonymous Internet access account for accessing resources over the network.

Always ensure that you have the latest *Microsoft Data Access Components* (MDAC) installed on the Web server to avoid database connection problems. Download the latest MDAC at

```
http://www.microsoft.com/mdac
```

Service Packs and Fixes

Service Pack 1 for Windows 2000

Just prior to this book going to press, Microsoft announced that they will be releasing Service Pack 1 for Windows 2000 in late spring of 2000.

Windows Update

Download and install the Critical Updates notification tool to be informed of the latest hotfixes to the Windows 2000 operating system. Select Start, Windows Update to go to Microsoft Windows Update Center after installing Windows 2000 to ensure that the operating system is current.

APPENDIX A

Essential TCP/IP

Introduction

The TCP/IP protocol suite is the core protocol underlying the Internet; therefore, installing and configuring World Wide Web, FTP, and other IIS services require a good understanding of TCP/IP. This appendix is a brief overview of the more essential aspects of TCP/IP as implemented in the Microsoft Windows 2000 operating system, and includes information on

- The history, nature, and purpose of TCP/IP
- The underlying architecture of Microsoft TCP/IP
- Installing and configuring TCP/IP on Windows NT 4.0
- TCP/IP addressing and subnetting
- *Microsoft Dynamic Host Configuration Protocol* (DHCP)
- Troubleshooting TCP/IP networks

What Is TCP/IP?

TCP/IP is not a single protocol but a *suite*, or collection, of protocols developed as an industry standard for *wide-area networking* (WAN) connectivity. Of the three standard networking protocols included with the Microsoft Windows 2000 operating system (NetBEUI Protocol, NWLink IPX/SPX Compatible Transport, and TCP/IP Protocol), TCP/IP is the widest in scope of implementation and the most complex to configure and maintain.

TCP/IP is generally used for

- Connectivity to the Internet, a worldwide network based on TCP/IP
- Heterogeneous networks, which combine Microsoft, UNIX, and other operating systems
- Enterprise-scale networks where a standard, reliable, routable protocol is needed

History of TCP/IP

TCP/IP originated with the *US Department of Defense Advanced Research Projects Agency* (DARPA) in the late 1960s, and it has been refined and extended by various agencies and governing bodies until the present. The standards for the TCP/IP protocol suite are established through a process of submitting and approving documents called *Request for Comments (RFCs)*. The development of TCP/IP involves the interworking of a number of agencies, including the *Internet Architecture Board* (IAB), the *Internet Engineering Task Force* (IETF), the *Internet Research Task Force* (IRTF), the *Internet Assigned Numbers Authority* (IANA), and the *Internet Society* (ISOC).

Some of the milestones in the development of TCP/IP have included

- Telnet (1972)
- File Transfer Protocol (FTP) (1973)
- Transmission Control Protocol (1974)
- Internet Protocol (1981)
- TCP/IP Protocol Suite (1983)
- Domain Name System (1984)

Requests for Comments go through a series of stages before becoming accepted standards:

- Proposed standard
- Draft standard
- Internet standard

When an RFC is published, it receives a number. For example, the original FTP protocol was defined in RFC 454. Often, a later RFC will supersede an earlier one due to revisions and extensions in the protocol. For more information on RFCs and to download or view RFCs, visit

```
http://www.isi.edu/rfc-editor/rfc.html
```

For an index of all RFCs, go to

```
ftp://ftp.isi.edu/in-notes/rfc-index.txt
```

Comparison with Other Protocols

The other protocol used for enterprise-level networks, NWLink IPX/SPX, is generally similar to TCP/IP in the number of Ethernet frames generated to accomplish basic networking processes such as transferring files, logging on, and so on. Where NWLink and TCP/IP differ is that TCP/IP is the native protocol of the Internet, and with the surge of interest in corporate connectivity to the Internet, it has become the default to install TCP/IP as the networking protocol, while reserving NWLink only for backward compatibility with NetWare systems.

NetBEUI is not suitable for enterprise-level computing because it is not routable and is hence unsuited for large internetworks.

Architecture of the TCP/IP Protocol Suite

The basis for developing networking protocols to link together dissimilar systems is the *Open Systems Interconnection (OSI) model,* developed in 1978 by the International Standards Organization (ISO). The OSI model serves as a starting point from which vendors can develop commercial networking protocols and software.

The OSI model utilizes a seven-layer model in which each layer on one machine communicates logically with the same layer on another machine, regardless of whether the two machines come from the same vendor or run the same networking operating systems. The OSI model is outlined in Figure A-1.

The TCP/IP protocol suite is based on a simplified version of the OSI model that has only four layers:

- Application layer
- Transport layer
- Internet layer
- Network layer

The correspondence between the OSI and TCP/IP models is shown in Figure A-2.

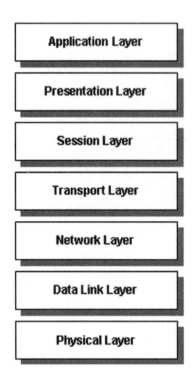

Within the four layers of the TCP/IP architecture model, a number of protocols have been defined (Figure A-3).

- *Application layer protocols* are protocols used by user applications to access Internet technologies. Of the many protocols here, some examples are

  - *FTP (File Transfer Protocol),* used for transferring files from one machine to another

  - *Telnet,* which enables terminal emulation for running remote applications

  - *HTTP (Hypertext Transfer Protocol),* which enables transfer of HTML Web pages

  - *SNMP (Simple Network Management Protocol),* for monitoring network data

- Application layer protocols interface with the Transport layer protocols through one of two methods in Microsoft TCP/IP:

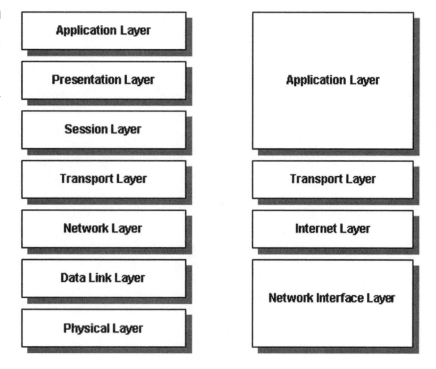

Figure A-2
Comparison between the OSI model (left) and the TCP/IP model right.

- *Windows Sockets (WinSock),* an interface between socket-based applications and TCP/IP
- *NetBIOS over TCP/IP (NetBT),* which enables NetBIOS sessions and naming functions
- *Transport Layer protocols* enable sessions between hosts so communication is possible. The two defined protocols are
  - *TCP (Transmission Control Protocol),* for one-to-one, connection-oriented, guaranteed-delivery, reliable sessions for transfer of large quantities of data
  - *UDP (User Datagram Protocol),* for one-to-many, connectionless, no-guarantee sessions for transfer of small quantities of data
- *Internet Layer protocols* enable routing of packets according to IP address as well as other protocol management functions. The four protocols here are

Figure A-3
The various protocols
in the TCP/IP protocol
suite.

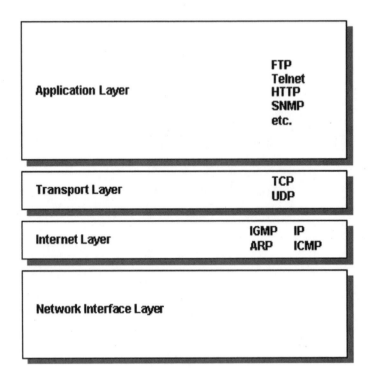

- *IP (Internet Protocol),* for addressing and routing of packets on an internetwork
- *ICMP (Internet Control Message Protocol),* for reporting delivery errors
- *IGMP (Internet Group Message Protocol),* used for multicasting
- *ARP (Address Resolution Protocol),* for resolving IP addresses into physical-layer network interface card addresses
- *Network Interface Layer protocols* deal with actually moving the data onto and off of the network wiring. No TCP/IP protocols are defined at this layer; instead, topology-dependent network interface card *drivers* are used to provide networking services here.

Structure of a TCP/IP Frame

Here is an illustration of how a typical TCP/IP frame is formed and transported over a network (Figure A-4).

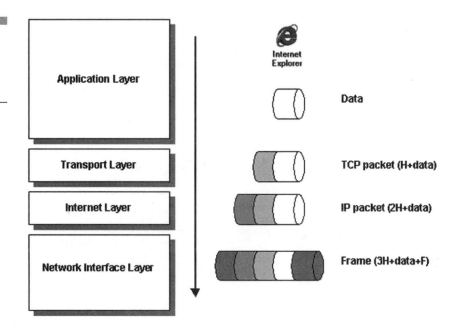

Figure A-4
Formation of a
TCP/IP frame by
protocol
encapsulation.

An application such as Internet Explorer running in the Application layer formulates an *instruction* such as HTTP GET and passes this instruction down to the next layer, the Transport layer.

The Transport layer segments the information sent down to it from the Application layer into data packets no larger than 1460 bytes and adds a TCP header of 20 bytes that specifies the source and destination ports, sequence number, and other information. The *TCP packet* thus constructed is then passed down to the Internet layer.

The Internet layer adds a header of 20 bytes to the TCP packet sent down to it from the Transport layer. The IP layer includes information concerning the source and destination IP addresses, the packet Time to Live (TTL), and other information relating to routing functions. The *IP packet* thus constructed is then passed down to the Network Interface layer.

The Network Interface Layer formats the packet passed down from the Internet layer in an appropriate fashion for the networking method (Ethernet, Token Ring, FDDI, and so on) that will be used. For example, if the IP packet is destined to travel on an Ethernet network, it is formatted into an 802.3 Ethernet frame by adding a 22-byte header containing the source and destination physical addresses and a four-byte footer containing checksum information. The result is an *Ethernet frame* of length up to 1514 bytes.

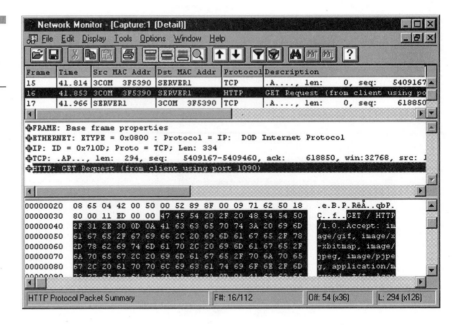

We can view the structure of TCP/IP frames in detail using the tool *Microsoft Network Monitor.* A limited version of this tool is included with Windows 2000 under the Administrative Tools Start menu item. Figure A-5 shows a Network Monitor capture with detailed information on the various encapsulated protocols for an HTTP GET request on an Ethernet network.

Here is the detailed packet information from the *detail pane* (middle pane) of Network Monitor's display window in Figure A-5. Note the encapsulation of the various protocols, the source and destination ports and addresses, and various other details. Note also the complexity of the TCP/IP protocol.

```
FRAME: Base frame properties
      FRAME: Time of capture5Feb 21, 1998 22:10:39.862
      FRAME: Time delta from previous physical frame: 39
      milliseconds
      FRAME: Frame number: 16
      FRAME: Total frame length: 348 bytes
      FRAME: Capture frame length: 348 bytes
      FRAME: Frame data: Number of data bytes remaining5348
      (0x015C)
ETHERNET: ETYPE50x0800 : Protocol5IP: DOD Internet Protocol
      ETHERNET: Destination address : 48543300CD6A
            ETHERNET: .......05Individual address
            ETHERNET: ......0.5Universally administered address
```

```
        ETHERNET: Source address : 02608C3F5390
            ETHERNET: .......05No routing information present
            ETHERNET: ......1.5Locally administered address
        ETHERNET: Frame Length : 348 (0x015C)
        ETHERNET: Ethernet Type : 0x0800 (IP: DOD Internet Protocol)
        ETHERNET: Ethernet Data: Number of data bytes remaining5334
        (0x014E)
    IP: ID50x710D; Proto5TCP; Len: 334
        IP:    Version54 (0x4)
        IP:    Header Length520 (0x14)
        IP:    Service Type50 (0x0)
            IP: Precedence5Routine
            IP: ...0....5Normal Delay
            IP: ....0...5Normal Throughput
            IP: .....0..5Normal Reliability
        IP:    Total Length5334 (0x14E)
        IP:    Identification528941 (0x710D)
        IP:    Flags Summary52 (0x2)
            IP: .......05Last fragment in datagram
            IP: ......1.5Cannot fragment datagram
        IP:    Fragment Offset50 (0x0) bytes
        IP:    Time to Live532 (0x20)
        IP: Protocol5TCP - Transmission Control
        IP: Checksum50x8003
        IP: Source Address5172.16.8.20
        IP: Destination Address5172.16.8.101
        IP: Data: Number of data bytes remaining5314 (0x013A)
    TCP: .AP..., len: 294, seq: 5409167-5409460, ack: 618850,
    win:32768, src: 1090 dst: 80
        TCP: Source Port50x0442
        TCP: Destination Port5Hypertext Transfer Protocol
        TCP: Sequence Number55409167 (0x52898F)
        TCP: Acknowledgment Number5618850 (0x97162)
        TCP: Data Offset520 (0x14)
        TCP: Reserved50 (0x0000)
        TCP: Flags50x18 : .AP...
            TCP: ..0.....5No urgent data
            TCP: ...1....5Acknowledgment field significant
            TCP: ....1...5Push function
            TCP: .....0..5No Reset
            TCP: ......0.5No Synchronize
            TCP: .......05No Fin
        TCP: Window532768 (0x8000)
        TCP: Checksum50x11ED
        TCP: Urgent Pointer50 (0x0)
        TCP: Data: Number of data bytes remaining5294 (0x0126)
    HTTP: GET Request (from client using port 1090)
        HTTP: Request Method5GET
        HTTP: Uniform Resource Identifier5/
        HTTP: Protocol Version5HTTP/1.1
        HTTP: Accept5image/gif, image/x-xbitmap, image/jpeg,
        image/pjpeg, application/mswo
        HTTP: Accept-Language5en
        HTTP: Undocumented Header5UA-pixels: 800x600
            HTTP: Undocumented Header Fieldname5UA-pixels
            HTTP: Undocumented Header Value5800x600
        HTTP: Undocumented Header5UA-color: color8
            HTTP: Undocumented Header Fieldname5UA-color
```

```
        HTTP: Undocumented Header Value5color8
HTTP: Undocumented Header5UA-OS: Windows 95
        HTTP: Undocumented Header Fieldname5UA-OS
        HTTP: Undocumented Header Value5Windows 95
HTTP: Undocumented Header5UA-CPU: x86
        HTTP: Undocumented Header Fieldname5UA-CPU
        HTTP: Undocumented Header Value5x86
HTTP: User-Agent5Mozilla/4.0 (compatible; MSIE 4.0; Windows 98)
        HTTP: Host5server1
        HTTP: Connection5Keep-Alive
```

Installing TCP/IP on Windows 2000

TCP/IP is the default network protocol for Windows 2000. When you first install Windows 2000 on a clean machine with a network card, it will prompt you for information on how to set up your TCP/IP connection. In this section, we will go over installing TCP/IP on a network interface that does not have TCP/IP installed.

Click Start, Settings, and Network and Dial-Up Connections to open the Network and Dial-up Connections Explorer (see Figure A-6). Right-click the Local Area Connection and select Properties from the context menu to con-

Figure A-6

The Network and Dial-up Connections Explorer.

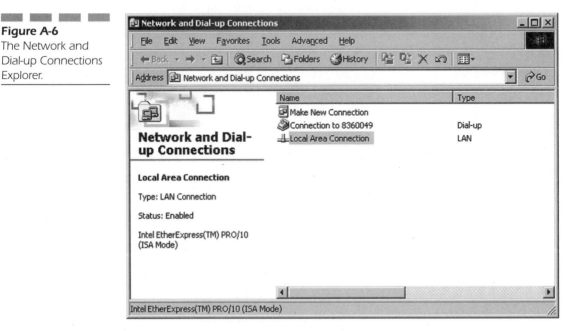

Figure A-7
Adding TCP/IP to the
local area
connection.

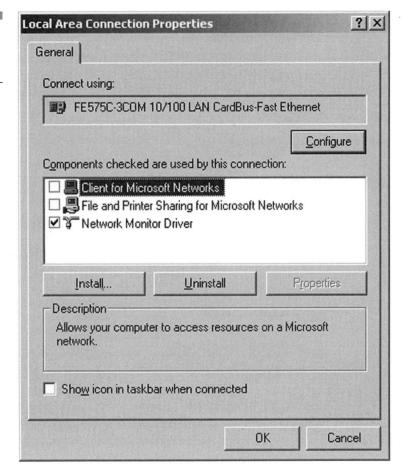

Figure A-7
Adding TCP/IP to the
local area
connection.

figure your internal network interface. This will bring up the Local Area
Connection properties dialog box (see Figure A-7).

Click the Install button to bring up the Select Network Component Type
dialog box (see Figure A-8). From here, you can select services and protocols
that will be used on your network client machine. Select Protocol and click
the Add button to bring up the Select Network Protocol dialog box (see Figure A-9).

Select Internet Protocol (TCP/IP) and click OK. Windows 2000 will proceed to install the TCP/IP protocol suite on your machine. When the installation is complete, the Local Area Connection Properties box appears
(Figure A-7); this time with the TCP/IP protocol listed.

Figure A-8
Selecting a network
component type.

Select Network Component Type

Click the type of network component you want to install:

📇 Client
📇 Service
🜲 Protocol

Description

A protocol is a language your computer uses to
communicate with other computers.

Add...   Cancel

Figure A-9
Selecting a protocol
to install on Windows
2000.

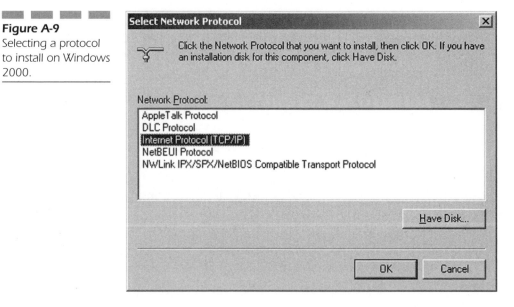

Select Network Protocol

Click the Network Protocol that you want to install, then click OK. If you have
an installation disk for this component, click Have Disk.

Network Protocol:

AppleTalk Protocol
DLC Protocol
Internet Protocol (TCP/IP)
NetBEUI Protocol
NWLink IPX/SPX/NetBIOS Compatible Transport Protocol

Have Disk...

OK   Cancel

The default setting of your newly installed TCP/IP will be to use DHCP (we'll discuss this later in this chapter). In the next section, we will go over configuring the TCP/IP protocol on a Windows 2000 machine.

Configuring TCP/IP on Windows 2000

Configuring TCP/IP is performed by using the Local Area Connection Properties box illustrated in Figure A-7, selecting the Internet Protocol (TCP/IP) from the available protocol listings, and clicking on the Properties button. This will bring up the Internet-Protocol (TCP/IP) dialog box (see Figure A-10).

Figure A-10
The Internet Protocol (TCP/IP) Properties dialog box.

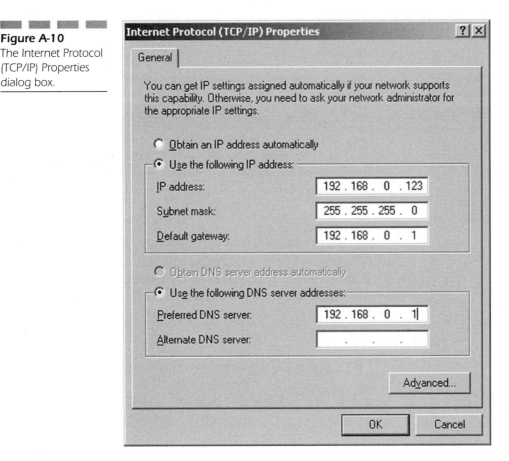

The Internet Protocol (TCP/IP) Properties Sheet

The General tab (Figure A-10) is used to configure the following TCP/IP settings:

Choose whether to manually specify an IP Address or to automatically obtain an IP address from a DHCP server. A *DHCP server* can be either a Microsoft Windows 2000 server running the DHCP Server service, or some other DHCP server. IP addresses can be obtained either over a local network or through a PPP dialup router (for example, when you connect to an ISP through Dial-up Networking, the DHCP server at the ISP will lease your machine an IP address over the serial PPP line).

If your machine is a server, it should have either a manually assigned IP address or a DHCP reservation so it always receives the same IP address from the DHCP server. If your machine is a client, it is easiest to have it obtain its IP address from a DHCP server.

If you configure your settings manually, you should enter three settings:

- *IP Address*   the unique 32-bit identifier for the machine on the TCP/IP network.
- *Subnet Mask*   a 32-bit number that divides the IP address into two numbers, a host number and a network number. The subnet mask is used during TCP/IP communications to determine whether the destination machine is on the local subnet or a remote one in order to route it appropriately.
- *Default Gateway*   the default gateway is a 32-bit number specifying where IP frames should be sent if there is no specified route to the destination machine. Note: Specifying a default gateway is optional, but if one is not specified, access may be restricted to the local subnet only. Click the Advanced button to open the Advanced TCP/IP Settings dialog box (Figure A-11).

The IP Settings Tab of the Advanced TCP/IP Settings Sheet

The IP Settings Tab (Figure A-11) is used to configure the following TCP/IP settings:

Figure A-11
Configuring IP setting
of the TCP/IP
connection.

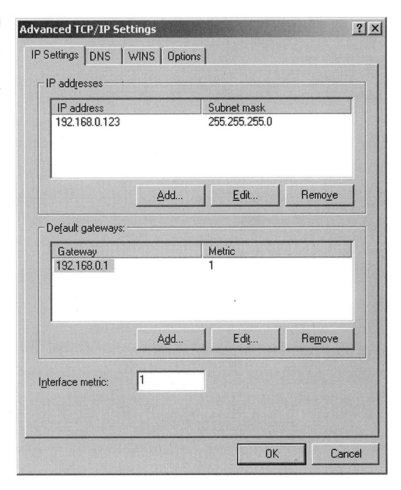

- *Additional IP addresses* for the connection selected: Add more IP addresses for this connection or network adapter.
- *Additional gateways* for the connection selected: Use the *metric* to define the best routes to take with the minimum amount of hops. If a machine needs to send a packet to a gateway and the gateway will not respond, the next gateway on the list will be tried.
- *Interface Metric* for the connection selected: If multiple routes exist, this defines which route to take with the metric that equals the default metric value. A metric defines how many hops it takes to get to the destination.

The DNS Tab of the Advanced TCP/IP Settings Sheet

The DNS tab (see Figure A-12) is used to configure the following TCP/IP settings:

- *DNS Server Addresses*   This will default to the IP address you assigned when first configuring your TCP/IP setting in the General tab of the TCP/IP Properties dialog box (see Figure A-10). You can add more DNS servers here by clicking on the Add button.

- *Domain Name Suffixes*   This is the Internet domain to which the host belongs. The domain name is the last half of the *Fully Qualified*

Figure A-12
Configuring DNS options of the TCP/IP connection.

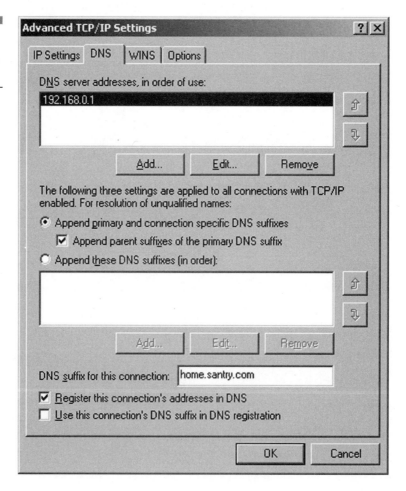

Domain Name (FQDN) of the machine. In this example, if our domain was `home.santry.com` and the machine's name was server1, the FQDN to access this server would be

`server1.home.santry.com`

- *Domain Suffix Search Order*   Specify additional DNS suffixes that should be appended to host names for DNS name resolution.

- *Dynamic DNS Registration*   At the bottom of this dialog box are options for registering your server's IP address and name in Dynamic DNS tables on your DNS server.

The WINS Tab of the Advanced TCP/IP Settings Sheet

The WINS tab (see Figure A-13) is used to configure the following TCP/IP settings:

- *WINS servers*   These are the IP addresses of the WINS servers that should be used by the selected network adapter. WINS stands for Windows Internet Naming Service and represents a Microsoft alternative to the Domain Name System suitable for small to medium-sized networks. If using TCP/IP, however, DNS is preferred to WINS. Although WINS supports a dynamic name database and thus has lower administrative overhead than DNS, DNS is still preferred for medium to large networks because of its compatibility with standard Internet functionality. WINS servers will be queried in order of appearance in this list box of IP addresses.

- *Enable LMHOSTS Lookup*   This enables the use of a local LMHOSTS file for NetBIOS name resolution. LMHOSTS files contain mappings of NetBIOS names to IP addresses and can provide a backup to or an alternative to WINS resolution of NetBIOS names. A sample LMHOSTS file is located in

`C:\winnt\system32\drivers\etc\`

- *NetBIOS over TCP/IP*   These options are used to specify how you wish to NetBIOS and WINS over the TCP/IP connection. Enable this option if your network consists of legacy NT clients and servers that use WINS to resolve NetBIOS names.

Figure A-13
Configuring WINS
Information.

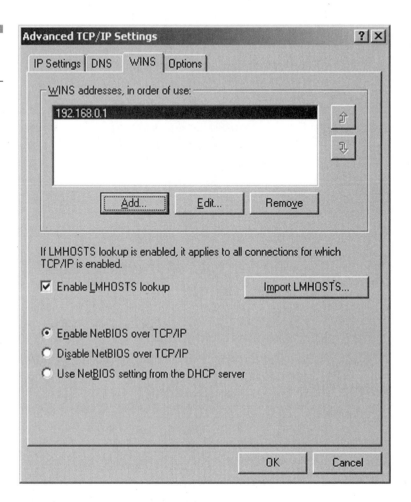

The Options Tab of the Advanced TCP/IP Settings Sheet

Use this tab (see Figure A-14) to specify other options for the connection. In this example, we have listed IP security and TCP/IP filtering. IP security is used for communicating with servers that have security enabled. You can select from different policies that are available on the system. TCP/IP filtering allows you to filter the port and protocol type of incoming and outgoing packets. Other options may be listed here depending on the services installed on the machine. Refer to the Windows 2000 documentation for reference.

Figure A-14
Configuring other
options for the TCP/IP
connection.

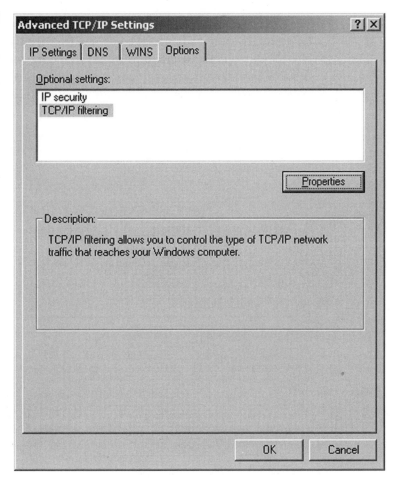

Figure A-14
Configuring other
options for the TCP/IP
connection.

Understanding IP Addressing and Subnetting

IP addresses are 32-bit binary numbers that are represented in decimal form as $w.x.y.z$, where w, x, y, and z may range from 0 to 255. IP addresses provide a unique way of identifying machines, routers, and other active networking hardware on a TCP/IP internetwork. A unique IP address is required by each machine on a TCP/IP internetwork. If two or more machines have the same IP address, communications on the internetwork may not work properly.

IP addresses can be split into two sections:

- *Network ID*   the portion of the address that identifies the subnetwork the computer is on. Computers on the same network can talk to each other using TCP/IP; computers on different networks must have their messages routed to each other by a dedicated router or multihomed Windows NT computer.

- *Host ID*   the portion of the address that identifies the host on the subnetwork. This must be unique to the subnetwork defined by the network number above.

IP Address Classes

Five classes of IP addresses are defined, of which you need to be familiar with only three: A, B, and C. Table A-1 outlines some information concerning these three classes. Note the following:

- 127.*x.y.z* is reserved for loopback functions.

- Network and host IDs cannot be either all zeros or all ones.

- The host ID must be unique on the locally defined network ID.

If your network is not connected to the Internet, or if you are using a firewall/proxy server combination to shield your network from the Internet, you can use any of the following IP address blocks, which are reserved for *private* TCP/IP networks:

Class A (one network): 10.*x.y.z*

Class B (16 networks): 172.16.*y.z* to 172.31.*y.z*

Class C (255 networks): 192.168.*y.z*

Table A-1

IP address classes.

Class	IP Address	Network Number	Host Number	Start of First Octet	End of First Octet	Number of Hosts per Network
A	w.x.y.z	w	x.y.z	1.x.y.z	126.x.y.z	16,777,214
B	w.x.y.z	w.x	y.z	128.x.y.z	191.x.y.z	65,534
C	w.x.y.z	w.x.y	z	192.x.y.z	223.x.y.z	254

Subnet Masks

IP addresses are split into network and host IDs by applying a subnet mask. The *default subnet masks* for the three classes of addresses described above are

Class A: 255.0.0.0

Class B: 255.255.0.0

Class C: 255.255.255.0

The IP address and the subnet are ANDed together in binary notation to determine the network number belonging to the IP address:

```
192.168.12.45      511000000 10101000 00001100 00101101
255.255.255.0      511111111 11111111 11111111 00000000
```

ANDing the IP address with the subnet mask results in the network number:

```
192.168.12.0511000000 10101000 00001100 00000000
```

The host number is the remaining portion:

```
45500000000 00000000 00000000 00101101
```

When TCP/IP wants to contact a host, it has to first determine if the host is local or remote. The host is *remote* if

```
(Source IP) AND (source subnet mask)
does NOT equal
(destination IP) AND (source subnet mask)
```

If a route to the remote host is found in the local routing table, the route is used; if no route is found, the IP frame is sent to the default gateway.

Subnetting IP Networks

To make better use of the limited number of available IP addresses, *custom subnet masks* can be constructed to further subdivide the network. The process of creating custom subnet masks is called *subnetting.*

As a simple example, consider the following class B IP address and default subnet mask:

```
172.16.119.5     510101100 00010000 01110111 00000101
255.255.0.0      511111111 11111111 00000000 00000000
```

Because 16 bits (the number of ones in the default subnet mask) are used for the network ID, the remaining 16 bits (the number of zeros in the default subnet mask) can be used for host IDs. What that means is that the network 172.16.0.0 can have a maximum of $2^{16}2 2565,534$ hosts because there are 16 bits in the host number and the cases "all zeros" and "all ones" are disallowed (hence, subtract 2).

With subnetting, we can "borrow" bits from the host ID and use them for the network ID. For example, consider the same IP address, this time used with the custom subnet mask 255.255.240.0, in the following example:

```
172.16.119.5510101100 00010000 01110111 00000101
55.255.240.0511111111 11111111 11110000 00000000
```

This arrangement gives more bits for network IDs (20 bits) and hence more subnetworks, but fewer bits for host IDs (12 bits) and therefore fewer possible hosts per subnetwork. In fact, the number of possible hosts per subnetwork is now reduced to $2^{12}2 254,094$ hosts.

In general, subnetting is somewhat complicated mathematically to perform, but Table A-2 provides a practical tool that can be used to perform simple subnetting calculations for class B networks. Similar tables can be constructed for class A and class C networks.

Table A-2

Subnetting calculation aid for Class B networks.

N, Number of Bits Borrowed from Host ID for Network ID	2^N-2, Number of Possible Subnets	Third Octet = $256-2^{(8-N)}$, Custom Subnet Mask	$2^{(8-N)}$, Network ID Increment	$2^{(16-N)}-2$, Number of Hosts per Subnet
1	Invalid	Invalid	Invalid	Invalid
2	2	255.255.192.0	64	16,382
3	6	255.255.224.0	32	8,190
4	14	255.255.240.0	16	4,094
5	30	255.255.248.0	8	2,046
6	62	255.255.252.0	4	1,022
7	126	255.255.254.0	2	510
8	254	255.255.255.0	1	254

The table item called *network ID increment* is important to understand. Building on the previous example, if the IP address and subnet mask for a host are configured as

IP address: 172.16.119.5

Subnet mask: 255.255.240.0

which range of IP addresses represents hosts on the *same subnet* as this host? The answer lies in the network ID increment. For a third octet of 240, the increment is given in the table as 16. There are 14 networks, each differing in the third octet by 16 from the previous one; the 14 possible networks are given in Table A-3.

From the bold entry in Table A-3, we can see that the network ID for the host in our example is 172.16.112.0 and that our host will be able to communicate directly (that is, without the need of a router) with all other hosts whose IP addresses range from 172.16.112.1 to 172.16.127.254.

	Network ID	Starting IP Address	Ending IP Address
Table A-3			
Possible Networks for the Example	172.16.0.0	Invalid (borrowed bits all 0s)	Invalid
	172.16.16.0	172.16.16.1	172.16.31.254
	172.16.32.0	172.16.32.1	172.16.47.254
	172.16.48.0	172.16.48.1	172.16.63.254
	172.16.64.0	172.16.64.1	172.16.79.254
	172.16.80.0	172.16.80.1	172.16.95.254
	172.16.96.0	172.16.96.1	172.16.111.254
	172.16.112.0	172.16.112.1	172.16.127.254
	172.16.128.0	172.16.128.1	172.16.143.254
	172.16.144.0	172.16.144.1	172.16.159.254
	172.16.160.0	172.16.160.1	172.16.175.254
	172.16.176.0	172.16.176.1	172.16.191.254
	172.16.192.0	172.16.192.1	172.16.207.254
	172.16.208.0	172.16.208.1	172.16.223.254
	172.16.224.0	172.16.224.1	172.16.239.254
	172.16.240.0	Invalid (borrowed bits all 1s)	Invalid

One application for using network IDs and custom subnet masks would be for granting or denying access to a Web site on IIS according to IP number. See Chapter 3, *Administering the WWW Service*, for information on where to configure these settings.

Installing Microsoft DHCP Server Service

If you want to use DHCP to automatically configure TCP/IP for machines on your network, you will have to make at least one of your servers a DHCP server.

To configure your Windows 2000 Server as a DHCP Server for automatically assigning IP addresses, subnet masks, default gateways, and other TCP/IP information to client machines on your network, you must first install the Microsoft DHCP Server service on your server. Note that the machine you want to install DHCP Server service on must have a manually configured (static) IP address.

Click Start, Settings, Control Panel, and Add/Remove Programs to start the Add/Remove Programs application. Click the Add/Remove Windows Components icon on the right side of the dialog box to start the Windows Components Wizard (see Figure A-15). Scroll down and select Networking Services. Click the Details button to open a list box containing the available networking services (see Figure A-16). Select *Dynamic Host Configuration Protocol* (DHCP) from the available services and click OK. This will bring you back to the Windows Components Wizard (see Figure A-15). Click Next to complete the installation.

Walkthrough: Creating a New DHCP Scope

A *scope* is a pool of IP addresses that are available to be leased by DHCP clients from the DHCP server. To create a new scope for your DHCP services, click Start, Programs, Administrative Tools, and DHCP. The DHCP MMC snap-in opens a listing of your local domain (see Figure A-17). To create a

Figure A-15
The Windows
Components Wizard.

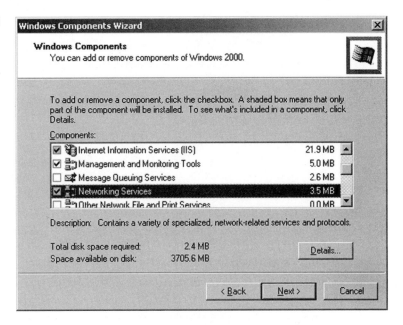

Figure A-16
Installing the DHCP
service.

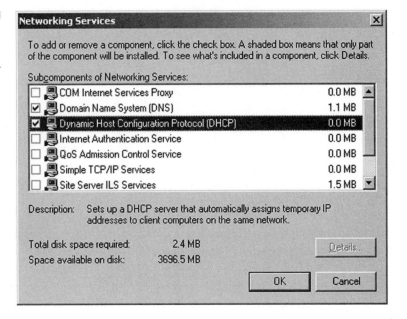

Figure A-17
The DHCP MMC
snap-in.

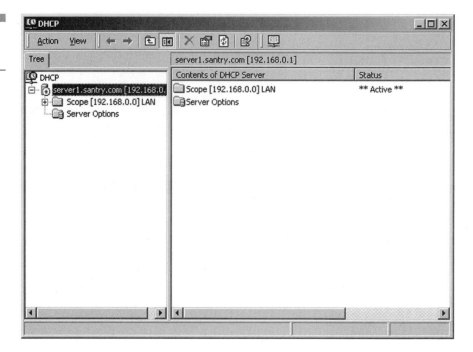

scope, right-click the local domain in the left pane of the MMC, in this example, `server1.santry.com`. Then select New Scope from the context menu. This will start the New Scope Wizard. Click Next to begin the wizard.

In this dialog box (see Figure A-18), enter a name and description for your scope. In this example, we used Santry Home LAN for the scope name. Click Next to add an IP scope.

In this dialog box (see Figure A-19), we will define a range for our scope. Enter 192.168.0.125 for a starting IP address. Enter 192.168.0.149 for an ending IP address. Confirm 255.255.255.0 has been entered for the subnet mask. Click Next to continue. This range contains the available IP addresses that a client can be assigned when making a request to our DHCP server.

In this dialog box (see Figure A-20), we can specify IP addresses that will be excluded from our original range. Say, for example, you have a mail server that has a static IP of 192.168.0.130 and you do not want this IP address to be assigned to clients making a request to the DHCP server. This will exclude the IP from the available IP addresses. Enter 192.168.0.130 in the Start Address range and click Add. This IP address will now appear in

Figure A-18
Giving the scope a name.

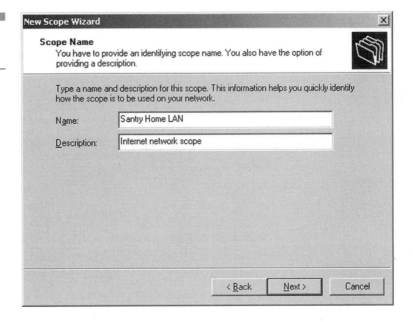

Figure A-19
Specifying a range of IP addresses for a new scope.

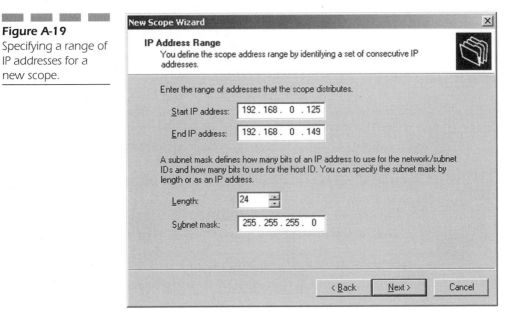

Figure A-20
Specifying a range of
IP addresses to
exclude from the
scope.

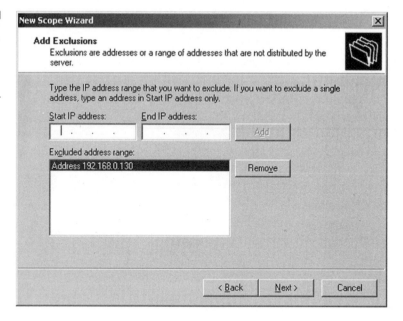

the excluded address range listings. This will avoid any conflicts that can occur when two machines have the same IP address. Click Next to continue.

In this dialog box (see Figure A-21), we will define the length of the *lease* that clients obtain when making a request to our DCHP server. You can specify the amount of days, hours, and minutes that the client will be able to *own* the IP address before making another request to the DHCP server. Accept the default value of eight days and click Next to continue.

This dialog box (see Figure A-22) gives you the option to continue on with the wizard and configure options such as the local DNS server, WINS server, gateways, and other TCP/IP network information. Select the No option and click the Next button to continue. This will complete the wizard, which will inform you that you will need to activate the scope and that you can configure scope options at a later time.

To activate this new scope, in the DHCP MMC snap-in, expand the local server node and right-click the new scope. Select from Activate the context menu. Your new scope is now active and clients can receive an IP lease from this DHCP server.

In the next section of this chapter, we will go over configuring the new scope and DHCP service.

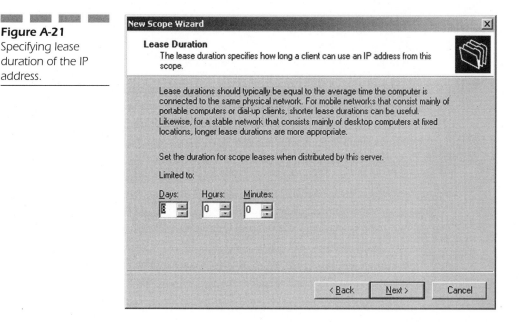

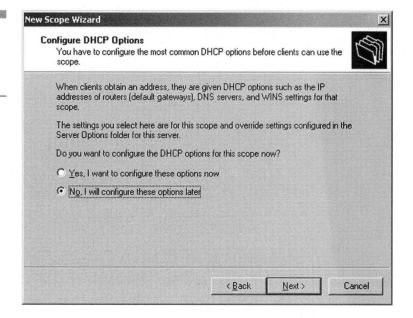

Configuring Microsoft DHCP Server Service

To modify an existing scope on your DHCP server, expand the local server node in the left pane of DHCP MMC snap-in (see Figure A-17). Select an existing scope under the server node and expand it. Underneath the scope are four nodes:

- *Address Pool*   This displays your IP range and exclusions if there are any defined.
- *Address Leases*   These are the clients that have made a request to the DHCP server and IP addresses that have been assigned to them.
- *Reservations*   If a client should have a specific IP address, you would see all existing reserved IPs in the right pane of this MMC view.
- *Scope Options*   This is a listing of the various options that can be assigned to your clients—information such as DNS servers, WINS servers, routers, and so on can be configured here. This information will be assigned to the clients along with their IP assignment.

So far, we have configured our DHCP server to automatically hand out IP addresses and a subnet mask. But how about configuring it to hand out other information like default gateways, IP addresses of WINS and DNS servers, and so on? To do this, select the active scope in the DHCP Manager MMC snap-in and expand the node. Select Scope Options node and right-click. Select Configure Options from the context menu. This opens the Scope Options dialog box.

To enable DHCP to assign a default gateway address to DHCP clients on your network, select the 003 Router Unused Option and click the checkbox next to it to make it an active option. Below the selected option will appear information that can be configured specifically to the option. Enter the IP address of the default gateway and click Add (see Figure A-23).

Other scope options you can define are

- *006 DNS servers*   IP address of DNS servers
- *046 WINS / NBT node type*   type of NetBIOS over TCP/IP (NBT) name resolution used by client (usually you will choose 85 H node)
- *044 WINS / NBNS servers*   IP address of WINS servers
- *047 NetBIOS Scope ID*   local NetBIOS scope ID

Figure A-23
Configuring the
default gateway.

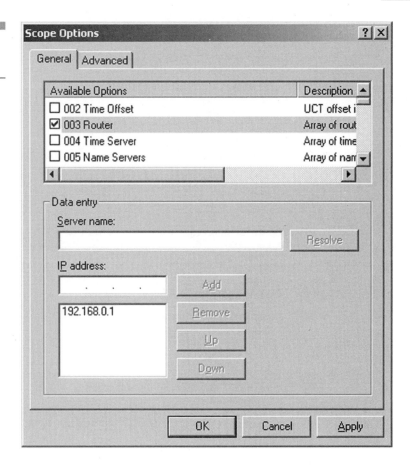

Figure A-23
Configuring the
default gateway.

After you have defined all your scope options, click OK to close the Scope
Options dialog box and return to the DHCP MMC snap-ins.

Troubleshooting TCP/IP

Finally, Microsoft TCP/IP includes a number of standard command-line
tools for troubleshooting TCP/IP. This section will briefly examine three
of them.

Using the `ipconfig` Utility

The `ipconfig` tool can be used to list the currently assigned TCP/IP settings for the host. Command-line options include

- `ipconfig`   shows basic TCP/IP settings
- `ipconfig /all`   shows all TCP/IP settings
- `ipconfig/release`   releases leased IP address (DHCP clients only)
- `ipconfig/renew`   requests new IP address lease (DHCP clients only)

Here is a typical output from the command `ipconfig/all`:

```
Windows NT IP Configuration
        Host Name . . . . . . . . . : server1.santry.com
        DNS Servers . . . . . . . . : 192.168.0.1
        Node Type . . . . . . . . . : Broadcast
        NetBIOS Scope ID. . . . . . :
        IP Routing Enabled. . . . . : No
        WINS Proxy Enabled. . . . . : No
        NetBIOS Resolution Uses DNS : No

Ethernet adapter NE20001:

        Description . . . . . . . . : 3Com Fast EtherLink XL Adapter
                                      (3C509).
        Physical Address. . . . . . : 48-54-33-00-CD-6A
        DHCP Enabled. . . . . . . . : No
        IP Address. . . . . . . . . : 192.168.0.131
        Subnet Mask . . . . . . . . : 255.255.255.0
        Default Gateway . . . . . . : 192.168.0.1
```

Using the `ping` Utility

Another helpful utility for testing and troubleshooting TCP/IP is `ping`. The following sequence of commands uses `ping` to progressively test TCP/IP on an internetwork:

1. `ping 127.0.0.1`   Ping loopback address to test if TCP/IP is properly installed and initialized.

2. `ping 192.168.0.111`   Ping your own IP address to verify it is correctly configured.

3. `ping 192.168.0.1`   Ping the default gateway to see if it is functioning correctly.

4. `ping 172.16.23.95`   Ping a remote host to see if it is reachable.

Here is a typical output from the first command above:

```
Pinging 127.0.0.1 with 32 bytes of data:
Reply from 127.0.0.1: bytes532 time,10ms TTL5128
Reply from 127.0.0.1: bytes532 time,10ms TTL5128
Reply from 127.0.0.1: bytes532 time,10ms TTL5128
Reply from 127.0.0.1: bytes532 time,10ms TTL5128
```

The time is the amount time from when the packet is sent until a response packet is received. The TTL is the remaining Time to Live of the packet. TTL is decremented for each hop across a router and may be decremented further if router congestion causes the packet to be delayed.

Using the `tracert` Utility

The `tracert` utility can be used to trace the route (that is, the hops through routers) from your machine to a destination host on the Internet. It is useful for troubleshooting WAN connections to determine if routers are functioning correctly.

The following example shows the result of typing the command `tracert ntt.co.jp`:

```
Tracing route to www.ntt.co.jp [210.130.164.102] over a maximum of
30 hops:
1     227 ms      185 ms      185 ms      tnt01.escape.ca
                                          [204.112.225.50]
2     196 ms      208 ms      211 ms      bb.escape.ca [204.112.225.4]
3     241 ms      209 ms      221 ms      escape.mbnet.mb.ca
                                          [204.112.54.194]
4     210 ms      252 ms      198 ms      e0.manitoba.mbnet.mb.ca
                                          [204.112.54.193]
5     207 ms      217 ms      199 ms      psp.mb.canet.ca
                                          [192.68.64.5]
6     240 ms      241 ms      254 ms      border1-atm1-0.quebec.canet.
                                          ca [205.207.238.45]
7     252 ms      258 ms      240 ms      psp.ny.canet.ca
                                          [205.207.238.154]
8     245 ms      239 ms      257 ms      borderx2-hssi2-0.Boston.mci.
                                          net [204.70.179.117]
9     817 ms      666 ms      245 ms      core2-fddi1-0.Boston.mci.net
                                          [204.70.179.65]
10    363 ms      325 ms      342 ms      core7.SanFrancisco.mci.net
                                          [204.70.4.93]
11    327 ms      323 ms      320 ms      mae-west3.SanFrancisco.mci.
                                          net [204.70.10.246]
12    328 ms      341 ms      320 ms      mae-west.iij.net
                                          [198.32.136.47]
13    337 ms      339 ms      334 ms      PaloAlto0.iij.net
                                          [202.232.0.109]
```

14	488 ms	478 ms	489 ms	iijgate.iij.net
				[202.232.0.245]
15	517 ms	678 ms	502 ms	otemachi00.iij.net
				[202.232.1.129]
16	498 ms	495 ms	493 ms	www-nttgw.iij.net
				[202.232.10.134]
17	550 ms	794 ms	539 ms	www.ntt.co.jp
				[210.130.164.102]

Trace complete.

APPENDIX B

Essential DNS

The *Domain Name System (DNS)* is a distributed hierarchical naming system used for naming hosts on the Internet and on enterprise-scale TCP/IP networks. It is therefore essential to be able to understand DNS if you plan to use IIS as an Internet server or for large-scale corporate intranets/extranets. This appendix is a brief overview of some of the more essential aspects of DNS as implemented in the Microsoft Windows 2000 operating system, and includes information on

- The history, nature, and purpose of DNS
- Host names and how to resolve them on Microsoft networks
- Installing and configuring Microsoft DNS Server service on Windows 2000 Server

Understanding DNS

DNS is a system for managing the naming of hosts primarily on the Internet and also on enterprise-scale TCP/IP networks. DNS is a client/server system, where DNS clients (called *resolvers*) send name resolution requests to DNS servers (called *name servers*). No single DNS server can handle all name resolution requests; instead, various DNS servers around the world are each responsible for administering a subset of DNS namespace called a *zone of authority*. Together, all the DNS servers around the world on the Internet form a distributed database for resolving host names anywhere in the world.

Name resolution is the process whereby a client (resolver) sends a request to a server (name server) requesting that the host name of a third computer (destination or target machine) be resolved into an IP address. For example, suppose you are connected to the Internet and type the command

```
ping www.yahoo.com
```

Your machine will first have to resolve the *Fully Qualified Domain Name* (FQDN) www.yahoo.com into its IP address (Figure B-1). To do this, a DNS *name lookup* request (for example, "Who the heck is www.yahoo.com?") is

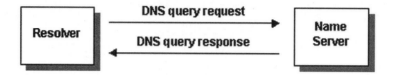

Figure B-1
A simple DNS name
lookup request.

sent to a DNS server, and the DNS server returns a *name resolution* response ("www.yahoo.com is 204.71.200.67") with the IP address of the target machine. At this point, ping is able to execute (actually, arp must be used next to resolve the IP address of the target machine into a physical layer network interface card address). If the name server is unable to resolve the request, it may forward the request to another DNS server to do so.

History of DNS

The history of DNS is tightly bound to the history of TCP/IP, discussed in Appendix A, *Essential TCP/IP*. The original ARPANET (DARPA's precursor to the modern-day Internet) only had a few hundred hosts in the 1970s, so name resolution was performed by copying a simple text file called HOSTS to every machine on the ARPANET. This *HOSTS file* had a static table of mappings between host names (or FQDNs) and their associated IP addresses.

As the ARPANET evolved into the Internet and the number of hosts grew tremendously, a new system for managing the namespace had to be devised because HOSTS files were growing so large that they took too long to process name resolution requests. This system was called the *Domain Name System* (DNS), and its new feature was that it divided the namespace of the Internet into a hierarchical structure with machines called name servers each being responsible for administering a small portion of this space. The most widely implemented version of DNS for many years was the *Berkeley Internet Name Daemon* (BIND) server running on UNIX. Windows 2000 has its own implementation called *Microsoft DNS Server service*, which is the main focus of this appendix.

Understanding the DNS Namespace

The namespace of all Internet hosts around the world is organized in a hierarchical structure (Figure B-2). At the top of the namespace is the *root domain*, which is symbolized by a period (.), although usually this is omitted and a null label is used instead.

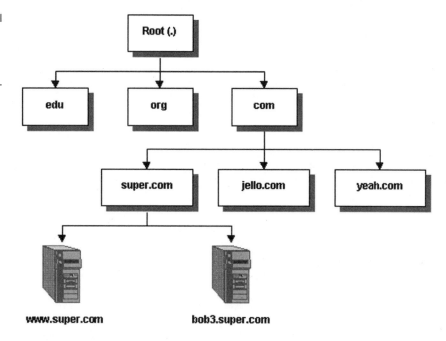

Beneath the root domain are the *top-level domains.* These include domains such as the following:

com	Commercial companies anywhere in the world
edu	Universities, mostly in the United States
org	Not-for-profit organizations
net	Networking companies
gov	U.S. government
mil	U.S. military

Other top-level domains include two-letter country codes such as these:

ca	Canada
uk	United Kingdom
fr	France

Beneath the top-level domains, individual companies and organizations can apply for and register their own *second-level domains,* such as

■ microsoft.com

■ yahoo.com

- `canola-council.org`

- `manitobanow.com`

and so on. If your company wants to register a domain name and will be connected to the Internet, you can view a list of registrars at

`www.internic.net/regist.html`

Beneath the second-level domains, you can either register *subdomains* or, more usually, register names of individual TCP/IP host computers, such as

- `ftp.mtit.com`

- `www.mtit.com`

- `charlie.mtit.com`

and so on. These last expressions are examples of *Fully Qualified Domain Names,* or *FQDNs.* Thus for example, in the FQDN `charlie.supercorpinc.com`, we have

- The host `charlie`

- The second-level domain `supercorpinc.com`

- The top-level domain `com`

To configure host names on a Microsoft Windows 2000 machine, click Start, Settings, Network and Dial-Up Connections. Select the connection you wish to modify and click Properties, select TCP/IP, and click Properties to open the Microsoft TCP/IP Properties dialog box. Click the Advanced button, select the DNS tab, and enter your desired Host Name in the textbox.

Host names should be composed only of letters, numbers, and hyphens. Do not use the underscore or other special characters. If you don't follow this rule, your host name resolution will fail. To determine the hostname of your computer from the command line, type

`hostname`

How the DNS Namespace Is Administered

Ideally, each domain in the DNS space would have its own DNS server. For example, if the company MTIT Enterprises has 20,000 computers, it would most likely have its own DNS server (or probably several) for resolving name lookup requests for anything in the `mtit.com` domain. The administrators of MTIT Enterprises would be responsible for setting up and administering their own name servers for local name resolution within the company. The local name servers would be responsible for a *zone of authority* that includes all hosts (or portions of hosts if there are multiple name servers) within the mtit.com domain.

In practice, however, many domain names either are used by small companies or apply only to a single Web server and at an *Internet service provider* (ISP) that houses the Web site for the company owning that domain. In this case, names in the domain would be resolved using the DNS server belonging to and administered by the ISP.

A *zone of authority* is the section of the DNS namespace that a particular DNS server is responsible for. DNS servers can have authority over

- One or more domains
- Some, all, or none of the subdomains for any domain

Regarding how they relate to other name servers and are configured, DNS servers can be configured as follows:

- *Primary name servers* store their *zone data* (hostname to IP mapping files) as local files.
- *Secondary name servers* receive their zone data from a *master name server* across the network by means of a process called a *zone transfer.* Secondary name servers provide redundancy and load balancing, but zone transfers can increase network traffic.
- *Master name servers* are a source of zone data for secondary name servers and may be either primary or secondary name servers themselves.
- *Caching-only name servers* are not authoritative for any domain, but merely cache name lookup queries and their results (the other kinds of name servers above also cache name lookups, but caching-only name servers *only* cache name lookups and do not have any zone information).

How DNS Queries Are Performed

Two types of queries can be sent by a resolver to a name server:

- *Recursive queries* basically mean, "Please give me the IP address corresponding to this host name; if you can't, please return an error indicating that the data does not exist."

- *Iterative queries* basically mean, "Please give me the IP address corresponding to this host name; if you can't, give me the IP address of another name server that might be able to help me."

There is also a third type of query that is a bit different. These are called *inverse queries* and basically mean, "Please give me the host name corresponding to this IP address." Inverse queries make use of a special domain called `in-addr-arpa` that is used for inverse name lookups. We won't be considering this type of query any further, however.

Here is a scenario to illustrate how name resolution might work in a large company that has its own DNS server and is also connected to the Internet (Figure B-3).

Let's say that someone in the company tries to browse the site `www.yahoo.com` using Internet Explorer. Before an HTTP GET request can be sent to the Web server hosting this site, the host `www.yahoo.com` must be resolved to an IP address. Here are the steps shown in Figure B-3, which are typical:

1. A *recursive* query is sent by the resolver (client) to the company local name server, which basically says, "Either resolve the host name `www.yahoo.com` or give me an error telling me it doesn't exist." This places the burden of the further work on the company local name server.

2. The local name server looks in its zone database and realizes it can't answer the query. Because it has to give an answer one way or

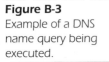

Figure B-3

Example of a DNS name query being executed.

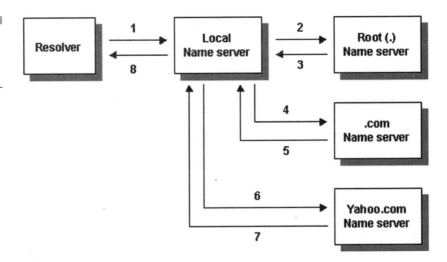

another, it sends an *iterative* query to a root name server, saying, "Who the heck is www.yahoo.com?" There are fewer than a dozen root name servers in the world, and their responsibility is to keep track of who the top-level domain name servers are.

3. The root name server receives the query and sends an answer to the local name server, saying, "I'm sorry, I don't know who www.yahoo.com is, but here is the IP of a .com name server that can probably help you."

4. The local name server then sends an iterative query to the .com name server saying, "Who the heck is www.yahoo.com?"

5. The .com name server replies to the local name server, saying, "I'm sorry, I don't know who www.yahoo.com is, but here is the IP address of the name server that is authoritative over the yahoo.com second-level domain." There are a number of .com name servers in the world, and they are responsible for resolving second-level domains under the .com top-level domain.

6. The local name server then sends an iterative query to the name server that is authoritative over the yahoo.com domain, saying, "Who the heck is www.yahoo.com?"

7. The name server that is authoritative over the yahoo.com domain replies to the local name server saying, "Oh yeah! I know just whom you're talking about. The IP address for the host www.yahoo.com is . . ."

8. The local name server *caches* the results of the whole series of queries and responses (in case something similar is requested soon) and returns the IP address for www.yahoo.com to the resolver (client) that requested it.

Microsoft Methods for Name Resolution

In a Windows 2000 network, computers are identified by their FQDN. When you install Active Directory, you will also be prompted to configure your DNS server on the network. Active Directory will then use DNS as its primary service for name resolution on your network. Planning and migrating the Active Directory and its use with DNS is beyond the scope of this book. For more information on planning your Active Directory and integration with DNS, refer to Chapter 6 of the Windows 2000 Resource Kit *Windows 2000 DNS*.

In this section, we will go over the basic concepts of how name resolution works on a Windows 2000 network. Figure B-4 illustrates the process by which host names (or FQDNs) are resolved on a TCP/IP network by Microsoft platforms. The process may or may not go through all seven steps, depending on how TCP/IP is configured on the computers and whether an earlier step succeeds or not. A step will be skipped if it is not configured in the TCP/IP settings of the client that is trying to resolve the host name.

Figure B-4
Microsoft methods
for resolving host
names or FQDNs.

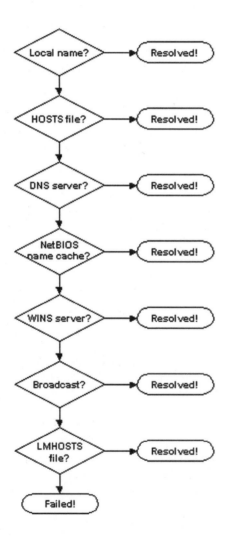

Here is a brief explanation of each step, assuming that for this scenario, the user typed

```
ping hal.santry.com
```

at the command line of the user's local machine:

1. The user's local machine first checks to see whether its *own* host name is `hal`. If it is, it returns its own IP address and `ping` and then executes.

2. If that fails, the local machine parses its HOSTS file (if there is one). The HOSTS file contains static host name to IP mappings and can be used as an alternative to DNS servers for small TCP/IP networks. On a Windows 2000 system, the HOSTS file is located in

   ```
   C:\winnt\system32\drivers\etc\HOSTS
   ```

   The sample HOSTS file that installed here when TCP/IP is installed on your Windows NT system initially contains instructions on how to construct a HOSTS file, plus one mapping:

   ```
   127.0.0.1=localhost
   ```

3. If that fails, the local machine sends a name lookup query to the DNS server specified in its TCP/IP properties (or by the DHCP server scope options). If the DNS server does not respond after five seconds, the query is resent after 10, 20, 40, 5, 10, and 20 seconds more.

   If these three methods fail, the local host may attempt to perform the following steps, if TCP/IP is configured to allow these. These steps are actually NetBIOS name resolution steps; that is, if host name resolution fails, the Microsoft platform will attempt to use NetBIOS name resolution to resolve the host name to an IP address. NetBIOS is primarily used in legacy NT networks and is still supported by Windows 2000 for heterogeneous networks consisting of Windows 2000 clients and legacy clients.

4. The local machine checks its local NetBIOS name cache to see if the mapping is present there.

5. If that fails, the local machine tries three times to contact a WINS server (if one has been specified in the TCP/IP settings for the local machine).

6. If that fails, the local machine sends out three broadcast NetBIOS name requests to the local network.

7. If that fails, the local machine parses its LMHOSTS file (if there is one). The LMHOSTS file contains static NetBIOS name to IP

mappings and can be used as an alternative to WINS servers for small networks. On a Windows 2000 system, the LMHOSTS file is located in

```
C:\winnt\system32\drivers\etc\LMHOSTS
```

The sample LMHOSTS.SAM file that is installed here when TCP/IP is installed on your Windows 2000 system initially contains no mappings but only instructions on how to construct a valid LMHOSTS file.

8. If that fails, an error is returned indicating that the host name cannot be resolved.

Considering the complexity of the above process, it could take as long as several minutes to successfully resolve a host name to an IP address, and that doesn't even include iterative queries to other DNS servers!

Installing DNS Server Service

Before you install Microsoft DNS Server service on a Windows 2000 Server, you must ensure that TCP/IP is properly installed on the machine, and that the host name and domain name are properly specified on the DNS tab of the Microsoft TCP/IP Advanced Properties sheet, and that the IP address of the DNS server is specified in the DNS Service Search Order on the DNS tab also. See Appendix A for instructions on how to perform these steps.

DNS services will automatically be installed when installing Active Directory services on your network using the Active Directory Installation Wizard. When you start the Wizard, it will query the network to see if there is a DNS server that supports dynamic updates. Dynamic DNS allows a client to notify the DNS server of its existence, and then DNS server will make an entry of the client in its name table. If the Wizard cannot find a DNS server that supports dynamic updates, it will then proceed to install and configure a DNS server to support the Active Directory.

To install Active Directory and DNS on your server, click Start, Programs, Administrative Tools, and then click Configure Your Server. Use the Configure Your Server Wizard to install Active Directory and DNS services on your machine. The Wizard will ask you questions about your network configuration and guide you through the process of setting up DNS and Active Directory on your server. In most cases, you will not need to configure DNS services in order to support your Active Directory; all configuration will be done using the Wizard. For more information on configuring Active Directory, consult the Windows 2000 documentation.

To install DNS separate from Active Directory, select Start, Settings, Control Panel, double-click on Add/Remove Programs, and then click Add/Remove Windows Components. The Add/Remove Windows Components Wizard will appear. Select Networking Services and click the Details button.

From the Networking Services dialog box (Figure B-5), check the *Domain Name System* (DNS) option, click the OK button, and then click the Next button to begin installation. After installation is finished, click the Finish button to close the dialog box.

Walkthrough: Configuring Microsoft DNS Server

A full treatment of configuring Microsoft DNS Server is beyond the scope of this appendix because it depends greatly on the portion of the DNS namespace over which the server will be authoritative, how the server will be configured for iterative queries and zone transfers with other DNS servers,

Figure B-5
Installing the
Microsoft DNS Server
service.

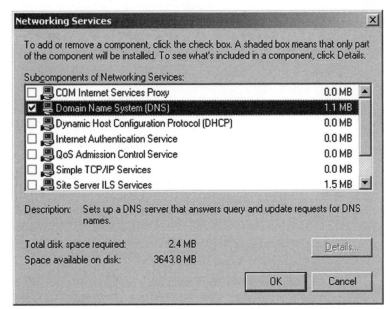

and its relation to the Active Directory. This walkthrough will be limited to creating a primary zone and adding a new host record to the server.

Click Start, Program Files, Administrative Tools, DNS to open the DNS MMC snap-in (Figure B-6). The *DNS MMC snap-in* is for configuring the DNS database files and other associated DNS files. These files are ASCII text files and are located in

```
C:\<system root>\system32\dns\
```

Included are the following text files:

- `<zone>.dns` files contain resource records for a given zone (an example of such a file would be mycorpinc.com.dns).
- `z.y.x.w.in-addr.arpa` contains the reverse lookup records.
- `cache.dns` contains the FQDNs and IP addresses of root name servers on the Internet.
- `boot` is not RFC-compliant and is not needed, but it can be used to control how the DNS server behaves upon startup.

Figure B-6
The DNS Manager
MMC snap-in.

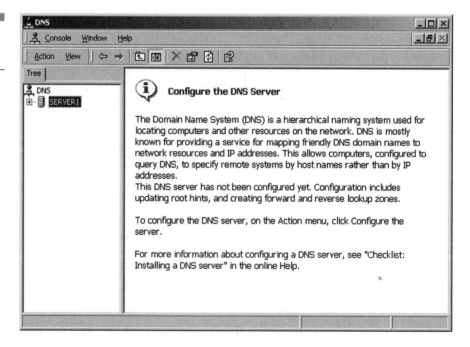

Included in the previous path are also sample files for each of the above and instructions on how you can create DNS files manually using a text editor like Notepad.

Right-click the server-node and select Configure the Server. This will start the Configure DNS Server Wizard (Figure B-7). Click the Next button to start the Wizard.

In this dialog box (see Figure B-8) select Yes, Create a Forward Lookup Zone. If you select No, this ends the Wizard and creates a DNS caching server and has no authority over any portion of the DNS namespace. Click the Next button to continue.

In this screen (see Figure B-9), you specify what type of DNS server this will be. Select Standard Primary to create a new zone. Click the Next button to continue.

In the next dialog box (see Figure B-10), enter the name for this zone. In this example, `home.santry.com` was used. Click the Next button to continue.

In this screen (see Figure B-11), select Create a New File with this File Name. This will create a new `dns` file with the root information.

In the next screen, select No, Do Not Create a Reverse Lookup Zone. Click the Next button to continue and then the Finish button to complete the Wizard.

Figure B-7
The Configure DNS
Server Wizard.

Figure B-8
Specifying the zone
option.

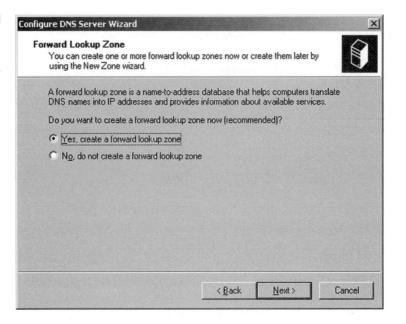

Figure B-9
Specifying the type of
DNS server.

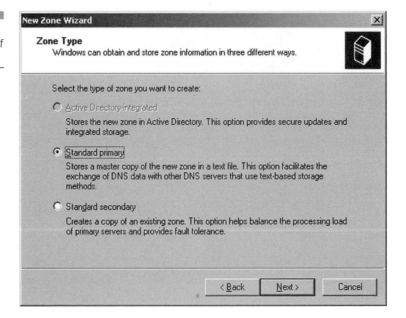

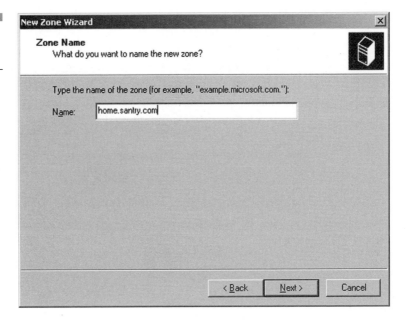

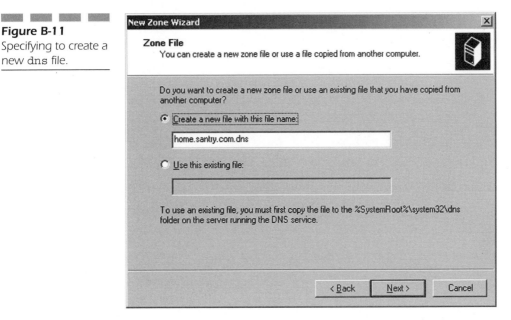

Some of the other options are included if you have Active Directory installed and wish to integrate the DNS server with the directory. In order to use the DNS server with Active Directory, you would need to configure the forward lookup zone to allow dynamic updates. Dynamic updates allow the workstations to update their IP address information in DNS so name resolution can take place on your network.

There is a *lot* more to configuring DNS, but this is all we can cover in the scope of this brief appendix. Refer to the *Windows 2000 Server Resource Kit* for more information on configuring DNS.

INDEX

ABOUT THE AUTHORS

Mitch Tulloch is a *Microsoft Certified Trainer* (MCT) and *Microsoft Certified Systems Engineer* (MCSE) living in Winnipeg, Canada. He is an independent consultant in Microsoft BackOffice products like Exchange Server and Internet Information Server and the author of a number of computer books including *Administering Exchange Server 5.5*.

Patrick Santry is a *Microsoft Certified Trainer* (MCT), *Microsoft Certified Systems Engineer* (MCSE), *Microsoft Certified Solutions Developer* (MCSD), *Microsoft Certified Professional + Site Building* (MCP+SB), and certified in CompTia's i-Net+ living in Erie, Pennsylvania. He specializes in developing e-business solutions using Microsoft technologies and is the author of a number of books and articles on the Microsoft Certified Professional program. Patrick can be contacted at `Patrick@Santry.com`.